Training Contemporary Commercial Singers

Training Contemporary Commercial Singers

Elizabeth Ann Benson

Foreword by Elizabeth Louise Blades

compton
PUBLISHING

This edition first published 2020 © 2020 by Compton Publishing Ltd.

Registered office: Compton Publishing Ltd, 30 St. Giles', Oxford, OX1 3LE, UK

Registered company number: 07831037

Editorial offices: 35 East Street, Braunton, EX33 2EA, UK

Web: www.comptonpublishing.co.uk

ISBN 978-1-909082-62-5

A catalogue record for this book is available from the British Library.

Cover design: David Siddall, http://www.davidsiddall.com

Cover image © Elizabeth Ann Benson.

Photograph: Jessi Rogers

Lighting design: Trevor Turner

Model: Ebony Strong

Set in 10 Candara by katepopplestone@gmail.com

1   2020

The CCM Serenity Prayer

Grant me the serenity to mix the notes that I cannot belt,
the courage to belt the notes that I can,
and the wisdom to know the difference.

Anonymous[1]

---

1   Adapted from Reinhold Niebuhr, 1932.

Contents

Reviews

Jeanie LoVetri, Creator of Somatic Voicework™ The LoVetri Method
As CCM Vocal Pedagogy becomes increasingly important in the 21st Century, singing teachers are seeking intelligent, grounded approaches to help students develop and flourish. In this book readers are exposed to a broad range of experts, both pioneers and those of the next generation, who provide a wealth of information about CCM. It is a welcome and wonderful resource for all singers and teachers of singing.

Sheri Sanders, Creator of the Rock Musical Revolution, Rock the Audition
Hungry for information and generous to share it, Elizabeth put together a KNOCKOUT book that will send you into pedagogical heaven. Get this book ONLY if you want to truly diversify your training in the most in-demand kind of singing: Contemporary Music.

Dr Melissa Forbes, University of Southern Queensland, Australia
Elizabeth Ann Benson's book arrives at a critical juncture in the development of CCM voice pedagogy as a discipline separate from classical voice pedagogy. The second generation of CCM singing teachers (many of whom have studied with the pioneering teachers interviewed for this book) are well-educated and effective pedagogues who are now rightfully taking their place within the academy, schools and in private studios. Training Contemporary Commercial Singers makes a valuable contribution to the field by drawing together various threads of CCM voice pedagogy and will assist future generations of CCM singing teachers to understand the foundations of their pedagogy.

Michelle Markwart Deveaux, Owner & Founder, faithculturekiss studios: Home of the SpeakEasy Cooperative
A fascinating and overdue peek into many of the personalities, histories, and methodologies that have helped to create a foundation for teachers everywhere. We've been teaching pop/rock/jazz/etc for a long time – and Teaching Contemporary Commercial Singers is a wonderful resource to have: A round-up of the most in-the-trenches pedagogues telling us their beliefs, findings, and experiences on singing the musics of the people!

Melissa Cross, Founder of the Zen of Screaming Instructional Series

Teachers of classical singing outnumber the opportunities available for classical singers. Non-classical singers and their respective career prospects outnumber the population of teachers to guide them. Elizabeth Ann Benson has provided an important resource and comprehensive survey of the collective wisdom of some of the world's most respected and esteemed instructors. This is a welcomed step forward towards evidence-based pedagogy for contemporary commercial music.

Dr. Maryann Kyle, Professor of Voice and Chair of Graduate Studies in the Alabama School of the Arts at the University of Mobile and Director of Teaching Fellowship, International Performing Arts Institute

Elizabeth Ann Benson's new book, Teaching Contemporary Commercial Singers is an innovative collection of ideas and methods pertaining to the vocal technique needed for a successful career in commercial music. Delving into issues faced in cross training the voice, Dr. Benson offers insight into how technology meets technique and artistry. She clearly presents philosophies and methods of different teachers without bias, allowing the reader to decide for themselves which is the most effective method for singing in the myriad styles of CCM.

Acknowledgements

I would like to thank Lisa Popeil and Jeanie LoVetri for their long-term investment in my development as a teacher and scholar. This book would not have been possible without their early contributions, mentorship, and inspiring tenacity. Matthew Edwards is responsible for planting the first seed which became this book, and he has continued to be a source of wisdom, humor, and creativity throughout its development. I am deeply thankful for my many friends and colleagues in the international community of singing teachers who have urged me forward and encouraged me. Thank you to Dale Cox for her keen eye and enduring positivity. Thank you to Auburn University's College of Liberal Arts and Department of Theatre for providing funding and teaching leave. Thank you to my colleagues Chase and Tessa for regularly asking me how it was going, and for filling me with confidence. I thank my parents, Suzanne and Tim, and my children, Lydia and Miriam, for believing that I can do anything. I thank my nurturing partner for sending me off to write while he took care of the dishes on countless evenings. The largest thanks must go to the 26 contributors to this text. It has been a remarkable privilege to soak up their wisdom, shared so generously.

Elizabeth Ann Benson

Foreword

July, 2016, 54th National Conference of the National Association Teachers of Singing (NATS), Chicago, Illinois:

> Mary Saunders-Barton (Bel Canto - Can Belto) and I sit down to chat about my idea for a second edition of A Spectrum of Voices: Prominent American Voice Teachers Discuss the Teaching of Singing. I intend to retain the original 2001 manuscript, but to expand on significant advances in vocal pedagogy over the years since publication. The plan is to include teachers whose specialty extends beyond classical art song/opera, particularly music theater and other genres nestled under the umbrella term coined by Jeannette LoVetri: Contemporary Commercial Music, or CCM.
>
> As Mary and I converse, she lists names of teachers she recommends I interview; in short order, I realize that I can only include a few in the revised Spectrum. To do the subject justice, I must consider writing a whole new book.

This is that book.

Fortunately, Elizabeth Benson beat me to it and the world of contemporary vocal pedagogy is better for it. Elizabeth walks the walk and talks the talk, having immersed herself in the CCM world as a performer, teacher, director, researcher and, now, author.

I first met Elizabeth when we were active members of the Colorado-Wyoming chapter of NATS. Her energy, curiosity and vibrant personality were evident. I've watched her life and career blossom over the past few years as her achievements collect: tabbed for the 2012 NATS Emerging Leader Award; hired in her current position at Auburn University; selected for the 2016 NATS Intern Program with study under master teacher, Jeannette LoVetri. Writing Training Contemporary Commercial Singers is the natural progression of those accomplishments.

Elizabeth has gathered an impressive group of teachers who represent the very best in their areas, which include multiple CCM styles: music theatre, gospel, jazz, pop, rock, and what is now called 'cross-training'. Following the same qualitative 'interview response' approach I used in A Spectrum of Voices, Elizabeth's questions cover a range of topics under general headings (Approach, Elements of Training, Special Demands from the Industry, and Aesthetic Context). As she has stated, 'some of these topics are unique to CCM pedagogy, having played no part in classical pedagogy, and the need to address their pedagogical implications comes directly from the demands of the commercial voice industry'.

July, 1997, International Congress of Voice Teachers, London, England:

> I am in the audience of over 1,000 voice teachers from the classical world. The day's schedule is devoted to 'Training British Singing Theatre' (aka, 'Music Theatre'). We are assembled not far from the West End, where Les Misérables, Phantom of the Opera, Blood Brothers and so many other record-breaking musicals continue their enormously successful runs.
>
> Murmurs and mutters of disapproval erupt into outspoken disqualification for this 'renegade form of voice teaching'. Revolution seems imminent as the masterclass comes to an abrupt halt.
>
> And then, amidst the uproar, Edward Baird rises and in his deep bass-baritone voice, calms the raging sea:
>
>> "Times are changing, and we must change with them. If our students are going to find employment, they must be able to sing and perform in these non-classical mediums - because that is where 75% of the jobs will be".
>
> Janice Chapman and Jo Estill stand to join him in agreement and solidarity... as do a significant number of us in the hall that day.

Such farseeing prophecy has more than proven true, and Elizabeth's book is clear validation of our profession's health and vitality. It fills a void that needed to be filled, and I am proud to have this opportunity to say, "brava"!

Elizabeth Louise Blades
Author of A Spectrum of Voices: Prominent American voice teachers discuss the teaching of singing 2ed.

Preface

I love voices. I sang before I talked. I was raised on Mozart and the Beatles. While performing "Country Roads" (John Denver) in third grade, I figured out that singing is what I wanted to do with my life. I studied classical singing in college because I was led to it by my teachers. That is what serious students did. I entered a master's program at New England Conservatory, where I hid the fact that I sang in a rock band on the weekends. I completed a DMA at the CUNY Graduate Center while listening to Metallica and Hugo Wolf on the subway. In the real world, I started teaching at a community music school. My high school students wanted to know how to belt, and there was just no way around the demand for this skill set. I realized that my students were going to belt with or without my support, so I decided to learn how it works, in order to support them. Finally, I brought my love of CCM genres out of the closet.

Lisa Popeil taught me how to belt. I studied her Voiceworks® method and I have not stopped asking her questions ever since. Later, I added Somatic Voicework™, the LoVetri Method and Estill Voice Training™ to my toolkit. I earned a spot in the NATS Intern Program, working on CCM singing with master teacher, Jeannette (Jeanie) LoVetri. The impact of her investment in my teaching is impossible to overstate. Both Jeanie and Lisa have been tremendous pillars of support throughout the process of researching and writing this book. I have also significantly benefited from conferences, professional development and the endless support of colleagues (whom I also call 'friends') from all walks of vocal life.

Eventually, I learned that my path is not unique. Many came before me and endured the same struggles. Many of the pioneers listened to their intuition, which told them to ask more questions, to dig deeper. I was driven by the same nagging thought in the back of my mind : 'Wait a minute, that can't be right...' I listened to that voice and it has taken me on the adventure of a lifetime.

Elizabeth Ann Benson

1

Introduction

Elizabeth Ann Benson

The type of pedagogical training for voice teachers varies widely. There is no uniform method for how to teach singing, nor how to train singing teachers. Some teachers have formal pedagogical training, while others have none. To qualify to teach at the university or conservatory level, academic hopefuls pursue graduate training. However, the predominant type of voice pedagogy training available in graduate programs is *classical* pedagogy. Due to the growing number of collegiate programs in music theatre and commercial singing, current teaching jobs are rarely limited to classical styles. The increased demand for contemporary commercial (CCM) pedagogical knowledge reveals that classical music's dominance in voice pedagogy and in higher-educational systems is being challenged. We are reinventing the field of voice pedagogy to fulfill the need for CCM training, and to preserve the formal study of singing, both classical and commercial. In order to produce the most employable generation of teachers, access to CCM training methods must increase. No book can teach an individual how to teach singing, but this text provides substantive information about several established methods of teaching CCM singing.

The term "contemporary commercial music" (CCM) was coined by Jeannette LoVetri as a critical alternative to 'non-classical'. LoVetri championed the term because it allowed these styles of music to be evaluated on their own terms, rather than being viewed through a classical lens.[1] In 2008, the American Academy of Teachers of Singing (AATS) stated that classical and CCM styles "are different aesthetically, psychologically, and acoustically, and thus demand different pedagogic approaches."[2] Several pioneer CCM pedagogues – including Lisa Popeil, Jeannette LoVetri, Jo Estill, and others included in this text – have developed their own methodologies through research, singing, and in many cases, through collaborative scientific studies. These methods are available to teachers in the form of workshop training with the method-creator. However, because the methodology functions as the creator's 'for-profit' business, the contents are often trademarked and protected. In the past, this has prevented comparative discussion of the methodologies which would serve to advance the field. This book lifts the veil on several prominent methods to facilitate detailed examination. Because there is no singular approach that the voice community has determined to be the best, readers are encouraged to explore the numerous methods presented in this book.

---

1   Jeannette LoVetri, "Contemporary commercial music: More than one way to use the vocal tract," *Journal of Singing* 58, no. 3 (2002), 249–252 and "Editorial: Contemporary commercial music," *Journal of Voice* 22, no. 3 (May 2008), 260–262, doi.org/10.1016/j.jvoice.2006.11.002.

2   American Academy of Teachers of Singing, "In support of contemporary commercial (nonclassical) voice pedagogy," *Journal of Singing* 65, no. 1 (September/October 2008), 10.

Inside this book

There are 26 contributing authors to this text. The interview subjects were identified as exemplary CCM voice pedagogues through an anonymous survey conducted in 2017. The interview subjects come from all over the world, representing Australia, the United Kingdom, Denmark, and the United States. They include the pioneering generation of CCM voice pedagogues and the generations that have followed. These next generations have benefited enormously from the groundbreaking work of their predecessors who paved the way for both the accessibility of knowledge and the legitimization of the field itself. The interview subjects come from a variety of stylistic specializations, including pop, rock, gospel, jazz, music theatre, popular culture musics[3], and cross-training (classical and CCM). Given the diversity of this pool, this text will present and celebrate a broad spectrum of responses. The chapters of the book are organized by interview question, allowing readers to see a variety of answers on each topic. This structure encourages readers to consider several approaches before embarking on a process of discovery towards their own.

At the start of the chapter, the topic of each interview question is contextualized through a brief introduction written by the author. This introduction provides an analytical overview of the responses and when appropriate, presents resulting data in column charts or pie charts. Significant points of agreement and disagreement are outlined and discussed. In some instances, lists of resources are provided. The individual pedagogues' responses are then presented in an order that highlights pedagogical trends. At the end of each chapter, a list of references and recommended reading on each topic is offered to encourage readers toward further exploration.

The bulk of the text is divided into four sections: (1) Approaches; (2) Elements of Training; (3) Special Demands from the Industry; and (4) Aesthetic Context. In Section 1: Approaches, teachers respond to questions about their particular method or approach, identify teaching philosophies, and share details about their own training and performing. Section 2: Elements of Training, includes several questions on how teachers address particular elements of vocal technique. Each teacher describes his/her approach to teaching posture and alignment, tension, breath, support, registration, (in)consistency, belt, vowels, and expression. In Section 3: Special Demands from the Industry, teachers discuss the use of audio technology in the CCM studio, how to teach improvisation, training beyond the voice studio, the role of voice science in the studio, and teaching CCM singing to younger students (under the age of 18). Some of these topics are unique to CCM pedagogy, having played no part in classical pedagogy, and the need to address their pedagogical implications comes directly from the demands of the commercial voice industry. Lastly, Section 4: Aesthetic Context, presents responses on admirable professional singers, teachers' perceptions of successful commercial singers, and the trademarks of excellent singing in commercial music. In response to the data, a brief discussion of where CCM pedagogy stands and where it may go is offered.

Several additional elements of training deserve specific exploration within a CCM pedagogical context, but they are beyond the scope of this text. In the future, the study of pedagogical approaches to extra-vocal techniques or distortions (such as creak, rattle,

---

3 Popular culture musics (PCM) is an Australian term equivalent to contemporary commercial music (CCM). More information may be found in Diane Hughes, "Contemporary vocal artistry in popular culture musics: Perceptions, observations, and lived experiences," in *Teaching Singing in the 21st Century*, ed. Scott D. Harrison and Jessica O'Bryan (Dordrecht: Springer, 2014), 287–301.

growl, grunt, scream, yodel, squall, or whoop) would be of particular relevance. There is no discussion of agility training for CCM riffs, runs, and licks, which often utilizes modal scales, blues scale, major and minor pentatonic scales, and the minor hexatonic scale. Also missing is the specific training of onsets, offsets, articulation, and the role of percussiveness, both in relation to consonants and to vocal agility in CCM styles. Additional complications specific to CCM which would be worthy of further research are: learning to hear and monitor one's own voice in an amplified sound environment; playing an instrument and singing at the same time; and improvising vocal harmonies. Until the results of such future research are available, a list of published resources on these topics is included at the end of this chapter.

Commercial singing

Within the Academy, classical music has been the predominant genre of study in music departments for a century, while popular music has been marginalized. In *The Crisis of Classical Music in America* Robert Freeman states: "Because the introduction of classical music to America in the mid-nineteenth century implied the social and intellectual superiority of those who supported such music, we have acted as though those repertories are *implicitly superior* to other kinds of music" (emphasis added).[4] The study of 'music' has actually meant the study of '*classical* music'. However, popular tastes are now challenging that structure with increasing demand for commercial music. According to the National Endowment for the Arts survey data, consumption of commercial music was reported at significantly higher rates than consumption of all other genres of music: 47% of U.S. adults use electronic media to consume broadcasts or recordings of rock, pop, country, folk, rap, or hip-hop music.[5]

The Academy has increased demand for those who teach multiple styles equally well, as noted by classical pedagogue Scott McCoy. He states: "Few, if any, of the pedagogy students at my university will have the option to pursue a teaching career as narrowly focused as mine".[6] Modern voice teachers must expand beyond the classical aesthetic.

Musical theatre programs have exploded since 1968 and are now established at 140 institutions in the United States.[7] Musical theatre singing can be viewed as a stylistic bridge between classical singing and CCM singing because it requires the application of technique in both classical styles (legit music theatre) and CCM styles (rock and contemporary musical theatre). Singers are being asked to become increasingly versatile in order to gain employment in musical theatre, requiring university programs to provide voice instruction in all rock styles, as well as legit and contemporary musical theatre styles. However, a survey published in 2009 found that only 19% of those teaching musical theatre had any pedagogical training in CCM.[8] As a result, hundreds of teachers seek independent CCM training each year.

There are now approximately 30 university programs in the U.S. which offer a degree in 'commercial' or 'popular' music with a singing emphasis or concentration, and that

---

4   Robert Freeman, *The Crisis of Classical Music in America: Lessons from a Life in the Education of Musicians* (Lanham, MD: Rowman & Littlefield, 2014), xix.

5   National Endowment for the Arts, *A Decade of Arts Engagement: Findings from the Survey of Public Participation in the Arts, 2002-2012* (Washington DC: National Endowment for the Arts, 2015), 27.

6   Scott McCoy, "Why I don't teach belting," *Journal of Singing* 70, no. 2 (November/December 2013), 182.

7   Wendy LeBorgne and Marci Rosenberg, *The Vocal Athlete* (San Diego: Plural, 2014), 225.

8   Edrie Means Weekly and Jeannette LoVetri, "Follow-up Contemporary Commercial Music (CCM) Survey: Who's teaching what in nonclassical music," *Journal of Voice* 23 (2009), 371.

number is growing.[9] Many programs have been established within the past 10 years, and most have been added to previously established classical music programs. Many programs do not employ dedicated CCM singing teachers but instead, rely on classical voice teachers to provide commercial singing instruction. This is not ideal because most classical teachers would not have had any formal CCM training and therefore, would be unlikely to possess the skills required to meet the needs of both classical and commercial students without seeking further training. However, it reflects an institutional-level desire to integrate classical and CCM voice training.

Currently, there are only two university programs in the U.S. with graduate degrees in non-classical voice pedagogy: Shenandoah Conservatory (CCM) and Pennsylvania State University (Musical Theatre Pedagogy). These programs are well-designed, but they yield very few graduates each year. An undergraduate degree does not qualify one to teach at the university level, so most academic hopefuls seek graduate study in a variety of classical or jazz performance programs, or sometimes Ph.D. programs in music education. However, these programs rarely offer thorough pedagogical training to teach CCM singing at the university level. At this time, there are zero doctoral programs in CCM voice pedagogy in the U.S. This creates a troubling disparity between the number of CCM teachers needed and the number of teachers who have specific formal training.

A course in voice pedagogy is increasingly being offered to undergraduate voice majors, but it is not always required. Moreover, this course is usually conflated with vocal anatomy and physiology. Knowledge of vocal anatomy and physiology is critical for the development of kinesthetic awareness, and this is beneficial for every singer not just every aspiring teacher. Therefore, the study of anatomy and physiology may serve singing students better if it were included as a required unit within applied voice lessons. Even when a voice pedagogy course is focused on actual pedagogy, the content of the course is often limited to *classical* aesthetics to serve *classical* repertoire. In these cases, the outdated presumption persists that technical training in the classical aesthetic is sufficient to sing in any style.

For more than three decades, the classical pedagogy community has officially recognized the need for teachers to be familiar with pedagogical skills beyond the classical aesthetic. In a 1985 column in the *Journal of Singing* (then called *The NATS Bulletin*), Robert Edwin posed the question "Are we the national association of teachers of *classical* singing?"[10] In a 2001 article, NATS past President Roy Delp asked "Could the mission of our new century be to turn our attention to teaching healthy singing in all styles?", and he continued, questioning his duty to provide opportunities for his students beyond his "own artistic tastes and preferences."[11] In a 2013 article, NATS Past President Scott McCoy states "Our curricula must be adapted to suit the needs and expectations of the real world, which includes skill in teaching both classical and CCM genres and techniques".[12] If undergraduates could be exposed to the application of vocal technique in a variety of styles, young teachers would indeed be more prepared for the real world.

---

9   Jessica Baldwin, "Commercial Voice Degrees, Diplomas, and Certificates," *Commercial Voice Resources Blog*, accessed on May 19, 2017, http://www.commercialvoiceresources.com/commercial-voice-programs-us.

10   Robert Edwin, "Are we the National Association of Teachers of Classical Singing (Revisiting 1985)," *Journal of Singing* 67, no. 5 (May/June 2011), 589–590.

11   Roy Delp, "Now that the belt voice has become legitimate…," *Journal of Singing* 57, no. 5 (May/June 2001), 1–2.

12   McCoy, "Why I don't teach belting," 182.

Integration

The integration of commercial and classical music programs has significant benefits which the Academey should seriously consider. In traditional university music departments, Freeman states "…we have failed to adequately broaden our students' interests and skills in non-European musics, in music of the twentieth and twenty-first century, and in the popular music beloved by the majors and non-majors alike".[13] By marginalizing the cultural and artistic importance of popular music, classical programs exclude countless prospective students. In an exclusively classical music program, students who enter college with a passion for popular music are unable to study their preferred genres. Unless they have had access to prerequisite skills and knowledge, they are also denied the opportunity to learn about classical music. This limits not only the number of music majors but also, the growth of new classical audiences.

As arts programs in primary and secondary public schools are cut, only the students who can afford private music study are receiving the foundational training which will allow them to compete in classical collegiate programs. Harvard University is one of the first institutions to publicly acknowledge that their traditional classical curriculum contained an implicit requirement that students come into the program with several years of previous study. The director of undergraduate studies at Harvard identified that requirement as "ultimately, a class-based implicit requirement"[14] which prevented growth in diversity among their student body. They have recently revised their curriculum to offer students the opportunity to pursue a music major in any genre of music according to each student's "artistic aspirations".[15] Most universities in the U.S. have an action plan to improve diversity and inclusion. Traditional classical music programs which continue to exclude commercial music from formal study are perpetuating class-based discrimination. While this discrimination may be unintentional, it is time to reexamine the status quo: an academic hierarchy which places classical music above all other styles. Integrating popular music into pre-existing classical programs can increase enrollment and ensure the viability of the entire department, but it will also require a commitment to consciously shaping the future of music education towards greater inclusivity.

The integration of commercial and classical programs does not pose a threat to classical programs. In fact, it could be the best way to ensure the survival of classical music programs, even as classical enrollment numbers decrease. John Covach states that the integration of pop music into a classical curriculum "offers the prospect not only of making significant advances in musical education, diversity, and inclusion but also of protecting and preserving the rich accomplishments of the American music-school tradition".[16] There will always be a path for the most talented classical singers at Juilliard, the Academy of Vocal Arts, and other top conservatories. Young artist programs such as Merola and Lindemann will continue to foster the highest echelon of young operatic talent. However, even in these elite programs, singers are asked to perform cabaret, jazz, musical theatre, and other CCM styles in order to fund-raise and reach a larger audience. Contemporary Art Song expert Sharon Mabry explains "We must capture the attention of a larger pool of listeners by offering a gourmet's

---

13 Freeman, *The Crisis of Classical Music in America*, xix.

14 Anne Schreffler, Director of Undergraduate Studies at Harvard University, quoted in Robin William, "What controversial changes at Harvard mean for music in the university," *The Log Journal*, accessed on 16 May 2017, http://thelogjournal.com/2017/04/25/what-controversial-changes-at-harvard-means-for-music-in-the-university/.

15 Ibid.

16 John Covach, "Rock Me, Maestro," *Chronicle of Higher Education* 61.21 (2015), accessed on 21 May 2017, http://www.chronicle.com/article/Rock-Me-Maestro/151423.

delight in musical style, mood, and vocalism, and by giving the audience more choices and new alternatives to the standard concert fare".[17] In university and conservatory programs, teachers should provide this training for all singers.

Training singers

The American Academy of Teachers of Singing states that no matter the style of music or pedagogical methods employed, the goal of any singing teacher should be to guide the student toward "efficient, healthy, and artistically expressive" singing.[18] Even when we can agree on the same goals, the methods used to attain them vary widely. Terminology itself has been a barrier to the debate and discourse critical to the development of the field. In academia, CCM pedagogues are already a marginalized population because they stand outside of the classical majority. This text seeks to move past terminological debate and into the substance of vocal function so that the field of CCM voice pedagogy may become aware of its own unity and embrace its inherent diversity.

In this text, 'technique' is defined as how one creates a desired sound with the voice, and 'style' is the application of learned techniques into musical repertoire. This critical distinction was presented by Cornelius Reid in 1975 when he advised pedagogues to clearly delineate between 'function' and 'aesthetics'.[19] If pedagogical approaches to technique can be separated from individual stylistic preferences, voice pedagogy could become a unified field, welcoming both classical and CCM approaches. In 1985, Robert Edwin asserted that a shift in pedagogic perspective from "exclusive (only certain vocalizations are acceptable)" to "inclusive (many vocalizations are acceptable)" is all that it takes to become a singing teacher of "great service".[20]

Voice science and voice pedagogy

When identifying technical and functional elements of voice use, scientific knowledge is critical. Voice science includes communication disorders, speech-language pathology, and laryngology. It can inform voice pedagogy, but voice science is a separate field. Voice pedagogy is and remains an *art*. The interview subjects in this text are all pedagogues. A few of them are also scientists, researchers, or clinicians, but the questions they answer have to do with their pedagogical methods. In this text, teachers describe how they use voice science in the studio, if at all. Some of the views expressed are rooted in voice science and some are not. It is important to note that university voice science courses are not regularly available to voice majors or music majors. Except for a few courses such as The Summer Vocology Institute offered through the National Center for Voice and Speech (NCVS), singing teachers must self-educate in the subject of voice science.

Discrepancies among the responses are to be expected; as the authors of *The Vocal Athlete* point out, both classical and CCM voice pedagogies still rely on "conventional wisdom and empirical observation combined with the research that does exist" in the process of perpetual

---

17 Sharon Mabry, *Exploring Twentieth-Century Vocal Music: A Practical Guide to Innovations in Performance and Repertoire* (Oxford: Oxford University Press, 2002), 5–6.

18 American Academy of Teachers of Singing, "In support of contemporary commercial (nonclassical) voice pedagogy," 10.

19 Cornelius L. Reid, *Voice: Psyche and Soma* (New York: Joseph Patelson Music House, 1975), preface.

20 Robert Edwin, "Are we the National Association of Teachers of Classical Singing?," *The NATS Bulletin* 41, no. 5 (May/June 1985): 40, reprinted in Robert Edwin, "Are we the National Association of Teachers of Classical Singing (Revisiting 1985)," *Journal of Singing* 67, no. 5 (May/June 2011), 590.

refinement.[21] Simply put, many of the responses are opinions based on significant experience, and the pedagogues reserve the right to change their minds at any point to keep up with the advancements in voice science. The most substantial discrepancies will be discussed and contextualized in the introduction of each chapter.

While some may argue that it is not possible, many master-level teachers report that they feel more aware of vocal function. These perceptions could be neurological, acoustic, or kinesthetic, or some combination thereof. It is reasonable to preserve the possibility that proprioception can increase with detailed study. Classical teachers have historically relied upon their eyes and ears to perceive vocal function, regardless of whether or not the perceived function reflected the actual function. Well-respected pedagogues still use the phrase "to sing off the breath," even though it is scientific fact that singing can only be achieved "on the breath." For hundreds of years, the eyes and ears were the best (and only) tools available to perceive vocal faults and to prescribe changes. Even if an approach is not fully aligned with the latest voice science, it can still be an effective means to achieve a desired result. Voice *science* cannot and should not replace the *art* of pedagogy. However, the two fields mutually benefit from an understanding of one another.

Collaborative scholarship between voice pedagogues and voice scientists is increasing. The singing voice specialist and the vocologist function to integrate "science, medicine and voice therapy with the artistry of singing and teaching".[22] Only a small number of singing teachers would call themselves singing voice specialists or vocologists, but this number is growing. Many of the pedagogues interviewed in this text are respected scholars who have collaborated in research and education with prominent voice scientists, including Johann Sundberg,[23,24] Peak Woo,[25] and Ingo Titze.[26] The studies cited here are only a representative sample, and readers are encouraged to explore each interview subject's own publications. Collaborative work demonstrates that these pedagogues are working to fortify the shared interests of the entire voice community.

Conclusion

Singing teachers should maintain flexibility in training methods as developments happen in science and pedagogy. In the concluding chapter of *Teaching Singing in the 21st Century*, the editors state: "We have a responsibility to encourage unorthodoxy, welcome diversity and embrace openness to create the cultural and structural conditions to kindle (or re-kindle) learning".[27] This is a monumental yet critical task for the future of voice pedagogy. The voice community has not identified any single method as the best or the most effective. Therefore,

---

21 Wendy D. LeBorgne and Marci Rosenberg, *The Vocal Athlete* (San Diego: Plural Publishing, 2014), 225.

22 Scott McCoy, "Singing Pedagogy in the Twenty-First Century: A Look Toward the Future," in *Teaching Singing in the 21st Century*, ed. Scott D. Harrison and Jessica O'Bryan (Dordrecht: Springer, 2014), 17.

23 Johan Sundberg, Margaretta Thalén, and Lisa Popeil, "Substyles of belting: Phonatory and resonatory characteristics," *Journal of Voice* 26, no. 2 (January 2012), 44–50, doi.org/10.1016/j.jvoice.2010.10.007.

24 Johan Sundberg, P Gramming, and Jeannette LoVetri, "Comparisons of pharynx, source, formant, and pressure characteristics in operatic and musical theatre singing," *Journal of Voice* 7, no. 4 (December 1993), 301–310, doi. org/10.1016/S0892-1997(05)80118-3.

25 Jeannette LoVetri, Susan Lesh, and Peak Woo, "Preliminary study on the ability of trained singers to control the intrinsic and extrinsic laryngeal musculature," *Journal of Voice* 13, no. 2 (1999), 219–226, doi.org/10.1016/S0892-1997(99)80024-1.

26 Jeannette LoVetri was a visiting faculty member at The Summer Vocology Institute in 2016.

27 Scott D. Harrison and Jessica O'Bryan, "Postlude: The Future of Singing Pedagogy" in *Teaching Singing in the 21st Century*, ed. Scott D. Harrison and Jessica O'Bryan (Dordrecht: Springer, 2014), 413.

it may be beneficial for teachers to explore several methods in order to maximize their pedagogical skill set.

Increased demand for CCM pedagogical knowledge reveals that we are challenging classical music's dominance in voice pedagogy and in higher-educational systems. We are reinventing the field of voice pedagogy in order to fill this void and to preserve the study of singing, both classical and commercial. Due to the growing number of collegiate programs in music theatre and commercial singing, current teaching jobs are rarely limited to classical styles. Until doctoral programs are developed to prepare university-level teachers to teach CCM singing, the field will rely on private training. This book will not teach the reader how to teach singing. However, as demand increases for teaching CCM styles and techniques, it may be a helpful resource to aid the understanding of significant differences and similarities between several CCM approaches and to develop a personal pedagogical approach.

References

American Academy of Teachers of Singing. "In support of contemporary commercial (nonclassical) voice pedagogy." *Journal of Singing* 65, no. 1 (September/October 2008): 7–10.

Baldwin, Jessica. "Commercial Voice Degrees, Diplomas, and Certificates." *Commercial Voice Resources.* Accessed May 19, 2017. http://www.commercialvoiceresources.com/commercial-voice-programs-us.

Covach, John. "Rock Me, Maestro." *Chronicle of Higher Education* 61.21 (2015). Accessed on May 21, 2017. http://www.chronicle.com/article/Rock-Me-Maestro/151423.

Delp, Roy. "Now that the belt voice has become legitimate...." *Journal of Singing* 57, no. 5 (May/June 2001): 1–2.

Edwin, Robert. "Are we the National Association of Teachers of Classical Singing?." *The NATS Bulletin* 41, no. 5 (May/June 1985): 40, reprinted in Robert Edwin, "Are we the National Association of Teachers of Classical Singing (Revisiting 1985)," *Journal of Singing* 67, no. 5 (May/June 2011): 590.

Edwin, Robert. "Are we the National Association of Teachers of Classical Singing? (Revisiting 1985)." *Journal of Singing* 67, no. 5 (May/June 2011): 589–590.

Freeman, Robert. *The Crisis of Classical Music in America: Lessons from a Life in the Education of Musicians.* Lanham, MD: Rowman & Littlefield, 2014.

Harrison, Scott D. and Jessica O'Bryan, eds. *Teaching Singing in the 21st Century.* Dordrecht: Springer, 2014.

Hughes, Diane. "Contemporary vocal artistry in popular culture musics: Perceptions, observations, and lived experiences." In *Teaching Singing in the 21st Century.* Edited by Scott D. Harrison and Jessica O'Bryan, 287–301. Dordrecht: Springer, 2014.

LeBorgne, Wendy D. and Marci Rosenberg. *The Vocal Athlete.* San Diego: Plural, 2014.

LoVetri, Jeannette. "Editorial: Contemporary Commercial Music." *Journal of Voice* 22, no. 3 (May 2008): 260–262. doi.org/10.1016/j.jvoice.2006.11.002.

LoVetri, Jeannette, Susan Lesh, and Peak Woo. "Preliminary study on the ability of trained singers to control the intrinsic and extrinsic laryngeal musculature." *Journal of Voice* 13 (1999): 219–226. doi.org/10.1016/S0892-1997(99)80024-1.

Mabry, Sharon. *Exploring Twentieth-Century Vocal Music: A Practical Guide to Innovations in Performance and Repertoire.* Oxford: Oxford University Press, 2002.

McCoy, Scott. "Singing Pedagogy in the Twenty-First Century: A Look Toward the Future." In *Teaching Singing in the 21st Century,* edited by Scott D. Harrison and Jessica O'Bryan, 13-20. Dordrecht: Springer, 2014.

McCoy, Scott. "Why I don't teach belting." *Journal of Singing* 70, no. 2 (November/December 2013): 181–182.

Means Weekly, Edrie and Jeannette LoVetri. "Follow-up Contemporary Commercial Music (CCM) Survey: Who's teaching what in nonclassical music." *Journal of Voice* 23, no. 3 (May 2009): 367–375. doi.org/10.1016/j.jvoice.2007.10.012.

National Endowment for the Arts. A Decade of Arts Engagement: Findings from the Survey of Public Participation in the Arts, 2002-2012. Washington DC: National Endowment for the Arts, 2015.

Reid, Cornelius L. *Voice: Psyche and Soma.* New York: Joseph Patelson Music House, 1975.

Sundberg, Johan, Margareta Thalén, and Lisa Popeil. "Substyles of belting: Phonatory and resonatory characteristics." *Journal of Voice* 26, no. 2 (January 2012): 44–50. doi.org/10.1016/j.jvoice.2010.10.007.

Sundberg, Johan, Patricia Gramming, and Jeannette Lovetri. "Comparisons of pharynx, source, formant, and pressure characteristics in operatic and musical theatre singing." *Journal of Voice* 7, no. 4 (December 1993): 301–310. doi.org/10.1016/S0892-1997(05)80118-3.

William, Robin. "What Controversial Changes at Harvard Mean for Music in the University." *The Log Journal.* Accessed on May 16, 2017. http://thelogjournal.com/2017/04/25/what-controversial-changes-at-harvard-means-for-music-in-the-university/.

Recommended reading

American Academy of Teachers of Singing. "In support of fact-based voice pedagogy and terminology." *Journal of Singing* 71, no. 1 (September/October 2014): 9–14.

American Academy of Teachers of Singing. "Research and creative accomplishment in promotion and tenure: A realistic look at expectations for teachers of singing in academia." *Journal of Singing* 71, no. 2 (November/December 2014): 141–143.

Bartlett, Irene. "Reflections on contemporary commercial singing: An insider's perspective." *Voice and Speech Review*, 8, no. 1 (2014): 27–35. www.doi.org/10.1080/23268263.2013.829711.

Benson, Elizabeth Ann. "Modern voice pedagogy: Functional training for all styles." *American Music Teacher* 67, no. 6 (June 2018): 10–17.

Borch, Daniel Zanger. *Ultimate vocal voyage: The definitive method for unleashing the rock, pop or soul singer within you.* Milwaukee: Hal Leonard, 2008.

Borch, Daniel Zanger, Johan Sundberg, P.-A. Lindestad, and M. Thalen. "Vocal fold vibration and voice source aperiodicity in 'dist' tones: Study of a timbral ornament in rock singing. *Logopedics, Phoniatrics, Vocology* 29, no. 4 (2005):147–153. doi.org/10.1080/14015430410016073.

Bos, Nancy. "Microphone technique: Cooking up complex vocals." In *The Voice Teacher's Cookbook: Creative Recipes for Teachers of Singing* ed. Brian J. Winnie, 11–12. Delray Beach, FL: Meredith Music, 2018.

Caffier, Philipp P., Ahmed Ibrahim Nasr, Maria del Mar Ropero Rendon, Sascha Wienhausen, Eleanor Forbes, Wolfram Seidner, and Tadeus Nawka. "Common vocal effects and partial glottal vibration in professional nonclassical singers." *Journal of Voice* 32, no. 3 (May 2018): 340–346. doi.org/10.1016/j.jvoice.2017.06.009.

Cazden, Joanna. "Dionysus, Demi Moore, and the cult of the distressed voice." *Voice and Speech Review* 3, no. 1 (2003): 243–246. doi.org/10.1080/23268263.2003.10739409.

Chandler, Kim. "Teaching popular music styles." In *Teaching Singing in the 21st Century* edited by Scott D. Harrison and Jessica O'Bryan, 35–51. Dordrecht: Springer, 2014.

Chandler, Kim. *Funky 'n' Fun Vocal Training Series, vol. 1-4.* CDs or MP3 file downloads. http://www.funkynfun.com/.

Corbett, Ian. *Mic it! Microphones, microphone technique, and their impact on the final mix.* Burlington, MA: Focal Press, 2015.

Cross, Melissa and D. Korycki. *The Zen of Screaming: Vocal Instruction for a New Breed.* DVD and CD. New York: Loudmouth, Inc, February 21, 2006. Alfred Music, February 1, 2007.

Cross, Melissa. *The Zen of Screaming 2: Vocal Instruction for a New Breed.* DVD. New York: Alfred Music, June 1, 2007.

D'haeseleer, Evelien, Iris Meerschman, Sofie Claeys, Clara Leyns, Julie Daelman, and Kristiane Van Lierde. "Vocal quality in theater actors." *Journal of Voice* 31, no. 4 (July 2017): 510.e7–510.e14. doi.org/10.1016/j.jvoice.2016.11.008.

Edgerton, Michael Edward. "Finding the ingredients towards yummy, unusual tastes: Extra-normal voice." In *The Voice Teacher's Cookbook: Creative Recipes for Teachers of Singing* edited by Brian J. Winnie, 36–38. Delray Beach, FL: Meredith Music, 2018.

Edgerton, Michael Edward. "The Extra-Normal Voice: EVT in Singing." In *Teaching Singing in the 21st Century.* Edited by Scott D. Harrison and Jessica O'Bryan 109-132. Dordrecht: Springer, 2014.

Edwards, Matthew. *So You Want to Sing Rock 'N' Roll: A Guide for Performers.* Lanham, MD: Rowman & Littlefield, 2014.

Edwards, Matthew. "Icing the song: Onsets and releases in rock singing." In *The Voice Teacher's Cookbook: Creative Recipes for Teachers of Singing* edited by Brian J. Winnie, 39–41. Delray Beach, FL: Meredith Music, 2018.

Edwards, Matthew. "The art of perfection: What every singer and voice teacher should know about audio technology." In *The Vocal Athlete* by Wendy D. LeBorgne and Marci Rosenberg, 271–294. San Diego: Plural Publishing, 2014.

Federman, Jeremy and Todd Ricketts. "Preferred and minimum acceptable listening levels for musicians while using floor and in-ear monitors." *Journal of Speech, Language, and Hearing Research*, 51, no. 1 (February 2008): 147–159.

Ferrone, Carol, Jessica Galgano, and Lorraine Olson Ramig. "The impact of extended voice use on the acoustic characteristics of phonation after training and performance of actors from the La MaMa Experimental Theater Club." *Journal of Voice* 25, no. 3 (May 2011): e123–e137. doi.org/10.1016/j.jvoice.2009.12.007.

1 Introduction

Frazier-Neely, Cathryn. "Live vs. recorded: Comparing apples to oranges to get fruit salad." *Journal of Singing* 69, no. 5 (May/June 2013): 593–596.

Granqvist, Svante, Stellan Hertegard, Hans Larsson, and Johan Sundberg. "Simultaneous analysis of vocal fold vibration and transglottal airflow: Exploring a new experimental technique." *Journal of Voice* 17, no. 3 (September 2003): 319–330. doi.org/10.1067/S0892-1997(03)00070-5.

Green, Lucy. *How Popular Musicians Learn: A Way Ahead for Music Education.* Abingdon-on- Thames: Routledge, 2017.

Hallqvist, Hanna, Filipa M.B. La, and Johan Sundberg. "Soul and musical theater: A comparison of two vocal styles." *Journal of Voice* 31, no. 2 (March 2017): 229–235. doi.org/10.1016/j.jvoice.2016.05.020.

Horning, Susan Schmidt. "Engineering the performance: Recording engineers, tacit knowledge and the art of controlling sound." *Social Studies of Science* 34, no 5 (October 2004): 703–731. doi.org/10.1177/0306312704047536.

Howard, David M. and Damian T. Murphy. *Voice Science, Acoustics and Recording.* San Diego, CA: Plural Publishing, 2008.

Howard, Elisabeth. *ABC's of Vocal Harmony: Improve Your Pitch, Rhythm, Sight-Reading, and Harmonies.* Los Angeles: Vocal Power Institute, 2006.

Lindestad Per-Ake, Maria Södersten, Björn Merker, and Svante Granqvist. "Voice source characteristics in Mongolian "throat singing" studied with high-speed imaging technique, acoustic spectra, and inverse filtering." *Journal of Voice* 15, no. 1 (March 2001): 78–85. doi.org/10.1016/S0892-1997(01)00008-X.

LoVetri, Jeannette. "Treatment of injured singers and professional speakers: The singer/actor, singer/dancer, and singer/musician." In *The Performer's Voice*, edited by Michael S. Benninger, Thomas Murry, and Michael M. Johns. San Diego: Plural Publishing, 2016.

Morange, Séverine, Daniele Dubois, and Jean-Marc Fontaine. "Perception of recorded singing voice quality and expertise: Cognitive linguistics and acoustic approaches." *Journal of Voice* 24, no. 4 (July 2010): 450–457. doi.org/10.1016/j.jvoice.2008.08.006.

Paradise, Kate. "Swinging lasagna." In *The Voice Teacher's Cookbook: Creative Recipes for Teachers of Singing* edited by Brian J. Winnie, 88–89. Delray Beach, FL: Meredith Music, 2018.

Peckham, Anne. "Vocalise patterns for the contemporary singer." *Journal of Singing* 59, no. 3 (January/February 2003): 215–220.

Proctor, Michael, Erik Bresch, Dani Byrd, Krishna Nayak, and Shrikanth Narayanan. "Paralinguistic mechanisms of production in human 'beatboxing': A real-time magnetic resonance imaging study." *Journal of the Acoustical Society of America* 133, no. 2 (February 2013): 1043–1054. doi-org.spot.lib.auburn.edu/10.1121/1.4773865.

Robinson-Martin, Trineice. *So You Want to Sing Gospel: A Guide for Performers.* Lanham, MD: Rowman & Littlefield, 2017.

Robinson-Martin, Trineice. "Soul Ingredients™: Onsets in African American folk-based music." In *The Voice Teacher's Cookbook: Creative Recipes for Teachers of Singing* edited by Brian J. Winnie, 99–101. Delray Beach, FL: Meredith Music, 2018.

Robinson-Martin, Trineice. "Performance styles and music characteristics of black gospel music." *Journal of Singing* 65, no. 5 (May/June 2009): 595–599.

Roy, Nelson, Karen S. Ryker, and Diane M. Bless. "Vocal violence in actors: An investigation into its acoustic consequences and the effects of hygienic laryngeal release training." *Journal of Voice* 14, no. 2 (June 2000): 215–230. doi.org/10.1016/S0892-1997(00)80029-6.

Rudolph, Thomas and Vincent Leonard. *The iPad in the Music Studio: Connecting Your iPad to Mics, Mixers, Instruments, Computers, and More!* Milwaukee: Hal Leonard, 2014.

Rykar, Karen S. "To train and test the voice in violence." *Voice and Speech Review* 2, no. 1 (2001): 66–73. doi.org/10.1080/23268263.2001.10761447.

Sadolin, Cathrine. *Complete Vocal Technique Application:* completevocal.institute/app/.

Sapthavee, Andrew, Paul Yi, and H. Steven Sims. "Functional endoscopic analysis of beatbox performers." *Journal of Voice* 28, no. 3 (May 2014): 328–331. doi.org/10.1016/j.jvoice.2013.11.007.

Strachan, Robert. *Sonic Technologies: Popular Music, Digital Culture and the Creative Process.* New York: Bloomsbury Publishing, 2017.

Tracy, Neal. "Music theater rocks! Organic Rock singing 101 and beyond." *Journal of Singing* 70, no. 2 (November/December 2013): 209–213.

Ufema, Kate and Douglas W. Montequin. "The performance scream: Vocal use or abuse?" *Voice and Speech Review* 2, no. 1 (2001): 74–86. doi.org/10.1080/23268263.2001.10761448.

SECTION I:
Approaches

2

Methods

A *method* is an organized process, a body of skills, and a systematic mode of inquiry. When defined broadly in this way, every voice pedagogue employs his or her own method formed by personal knowledge and experience. By contrast, a *methodology* is a "particular set of procedures" or "body of rules employed by a discipline".[1] While it is difficult to categorize each pedagogical approach because each is unique and multi-faceted, some effort has been made to group the approaches into categories. They range from strict methodologies to the complete rejection of methodology in favor of an eclectic or independent model. Readers are encouraged to study each approach in more depth so that nuances may be understood at a deeper level than the scope of this text may offer.

Six pedagogues have developed methodologies of CCM singing, which are available to students of singing through workshops and masterclasses, and to teachers of singing through teacher training or certification. These methodologies are listed below, and some examples include Somatic Voicework, The LoVetri Method™ and Estill Voice Training®. These methodologies are the first of their kind in CCM voice training, and their founders have pioneered and defined the field. A CCM voice pedagogue should explore and study all of these invaluable methodologies as they form the foundation of "comparative" CCM voice pedagogy.

Four pedagogues have a well-organized point of view which may have a trademarked label but do not represent a rigid methodology of training. These models may or may not offer practitioner training. These more flexible approaches are listed below, and examples include *Bel Canto/Can Belto* and Soul Ingredients® Method. Details of each approach will be presented here and in the following chapters.

As the field has progressed, an increasing trend towards flexibility has emerged. The majority of pedagogues (60%) identify as practitioners who do not teach a particular methodology but instead, draw upon many eclectic sources, such as several methodologies included in this text, performing and pedagogical experience, and study of voice science. As more voice science research emerges on the topic of CCM singing, practitioners wish to remain flexible in order to be able to respond to these changes.

Ten of the pedagogues (40%) eschew the use of a single methodology in CCM voice training. They argue that every student is unique, and they draw from many sources to find solutions. Several pedagogues state that due to the complexity of the voice, there is no particular set of procedures which is vast enough to provide answers to every challenge. In response to this trend, some of the newer teacher training programs have no central approach to their

---

1   Merriam-Webster, www.merriam-webster.com/dictionary/methodology, accessed on August 29, 2018.

offerings, such as the CCM Vocal Pedagogy Institute at Shenandoah Conservatory or the Boston Conservatory Vocal Pedagogy Professional Workshop.

It is important to note that many of the pioneering methodologies are quite flexible and do allow for and implement revisions as development in science progresses. Many of the founders of the methodologies are at the forefront of CCM voice research themselves as authors or test subjects, who then generously share findings through conferences, workshops, and seminars. The same generosity will be found in this text, as these expert pedagogues have shared extensive information about the practical details of their methodologies, methods, models, and approaches. Readers are encouraged to explore each pedagogue's individual scholarly contributions in depth. Many such contributions have been referenced throughout this text, but they are too numerous to be covered comprehensively.

Contributors (Alphabetical)
Irene Bartlett: PhD, Coordinator of Contemporary Voice and Vocal Pedagogy, Lecturer in Jazz/ Contemporary Voice: Griffith University, experts.griffith.edu.au/academic/i.bartlett
Mark Baxter: Vocal Coach, voicelesson.com/
Tracy Marie Bourne: Diploma of Dramatic Arts (Acting), Bachelor of Music (Voice), Master of Music (Perf.), PhD, Private Studio teacher and Voice/Singing teacher: Canberra Academy of Dramatic Art, www.tracybourne.com
Dane Chalfin: Vocal Rehabilitation Coach and Singing Teacher, www.vocalrehabilitation.com
Kim Chandler: MMus (Distinction) BMusEd, www.kimchandler.com, www.funkynfun.com
Matthew Edwards: DMA, Associate Professor and Coordinator of Musical Theatre Voice: Shenandoah University, Artistic Director: Contemporary Commercial Music Vocal Pedagogy Institute, www. EdwardsVoice.com
Robert Edwin: BA, Owner: Robert Edwin Studio, LLC, www.robertedwinstudio.com
Cate Frazier-Neely: Voice Teacher and Singing Specialist, www.CateFNStudios.com
Marcelle G. Gauvin: Associate Professor of Voice: Berklee College of Music; Faculty: Contemporary Commercial Music Vocal Pedagogy Institute, Shenandoah University; Owner: Double Bar Music, Westport, MA
Elisabeth Howard: Bachelor and Master (voice): The Juilliard School; Former faculty: Hunter College and Pepperdine University, Founder of the Vocal Power Academy, Voting member of the Grammys. www.vocalpoweracademy.com
Gillyanne Kayes: PhD, Visiting Professor London College of Music: University of West London; Co-founder of Vocal Process Ltd. www.vocalprocess.co.uk
Wendy DeLeo LeBorgne: PhD, CCC-SLP, Clinical Director, Voice Pathologist & Singing Voice Specialist: The Blaine Block Institute for Voice Analysis and Rehabilitation, Dayton, OH, The Professional Voice Center of Greater Cincinnati, Cincinnati, OH, Adjunct Assistant Professor: Cincinnati College-Conservatory of Music, http://www.drwendy.me
Jeanette LoVetri: Founder of Somatic Voicework™, The LoVetri Method, Director: The Voice Workshop, Singing Voice Specialist, http://www.thevoiceworkshop.com/
Edrie Means Weekly: M.M., B.M.E., Co-founder: Contemporary Commercial Music Vocal Pedagogy Institute, Adjunct Associate Professor of Voice Pedagogy, Music Theatre Styles Specialist: Shenandoah University, http://edriemeans.wix.com/edriemeans
Kathryn Paradise: BM, MM: Belmont University, Instructor of Commercial Voice: Belmont University, www.kateparadise.com
Lisa Popeil: MFA: California Institute of the Arts, Founder of Voiceworks® Method, http://www. popeil.com/

Jeff Ramsey: BM: Berklee College of Music, Associate Professor of Voice: Berklee College of Music, www.jefframseymusic.com
Seth Riggs and Margareta Svensson Riggs: Speech Level Singing™, http://www.theriggsvocalstudio.com
Trineice Robinson-Martin: MM, EdM, EdD, Faculty: Princeton University, Founder of Soul Ingredients™ Voice Studio, www.DrTrineice.com
Marci Rosenberg: MS, CCC-SLP, Speech Pathologist & Clinical Singing Voice Specialist
Cathrine Sadolin: Founder of Complete Vocal Technique (CVT), http://completevocal.institute/
Mary Saunders Barton: BA, MA, Professor Emeritus Voice and Voice Pedagogy for Musical Theatre: Penn State University, Chair: American Academy of Teachers of Singing, www.belcantocanbelto.com
Jan Shapiro: Bachelor's in Music Ed.: Howard University, Master's in Education: Cambridge College, Former Department Chair and Professor of Voice: Berklee College of Music, www.JanShapiro.com
Kimberly Steinhauer: PhD, President: Estill Voice International, www.estillvoice.com
Kevin Wilson: BM Vocal Performance: University of Central Oklahoma, MM Vocal Pedagogy: New England Conservatory of Music, Director of Vocal Pedagogy: The Boston Conservatory @ Berklee, www.KevinWilsonVoice.com

Methodologies
Elisabeth Howard: Vocal Power Method http://www.vocalpoweracademy.com/
Jeannette LoVetri: Somatic Voicework™ The LoVetri Method http://www.thevoiceworkshop.com/somatic.html
Lisa Popeil: Voiceworks® Method http://www.popeil.com/
Seth Riggs and Margareta Svensson Riggs: Speech Level Singing™ http://www.speechlevelsinging.com/, http://theriggsvocalstudio.com/
Cathrine Sadolin: Complete Vocal Technique (CVT) completevocal.institute/cathrine-sadolin/
Kimberly Steinhauer, President Estill Voice International, Founder: Jo Estill, 1921-2010, Estill Voice Training® www.estillvoice.com/

Well-organized points of view
Mark Baxter: Split Second Singing, voicelesson.com/
Dane Chalfin: Primal Voice, Practitioner Training, www.vocalrehabilitation.com/courses-workshops
Trineice Robinson-Martin: Soul Ingredients® Method, Workshops and Masterclasses www.drtrineice.com/soul-ingredientsreg-workshops-and-master-classes.html
Mary Saunders Barton: Bel Canto Can Belto, Practitioner Training, http://www.belcantocanbelto.com/

Teacher training with no central method
Matthew Edwards: Artistic Director of the Contemporary Commercial Music Vocal Pedagogy Institute at Shenandoah Conservatory: www.ccminstitute.com/
Cate Frazier-Neely: Workshops and Masterclasses, www.catefnstudios.com/workshops-masterclasses
Gillyanne Kayes and Jeremy Fisher: Founders of Vocal Process, Multidisciplinary, Multimedia Voice Educators, vocalprocess.co.uk/
Wendy DeLeo LeBorgne: Workshops and Masterclasses, http://www.drwendy.me/workshops-masterclasses
Kevin Wilson: Director of Vocal Pedagogy, Boston Conservatory Vocal Pedagogy Professional Workshop: bostonconservatory.berklee.edu/extension-programs/vocal-pedagogy-professional-workshop

Other training resources
Acoustical Society of America (ASA), acousticalsociety.org/
American Speech-Language-Hearing Association (ASHA), www.asha.org/
Association for Popular Music Education (APME), www.popularmusiceducation.org/about-apme/
The Australian National Association of Teachers of Singing (ANATS), www.anats.org.au/about-anats-ltd
Australian Voice Association (AVA), www.australianvoiceassociation.com.au/
The British Voice Association (BVA), www.britishvoiceassociation.org.uk/
Canadian Voice Care Foundation (CVCF), http://www.canadianvoicecarefdn.com/
The College Music Society, www.music.org/
Commercial Voice Resources (Jessica Baldwin): http://www.commercialvoiceresources.com/
The European Voice Teachers Association (EVTA), http://www.evta-online.eu/
The Fall Voice Conference, http://www.fallvoice.org/
International Congress of Voice Teachers (ICVT)
The International Society for Music Education, www.isme.org/
International Voice Teachers of Mix (IVTOM), http://www.ivtom.org/about-2/
Music Theatre Educators' Alliance International (MTEA), www.musicaltheatreeducators.org/
National Association of Teachers of Singing (NATS), www.nats.org/
The National Center for Voice and Speech (NCVS), http://www.ncvs.org/svi_infous.html
New Zealand Association of Teachers of Singing (NEWZATS), newzats.org.nz/
Pan American Vocology Association (PAVA), http://www.pava-vocology.org/
Pan-European Voice Conferences, http://www.pevoc.org/about.php
The Society for Ethnomusicology, www.ethnomusicology.org/
The Voice Foundation Symposium, voicefoundation.org/annual-symposium/
Voice and Speech Trainers Association (VASTA), www.vasta.org/

This chapter includes responses to the prompt "Do you teach a specific pedagogical method? If so, what are the foundational principles of this method?". Responses are presented in order from methodologies, well-organized points of view, and end with those who draw on eclectic sources or eschew single methodology in practice. The range of responses celebrates the "many roads to Rome" approach to CCM voice pedagogy, which is echoed many times throughout this text.

Elisabeth Howard

I am the originator of the Elisabeth Howard Vocal Power Method.[2] I am the author of the *Teachers' Vocal Power Method Toolkit for CCM*[3] and the *Singers' Vocal Power Method Toolkit for CCM*.[4]

The foundational principles of the Vocal Power Method are as follows:

---

2 More information is available at http://www.vocalpoweracademy.com/ or in Elisabeth Howard, *Sing! The Vocal Power Method* (New York: Alfred Music, 2006).

3 More information is available at www.vocalpoweracademy.com/teacher-sale-s-page.

4 More information is available at www.vocalpoweracademy.com/student-sale-s-page.

Vocal power techniques

1. Breathing and support – using intercostal and subcostal muscles for ribcage expansion and for deep, low breathing and support.
2. Dynamics – Forte, piano, crescendo, decrescendo. Co-ordination of breath flow with appropriate vocal fold adduction.
3. Power and projection using the least amount of effort through the balance of vocal fold adduction, breath pressure, and resonance space.
4. Diaphragmatic vibrato for long, sustained tones. Four vibrato techniques used specifically in classical singing, R&B, rock, country, and jazz.
5. Safe belting - the mix.
6. Specific vocal tract configurations used for emotional expression.
7. "Licks" and "runs" techniques used in classical singing applied to "licks" and "runs" in R&B and jazz.

Vocal power approach to vocal style

Analyze songs of recording artists with respect to the following:
1. Vibrato speed, width, delayed vibrato, straight tone.
2. Vibrato type – flutter, throat, shimmery, diaphragmatic, Mediterranean.
3. Voice quality – clear, breathy, rough, etc.
4. Special effects – vocal tract configuration for specific emotions.
5. Coloration – chest, mouth mask, head colors.
6. Registers – head, chest, MIX, blended, broken etc.
7. Dynamics – use of piano, forte, crescendo, decrescendo etc.
8. Pronunciation – consonant, vowels, pronunciation of words authentic to the style.
9. Phrasing – back phrasing and anticipation.
10. "Licks" and "runs".

Jeannette LoVetri

I have my own method called Somatic Voicework™[5] which I created in 2002. It was originally based on my 35 years of teaching singing; it now includes an additional 15 years' experience of teaching this approach and, of course, my entire life (since age 15) of being a singer.

Somatic Voicework™ rests upon my understanding of voice science, vocal health and voice medicine as I have learned about those disciplines from multiple sources since 1978. The work has been vetted by numerous national and international Speech-Language Pathologists, medical doctors and voice science researchers, and by hundreds of well-established teachers of singing in many styles, quite a few of whom hold doctoral degrees. Ten internationally recognized laryngologists have lectured during the training program, and five speech-language pathologists have presented vocal hygiene and voice science as well.

It is also based on my years of teaching in New York City in a private practice where I must help singers to meet the needs of the music marketplace on Broadway, in jazz, in rock, folk, gospel, R&B, and alternative styles. My own training was in classical music, and I have always been a lyric coloratura soprano who could belt and who was very comfortable in music theatre. I still perform (non-professionally) music from each style.

---

5 More information is available at http://www.thevoiceworkshop.com/somatic.html.

The work is based on the deliberate use of three registers (vocal qualities), which are traditionally referred to as chest, mix, and head, but which also have other descriptive terms to identify them as well as vowel sound purity, postural balance and breathing co-ordination. The goal is to balance the voice across at least two octaves and to develop a free sound that is authentic, communicative and personally satisfying. Somatic Voicework™ cultivates physical and aural awareness and is a heart-centered approach to singing and teaching.

Lisa Popeil

There are certain skills I believe every singer should understand and master: posture, breathing, support, what resonance means, how to control ring, brightness, nasality, and how resonance changes by varying laryngeal heights. Even changing the hypo-pharyngeal space from neutral, constricted, or wide positions is a fun and important resonance controller. Understanding and controlling vibrato types and speeds is part of the basic skills of singing, as well as how to control vocal fold abduction and adduction for different effects (I teach five positions). Also vital to technical excellence is having reliable and even transitions between vocal registers throughout the range, being able to change a register regardless of pitch, and even how to break as in yodeling or falsetto flips, all of which can quite easily be taught. Most students want to know the mechanism of easy high notes, in chest or head voice, and also how to project their voices. Finally, all singers should know their absolute range, their lowest and highest phonatable notes.

These topics, which I sometimes call "The Concepts", are included in the Voiceworks® Method[6] which is really everything I know and everything I may learn in the future.

Seth Riggs and Margareta Svensson Riggs

Artistically speaking, singing is using the voice in a manner which communicates ideas and emotions to an audience. Technically, however, singing is nothing more than sustained speech over a greater pitch and dynamic range. You do not sing like you speak, but you need to keep the same comfortable, easily produced vocal posture that you have when you speak so that you do not "reach up" for high notes or "press down" for low notes.

The Seth Riggs Vocal Technique, trademarked as Speech Level Singing™[7], is a connected sound, with the anchor in the chest no matter how high the notes. It has its foremost foundational principle in allowing the larynx to rest in a speech level condition, the general area where you speak, without manipulation, throughout at least three octaves of involvement. If a well-balanced bridging process is adhered to throughout the first, second, third and fourth bridging, and beyond, also known as *passaggi* or simply "breaks," there will be an ease, pure vowels and effortless emission from chest voice into head voice, which will remain uncluttered and un-aged.

Seth Riggs formed and started developing his technique while still performing on Broadway in the 50s and 60s, and has since worked with artists who have shaped the history of music including Michael Jackson, Barbra Streisand, Stevie Wonder, Natalie Cole, Ray Charles, and many others. His clients have collectively received more than 135 Grammys while working with him.

---

6   More information is available at http://www.popeil.com/.

7   More information is available at http://www.speechlevelsinging.com/.

Today Seth Riggs and his wife Margareta Svensson Riggs, who is trained both as a singer and as a singing teacher by her husband with more than 6000 performances as a singer behind her, give master classes and workshops together at which participants will not only vocalize through three octaves but also sing songs connected through the otherwise so often problematic first bridge within a matter of days.

"Speech Level Singing" has become a term widely used and not always well applied.[8] If taking lessons from someone claiming that they teach Speech Level Singing, regardless of diplomas on the wall or whom they claim that they were taught by, make sure to ask the teacher to vocalize evenly through three octaves and sing a full song through at least the first bridge. If the teacher can do it you should be in good hands, and if you follow instructions you should see improvement in your vocal ability within a short time.

Cathrine Sadolin

I am the founder of Complete Vocal Technique or CVT.[9] This method is taught at the Complete Vocal Institute in Copenhagen and is also available in published book form in 10 languages; since last year it has also been available as an interactive mobile application in several languages.[10] We have grown to a community of 432 certified teachers from 26 countries. I believe that singing is not difficult, and anyone can learn to sing. Within CVT, I have organized and simplified the approach to be as clear and direct as possible. More details may be found on the CVI website.

There is a version of our app which is free. Here you can find information on the technique, the teaching, and most of our scientific research. This is a big dream come true for me, because my main goal when working with all these techniques and research has always been to make it easier for singers to get help on whichever issue they might have. Now, with the free app, any singer anywhere in the world with a smartphone can have free access to the technique, teaching, updates, and research, so that they can study the evidence for themselves. Many do not understand why we release so much information for free, but it is because we believe that everyone should have access to the scientific research we conduct. Every study we perform will be made available to everyone. Also, people who do not have money to come to Copenhagen and receive training can study on their own. Science and evidence, logic, and rational exploration should be accessible to everyone. I hope that this will be a revolution in singing. Everyone should be able to learn, not just those with money.

The development of this method started with my own challenges with asthma. It was suggested to me that I take some singing lessons to try to improve my asthma. I took one singing lesson, and I knew that I needed to continue to sing for the rest of my life. Everyone doubted my abilities because my asthma was so severe. I was often hoarse and had no voice. I had only a five-note range, and my voice cracked constantly. Of course, if you are coughing all the time, the voice is really damaged. I wanted to learn more. I took lessons, and it was very difficult. Usually, singing training starts with some kind of talent, but I had none, I could not even breathe. I was really starting from scratch, and the teachers did not know what to do. They were used to students that could copy what they did. I worked with several teachers but they could not help me because of my breathing problems. I ended up with nodules.

---

8   Due to the widespread use of the term "Speech Level Singing," the original method is in development. More information is available at http://theriggsvocalstudio.com/.

9   More information is available at http://completevocal.institute/.

10   More information is available at completevocal.institute/app/.

I wanted to know why the different approaches to singing all seemed to operate without any kind of science behind them, and I wondered why it had to be so metaphoric. Phrases like "sing like you're in the wind" made no sense to me. I had to figure this out for myself. I went to London and started studying there because there was a teacher who would work with me, Vera Rózsa. However, as she usually taught professional singers, I had a hard time understanding what she was saying.

I started to research everything myself. I read everything on anatomy and physiology and the voice and I realized that there are some rules and foundational principles. At that time, I could not find anything written which explained what to do in a concrete way, so I had to invent it myself. As I understood more of the anatomy and physiology, and by experimenting, I gradually managed to solve many of my singing technical problems. Then I began performing (at that time classical singing). My friends were rock singers, and they asked questions about singing. I realized that the color of the sound comes not from the vocal cords, but the vocal tract. It was logical to think that you could sing in any style just by modifying the sound color. Then friends asked about vocal distortions, such as grunting and growling. I did not know but I wanted to look into it. Then I began to study and sing other styles and gradually I became so involved in research that I was spending more time on research than on singing. It evolved into a structure with some foundation, which could then be built upon.

Kimberly Steinhauer

I use the Estill Voice Model as a Rosetta Stone for the translation of vocal sounds to the underlying biomechanical properties of those productions – it is not a pedagogical method for teaching music, but a tool for describing voice production. *The beauty* is that established voice methods are not discounted – just clarified in a common language for further growth. When everyone is speaking the same language, the vocal possibilities are endless and achievable. I teach voice motor control via Estill Voice Training® (EVT®)[11], a system that separates the craft of voice from artistry. If the Estill Voice Model describes "how the voice works," then Estill Voice Training® prescribes "how to work the voice". EVT combines principles from vocal and athletic sciences to empower speakers and singers to gain conscious mastery of the voice for any musical style. Students of EVT visit the "gym" daily to extend vocal range, strength, flexibility, and endurance via targeted exercises for 13 anatomic structures called EVT Figures for Voice™. Each of these 13 structures moves to produce changes in voice quality that can be heard, felt, and seen. EVT is different from other voice methods because it focuses on the craft of hearing, feeling, and seeing these voice Figures throughout the range without attending to music or accompaniment by a piano. A vocalist's choice of Figure option will determine the final "mix" of voice quality for the specific context. After the voice craft is mastered through focused and deliberate practice of the Figures, a performer possesses the vocal freedom to make artistic choices and comfortably meet the vocal demands in repertoire, from opera to pop to musical theatre.

Mark Baxter

I refer to my approach as "Split-Second Singing," a moniker derived from the time it takes chemical and electrical signals to travel from the brain to the muscles of phonation. The

11   More information is available at www.estillvoice.com/.

founding principle is that the sounds of popular singing are innate and universal to the human experience. Therefore, those who struggle to produce them are restricted by inhibition – not ignorance. The inhibition is the result of perceived disapproval from one's culture, typically starting with the family or home environment, and can extend up to one's country or religious beliefs. Unfortunately, I was a prime example of the restrictions culture can impose on a young voice.

My parents firmly believed that the "singing gene" was not present in my DNA. Therefore, they felt my aspiration to sing professionally was delusional. Undaunted, I persevered to prove them wrong. My vocal professors in college constantly warned me that if I did not adhere to classical training I would most certainly suffer permanent vocal damage. Undaunted, I sang in rock bands through my 20s and beyond. Although I proved them wrong by sustaining no pathologies during a decade of performing multiple nights a week, my singing often felt effortful – like I was swimming against the current. I knew other rock singers who struggled but I also knew a few that did not. I became curious about the difference. I trained with various voice teachers privately and explored non-musical disciplines such as physical therapy, orthopedics, chiropractic care, yoga, and deep tissue massage. The fruits of these studies, blended with the lessons learned during my performing years, are what fed me as a young voice teacher and became the content of my first book, *The Rock-n-Roll Singer's Survival Manual*.[12] However, I had yet to answer the question as to why singing is fluid for some but not all. It was not until I turned my curiosity towards the brain that I found the culprit.

The phenomenon of culturalization is known to permeate the synaptic connections within a developing brain and ultimately influence adult thoughts and behaviors. This cultural code of conduct acts as a traffic cop within the brain, releasing a neurotransmitter called gamma-aminobutyric acid (GABA) as a red light to inhibit the motor signals of singing from speeding down the neural pathways to the muscles below. My current pedagogical method is to green-light those pathways using a multitude of vocal exercises instead of repertoire work. The exercises featured in my forthcoming book *Split-Second Singing* allow singers to focus on developing co-ordination between the voice's actuator, vibrator, resonators, and articulators before dipping into the cultural waters of their chosen genres. The repetition of non-emotional exercises reduces GABAergic interference over time and re-establishes the innate spilt-second connection between inspiration and sound. This is not a new approach; it is how every musician learns to play an instrument. The difference is that singing does not *require* skill-building exercises because it is innate. I am not against unskilled folks singing songs. I just find a voice develops much faster if you first "un-train" any cultural restrictions singers may be harboring by allowing them to sound as bad as a child learning to play a saxophone, violin or trumpet. Musicians-in-training are allowed to fail. Singers are not. I did not lack a passion for learning when I was young – I lacked permission to fail.

Dane Chalfin

I am more interested in models because using a pedagogical model based on whatever your current understanding of anatomy, physiology, acoustics, and the appropriateness of that information to repertoire and performance, provides a framework in which you can get creative. Although, I would say that there are models out there that call themselves models but have become very method-like. A method has a prescribed approach and provides a limited number

---

12 Mark Baxter, *The Rock-n-Roll Singer's Survival Manual* (Milwaukee: Hal Leonard, 1990).

of tools which have been sanctioned, and you are not allowed to break from this mandate. Methods have commercial goals attached to them, and they can create zealots. When you start using your method as the "truth", and you sell that "truth" in a way that is based on creating fear among singers regarding vocal health being dependent on using your method, this is unethical.

I am concerned about some methods which have become outdated and are no longer aligned with science. Manipulating science in public relations is not good practice. If one voice scientist says your method is good, that is only *one* person saying so. A voice scientist is not a professional singer and may not even work with professional singers. Voice scientists have spent no time on tour with professional singers, nor worked with them in a studio, nor sat at the side of the stage with them. I sit on two boards which are medically related. I feel that I need to be a voice of reason sometimes in our community, even if that is unpopular. When methods also advertise products, such as throat sprays and lozenges, I start to question the moral compass.

I was watching Janice Chapman[13] (Royal Academy of Music, Guildhall School of Music and Drama) teaching in about 2003. She was using primal sounds like laughing, crying out, whimpering, calling out, and yelling, to elicit reflexive responses in the muscles of respiratory support. The premise of this technique is that human babies have evolved to have a set of noises that communicate their needs to care-givers, and these are hard-wired. These are survival-dependent, and emotionally-led, which creates nice reflexive responses in the muscles of support. Janice would use these responses to get people connected to their bodies and then move into a more classical approach. As I listened to her using these tactics, I was thinking that contemporary singers in pop/rock and theatre make these noises all the time. I decided to take it to the laboratory, stick some cameras up people's noses and find out what is happening in the vocal tract.

We started looking at Primal Sound[14] at the University Hospital of South Manchester, where I am the Vocal Rehabilitation Coach (Singing Voice Specialist). We put together a protocol to look at the gestures of the larynx and pharynx in primal sounds. We started this study in 2006 and to date, we have done over 450 protocols on a huge range of professional, semi-professional, and amateur singers, healthy and disordered, and some non-singers. To my knowledge, it is the largest study that has ever been done on the contemporary singing voice in the world. We have not published yet, because it is not yet concluded. We have been refining parameters the whole time. We started with lots of sounds and as we narrowed it down, we found four basic families of gesture: sigh, whimper, whinge (crying out), and yelling.[15] Small changes to the vocal tract can make those sounds brighter or darker, and that might sound more like a sob or a whine, or a groan, and so on. However, all the gestures look similar in terms of vocal fold activity and vocal tract shape. We have a set of parameters for those sounds that identify where they are most optimally efficient.

Trineice Robinson-Martin

Soul Ingredients™[16] Methodology aims to address voice training from the perspective of understanding and acknowledging the person and personality, developing the voice as an instrument, conditioning the voice to execute stylistic components of the music chosen to sing, and nourishing the musical execution of honest emotional expression of the content.

---

13 More information is available at http://www.janicechapman.co.uk/.

14 More information is available at www.vocalrehabilitation.com/.

15 More information is available at www.vocalrehabilitation.com/.

16 More information is available at http://www.drtrineice.com/index.html.

Soul ingredients™ uses pedagogic research and voice science to develop the voice as an instrument, and applies that knowledge to conditioning the voice to sing in a specific style – as determined by those vocal parameters valued in said style.

Conceptually, "soul singing" from the standpoint of African-American folk-based music (i.e. gospel, blues, jazz, R&B, etc.) is a style of singing in which the expression and communication of how one *feels* about what one is singing dominates the actual words and melody being sung. In other words, in soul singing it is not enough to simply sing a melody with the words "I'm still hurting". The virtuosity of a soul singer stems from his or her ability to musically and emotionally communicate the hurt and frustration behind the words "I'm still hurting" with as much, if not more, conviction than would be expressed in spoken dialogue. Most of the sung tones and vocal nuances used in the musical communication in African American folk-based styles are directly related to sounds and vocal nuances used in everyday charismatic colloquial speech. It is this concept of natural emotions and natural sounds, being easily executed that forms the foundational principles of Soul Ingredients™ Methodology.

Soul Ingredients™ asks the questions: Who are you and what do you want to say? What musical language do you want to communicate? Is your *real* voice being heard (both figuratively and physiologically)? Is your voice physically prepared to have this conversation? How do you *feel* about what you have to say? How do you want the audience to respond to what you have to say (i.e. do you want their empathy, sympathy, or are you making a call to action)?

Every aspect of voice training aims to answer these questions.

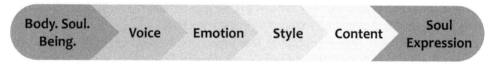

My approach to functional voice training stems from pedagogic practices learned from Jeannette LoVetri and Somatic Voicework™, The LoVetri Method.

My approach to style is to expose singers to various improvisatory tools used for music interpretation so they do not feel limited when telling their own stories.

Mary Saunders Barton

I am a musical theatre voice teacher by trade. My overarching responsibility is to train actors to sing. Allegiance to dramatic storytelling is paramount. The term *bel canto can belto*[17], which has come to be associated with my name, evolved quite naturally over the years from empirical observation and practical application in studio work. It represents a pedagogical "cross-training" point of view rather than an exclusive training method.[18] The foundational technical principle is the balance of registration and resonance in order to maximize range and assure the health and longevity of the vocal instrument. As musical theatre continues to re-invent itself by absorbing new styles to tell its stories, performers are challenged to find healthy ways to meet industry demands authentically. The technique shares many of the same principles governing healthy dynamic speech. It is vowel/resonance based and takes advantage of subtle laryngeal balancing between thyroarytenoid (mode 1, chest) and cricothyroid (mode 2, head/falsetto) functions. Speaking and singing become inextricably

---

17 More information is available at http://www.belcantocanbelto.com/.

18 More information is available in Norman Spivey and Mary Saunders Barton, *Cross-Training in the Voice Studio: A Balancing Act* (San Diego: Plural Publishing, 2018).

linked. The current generation of musical theatre singers needs to be powerfully conditioned, like any elite athletes.

Cate Frazier-Neely

No, I do not teach a specific pedagogical method. I am an amalgam of everything I have ever heard, seen, studied or experienced.

Tracy Marie Bourne

I principally teach music theatre vocal styles, including belt, legit, and mix qualities. I do not teach just one particular method, but I have attended Somatic Voicework™ training with Jeannette LoVetri. I have been influenced by other methodologies including Estill Voice Training® and Speech Level Singing™, but I have not undertaken specific training in these methods. I was originally trained as a classical singer and use some of these principles in my teaching.

Marcelle Gauvin

I combine a number of pedagogical methods in my teaching. Each method I utilize is based on voice science and informed by bodywork mechanics. I work from two assumptions. The first is if you speak, you can sing. The second is that each voice is unique unto itself and has something to contribute to this life experience.

Kathryn Paradise

I became certified in Somatic Voicework™, The LoVetri Method in 2008, and by the National Center for Voice and Speech in Vocology in 2010. Both of these methods are grounded in a foundation of science-based, functional singing. I have found functional voice training to be adaptable to all styles of singing and the wide variety of artistic, emotional, mental and physical needs presented by students in the commercial voice studio. I have also informally explored or researched other systems of commercial voice pedagogy, including Speech Level Singing™ (Seth Riggs), Singing Success[19] (Brett Manning), Complete Vocal Technique (Cathrine Sadolin), Estill Voice Training®, *The Phenomena of the Belt/Pop Voice*[20] (Jan Sullivan), and various writings and research by Lisa Popeil.

Jeff Ramsey

I teach functional voice training learned from many years of studying with Mark Baxter. I have also supplemented my knowledge with Somatic Voicework™, The LoVetri Method.

Jan Shapiro

I use my own way to describe vocal technique and style. However, in general, the way I teach technique, regardless of style, is the same. This is based on general classical training – breath management, singing freely without tension in the whole body.

---

19 More information may be found at www.singingsuccess.com.

20 Jan Sullivan, *The Phenomena of the Pop/Belt Voice* (3rd ed., Logos Ltd, 1996), and Janet Sullivan, "How to teach the belt/pop voice," *Journal of Research in Singing and Applied Vocal Pedagogy* 13, no. 1 (1989): 41-56.

Marci Rosenberg

I do not teach a specific trade-marked or certified method in isolation, though I am familiar with several. My approach is a hybrid, functional approach based on my own experience as a singer, an SLP who is a clinical singing voice specialist, a voice teacher, and the numerous wonderful workshops I have attended over the years. My pedagogy has certainly evolved over the last 20 years and is very much informed by my knowledge of singing science and biomechanics, exercise physiology, and motor learning principles. There has never been a time when I have been content that I have learned what I need to know. I will always continue to further my knowledge and evolve my pedagogy as research and clinical practice/studio application reveals more insight into the voice.

Kevin Wilson

I do not teach anything attached to a dogma or trade-marked practice. Most of my teaching techniques developed by trial and error in the studio. I have acquired many tools along the way from various pedagogical writings, as well as from contemporary pedagogues and colleagues. I teach to an aesthetic that I perceive as balanced, flexible, and sustainable over time.

Irene Bartlett

No, I do not teach any particular method. My personal belief is that methods become fixed and inflexible while the science-based knowledge of the voice is constantly evolving. I am an eclectic teacher – a collector of ideas and technical exercises that I adapt to suit the student's style choices, natural singing abilities, and voice maturation level. My greatest influences have come from the literature of Voice Science including the research of Ingo Titze, Robert Sataloff, Michael Benninger, Johan Sundberg, and Tom Cleveland. In line with my research of voice science principles, my pedagogical approach is firmly underpinned by bodywork models – predominantly, the Alexander Technique and Barbara Conable's "Bodymapping". I have borrowed deeply from pedagogues in the singing voice literature including Oren Brown, Janice Chapman, Leon Thurman & Graham Welch, Robert Edwin, Jeanette LoVetri, and from my research of the early work of Jo Estill.

Kim Chandler

I do not believe that any one vocal method or vocal "map" (as I call it) is comprehensive enough at this point in time. The voice is so much more complex than we teachers or singers can ever truly understand, so a vocal methodology can provide some sort of "navigation" ability. Either the map connects with your view of your voice or it does not. That is why I think it's good to have different approaches available because not everything works for everybody. It's not "one size fits all". I personally advocate a "pick and mix" approach where I can choose from the various methodologies that I have had some training in (or at least some encounter with) if it's useful to my clients. I see vocal methods as a set of tools and the bigger the set of tools, the more useful you are going to be as a coach, in my opinion. Even though we may have our favorite set of tools that we use most of the time, undoubtedly someone will come along for whom your usual tools do not work, and so you may need to grab something from the back of the toolbox to find exactly what will help that person. So, if there is a strict methodology that cannot be ventured outside of, that smacks of limitation rather than educational freedom to me. This is why I have kept myself methodologically independent so that I can use whatever my clients need and keep changing, growing and evolving. I am not limited to just one approach and no one can dictate to me what I can and cannot teach. Every single methodology, no matter how complex, is still a simplification of the truth. Teaching should be entirely client-focused, not requiring the teacher and client to fall into line behind the dictates of a method.

Matthew Edwards

I consider myself a vocologist. The term vocology has been around for a while but is gaining more prominence with the development of the Pan American Vocology Association and its efforts to create a recognition for those who believe in fact-based training for all types of vocalization. Vocologists study the human voice and use research to inform their practice. To that end, I do not teach one specific method but rather, use my knowledge of vocal function to choose exercises for each student's needs. I have studied several methods and think there is a lot to be said for codifying one's life experience. However, I prefer to use anything that works rather than commit to a singular approach.

Edrie Means Weekly

I teach healthy vocal function based on voice science and voice medicine. With vocal research and voice science, we know a lot more about the function of the voice today. I work on the function at the vocal fold level, the breath flow and pressure, and the shape of the vocal tract for different styles and vowel formation. I teach the individual and adapt to how they learn, whether they are young or old. Each singer is unique with different needs. There is no cookie cutter recipe for all singers. I adjust to their individual learning style, aural, visual, or kinesthetic. I maintain working on healthy vocal function, evenness of register balance, and flexibility.

Robert Edwin

I am not a big fan of branded pedagogic methods or approaches. I prefer to take my cue from one of the teaching giants of the 20th century, Richard Miller. Professor Miller, who was my sponsor for membership in the National Association of Teachers of Singing (NATS) and my first Editor-In-Chief when I started writing for *The NATS Bulletin* (now called *Journal of Singing*) in 1985, never branded his pedagogy. There was never "The Richard Miller Method". Rather, he taught and wrote using the collected wisdom of the ages held under the light of modern voice science and technology. I have tried to emulate Richard in that regard by describing my pedagogy as fact-based, gender-neutral, age-appropriate, and style-specific.

Gillyanne Kayes

No, I do not use a specific pedagogical method because the idea of a single "method" is anathema to me. I think it's important to draw from different methodologies in teaching. Methods have advantages in that they provide a structured approach, but these are also, of their nature, limiting. In my opinion, good pedagogical training exposes the teachers to a number of different approaches, as well as the foundational knowledge of vocal function, musicianship, and basic acoustics.

Wendy DeLeo LeBorgne

In my private studio, I do not teach a single specific pedagogy as there is no "cookbook" approach to teaching singing. I use a combination of pedagogies depending on the needs of the artist. Because I teach both classical and commercial artists, I will draw from the classical pedagogy literature and terminology when working with classical-based singers, and when I train commercial artists, I pull from the current literature combined with my own knowledge of commercial voice production (from a physiological standpoint). In commercial voice pedagogy, I will use combined pedagogical teachings from a variety of commercial voice pedagogues including, but not limited to: Jeanie LoVetri, Mary Saunders Barton, Jo Estill, Marybeth Bunch, Lisa Popeil, and my own exercise physiology and pedagogy knowledge. I try to draw relevant teachings from each of the pedagogical teachings historically and currently as it applies to the current level of the artist and the ultimate vocal goals of the singer. When I teach vocal pedagogy at CCM (Cincinnati College Conservatory of Music), I work to expose my students to historical pedagogical teachings as well as current day pedagogical materials.

3
Philosophy

A teaching philosophy is a pedagogical guide for what is valued and goes to the heart of this text. The responses of this chapter are more similar to one another than those of any other chapter in this text. There is a set of shared core values that runs deep in this group. These pedagogues are united in their desire to be of service to their students. Through functional and healthy voice training, they empower their students to reach their own specific goals. Teachers remove their personal stylistic preferences from the process and engage in a collaborative journey with the student. They do not work towards a preconceived notion of what sounds "good" or "correct" but rather, guide the student towards a fully realized version of their own unique and most-expressive sound. Teachers engage in lifelong learning and appreciate opportunities to improve their own pedagogical skills. Teaching is regarded as a "privilege" and a profound source of satisfaction.

Within the Academy, a movement towards more inclusive and diverse music training may still be a revolutionary concept. Fortunately, inclusive student-centered teaching is already happening in the CCM voice studio. These pedagogues describe a learning atmosphere in which any student would thrive. Genre preferences are removed from technical training, and work towards individual goals is completely customized. Simply put: The master–apprentice model has no place in contemporary commercial voice training. Instead, master pedagogues work from a vast base of knowledge and experience to provide hand-crafted artisanal voice training.

This chapter includes responses to the prompt: "Describe your teaching philosophy. This may include personal goals, objectives, and priorities". The responses are presented in order from most concise to most detailed.

Wendy DeLeo LeBorgne

My teaching philosophy is to maximize performance, minimize injury, and maintain artistic vision in each artist. These are the three goals that I work to achieve with each of my artists.

Kevin Wilson

I am most interested in a sustainable and flexible technique that allows a singer to become purely expressive both physically and emotionally in any genre. I believe that we have one voice that can be flexible, informed, and nuanced for all opportunities.

Robert Edwin

Simply put, my job as a teacher of singing is to help my students explore and pursue efficient, artistic singing in the genre/s they have chosen. Since each and every student comes into my studio with a unique life story, distinct personality traits, and a certain level of talent, technique, and motivation, I have to design a pedagogic approach that will work for that individual so they can find their own voice. "One size fits all" has never been a mantra in this teacher's world.

Gillyanne Kayes

I would describe myself as a "functional voice" teacher in the sense that I deal with functional aspects of singing voice production in my training. I am known as a technique troubleshooter and vocal skills developer. I listen to and work with the singer, the personality and the voice in front of me. I am especially interested in "voice type" in the broader sense i.e. not just voice category but power, depth, brightness, heaviness/lightness plus vocal pitch range capabilities. The most important thing is to work with the singer in front of you always.

Marcelle G. Gauvin

My teaching is grounded in service to my students' development and well-being. I enter that service first by qualifying their personal goals and professional needs. Vocal health is a high priority for me. But I do realize that, at times, professional demands may be pressing. As a voice teacher, my objective is twofold. First, I assist students in building a functional and flexible instrument which is strong enough to handle their professional and artistic demands. Second, I encourage students to discover their individual "voice print" by exploring the unique characteristics and colors their instrument has to offer.

Cate Frazier-Neely

I believe that habilitating (or rehabilitating) the singing voice is a transformational path and connects someone to his or her Best Self. They can then bring that "Best Self" out into the world in a myriad of ways that can help others transform into their Best Selves. This occurs through processes that connect a singer's limbic system (spontaneous and unencumbered emotional expression) to their learned auditory environment (what they hear and perceive and the music they want to sing.)

Singing, performing, teaching, and learning are spiritual paths for a lifetime. To this end, I serve as an artist/educator who is also a functional vocal technician and a singing voice rehabilitation specialist.

Seth Riggs and Margareta Svensson Riggs

Whether superstar or a serious amateur, there is only so much time. Everybody has hopes, dreams, goals, and desires. Therefore, it is vitally important to address what it is that the singer does to cause problems or limitations, and immediately get him or her to sing the correct way instead. When the singer experiences the ease and extended range that is accomplished, the objective is to give him/her the tools to become independent as soon as possible.

To see someone with the gift and passion for singing, regardless of age and struggles, have a new life as a singer, and be able to be the best artist they can be, is what makes it all worthwhile.

Jeff Ramsey

I think any teacher's goal would be to get the student to be able to get the most out of their instrument, with the least amount of muscular effort or resistance. This is how I work with my own vocal development, as I still continue to study with Mark Baxter. One of the concepts Mark and I have talked about is the concept of asking for the sound that you want and allowing the vocal folds to choose the way in which it gives the sound back to you (head, chest, mix). The idea though is not to choose the register but rather, choose the volume you want. I have used this concept for years to reduce wear and tear.

Mary Saunders Barton

My goal in teaching musical theatre performers is to encourage them to trust themselves and their unique gifts, and to respect the technical process.

It is my highest priority to empower students to "teach themselves", to give them the keys to the kingdom as they mature into artists. Once a technique is understood fully, it can be practiced and reinforced and, ideally, used to encounter new vocal challenges with confidence. But there is no timer that pops up at graduation and says "Done. No more training needed". Once they launch into their careers, our students will be the primary advocates for their own vocal health. This implies a commitment to lifelong learning and continued training, which is the surest way to stay inspired and involved.

Mark Baxter

It is the brain that sings. So, my philosophy is to first address the cultural and emotional stigmas that hold the voice hostage. Creating an environment that forgives unintentional and awkward behavior is a priority. Inhibited singers need permission to explore their instruments without the pressure of producing aesthetically pleasing sounds at first. Once physical and emotional comfort is established, we then work on creating intentional vocal sounds. For beginners, I often use cartoon characters as vocal references, such as a teddy bear for depth or a little Martian for a piercing quality. Intermediate and advanced singers are appropriately challenged via exercises until deep skill-sets are established. The goal for each singer is to develop a strong foundation of vocal reflexes so that artistic identity may be explored without restriction.

Edrie Means Weekly

My teaching philosophy is continuously developing and is a journey of self-reflection. I feel confident in my abilities to help singers through the process of developing a healthy functional foundation from which they can explore their own voice with the hopes of succeeding in their life dreams. I am dedicated to healthy functional vocal training based upon voice science and voice medicine. I try to guide singers in creating their sound and building their confidence and performance style. I continue to remain active, gathering invaluable performance, research, and pedagogical experiences. This allows me to continue the journey of refining my own developmental philosophy of teaching, and to develop courses to further vocal education globally. I believe you never stop learning and continue to pass it on to the next generation of performing artists in this ever-changing world of singing styles.

Lisa Popeil

As a teacher (though it may sound corny), I live to serve. I am committed to providing each student with an experience that is invigorating, fun, and empowering. My goal is to provide clear answers to any questions posed to me, and to share tools and techniques which work immediately to help my students reach their vocal goals. I am not imposing a method or a series of exercises. My method simply is my Plan A approach. I am willing to try whatever it takes to guide a student towards a certain skill or sonic aesthetic or expressive ability. I try to teach with precision and clarity to help take the mystery out of the singing experience. In the past, I have tried to develop my own vocal skills to a certain level so that I can demonstrate an idealized sound quickly and accurately.

I consider teaching a noble profession and feel deeply grateful for having had the opportunity to work, over the decades, with such a diverse group of singers who have the same passion for singing as me.

Elisabeth Howard

My goals for myself and for my students are:
1. Build a solid foundation in vocal technique so that you can honor the music and communication of feelings through the music.
2. Work hard, be disciplined, believe in yourself and always strive to be better. There is always room for improvement.
3. Give yourself credit for what you have accomplished. Set high standards and always be grateful for what you have achieved.
4. Never dwell on wrong choices in the past. Your decisions are part of your path.
5. Be open, be flexible, and listen to those who are role models. Learn from them.
6. Be realistic. One has to weigh the pros and cons of having a professional career. Lifestyle or having a family are some of the considerations.
7. When we were born, where we grew up, our parents, our siblings, our friends, the schools we attended, our teachers, our mentors, our religious beliefs, all play an important part in our decisions.
8. We are on a journey to learn from our successes and failures and from each other.
9. Always be the best you can be and always... Let it Shine!

Dane Chalfin

What we know today in anatomy, physiology, acoustics and the genre-specific sounds required by the industry is always difficult to pin down because of how rapidly that information is changing thanks to new research. In my view, the human body operates in a hierarchy where voice production is concerned. Unless you have one thing in place, the next thing does not work as well. I think we can broadly define the hierarchy as alignment, respiration, phonation, resonance, articulation, and style. Interpretation of the text/lyrics should be guiding all of this as well.

I am constantly revising my research and teaching. My book is two years overdue with my publisher because I keep doing more research and proving myself wrong. As a scientist, this is the best thing in the world, but it means that I am continually revising my information. I do not keep people coming back because they are chasing an ideal; I keep them coming back because they trust that I am going to tell them the truth as far as I understand it today. That is always the over-riding principle, and I think that it is part of being a good teacher.

Kathryn Paradise

Great teaching is a creative endeavor, a profession that, at its best, balances structure with out-of-the-box thinking. I aim to achieve this balance while also acknowledging that teaching tends to expose our own weaknesses. My goal in teaching voice is to be a guide as the student explores his or her voice. I view my role as that of a mentor, seeking to empower each student to reach for, or even beyond, her own musical, personal, and professional goals. I do this by embracing and encouraging what is unique and surprising in each student's experience and by fostering trust between the student, her instrument, and her creative imagination. My personal goal in each lesson is to stay present, and respectful of the student's experience, with a mindset that explores and questions alongside. My priority is to identify what each student already does well and work intentionally and gently outwards into areas of weakness and challenge. I have found that asking students questions and validating their personal experience leads to investment and enthusiasm on the part of the student. I am quick to abandon methods or repertoire that do not speak to a specific individual in favor of ideas and materials that resonate and excite. My long-term goal for all students is that they become their own best teachers.

Tracy Marie Bourne

As a music theatre teacher, I am training singers to be vocal actors. This requires an expressive and free sound that can produce a broad range of sounds with a healthy and efficient technique. Music theatre is a multi-disciplinary form, and singers must have a relationship to the text, to character, and to their body. It is not good enough for them to just produce a beautiful sound. Sometimes they need to sing sounds that carry hard emotions, such as anger or fear. It is my job to teach them how to produce sounds in all parts of their range so that they have the versatility to sing and act with authenticity in performance.

When teaching, I encourage my students to build awareness of their instrument and develop the capacity to adjust the way they produce sounds. I do this by asking them questions about how they sensed or felt the sound: "Where did you notice the sensation of resonance?". I also ask them to monitor tension by using the mirror to observe visual signs, or by using their hands to feel for jaw tension. When singers do something correctly, we stop and identify what it was that worked and what they did to achieve that. I often jokingly say "press save" so that we can find that successful sound again in the future.

Kim Chandler

Clients are each seen on their own merit. I am on a collaborative, unique journey with every client I have the privilege of coaching. I will do whatever needs to be done and dip into whatever skills, tricks, techniques, concepts, analogies and advice, from many years as a performer and as a coach, to help the person in front of me. Like a locksmith, it is my job to find the "key" that unlocks a singer's issues. I favor an equal emphasis on training the ears and voice. Aural development is every bit as important to someone's singing career as their vocal development is. It is this philosophy that underpins the content of my "Funky 'n Fun" vocal exercise series[1] where I have put a musical concept and technical concept together in the same exercise wherever possible. The exercises are also sung in a pop way (not classical), backed by funky tracks (not piano), and are based on a range of musical patterns (not just the major scale), e.g.

---

1   More information may be found at http://www.funkynfun.com/.

modes, pentatonic scales etc. Musical relevance and applicability to repertoire is paramount in creating useful and exciting vocal exercises that singers will actually enjoy doing and see the point in practicing. It helps immensely with motivation and compliance. Contemporary singers certainly deserve their own tailored exercises, and should not have to make do with classical "hand-me-down" exercises that generally do not fit their needs.

Marci Rosenberg

Mine is a hybrid approach based on sound singing science, exercise physiology and motor learning principles. The analogy that I use with students is that we all have a mental rolodex for voice production. Over time, we collect index cards with various types of information. Some of those index cards serve us well and some do not. The process of studying voice is geared toward organizing the mental rolodex so that the singer has better access to efficient options for movement. My over-arching goal is to look at each voice student in terms of what is happening biomechanically from head to toe when they are producing sound. What movement patterns are serving them well, what movements patterns are working against healthy efficient voice production, and how deeply ingrained do these movement patterns appear to be. I typically work in a hierarchical manner, adding complexity to a task as the student (or patient) demonstrates facility. The techniques or exercises I use might be quite different from student to student, but the goal is always geared toward bringing the student's awareness to what is happening in his body during sound production to establish better kinesthetic references for more efficient movement patterns over time. I view voice work as not only co-ordinating, strengthening and balancing musculature, but also training the nervous system so that the student's "mental rolodex" for voice production is better organized with more options for efficient movement.

Jan Shapiro

My teaching philosophy comes from my own personal vocal training, my experience as a performer (working/touring six nights a week for 15 years, one to four nights/week of performances during my early years at Berklee), and my teaching experience working with an array of different singers. In simple terms, my philosophy is that one's singing should always be free, without any tension. In order to achieve this, the student singer needs to develop fine co-ordination of breathing muscles and a natural vocal sound.

Almost always, there is a need to work further on better breath support to carry one's voice freely out to the listener.

Concentration on the basics is essential. I sometimes ask my students to hand write a sign listing three basic components. I dictate this to them while they write.

The "sign" to use for practice has a three-tiered bracket. This bracket is actually three components that should be co-ordinated to equal one thought: "To Sing":

1. Relax (jaw muscles, neck, shoulders, upper chest).
2. Take a RELAXED deep breath from the diaphragm.
3. When singing in the mid and upper register, keep an open space (i.e. lifted palate, like yawning).

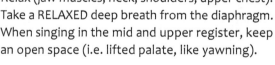

The idea is to have the student concentrate only on the three things listed. They are not to think about notes, words, or how he or she sounds while singing. This often helps students who basically "think too much" while singing! I do not always use this method; sometimes simply telling the student to relax is enough.

Matthew Edwards

I approach each student as an individual with no preconceived notion of what they are supposed to sound like. My number one objective is to help the students achieve their goals, whatever those may be. In the case of a commercial artist, it may be teaching them to improve their stamina while reducing the risk of injury without significantly changing their vocal quality. For a college-age musical theatre major, it may be teaching them how to sing legit, contemporary, and pop/rock repertoire, from the ground up. I believe students sing better when they understand what is happening in their bodies, so I make it a point to describe exactly what it is I am trying to accomplish. You see this same approach in physical therapy when the therapist tells you how your body is functioning and how the exercises he/she is prescribing will improve that function.

However, too much attention to functional jargon can get in the way of artistic expression. So, while I use technical terms at the beginning of my work with a student, I eventually transition to terms that they identify as most helpful. In some cases, students prefer technical terms but for many others, placement or imagery is more effective. I always go with what works best for each individual. My ultimate goal is to be able to focus on story-telling and have the voice fall into place as the performers communicate their human experience through song. Finally, I believe that if you are in doubt, you must refer out. There are so many sub-specialties in our field today and it is impossible for any one teacher to know all of the information that is out there.

Irene Bartlett

My philosophy is based in the belief that learning outcomes improve greatly when teachers encourage students' intrinsic motivation[2] and self-efficacy[3]. In applying philosophy to practice, I have witnessed major positive improvements in students' effort and persistence, and ultimately, in achievement. Rather than following the traditional master/apprentice model, I consider myself to be a voice builder rather than a singing teacher. I build voices based on students' existing vocal development, knowledge of voice function and their style preference, in a belief that collaborative activities between teacher and student will promote deep sense-making, life-long learning, and sustainable vocal health for the singer.

Reliable, adaptive, and style-relevant vocal technique is key to my teaching philosophy where "good singing, is good singing" regardless of style or genre. I believe that inappropriate or poor technique (rather than style in itself) is most likely to induce voice damage in singers of CCM styles. This philosophy requires pedagogical agility, including a knowledge and appreciation of a wide range of music genres, and a non-judgmental attitude to singers' music preferences which is free from any personal, aesthetic bias on my part. My

---

2   Edward L. Deci and Richard M. Ryan, "Self-determination theory: A macrotheory of human motivation, development, and health," *Canadian Psychology* 49, no. 3 (2008): 182-185.

3   Dale H. Schunk and Carol A. Mullen, "Self-efficacy as an engaged learner," in *Handbook of Research on Student Engagement* edited by Sandra L. Christenson, Amy L. Reschly, and Cathy Wylie, 219-235, New York, NY, US: Springer Science + Business Media, 2012, http://dx.doi.org/10.1007/978-1-4614-2018-7_10.

long-term goal is to maximize students' learning potential through open communication of ideas and factual information.

For professional singers that I teach, I work to foster self-recognition of their individual artistic talents through an understanding and acceptance of both successes and failures in their artistic development. In my experience, all performances are learning opportunities where reflection on perceived failures creates a necessary resilience and industry-readiness when the next performance and/or career opportunity appears.

Trineice Robinson-Martin

In terms of voice training, Soul Ingredients™ looks at voice training from four aspects: Anatomical Awareness (know your instrument), Voice Fitness and Conditioning (strengthen your instrument), Style Conditioning (condition your instrument), and Interpretation Coaching (tell your story).

Anatomical Awareness	Voice Fitness and Conditioning
Style Conditioning	Interpretation Coaching

My teaching philosophy is that vocal training should enhance a singer's ability to tell a story in the most natural, emotionally honest way. Therefore, I aim to meet students where they are, and gradually expand their abilities and provide them with more efficient ways of projecting their voice (both figuratively and physically).

- Vocal health is important, and thus I believe a singer's voice must be properly conditioned for the style of music he or she chooses to sing. However, a "proper sound", or what is ultimately considered to be a healthy sound, should not compromise the cultural expectations of the sound, nor the natural characteristics/qualities that make a person's sound unique. In other words, although some teachers may consider a classical sound a "proper and healthy sound", as this sound does not match the cultural expectations of soul music, a classical sound would not be a "proper sound" for a soul singer. Therefore, it is necessary for singers to sing healthy vocal sounds that are also culturally appropriate for the style of music they wish to perform.
- A trained singer has choices in terms of what sounds they make and is not limited in their ability to tell a story.
- The more singers understand how their body works when singing, the better choices they can make about maintaining their voice.
- Singers should understand the difference between a default singing mode and stylistic choices.
- After a technique is learned, it should be immediately put in the context of repertoire.

- A style of music cannot be learned in a voice studio. Thus, understanding the role and necessity of cultural immersion as a primary form of learning musical style, Soul Ingredients™ aims to nurture one's ability to musically communicate emotion in a vocally responsible manner while still upholding the cultural expectations of the musical style.

Kimberly Steinhauer

My philosophy of teaching uses theories of cognitive and motor learning to train a total artist, not just a great singer. Students succeed when given specific goals and clear objectives for meeting those goals throughout the learning process. Implicit and explicit goal setting is especially crucial for increases in any type of motor learning, especially the very complex task of voice motor learning for the performer. My dissertation and subsequent research grants explored voice motor learning using parallels from the highly demanding training programs of airline pilots and athletes. These disciplines require sophisticated and elegant coordination of body and brain that must become automatic under pressurized situations, i.e., flying in a storm, throwing a touchdown pass in the final play of a football game, or singing for an audition or opening night. Learning to sing or speak in multiple styles, as demanded by the rigors of vocal performance programs, requires co-ordination of respiratory, phonatory, and resonatory systems of the body, as well as integration of the cognitive processes of the brain involved in motor skill acquisition and retention. Increasing versatility among these systems during high-level performance can be taught exploiting the strategies of *feedback provision*, *practice structure*, and *contextual practice*. In other words, the amount and type of feedback, the order of tasks during practice, and the situation in which you practice have a huge impact on the transfer of chaotic, short-term acquisition to long-term, permanent change in voice motor behavior (speaking and singing on stage). Integrating these principles in voice training produces not only accurate but also, consistent singing which takes the novice to the expert level quickly. For years, athletic training has embraced these advances in research more than artists who are unnecessarily skeptical of science. However, my research has shown that increases in voice motor learning occur as a result of employing acoustic biofeedback along with carefully structured practice order and context. Using these principles to teach voice provides clarity, fun, and flexibility, and they are highly appreciated by the students who have felt that voice is a mystery. Finally, when the craft of voice is mastered, the artist can feel free to express text and music in any manner and in any circumstance with confidence, consistency, and stability.

Jeannette LoVetri

A great deal of training for singing is aimed at making sound for sound's sake, or is largely driven by attention to "breath support" and "resonance". In CCM styles, at least two popular methods advocate direct manipulation of various structures within the throat and mouth. I am vigorously opposed to these approaches. Further, there is an idea that training is counter-indicated in CCM styles, lest the person's voice be "changed" and sound "too classical". This is a valid objection since all available singing voice training throughout most of the 20th century was aimed at classical literature.

Sometimes, in theatre, people have the idea that being strongly involved in the acting is enough to catapult the vocalist into any desired vocal quality. That is ridiculous, but I have run into it. Many of these ideas and practices are in the midst of a big sea change, but the tendency is still to regard classical training as an all-purpose approach to any musical style, and that is simply not possible. CCM artists do not want to sound like opera singers. Jazz singers do not want to sound like Broadway belters. Pop/rock vocalists cannot sound like opera singers, even if they try.

There are many online methods of training that claim to have the "10 best tips" to singing training, or offer CD or DVD training courses that will make you "a star". I do not believe you can learn to sing well by reading a book or watching a video, no matter who makes it. You need guidance from someone with good eyes and ears. This process, done well, takes time. Mastery takes a minimum of five years but can easily run to ten years in a really serious vocal artist, even for those who are very talented. I also have little faith in teachers who cannot make the sound they are seeking to teach. We learn a great deal by listening, and a description in words is never going to substitute for making the correct sound in front of the student. I have a problem with those who teach CCM styles who have an only classical background, even if they understand the science behind the sound. That is not enough.

I believe the voice works best when sound is balanced across many parameters. If the larynx is free to move and the throat can be adjusted by making changes in the responses that impact the sound, many kinds of vocal production are possible. The well-trained singer can choose the vocal quality that he or she likes best and that serves both the needs of the voice in terms of vocal health and the music in terms of the style.

Working with register balance allows the teacher to address every obstacle to vocal freedom, one issue at a time, until the instrument's true character emerges on its own. I never have any preconceived idea about how someone *should* sound, only a mental guide that allows me to assess function in terms of freedom and strength; and that, in turn, allows me to evaluate how well things are working overall. Any vocalist in any style will achieve his/her goals with these simple tools, consistently and accurately applied.

Cathrine Sadolin

To begin with, singing is not difficult, and everyone can learn how to sing. There are also some ground rules:

1. Singing should always feel comfortable. If it feels wrong, then it is wrong. Singers should trust themselves, not the teacher. It is important that the technique works immediately. If I give advice to a singer, he/she should be able to apply it right away and see the difference. Practice may still be needed to make the adjustment work long-term, but the singer should be able to apply the adjustment and see a difference right away. Every singer should feel at every lesson that they have made some progress.
2. Technique should be concrete and efficient in practice.
3. It is important that singers do not fear the sound because it "sounds damaging" or "sounds wrong". They can fear uncontrolled constriction, but not the sound itself. Every sound can be produced in a healthy way.
4. A technique should work for any style. This is why we call it "complete" vocal technique. This may sound a little arrogant because "complete" can also mean "perfect" in some languages, but that is not my intent. It is thought of as "comprehensive" or "all-encompassing". My aim is to include all the sounds that the voice can produce. This is why we have techniques for everything, from a Baroque trill to a scream.
5. The technique should comply with anatomy and physiology.

6. I think that it is important that we can provide logical and rational explanations supported by evidence for the things we are claiming when we teach. If technique is based on concrete and proven facts, then it usually works much faster and you know you are protecting the voice from damage.

7. The terminology must be clear. Every term must have a definition. Every sound must have only one term. Every term must mean only one thing.

8. We seek to create an environment of critical thinking, where we continuously scrutinize our own method.

9. I think it's important that we do not have any dogmas and that everything is open for debate and subject to change. It is important to be respectful of other methods and remain open-minded. Even among the 16 teachers in the institute, someone might say "Well this, we could not possibly change". I always say we can change everything for which we find evidence. Within the community, we ask for criticism to create an environment of critical thinking. We scrutinize ourselves to try and find the best way to do things. When we create a "policy" of discussion and renewal, everyone is willing to tear things down, so we can build them up again in a better way.

10. Technique should be genre free, and should work for classical and death-metal, pop/rock, folk, or any style because the voice is the same. The technique should work for the voice, not the genre. A singing technique lesson should be different from a genre lesson. An authorized CVT teacher can help the singer technically in all styles, because the technique is founded in anatomy and physiology, and we know how to produce all sounds in a healthy way. When working with repertoire I only work in styles in which I am comfortable, or I refer the student to a specialist in that style.

11. We must separate taste and technique. Many times, techniques are presented as a preferred aesthetic, which I think is a mistake. The singers often have goals, and even if they are vague, they are usually connected to an aesthetic that singers want for themselves. It is important that teachers do not take that away. You should be able to help a singer get from A to B without putting your own taste into the journey. Even if you do not like what they are doing, you should be able to teach it. We do not know which singer will be the next big star and neither does the singer. It's important not to take away specialty or unique qualities from a singer, because who are we to judge? We often see that even with sounds we do not like at all, millions of people buy the records. We must admit that we cannot predict what people will want.

12. A teacher should not impose personal taste onto the singing student. We might kill the next famous fantastic thing in singing. Even if the singer asks you "which sound is better?", we still should not tell them. That is giving a singing teacher an authority which they do not have. We have a lot of techniques to help singers achieve their goals, but we do not tell a singer how they should sound. This destroys originality and uniqueness. If I am hired as a producer, then I am hired for my taste. But as a teacher, my taste does not enter into the training.

13. When individual elements of technique are pin-pointed for work, everything else can stay as it is. Keep what you like and leave the rest. I do not believe in tearing everything down and building it from scratch because this will fundamentally change the singer.

14. Singers should design their own sound, and only change what they want to change. At the CVI, we consider ourselves to be servants to the singer. We help them achieve their own individual goals.

15. All sounds can be produced in a healthy way.

References and recommended reading

American Academy of Teachers of Singing. "In support of contemporary commercial (nonclassical) voice pedagogy." *Journal of Singing* 65, no. 1 (September/October 2008): 7–10.

American Academy of Teachers of Singing. "Research and creative accomplishment in promotion and tenure: A realistic look at expectations for teachers of singing in academia." *Journal of Singing* 71, no. 2 (November 2014): 141–143.

American Academy of Teachers of Singing. "In support of fact-based voice pedagogy and terminology." *Journal of Singing* 71, no. 1 (September/October 2014): 9–14.

Austin, Howard and Elisabeth Howard. *Born to sing: The Vocal Power Method (the next generation) – A fully integrated, cross-referenced multimedia program.* United States: Music World, Vocal Power School, 2007.

Bartlett, Irene. "One size doesn't fit all: Tailored training for Contemporary Commercial Singers." In *Perspectives on Teaching Singing: Australian Vocal Pedagogues Sing their Stories*, edited by Scott D. Harrison, 227–243. Bowen Hills, Qld.: Australian Academic Press, 2010.

Bartlett, Irene. "Unique problems and challenges of contemporary voice: What do teachers think?" *Australian Voice* 5 (1999): 45–49.

Bartlett, Irene. "More than just a style: A profile of professional contemporary gig singers. In *Teaching Singing in the 21st Century*. Edited by Scott D. Harrison and Jessica O'Bryan, 367–382. Dordrecht: Springer, 2014.

Bartlett, Irene. "Reflections on contemporary commercial singing: An insider's perspective." *Voice and Speech Review*, 8, no. 1 (2014): 27–35. www.doi.org/10.1080/23268263.2013.829711.

Baxter, Mark. *The Rock-And-Roll Singer's Survival Manual.* Milwaukee: Hal Leonard, 1990.

Benson, Elizabeth Ann. "Modern voice pedagogy: Functional training for all styles." *American Music Teacher* 67, no. 6 (June/July 2018): 10–13.

Bos, Nancy. "Where we were then and where we are now: A singing teacher's perspective." *Journal of Singing* 71, no. 3 (January/February 2015): 347–348.

Chalfin, Dane. "From 'me' to 'we': Audience-focused practical tools for interpretation and performance." In *The Singer-Songwriter Handbook*, edited by Justin A. Williams and Katherine Williams. New York: Bloomsbury Academic, 2017.

Chandler, Kim. "Teaching popular music styles." In *Teaching Singing in the 21st Century* edited by Scott D. Harrison and Jessica O'Bryan, 35–51. Dordrecht: Springer, 2014.

Deci, Edward L. and Richard M. Ryan. "Self-determination theory: A macrotheory of human motivation, development, and health." *Canadian Psychology* 49, no. 3 (2008): 182–185.

Eckert, Rosana. "Everything but the kitchen sink: Singing in all styles." In *The Voice Teacher's Cookbook: Creative Recipes for Teachers of Singing* edited by Brian J. Winnie, 33–35. Delray Beach, FL: Meredith Music, 2018.

Edwin, Robert. "Personal and pedagogic aesthetics." *Journal of Singing* 66, no. 5 (May/June 2010): 575–577.

Edwin, Robert. "Are we the National Association of Teacher of Classical Singing? (Revisiting 1985)." *Journal of Singing* 67, no. 5 (May/June 2011): 589–590.

Edwin, Robert. "Vocal animal crackers." In *The Voice Teacher's Cookbook: Creative Recipes for Teachers of Singing* edited by Brian J. Winnie, 42–43. Delray Beach, FL: Meredith Music, 2018.

Frey-Monell, Robyn. "Motivation in the applied voice studio: An overview." *Journal of Singing* 67, no. 2 (November/ December 2010): 147–152.

Hallqvist, Hanna, Filipa M.B. La, and Johan Sundberg. "Soul and musical theater: A comparison of two vocal styles." *Journal of Voice* 31, no. 2 (March 2017): 229–235. doi.org/10.1016/j.jvoice.2016.05.020.

Harrison, Scott D. ed. *Perspectives on Teaching Singing: Australian Vocal Pedagogues Sing their Stories.* Bowen Hills, Qld.: Australian Academic Press, 2010.

Harrison, Scott D. and Jessica O'Bryan. "Postlude: The future of singing pedagogy." In *Teaching Singing in the 21st Century*, edited by Scott D. Harrison and Jessica O'Bryan, 411–413. Dordrecht: Springer, 2014.

Howard, Elisabeth. *Sing! The Vocal Power Method.* New York: Alfred Music, 2006.

Hughes, Diane and Jean Callaghan. "Advocating for change: Interdisciplinary voice studies in Australian school education." In *Perspectives on Teaching Singing: Australian Vocal Pedagogues Sing their Stories*, edited by Scott D. Harrison, 306–316. Bowen Hills, Qld.: Australian Academic Press, 2010.

Kayes, Gillyanne. *Singing and the Actor.* New York: Routledge, 2004.

LeBorgne, Wendy D., and Marci Rosenberg. *The Vocal Athlete.* San Diego: Plural Publishing, 2014.

LoVetri, Jeannette. "The necessity of using functional training in the independent studio." *Journal of Singing* 70, no. 1 (September/October 2013): 79–86.

LoVetri, Jeannette. "Contemporary commercial music: More than one way to use the vocal tract." *Journal of Singing* 58, no. 3 (2002): 249–252.

McPherson, Gary and Graham Welch, eds. *The Oxford Handbook of Music Education.* New York: Oxford University Press, 2012.

Meyer, David and Matthew Edwards. "The future of collegiate voice pedagogy: SWOT analysis of current practice and implications for the next generation." *Journal of Singing* 70, no. 4 (March/April 2014): 437–444.

Reid, Kate. "A recipe for jazz voice quality." In *The Voice Teacher's Cookbook: Creative Recipes for Teachers of Singing* edited by Brian J. Winnie, 95-96. Delray Beach, FL: Meredith Music, 2018.

Riggs, Seth and John Dominick Carratello. *Singing for the Stars: A Complete Program for Training Your Voice.* Van Nuys, CA: Alfred, 1998.

Riggs, Seth. *Singer's Advantage: Female.* DVD. In Tune Product, 2007.

Robinson, Daniel K. "Teaching the contemporary worship singer." In *Perspectives on Teaching Singing: Australian Vocal Pedagogues Sing their Stories,* edited by Scott D. Harrison, 276-292. Bowen Hills, Qld.: Australian Academic Press, 2010.

Robinson, Daniel K. "Voice in worship: The contemporary worship singer." In *Teaching Singing in the 21st Century,* edited by Scott D. Harrison and Jessica O'Bryan, 319–334. Dordrecht: Springer, 2014.

Robinson-Martin, Trineice. "Take my hand: Teaching the gospel singer in the applied voice studio." In *Teaching Singing in the 21st Century,* edited by Scott D. Harrison and Jessica O'Bryan, 335–350. Dordrecht: Springer, 2014.

Rosenberg, Marci and Wendy D. LeBorgne. *The Vocal Athlete: Application and Technique for the Hybrid Singer.* San Diego: Plural Publishing, 2014.

Sadolin, Cathrine. *Complete Vocal Technique.* Copenhagen: CVI Publications, 2012.

Sadolin, Cathrine. *Complete Vocal Technique.* CVT App: completevocal.institute/app/.

Saunders Barton, Mary. *Bel Canto, Can Belto.* DVD. University Park, PA: Penn State Media Sales, 2007.

Saunders Barton, Mary. *What About the Boys?* DVD. State College, PA: Mary Saunders Barton, 2014.

Schunk, Dale H. and Carol A. Mullen. "Self-efficacy as an engaged learner." In *Handbook of Research on Student Engagement* edited by Sandra L. Christenson, Amy L. Reschly, and Cathy Wylie, 219-235. New York, NY, US: Springer Science + Business Media, 2012.

http://dx.doi.org/10.1007/978-1-4614-2018-7_10.

Shapiro, Jan, *So You Want to Sing Jazz: A Guide for Professionals.* Lanham, MD: Rowman & Littlefield, 2016.

Sieck, Stephen. "Inclusive pedagogy: Cooking in a way that feeds all singers." In *The Voice Teacher's Cookbook: Creative Recipes for Teachers of Singing* edited by Brian J. Winnie, 109-110. Delray Beach, FL: Meredith Music, 2018.

Spivey, Norman. "Building bridges: Paths to a multifaceted career." *Journal of Singing* 72, no. 1 (September/October 2015): 1–5.

Spivey, Norman and Mary Saunders Barton. *Cross-Training in the Voice Studio: A Balancing Act.* San Diego: Plural Publishing, 2018.

Steinhauer, Kimberly, Mary McDonald Klimek, and Jo Estill, *The Estill Voice Model: Theory and Translation.* Pittsburgh: Estill Voice International, 2018.

Titze, Ingo R. "Some reflections on speech-like singing and related contemporary approaches." *Journal of Singing* 70, no. 1 (September/October 2013): 57–58.

Wigginton, James R. "When 'proper' is dead wrong: How traditional methods fail aspiring artists." *Journal of Singing* 66, no. 4 (March/April 2010): 447–449.

Wilson, Pat H. "Showtime: Teaching music theatre and cabaret singing." In *Perspectives on Teaching Singing: Australian Vocal Pedagogues Sing their Stories,* ed. Scott D. Harrison, 293–305. Bowen Hills, Qld.: Australian Academic Press, 2010.

4

Teacher training

Anyone can teach singing, and there is no required certification or license. Any combination of training and experience could yield a great teacher. However, 84% of the pedagogues in this text undertook informal or formal classical training at some point in their careers, either as a starting point because classical singing was the only training available, or to earn a degree which would allow them to establish themselves professionally. None of them were satisfied with limiting themselves to one style of music, so they continued to explore other styles and sounds. Some pedagogues pursued music theatre training (32%) and some self-educated (32%); very few received jazz training (24%) or pop music training (20%), and the majority of that was learned "on the job" either as performers in the genre or as teachers trying to meet the needs of their CCM students through trial and error in the voice studio. Each journey is interesting and unique, but they are all bound by relentless curiosity and a drive to reconcile the misinformation they had been fed: if classical singing was the only safe way to sing, then why were so many people sustaining long careers in other genres? Why was there so much demand for teachers in CCM styles?

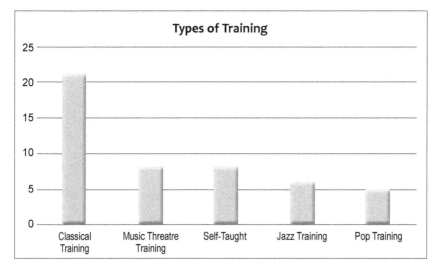

The common factor among these great pedagogues is a commitment to lifelong learning. Of these, 32% made a point of saying that their own training is ongoing, and many more demonstrated this fact through research, publications, conference presentations, teacher training, workshops, and seminars. Only 20% have formal training in voice research, yet 48% have participated in formal voice research and scholarship. An extensive reading list may be found at the end of this chapter. However, this list is not comprehensive. The scholarly contributions of all of the pedagogues in this text are ongoing, and far too numerous to include. Readers are encouraged to explore each pedagogue's individual publications.

Despite an intense bias from the classical music academic community, the CCM pioneer pedagogues have dedicated their lives to the codification of their own work and to the training of the next generations of teachers. Readers will see that these teachers have often studied several of the pioneering methodologies and have benefited enormously from these pre-established systems of training. In fact, 60% of pedagogues emphasize that a significant mentor or open-minded teacher encouraged, supported, or facilitated their entry into the field of CCM voice pedagogy. These data reveal that the CCM voice pedagogy community is already unified, interwoven, and reinforced through our support of one another.

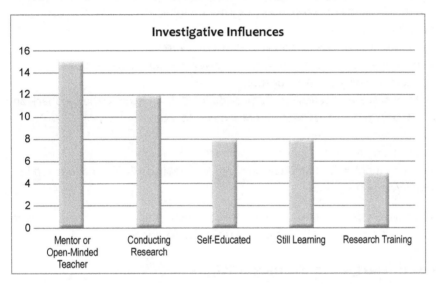

In order to meet the growing demand for teachers with CCM and music theatre singing specializations, both in the private/independent studio and at colleges and universities, teachers may continue on unique and unexpected journeys. There are still only two non-classical pedagogy degrees in the U.S. (Shenandoah University[1] and Pennsylvania State University[2]). However, certificate programs or the option to emphasize in musical theatre pedagogy are starting to emerge in graduate programs throughout the U.S.[3] In Australia, the Queensland Conservatorium at Griffith University (Australia) has CCM voice pedagogy and research doctoral studies programs. Until U.S. universities follow suit, the data collected here indicate that a generally good course of study to become an excellent CCM pedagogue is the following (not necessarily in this order):

- Be open-minded, flexible, tenacious, and keen to learn all there is to know about CCM singing, forever.

---

1   More information may be found at www.su.edu/conservatory/areas-of-study/pedagogy-voice/master-of-music-in-pedagogy-ccm-voice/.

2   More information may be found at theatre.psu.edu/programs/musical-theatre-mfa-voice-pedagogy.

3   This list is not comprehensive. New York University Steinhardt offers a master of music in vocal performance with a concentration in music theatre and an advanced certificate in vocal pedagogy: steinhardt.nyu.edu/music/vocal/music_theatre/dual_degree. The University of Mobile, Alabama School of the Arts offers a DMA in Vocal Performance which prepares students for performance and teaching across multiple styles, including contemporary, musical theatre, opera, and others: umobile.edu/academics/alabama-school-arts/doctor-of-musical-arts/.

- Listen to masterful singers from all genres, forever. Attend live performances of great singers, forever.
- Get the training and performing experience to become a great musician, forever.
- Take voice lessons with a CCM singing expert.
- Figure it out in your own voice and body, forever.
- Get performance experience in one or more CCM genre(s).
- Start to teach CCM singing.
- If you want to teach at a university, get the formal training that will make this possible. Otherwise, this step is not necessary.
- Read all the research on voice pedagogy and voice science, continually, forever.
- Study many of the codified CCM voice pedagogy methodologies.
- Continue to teach CCM singing.
- Find a mentor or network of mentors and ask questions, forever.
- Participate in or conduct voice research to seek answers to your own questions.
- Observe great CCM teaching and ask questions, forever.
- Ask a mentor to observe your teaching and provide feedback. Listen to the feedback and ask questions. Repeat the process with other mentors, forever.
- Learn from your students, forever.
- Continue to train, learn, and refine teaching approaches, forever.
- Give back: Become a mentor. Conduct teacher training. Establish a CCM pedagogy seminar, workshop, or university program.

This chapter contains responses to the prompt "What is your training?". The responses are presented in a loose order according to decades of teaching experience.

Seth Riggs and Margareta Svensson Riggs

Seth Riggs was born in Washington D.C. in 1930. As a 9-year-old he was in the boy choir at the Washington National Cathedral conducted by Paul Calloway and it has influenced his life.

Seth has earned degrees from Manhattan School of Music, Johns Hopkins University, and Peabody Conservatory of Music, none of which taught him how to get from chest to head voice. He studied singing technique – which was all classical opera – with John Charles Thomas, Robert Weede, Helge Röswanger, Tito Schipa and Keith Davis; repertoire with Pierre Bernac, Martial Singher, Leo Taubman, Charles Wadsworth, John Brownlee, Hans Heintz and Louis Graveure; acting with Lee Strasberg, Sandy Meisner, Bobby Lewis and Frank Silvera; and dancing with Peter Gennaro and Matt Mattox. Seth feels he is always learning.

Margareta Svensson Riggs was born in 1968 in a small town on the west coast of Sweden. After 10 years in Varberg Music School from age 9, (studying classical piano with Lydia Makarova, pop, jazz and improvisation piano with Dag Hallberg, guitar with Kenneth Grönberg, music harmony and theory with John Clemson, voice with Inga Johansson, choirs and bands with among others Erik Molin), she was recruited to be a singer-pianist and headliner on board a cruise ship at age 19. This work propelled her into an on-going career that soon became international; her training thereafter was attained alongside performing, and is always on-going.

In performing arts, Margareta has studied voice with independent singing teachers Kurt Jacobsson, Jeanie LoVetri and Seth Riggs. She has earned a degree in acting from Calle Flygare Teaterskola Stockholm, as well as acting training at Tisch School of the Arts, NYU, Musical

Theater Works Conservatory, Stonestreet Studios, and coaching by Brian Reise, Doug Warhit and Thom McFadden; dance training at The Ballet Academy Stockholm, Harvard University and Broadway Dance Center; songwriting and production at UCLA, Pasadena City College and Musicians Institute. Margareta has appeared as an expert judge on the CBS global talent show *The World's Best*, hosted by James Corden.

Margareta finds, however, that there is crucial learning that can come only through experience as a professional singer. Among those experiences high on Margareta's list was the development of nodules on her vocal folds six years into her hectic and intense performing career, and surgery and vocal rehabilitation. This gave her a first-hand understanding of the journey so many professional singers face at some point before coming to her and her husband for training.

Mary Saunders Barton

I always sang as a child and began piano lessons at an early age. When I was 9, my mother encouraged me to join the church choir in my home town, where I remained until college. I began formal classical voice training at 13 and continued in college. Enamored with all things French, I pursued graduate study in French language and literature in Paris. During my time there, I had the opportunity to study with Pierre Bernac. That experience had a profound and lasting influence on my career as an artist and teacher. After graduate school, I followed a winding path before landing in New York City to pursue musical theatre in the early 1970s. I took acting, singing and dancing "à la carte", as we did in those days, and acquired enough skill to begin a professional career. I began teaching singing serendipitously when fellow actors began to ask me to help them with their auditions. I discovered that I had a gift for diagnosing problems and was fascinated by the process of solving them. There were no formal musical theatre pedagogy programs and voice science was in its infancy. I began to teach in the Voice Studio in NYC, then known as the Paul Gavert Studio, where I had a number of compatriots. We were all trying to figure out those Broadway sounds, especially the belt.

Paul Gavert was a classical baritone who began working with Betty Buckley when she was performing Grizabella in Andrew Lloyd Webber's *Cats*, and he became known for his ability to coach healthy Broadway belting, although I do not think Betty ever called it that. Jo Estill had also made a significant impression on many of us with her voice training method and the notion of "voice qualities". We looked to colleagues like Joan Lader to help us translate some of this information. Looking back, I realize we were all flying by the seat of our pants in terms of non-traditional vocal techniques. By the time I was married with two children, I had a full-time studio in NYC and was also teaching students of all ages and inclinations in my home in Rockland County. This was an invaluable "lab" for me. My first experience with pre-professional college students was at the Hartt School in the 90s. Inspired by my good friend Marianne Challis, I also began creating one-woman cabaret performances during that time, which reminded me of the importance of balancing teaching with artistry. In 1999, I received a call from my soon-to-be colleague Bev Patton in the theatre department at Penn State who had heard about me from a student we had in common. Penn State had decided to hire a musical theatre "specialist" for their fledgling BFA program. I applied, got the job, and just like that, we packed up the whole family and moved to State College. Penn State was a gift to me as a teacher. I became part of an immensely collegial faculty who embraced me with open arms and never a hint of suspicion or negative judgment. We learned an immense amount from each other during those 18 years. The *"bel canto can belto"* pedagogy was born there as a result of the inspiration classical and musical theatre faculties took from each other.

I created two video tutorials on teaching musical theatre singing. Then, in 2011, with colleague Norman Spivey, launched an MFA for musical theatre voice pedagogy to meet the very significant need for voice teachers in university musical theatre programs who specialize in vernacular techniques.

The initial proposal for this degree stated: "A graduate of this course of study should feel equally at home teaching classical and musical theatre repertoire, respecting the important distinctions between them". I remember saying that we should be able to expect 100% job placement for these graduates and we have not been disappointed.

Cathrine Sadolin

I studied singing privately, and then I went to university to study. I had no background, so I had to catch up. I came into the university and I loved it because everyone else was also as interested in music as I was. It was purely classical at that time. I moved to London and continued to study voice privately with Vera Rózsa. I could only afford one lesson every 10th day. The rest of the time, I studied anatomy and physiology on my own. I started to put things together and gradually found a technique that worked. I was also singing a lot of classical concerts at this time. People started asking me about other vocal sounds, and I experimented on my own. There was no place to study these things formally so I began to form the Complete Vocal Technique system and it helped me and later, other people.

I attended a lot of conferences and in 2006 an ENT, Dr. Julian McGlashan from Queens Medical Center in Nottingham, UK complimented my approach and thought it made a lot of sense. We teamed up and have conducted a lot of research together. We try to explain what is going on, how certain sounds are produced. We did one study together where he performed endoscopy while singers demonstrated every vocal mode: Neutral, Edge, Overdrive, and Curbing.[4] This confirmed the anatomy and physiology of exactly how each mode is produced. It was remarkable to see how consistent the singers were.

Because we have a common terminology, we can create this level of consistency, and so there are always many teachers who can teach the same singer. At the CVT institute, we have 16 teachers. We communicate about the singers through a log book and are able to describe precise technical problems so that one teacher can pick up where another left off. We can communicate exactly what the challenges are, even in the absence of sound. It is very practical and shows that it is possible to create a mutual terminology.

Robert Edwin

I was born into a professional musical family. Both my father, Edwin R. Steinfort, and my mother, Helena W. Monbo, were performers and singing teachers. They taught in New York City at the fabled Ansonia Hotel on Broadway. I was their youngest student and went on to a fine and very diverse singing career. That diversity in performing certainly helped me transition into pedagogy many years later when I apprenticed and was mentored in my mother's independent studio in NYC, a studio that included classical cantors, rock and pop singers, and Broadway stars.

---

4   More information on this study may be found in the research section of the CVT mobile application.

Elisabeth Howard

I have a Bachelor's and Master's degree from the Juilliard School and I attended Indiana University on a Graduate Assistantship in Voice.

Irene Bartlett

My training is interesting and unconventional!! Once I began teaching, I quickly realized that I did not want to be the teacher who teaches everyone to sing "like me" – the performer. I wanted to learn and understand how the voice was produced (anatomy and physiology) and how, as a teacher, I could recognize and honor each individual voice as it was presented to me (in terms of natural, idiosyncratic tone and timbre) while teaching efficiency of voice production alongside style-specific effects. So, through the study of voice anatomy, physiology, function, and pedagogy, I began to develop a personal model of singing technique.

I began this life-long journey of knowledge building by reading journal articles and books, speaking to speech pathologists and attending pedagogy and voice science workshops, conferences, and symposia on both the speaking and singing voice. To do this, I sought events from within Australia and the U.S.A. I enrolled in a Masters and finally a Doctoral degree, surveying 102 professional Australian CCM singers to fully research their *lived experience* of singing across a range of genres and styles.

The "unconventional" part is that as a professional singer, I did not have any formal singing lessons – I trained "on the job". I began my professional performance career when I was 16 years old by auditioning successfully for a resident singer position on a television pop music show. From the beginning, I was guided by the professional musicians and I learned my craft through the master/apprentice practice of the time. At that time, there were no contemporary voice teachers, so the musicians' advice was "don't have singing lessons!" as classical training would change my unique and natural speech-quality voice production. However, I actively listened to a wide range of great singers and instrumental recording artists and developed perfect relative pitch (singing along with the recordings in any key male or female), an ear for various style elements, and a wide flexibility in vocal range and tonal colors.

Coming from a large family, from a very young age I was introduced to music through my parents' and brothers' style preferences including: "Classical" – Joseph Schmidt, Luciano Pavarotti, Maria Callas, and Jessie Norman; "Music Theatre" – Ethel Merman, Barbara Cook, Elaine Paige, Bernadette Peters, and Audra McDonald; "Jazz" – Ella Fitzgerald, Sarah Vaughan, Carmen McCrae, Jo Stafford, Frank Sinatra, Tony Bennett, Mel Tormé, and Nat King Cole; "Popular music and screen singers" – Judy Garland, Connie Francis, Patsy Cline, Dusty Springfield, Aretha Franklin, Dionne Warwick, and Shirley Bassey; "Jazz instrumentalists" – Thelonious Monk, Charlie Parker, Miles Davis, Coleman Hawkins, George Shearing, Herbie Hancock, and Chick Corea, to name only a few. The list goes on, and on, and on. Through this listening and simultaneous singing practice (years of performance), I developed an innate and deep sense of musicianship with music appreciation across a wide range of styles.

Jan Shapiro

Starting at age 15, I was classically trained. I studied with several voice teachers throughout my career, but three teachers made a big impact on me. Essentially these three teachers shared the same overall philosophy: sing freely and breathe in a low, relaxed way.

Mark Baxter

The most valuable education for singers occurs on stage. After receiving some formal instruction in music at The College of New Jersey, I performed for a living for 15 years. To date, I have logged well over 3,000 performances. When you are singing for your next meal, canceling is not an option. Throughout my performing years, I diligently explored various singing methods and strategies for maintaining vocal health. I completed hundreds of private voice lessons with various teachers and attended countless seminars including: vocal pedagogy by the Functional Voice Foundation of West Germany, neuromuscular massage, nutrition, The Alexander Technique, acupressure, reflexology, along with various psychological and visualization techniques. My performing experience allows me to empathize with my students. I know first-hand what it's like to deal with vocal problems and the difference affective instruction can make.

Jeannette LoVetri

I sang my first performance at a Brownie meeting in third grade. I started voice lessons at 15 with a classical teacher in my home town. I attended Manhattan School of Music in 1967–68. My Wagnerian soprano teacher was less than impressed with me and by the end of the school year, I could barely sing. I was very demoralized, so I quit. From then on, all my studies were private ones. I continued to take lessons until 1978, from many different teachers in New York, at which time I stumbled upon The Voice Foundation *Symposium: Care of the Professional Voice* at Juilliard. That changed my life.

Subsequently, I attended voice-oriented seminars, workshops, classes, and conferences all over the world. I read hundreds of books and articles. I worked with coaches in both classical and music theatre rep and I continued to perform, but not professionally. Eventually, I worked with world-renowned scientists, doctors, speech-language pathologists, and other singing teachers, gaining both knowledge and experience. I started teaching in 1971 and in 1980, I took my first Broadway performers. In 1988, I participated in research as a subject and in 1998, as a researcher.

My education was unorthodox, outside-the-box, grounded in the real world of the music industry and its demands. I also investigated numerous kinds of bodywork and alternative therapies. I expanded the dance training that I had begun at age three and began investigating jazz through my many professional jazz students who were vocalists and teachers.

I still go to conferences and workshops, I still do research and collaborate with others in the various other voice disciplines in many ways. I feel that my education continues every day, as I am always learning from my students how to be a better teacher.

Lisa Popeil

I began piano lessons when I was four and musical theatre voice lessons at age six, growing up in Chicago. After some fairly obvious voice problems resulting from the instruction "Louder Lisa, louder!!", my mother found a classical voice teacher for me, the indomitable Gisela Goettling. Since I was only seven, Mrs Goettling was understandably reticent to work with me, but my mother simply bullied her into giving me a chance. Then began a beautiful personal and musical relationship that lasted until I was 15 and moved to Southern California.

Once on the West Coast, I continued private voice lessons and pursued my interest in pop singing, writing my own songs and recording in studios at 15 years of age. At that point, I knew very little about any style aside from classical but was driven to learn more and searched for teachers who could help me.

My original plan was to go to Stanford and study Linguistics but after an emotionally disastrous experience in France, I decided to study Psychology at Prescott College in Arizona for a couple of years. My mentor there said "Time for you to go to music school" and suggested California Institute of the Arts. Fortunately, that school offered a Bachelor of Arts Degree in General Music which allowed me to divide my time between piano, composition, and voice, and which gave me an opportunity to perform a wide variety of music, from Medieval to Avant-Garde. When it came time to get my master's degree, I had to choose one focus and felt that even though I was no world-class singer by a long-shot, I was a bit more accomplished in voice than in piano and composition!

Kimberly Steinhauer

I combined my love of singing and inquiry into the science of singing for a B.S. in Music Education at Indiana University of Pennsylvania, M.A. in Speech Communication at The Pennsylvania State University, and Ph.D. in Communication Science and Disorders at the University of Pittsburgh. But, my core voice training came from my private study with Jo Estill, beginning in 1985. I sang in all styles and venues during my education and sought voice teachers for pop/classical at each of my institutions. At Penn State during my masters, I studied classical voice and performed with the orchestra as a concerto competition winner; I also music-directed and performed principal roles in musical theatre productions. While earning my Ph.D. at the University of Pittsburgh, I cross-registered at Carnegie Mellon University to study classical voice with Mimi Lerner, as I prepared for the regional Met auditions, and performed with local opera, sacred, and acoustic shows.

Edrie Means Weekly

In high school, I was trained with a classical technique. When I was in college, the training was primarily classical, and the repertoire required for juries was all classical. Fortunately for me, I had a wonderful voice teacher, Janette Ogg, a Van Lawrence recipient, who encouraged me to explore vocal sounds and allowed me to sing in different styles, while maintaining good healthy vocal function. At the time, I never thought the way I was using my voice to sing was a certain "technique" but rather, as the way my voice is functioning in this particular style of singing. From the beginning, I felt I used the same subglottic air pressure for an operatic fortissimo high note as I did for high belt note – and still do. At the time, I understood I was not giving as much space, and my vowels were not as round and pure, as they were for classical singing but were more speech-like. I also knew I was altering the shape of the vocal tract for the different styles I was singing.

Only later, when I began to teach what I had taught myself, which was to sing in multiple styles, would I be more interested in how the voice functioned at a deeper level in these styles. At the same time, I had a hunch that there were others teaching themselves and wanted more information. This prompted my 2003 research article with Jeannette LoVetri, which was published in the *Journal of Voice*.[5] The results indicated that a large percentage of those teaching CCM had neither formal education in teaching these styles, nor did they have professional experience in singing these styles. Many of the respondents indicated conflict between classical and CCM styles. It led to the development of the Contemporary Commercial Music (CCM) Vocal Pedagogy Institute at Shenandoah University offering the first-ever CCM courses as part of the required curriculum for a Master of Music in Vocal Pedagogy and Doctor of Musical Arts in Vocal Pedagogy. Since 2003, people from all over the world have come and received graduate credit from taking courses at the CCM Vocal Pedagogy Institute. Other universities, such as Penn State, have implemented CCM pedagogy in their graduate degree programs.

I attended my first Voice Foundation Symposium in 2001 to present research. At the Voice Foundation, I met the leading voice scientists and heard the ground-breaking research and education about the human voice. Through reading articles, reading books, attending research presentations, viewing spectral analysis, workshops and discussions with experts and colleagues, I began to understand the mechanical, physiological, aerodynamics, and vocal acoustic differences of what I was doing to sing in different styles, and could effectively explain these things to my students. Apart from my degrees and experience, I have taken a course in retraining the injured voice and sat in ENT examinations of clients. I also have wonderful doctor and SLP mentors.

Gillyanne Kayes

I trained as a classical singer, focusing especially on *Lieder* and song. I have attended numerous training courses during my career – I was a senior Estill™ trainer for several years, but no longer work with that approach. I have trained with Janice Chapman and attended short courses in vocal function run by the British Voice Association, courses in the Accent Method approach to breathing, and Function of the Singing Voice run by Johan Sundberg in Sweden. I also completed a 2-day training with the British Laryngological Society. I am fully trained as a musician and play keyboard. I have a BA Hons in music and a PhD in voice research.

Marcelle Gauvin

I began my official vocal training as an undergraduate studying classical technique with Jaqueline Bazinet Cobert. At the time, jazz and contemporary music programs for vocalists were not available at the college level and since my established career was singing this type of music, I continued private study with Eddie Watson and Dante Pavone, instructors in the Boston area. Like many of us, I had to figure out a lot about contemporary commercial singing on my own. I was introduced to McCloskey® technique[6] which triggered an interest in body mechanics for me, leading to certification in craniosacral therapy through the Upledger Institute.[7] I practiced bodywork at the Acupuncture Clinic of Daniel R. Schwartz, continuing my education in alternative health modalities, and eventually left the practice due to the demands of my performing and recording career as a jazz singer.[8]

---

5   Jeannette L. LoVetri and Edrie Means Weekly, "Contemporary commercial music (CCM) survey: Who's teaching what in nonclassical music," *Journal of Voice* 17, no. 2 (June 2003), 207-215, doi.org/10.1016/S0892-1997(03)00004-3.

6   More information may be found at www.mcclosky.org.

7   Upledger Institute International, www.upledger.com/about/index.php

8   Acupuncture Clinic of Daniel R. Schwartz, www.danielschwartzacupuncture.com/

At that time, I had the opportunity to work for a week with Bobby McFerrin which was a life-changing experience and one that has never left me. In search of a method that would meet my needs as an artist and a teacher, I explored the Seth Riggs method and eventually was introduced to Jeannette LoVetri by a colleague. I became certified in the Somatic Voicework™ Method at Shenandoah University's Contemporary Commercial Music Institute, and after completing the initial certification, continued with post-graduate courses. Eventually, I became a faculty member at Shenandoah's CCM Institute where I continue to be exposed to the most current research and training trends in the industry.

Tracy Marie Bourne

I initially trained as a classical singer at the Queensland Conservatorium, and then went on to three years of training as an actor at the Victorian College of the Arts, which is now part of Melbourne University. I completed a Masters of Music at Melbourne University, and chose to focus on contemporary classical singing during this time. I have recently completed a PhD on music theatre vocal techniques through the Sydney Conservatorium, University of Sydney. My dissertation is entitled *The Perceptual, Acoustic and Physiological Characteristics of Music Theatre Singing*. I have published four articles from these studies in international science and singing journals. I have also trained in Somatic Voicework™, The LoVetri Method, and undertaken a voice function course in Sweden with Dr Johan Sundberg.

Cate Frazier-Neely

I received the M.M. in Vocal Performance and Pedagogy from the University of Maryland, College Park, and the B.M. in Vocal Performance from The College of Wooster in Ohio.

I come from a family of professional musicians and music educators, and a singing home and community. In college, I worked as an accompanist in the music department and as a piano and voice teacher to professors' children. In graduate school, a few faculty members passed on theatre singers to me, which is when curiosity for popular music pedagogy blossomed.

Those of us interested in "non-classical" pedagogy were isolated for many years – remember, no Internet. The academic community was oriented towards opera, oratorio, art song, or choral performance, and singers working in various popular genres did not work with the language or processes of vocal technique.

I worked "in the trenches" after grad school, starting in 1980, by teaching large numbers of singers of all ages and stages that wanted to sing musical theatre, jazz, folk, rock, as well classical genres. By age 26, teaching was split between a private voice studio and college adjunct positions, later moving from academia to a large community music school. I played through musical theatre scores, created time-lines of various popular music developments, and read biographies of choreographers. At the Library of Congress, I listened to LPs of Broadway cast recordings, the *Smithsonian Folkways' Collections*, early country recordings, jazz and blues, and songs of resistance from the 1960s. I listened to and imitated street cries (the calls used by vendors to advertise their street wares), as well as call and response from African and African-American traditions. Observing Paul Kengmo, a Cameroonian dancer who worked with young children in West African dance, influenced my move towards a more holistic approach to teaching music and movement.

I was very active as a classical singer and studied regularly through 2010. My principal teacher was Elizabeth Daniels but I was also influenced by Elizabeth Vrenios and workshops in jazz improvisation with Jay Clayton. I performed *Fach*-crossing opera roles to contemporary modern works to ensemble singing to cabaret. I worked with John Cage, Lori Laitman, Richard Miller, Randolf Maudlin of The Washington Opera, Martin Katz, and many conductors, coaches, and colleagues. I also founded four arts' organizations, and sustained two of them for over 20 years.

Even with this background, I felt it necessary to earn certification in Somatic Voicework™, The LoVetri Method, and followed by a certificate in Leadership Through Emotional Intelligence from Case Western Reserve's Departments of Psychology and Business. I have practiced Yoga since 1985, and grow through somatic re-education and the neuroplasticity of the brain to experience my body as a primary source of wisdom and strength and not something to overcome or cope with. LoVetri has been my rehabilitation specialist since I was diagnosed with bi-lateral vocal fold paresis, a neurological condition where the vocal folds are still pristine. The ways I have chosen to handle this experience have taught me more about singing, health and wellness than I thought possible.

Kim Chandler

My academic qualifications are a Bachelor of Music Education from Queensland University and Master of Music (with distinction) in Performance from the London College of Music. I regularly attend training days, and national and international voice symposia and conferences. Whilst these sorts of conferences are not geared specifically to CCM practitioners, they provide essential learning of the latest findings in voice science, physiology, and pedagogy in general, with some specific presentations for CCM. However, for coaching CCM singers, my main training has been "in the field" as a high-level performer for almost 30 years. This helps me to know first hand what the demands are of the music industry.

Jeff Ramsey

My initial training was classical. It was called the open-close method, which was a very deliberate modification of the vowels. Unfortunately, this particular method, while good for classical, did not work well for me with contemporary music. After having surgery to remove a nodule, my speech therapist suggested Mark Baxter, who has been teaching for the past 30 years or so. I have been studying with him ever since (17 years).

Kevin Wilson

I have a Master of Music in Vocal Pedagogy from New England Conservatory, and a Bachelor of Music in Vocal Performance from the University of Central Oklahoma. I continued my studies at the Sargent School of Health at Boston University in Speech, Language, and Anatomy. I have attended various workshops through the New York Singing Teachers Association's (NYSTA) distinguished voice professional program, National Association for Teachers of Singing (NATS), and Voice and Speech Teachers Association (VASTA). Additionally, I have studied Fitzmaurice, Lessac, and Linklater voice and speech methods.

Matthew Edwards

I have a bachelor's degree in vocal performance from the Cleveland Institute of Music and a master's in vocal performance from Louisiana State University. When I was hired at

Shenandoah Conservatory, a condition of my employment was to complete a doctorate. So, I also have a Doctor of Musical Arts in voice pedagogy from Shenandoah.

My undergraduate training was absolutely amazing. It was basically designed as a musical theatre degree for classical singers. We were in acting classes six hours a week and studied all of the great teachers: Stanislavsky, Chekhov, Meisner, Uta Hagen, etc. Gary Race, who was the head of the opera program at the time, was the true definition of a master teacher. It is because of him that I can coach actors and prep students for professional auditions. My voice teacher at CIM was Beverley Rinaldi. At the end of my junior year she said "I think you are going to be a very good voice teacher one day", and she asked me if I would be her work-study teaching assistant during my senior year. I observed her teaching of the freshmen and would meet with them later in the week to teach a supplementary lesson. Ms Rinaldi would observe my teaching, give me feedback, and offered a lot of support. It was because of her encouragement that I seriously considered teaching as a career.

When I went to LSU, I took my first voice pedagogy class with Dr Loraine Sims and got hooked on science. I started reading everything I could get my hands on and began experimenting with myself, my girlfriend (who is now my wife), and my students. The big breakthrough for me was the NATS Intern program. When I saw Jeanette LoVetri was going to be one of the master teachers, I applied with a long letter explaining why I needed to be paired with her. I was, and it was absolutely magical; it completely changed my approach to teaching. Jeanie taught me to look beyond placement, posture, and breath, and to always think about vocal function. She insisted you must always know why you are using an exercise and what type of change you expect to elicit. After the internship, I started reading every resource I could find, and began sorting out why specific exercises did or did not work. I used this knowledge to begin developing my own approach, which I continue to refine as new research sheds light on the mysteries of the voice. Of all my educational experiences, the NATS Intern program had the greatest impact on my professional life.

Dane Chalfin

I started teaching at 18. I had been trained in a method which is very popular in North America. I was living on the west coast and was studying under a famous pedagogue. I was always in trouble as a teacher of that particular method for not following the rules. This really formed my views on the limitations of rigid methods.

I moved into a more science-based model for some time. I asked a lot of questions. I saw the same kind of zealous behavior going on, in a supposedly scientific model, and I wanted to see the research. I had ingratiated myself into one of our bigger voice clinics in the United Kingdom at that time, and so we were able to perform an audit of the research that was available.

I learned a lot on the job, working in the voice clinic. This taught me so much about being a singer, a teacher, a coach, a human being, a counselor, generally a better person, and a better practitioner. I had a bit of part-time educational work, and a really busy studio. I had an "up" moment for a while in my career where I was seeing a lot of really big bands. The record labels were still paying good money at that point. I could afford to take a lot of time off and just go sit in the clinic. I did this without opening my mouth for about three years, at least four to five days per month. There was no singers' clinic at that point, so I was there for all of the voice clinics watching and learning. They let me ask questions, and they would answer them. Eventually, they offered me a job, and we really started to research.

I have had a lot of my best education where the voice is concerned, through the British Voice Association, which allowed me access to a lot of really brilliant thinkers. I learned a lot from Tom Harris and Sara Harris, who wrote *The Voice Clinic Handbook*,[9] and they asked me to contribute to the second edition. I learned from Janice Chapman. I learned from Linda Hutchison and Ron Morris. Even though sometimes I get to co-present with my heroes, I am still that very hungry student. This is probably the secret to learning, never to think that you know everything. Johan Sundberg has a wonderful quote where he said, "Always seek people who are searching for the truth, but avoid people who have found it". Going to conferences and spending time with people from other fields is critical. I have been so lucky to have access to those people.

I am lucky to have so many great colleagues. Sometimes we all just kind of get into a clinic room with our equipment and play. This is how I have answered a lot of my questions, through informal collaboration that turns into research.

Wendy DeLeo LeBorgne

I have a BFA in musical theatre from Shenandoah Conservatory. My masters and Ph.D. are from University of Cincinnati in Communication Sciences Disorders. My research has been exclusively on the professional belting voice. I have worked on perceptually defining the belt sound, and then worked to objectively define those perceptual parameters.

Kathryn Paradise

I received my BM and MM from the University of Miami, Frost School of Music in Studio Music and Jazz Vocal Performance. I am currently completing a DMA in Jazz Vocal Performance from the University of Illinois, Urbana-Champaign. I have additional certifications in Somatic Voicework, The LoVetri Method™ and in Vocology from the National Center for Voice and Speech.

Trineice Robinson-Martin

I grew up singing in church and began singing jazz in high school. I did not take singing seriously as a career choice until my second year of college. During undergraduate work, I primarily worked with a jazz teacher. During my master's degree in jazz I worked with a classical teacher, first began to consistently receive more developmental voice training (i.e. working towards classical voice training parameters strengthening head voice, balanced phonation, breath management) and eventually, classical repertoire. Upon finishing my master's degree, I continued my graduate studies in music education where I focus on the applied voice. My goal during these years was to better understand how to sing the styles of music I performed and grew up singing, in a healthy manner, and I was not willing to accept that "healthy" meant "classical". As a result, my final graduate years were dedicated to research about voice science and pedagogy, then CCM voice pedagogy, and finally, the performance practices for African American folk-based music styles. Recognizing the role gospel music has in the development of black music and culture, I used the development

---

9   First edition: Tom Harris, Sara Harris, John S. Rubin, David M. Howard, eds., *The Voice Clinic Handbook* (Hoboken: Wiley, 2006). Second edition: Tom Harris and David M. Howard, eds., *The Voice Clinic Handbook* (Oxford: Compton, 2017).

of voice pedagogy for gospel music as the center from which African American folk-based music could also stem. After I finished my doctoral degree, I continued working with Jeanette LoVetri and became a certified instructor under Somatic Voicework™ The LoVetri Method. With the encouragement and help of Jeanette LoVetri, Soul Ingredients™ methodology was developed, applying many of her pedagogic principles to the functional development of the gospel/soul and jazz voice.

Marci Rosenberg

I began studying voice and performing professionally when I was about seven years old, in local professional dinner theatres, and continued throughout high school. I went to a conservatory for my undergraduate degree in voice performance. In my senior year, I took a vocal pedagogy course and as a class, we went to a local laryngologist and learned about the field of laryngology and speech pathology. I volunteered for a research study in this clinic so that I could get a free laryngeal exam. Once I learned about the world of clinical vocology, I knew that I wanted to work clinically to rehabilitate voices. One of my earlier teachers and mentors, Thom Hauser, had a background in singing science and encouraged me to pursue the field of speech pathology. I completed a second bachelor's degree in speech-language pathology and then spent a year doing research in the voice and speech lab at The National Institute on Deafness and Communication Sciences and Disorders before completing my masters in speech pathology. I was very fortunate to complete a six-month clinical externship at University of Michigan and was hired right out of graduate school. I have been working as the primary clinical singing voice specialist at The Vocal Health Center since 2003. I continue to maintain a private consulting voice studio as well.

References and recommended reading

American Academy of Teachers of Singing. "In support of contemporary commercial (nonclassical) voice pedagogy." Journal of Singing 65, no. 1 (September/October 2008): 7–10.

Bartlett, Irene. "Reflections on contemporary commercial singing: An insider's perspective." *Voice and Speech Review*, 8, no. 1 (2014): 27–35. www.doi.org/10.1080/23268263.2013.829711.

Bartlett, Irene and Pat H. Wilson. "Working 9-5: Causal relationships between singers' 'day jobs' and their performance work, with implications for vocal health." *Journal of Voice* 31, no. 2 (March 2017): 243.e27–243.e34. doi.org/10.1016/j.jvoice.2016.04.003.

Bartlett, Irene and Diana Tolmie. "What are you doing the rest of your life? A profile of Jazz/Contemporary Voice graduates." *International Journal of Music Education* 36, no. 2 (2018): 197–216.

Bennett, Dawn and Andrea Stanberg. "Musicians as teachers: Developing a positive view through collaborative learning partnerships." *International Journal of Music Education* 24, no. 3 (2006): 219–230. doi:10.1177/0255761406069646.

Benson, Elizabeth Ann. "Modern voice pedagogy: Functional training for all styles." *American Music Teacher* 67, no. 6 (June 2018): 10–17.

Bos, Nancy. "Where we were then and where we are now: A singing teacher's perspective." *Journal of Singing* 71, no. 3 (January/February 2015): 347-348.

Bourne, Tracy and Maëva Garnier. "Physiological and acoustic considerations of the female music theater voice." *The Journal of the Acoustical Society of America* 131, no. 2 (February 2012): 1586–1594. doi.org/10.1121/1.3675010.

Bourne, Tracy, Maëva Garnier, and Adeline Samson. "Physiological and acoustic characteristics of the male music theatre voice." *The Journal of the Acoustical Society of America* 140, no. 1 (July 2016): 610–621. doi.org/10.1121/1.4954751.

Bourne, Tracy, Maëva Garnier, and Dianna Kenny. "Music theatre voice: Production, physiology and pedagogy." In *Perspectives on Teaching Singing: Australian Vocal Pedagogues Sing their Stories*, edited by Scott D. Harrison, 170–182. Bowen Hills, Qld.: Australian Academic Press, 2010.

Bourne, Tracy, Maëva Garnier, and Diana Kenny. "Musical theatre voice: production, physiology and pedagogy." *Journal of Singing* 67, no. 4 (March/April 2011): 437–444.

Bourne, Tracy and Dianna Kenny. "Vocal Qualities in Music Theater Voice: Perceptions of Expert Pedagogues." *Journal of Voice* 30, no. 1 (January 2016): 128.e1–128.e12. doi.org/10.1016/j.jvoice.2015.03.008.

Chandler, Kim. "Teaching popular music styles." In *Teaching Singing in the 21st Century* edited by Scott D. Harrison and Jessica O'Bryan, 35–51. Dordrecht: Springer, 2014.

Echternach, Matthias, Lisa Popeil, Louisa Traser, Sascha Wienhausen, and Bernhard Richter. "Vocal tract shapes in different singing functions used in musical theater singing: A pilot study." *Journal of Voice* 28, no. 5 (September 2014): 653.e1–653.e7. doi.org/10.1016/j.jvoice.2014.01.011.

Edwards, Matthew. *So You Want to Sing Rock 'N' Roll: A Guide for Performers.* Lanham, MD: Rowman & Littlefield, 2014.

Edwards, Matthew. "The art of perfection: What every singer and voice teacher should know about audio technology." In *The Vocal Athlete* by Wendy D. LeBorgne and Marci Rosenberg, 271–294. San Diego: Plural Publishing, 2014.

Edwin, Robert. "A broader Broadway." *Journal of Singing* 59, no. 5 (May 2003): 431–432.

Edwin, Robert. "Contemporary music theater: Louder than words." *Journal of Singing* 61, no. 3 (January 2005): 291–292.

Edwin, Robert. "Belt is legit." *Journal of Singing* 64, no. 2 (November/December 2007): 213–215.

Edwin, Robert. "Cross training for the voice." *Journal of Singing* 65, no. 1 (September/October 2008), 73–76.

Edwin, Robert. "Are we the National Association of Teacher of Classical Singing? (Revisiting 1985)." *Journal of Singing* 67, no. 5 (May/June 2011): 589–590.

Estill, Jo. "Belting and classic voice quality: Some physiological differences." *Medical Problems of Performing Artists*, 3 (1988): 37–43.

Estill, Jo. "Observations about the quality called belting." In *The Ninth Symposium, Care of the Professional Voice*, ed. B. Weinberg & V. Lawrence, 82-88. New York City: Voice Foundation, 1980.

Estill, Jo, O. Fujimura, M. Sawada, and K. Beechler. "Temporal perturbation and voice qualities." In *Vocal Fold Physiology: Controlling Complexity and Chaos* edited by Pamela J. Davis and Neville H. Fletcher, 237–252. Singular Publishing, 1996.

Frazier-Neely, Cathryn. "Live vs. recorded: Comparing apples to oranges to get fruit salad." *Journal of Singing* 69, no. 5 (May/June 2013): 593–596.

Gill, Brian P., and Christian T. Herbst. "Voice pedagogy—what do we need?." *Logopedics Phoniatrics Vocology* 41, no. 4 (December 2016): 168–173.

Green, Kathryn, Warren Freeman, Matthew Edwards, and David Meyer. "Trends in musical theatre voice: An analysis of audition requirements for singers." *Journal of Voice* 28, no. 3 (May 2014): 324–327.

Harris, Tom and David M. Howard, eds. *The Voice Clinic Handbook.* 2nd ed. Oxford: Compton Publishing, 2017.

Harrison, Scott D., ed. *Perspectives on Teaching Singing: Australian Vocal Pedagogues Sing Their Stories*, Brisbane: Australian Academic Press, 2010.

Harrison, Scott D. and Jessica O'Bryan, eds. *Teaching Singing in the 21st Century*. Dordrecht: Springer, 2014.

Kayes, Gillyanne. *Singing and the Actor*. 2nd ed. New York, NY: Routledge, 2004.

LeBorgne, Wendy, Linda Lee, Joseph C. Stemple, and Heather Bush. "Perceptual findings on the Broadway belt voice." *Journal of Voice* 24, no. 6 (November 2010): 678–689. doi.org/10.1016/j.jvoice.2009.02.004.

LeBorgne, Wendy D. and Marci Rosenberg. *The Vocal Athlete*. San Diego: Plural Publishing, 2014.

Lombard, Lori E. and Kimberly M. Steinhauer. "A novel treatment for hypophonic voice: Twang therapy." *Journal of Voice* 21, no. 3 (May 2007): 294–299. doi.org/10.1016/j.jvoice.2005.12.006.

LoVetri, Jeannette. "Essay Somatic Voicework™: The LoVetri Method." *Voice and Speech Review* 6, no. 1 (2009): 436–442. doi.org/10.1080/23268263.2009.10767606.

LoVetri, Jeannette. "Contemporary commercial music: More than one way to use the vocal tract." *Journal of Singing* 58, no. 3 (January 2002): 249–52.

LoVetri, Jeannette. "Contemporary commercial music." *Journal of Voice* 22, no. 3 (May 2008): 260–262. doi.org/10.1016/j.jvoice.2006.11.002.

LoVetri, Jeannette, Susan Lesh, and Peak Woo. "Preliminary study on the ability of trained singers to control the intrinsic and extrinsic laryngeal musculature." *Journal of Voice* 13, no. 2 (June 1999): 219–226. doi.org/10.1016/S0892-1997(99)80024-1.

LoVetri, Jeannette, Mary Saunders Barton, and Edrie Means Weekly. "A brief overview of approaches to teaching the music theatre song." In *Teaching Singing in the 21st Century*. Edited by Scott D. Harrison and Jessica O'Bryan, 53–66. Dordrecht: Springer, 2014.

LoVetri, Jeannette L. and Edrie Means Weekly. "Contemporary commercial music (CCM) survey: Who's teaching what in nonclassical music." *Journal of Voice* 17, no. 2 (June 2003): 207–215. doi.org/10.1016/S0892-1997(03)00004-3.

McGlashan, Julian, Mathias Aaen Thuesen, and Cathrine Sadolin. "Overdrive and Edge as refiners of 'belting?' An empirical study qualifying and categorizing 'belting' based on audio perception, laryngostroboscopic imaging, acoustics, LTAS, and EGG." *Journal of Voice* 31, no. 3 (May 2017): 385.e11–385.e22. doi.org/10.1016/j.jvoice.2016.09.006.

Means Weekly, Edrie and Jeannette LoVetri. "Follow-up Contemporary Commercial Music (CCM) Survey: Who's teaching what in nonclassical music." *Journal of Voice* 23, no. 3 (May 2009): 367–375. doi.org/10.1016/j.jvoice.2007.10.012.

Meyer, David and Matthew Edwards. "The future of collegiate voice pedagogy: SWOT analysis of current practice and implications for the next generation." *Journal of Singing* 70, no. 4 (March/April 2014): 437–444.

Naseth, Andrew. "Constructing the Voice: Present and Future Considerations of Vocal Pedagogy." *Choral Journal* 53, no. 2 (September 2012): 39–49.

Nix, John. "'You want me to do what?' Twenty-First-Century Voice Pedagogy Encounters Pedagogical Fundamentalism." *Choral Journal* 53, no. 10 (May 2013): 43–51.

Popeil, Lisa. "Comparing Belt and Classical Techniques Using MRU and Video Fluoroscopy." *Journal of Singing* 56, no. 2 (November/December 1999): 27–29.

Popeil, Lisa. "The Multiplicity of Belting." *Journal of Singing* 64, no. 1 (September/October 2007): 77–80.

Robinson-Martin, Trineice. *So You Want to Sing Gospel: A Guide for Performers*. Lanham, MD: Rowman & Littlefield, 2017.

Robinson-Martin, Trineice. "Performance styles and music characteristics of black gospel music." *Journal of Singing* 65, no. 5 (May/June 2009): 595–599.

Sadolin, Cathrine. *Complete Vocal Technique Application*: completevocal.institute/app/.

Saunders Barton, M. *Bel canto/can belto: Teaching women to sing musical theatre*. DVD. University Park, PA: Penn State Media Sales, 2007.

Saunders Barton, M. *Bel canto/can belto: What about the boys? Teaching men to sing musical theatre*. DVD. University Park, PA: Self Published, 2014.

Shapiro, Jan, *So You Want to Sing Jazz: A Guide for Professionals*. Lanham, MD: Rowman & Littlefield, 2016.

Spivey, Norman and Mary Saunders Barton. *Cross-Training in the Voice Studio: A Balancing Act*. San Diego, CA: Plural Publishing, 2018.

Steinhauer, Kimberly, Mary McDonald Klimek, and Jo Estill. *The Estill Voice Model: Theory and Translation*. Pittsburgh: Estill Voice International, 2018.

Steinhauer, Kimberly, Judith Preston Grayhack, Ann L. Smiley-Oyen, Susan Shaiman, and Malcom R. McNeil. "The relationship among voice onset, voice quality, and fundamental frequency: A dynamic perspective." *Journal of Voice* 18, no. 4 (December 2004): 432–442. doi.org/10.1016/j.jvoice.2004.01.006.

Thuesen, Mathias Aaen, Julian McGlashan, and Cathrine Sadolin. "Investigating laryngeal 'Tilt' on same-pitch phonation: Preliminary findings of vocal mode metal and density parameters as alternatives to cricothyroid-thyroarytenoid 'Mix.'" *Journal of Voice*, in press. doi.org/10.1016/j.jvoice.2018.02.023.

Turnbow, Christy, Mary Saunders Barton, and Norman Spivey. "Training the next generation of music theater voice teachers: Penn State's first MFA Pedagogy grad takes stock." *Journal of Singing* 71, no. 2 (November/December 2014): 217–220.

Wigginton, James R. "When 'proper' is dead wrong: How traditional methods fail aspiring singers." *Journal of Singing* 66, no. 4 (March/April 2010): 447–449.

Winnie, Brian J. "Bridging the gap between classical and contemporary vocal technique: implications for the choral rehearsal." *Voice and Speech Review* 11, no. 1 (2017): 55–71. www.doi.org/10.1080/23268263.2017.1370803.

Winnie, Brian J., ed. *The Voice Teacher's Cookbook: Creative Recipes for Teachers of Singing*. Delray Beach, FL: Meredith Music, 2018.

5

Performing

At one point in time, responses to the question "Do you perform regularly?" might have been an unequivocal "Yes, of course". Those in academia are well-acquainted with the pressure to "do it all" as a performer, scholar, and teacher. However, performing often requires travel and time away from the teaching studio. The American Academy of Teachers of Singing (AATS) states "extended and repeated absences... are at odds with the regular, systematic training needed by students in the studio and classroom" and continues to say that an extensive ongoing performance schedule "may not even be desirable given the demands of effective studio teaching".[1] For independent studio teachers, travel means loss of teaching income and may be cost-prohibitive. As a result, half of the pedagogues in this group have chosen to focus on teaching rather than simultaneously pursue a performing career alongside a teaching career. This reflects a shift towards a student-centered model in the pedagogical voice community. AATS states that in academia, teachers of singing should be evaluated on the "pedagogic success" and "developing artistry of their students"[2] above all else.

Half of the pedagogues interviewed still perform regularly, and underline that it is vital for a teacher to feed their soul in some way. Teachers must maintain their own passion and inspiration in order to be able to give the same to their students. Many pedagogues mention the importance of being able to demonstrate the sounds that one is teaching, so staying in top vocal shape is still essential for the job. The absurd adage "Those who can't do, teach" needs an update: "Those who can't do, really shouldn't teach".

Some pedagogues have found fulfillment in related clinical work, becoming singing voice specialists and working in voice research and publication. Several have developed teacher training programs, and their life's work is spent developing the next generations of teachers. Some find opportunity and stability in studio recording work. As with many topics presented in this text, there is no one best option, only a fascinating range of individual choices.

This chapter includes responses to the prompt "Do you perform regularly?". The responses are presented starting with those who regularly perform, followed by those who maintain a combination of both performing and teaching, and finally, those who perform rarely or not at all.

Jeff Ramsey

I perform at least two to three times a month in some capacity, be it singing leads, or backing vocals for a band, or for a recording session I am running, or someone else's session.

---

1 American Academy of Teachers of Singing, "Research and creative accomplishment in promotion and tenure: A realistic look at expectations for teachers of singing in academia," *Journal of Singing* 71, no. 2 (November/December 2014), 142.

2 Ibid.

Edrie Means Weekly

I continue to perform professionally in musical theatre, jazz, pop, country, and classical styles.

Trineice Robinson-Martin

I sing about 60 performances per year in jazz, gospel, and R&B styles.

Lisa Popeil

Though I had no intentions to perform again, after a recent successful and enjoyable outing (reprising a performance from 35 years ago), much to my surprise, I have begun accepting performing invitations. I have begun performing cabaret material at a night club and will be singing jazz at wine bars and even "weird opera" at an outdoor rock festival in Germany.

Elisabeth Howard

I perform regularly in my Vocal Power Workshops. I won the National Crown "Ms. Senior America 2012"; my talent was singing. I sang "Sempre Libera", Violetta's aria from *La Traviata*, a role I performed with orchestra in Los Angeles. I plan to sing some jazz standards in the near future as I am studying jazz piano with one of the top in his field, Frank Caruso.

Irene Bartlett

I am very pleased to say that I am still singing for concert and corporate gig performances. Now I mostly sing jazz and classic pop styles, with some music theatre and classic rock thrown in for good measure. For 40 years, I was performing in CCM venues four to five nights per week. Due to my teaching and research work, it is now most usually around 15-20 performances per year. I am first and foremost a singer. It is my spirit and my soul, so I will continue to sing as long as people want to listen. My family believes that I will be singing with my last breath!

Kim Chandler

Yes, as I've done for the past 30 years, I still do sessions most days a week, thanks to having a recording studio in my house and a producer husband. The recording work is an eclectic mix that includes singing on jingles, film music, demo songs, children's educational resources, background vocals on albums, sight-reading guide parts & backing vocals for cruise line shows etc. I also regularly conduct large recording sessions at the famous Abbey Road Studios – a dream gig for a session singer! As regards live performance, I do some big band gigs, show gigs and support slots for international artists, most recently for The Jacksons. But in the past I've had the privilege to doing live backing vocals for some of the best singers in the world, such as Michael McDonald, Natalie Cole, Michael Bolton, The Bee Gees, Neil Diamond, Susan Boyle, Rick Astley, Thelma Houston, and I've performed at the Royal Albert Hall, Downing Street, Wembley Arena & Stadium, the O2 Arena and Buckingham Palace. All this performance experience can't help but inform my coaching.

Robert Edwin

I am happy to report that after over 50 years as a "Bach to rock" professional singer, I still continue to practice what I preach. In fact, my latest album of original music, "Take Them

Along, Our Songs",[3] got a rave review from Gregory Berg in the September 2016 issue of the *Journal of Singing* "Listener's Gallery". The album includes pop, rock, classic music theatre, jazz, folk, and country, and is available at CDbaby.com.

Kathryn Paradise

Yes. I perform regionally and nationally as a jazz vocalist and also do studio and background vocal work in Nashville, TN.

Mark Baxter

At 62, I perform irregularly but record often. Performances require promotion and unfortunately, I do not have the time to effectively promote a show.

Kimberly Steinhauer

My performing/teaching load ratios shift, but I am still active with an acoustic duo, periodic church solos, and other local performances such as pop soloist with the Musician's Concert Band, as the "Queen of the Night" with the Edgewood Symphony Orchestra, and a "Walküre" in Opera Theater of Pittsburgh's *Die Walküre*. Roles have ranged from "the Witch" in *Into the Woods* to "Grandma" in *Phantasmagorilla*? No! *Phantasmagoria* , a new opera by Efrain Amaya.

Seth Riggs and Margareta Svensson Riggs

Yes, we are both performers from the get-go. Seth started in 1939, at nine years of age, in the boy choir at the Washington National Cathedral. He later performed on Broadway and the New York City Opera for 10 years while at the same time forming, developing and teaching his vocal technique. He has since worked with artists who have shaped the history of music including Michael Jackson, Barbra Streisand, Stevie Wonder, Natalie Cole, Ray Charles, and many others. His clients have collectively received more than 135 Grammys while working with him.

Margareta did her first public performance when she was five and never stopped. Once grown up, and by the time she and her husband, Seth Riggs, started giving vocal workshops together, she had already done 26 years of an average of 275 gigs a year as a singer-pianist around the world, ranging from small to large venues and audiences, including opening seven Las Vegas and Beverly Hills Hotels, and maintaining a clientele of 'who's who' in her audiences. Margareta continues to do concerts and shows where often, Seth is a guest performer.

As a note in general, it is not a given that just because someone is a successful performer, he or she can teach the technique of singing. They might just transfer what they do themselves with their vocal ability, and unless they have a balanced registration and know how to get the same result in others, their principles might not be working for everyone else.

The other is also true. It is easy to be impressed by someone with diplomas on their wall. But if they have not been successful performers on any level at any time, their knowledge is going to be limited, at best.

---

3   "Take Them Along, Our Songs": Robert Edwin sings Crosby & Edwin Songs (2016) available at CDbaby and iTunes. Also, "Legacy" (2016), "More to Life" (2008), and "Robert Edwin-Christian Songs" (2008). "Keep the Rumor Going" (1966) is out of print.

Marcelle Gauvin

Yes. It is difficult with the teaching schedule I keep but I feel it's important to maintain my own artistry as it sustains my enthusiasm for teaching and my overall life force. I limit myself to concerts or recording projects, and keep my club engagements minimal at this point, due to heavy teaching demands. Practice time is always challenging. I will sing occasionally with my daughters who cover pretty much the gambit of CCM styles, but my love lies in the depth and freedom of jazz. It is my artistic fuel.

Cathrine Sadolin

Yes, I do perform but I have been extremely busy in recent years and have had to cut down on live performing. However, I still sing and play instruments in live performance. I have not done much recording recently, due to my busy schedule. My own personal performing styles are folk music and hard rock, and I merge these two styles in live performance.

Mary Saunders Barton

I have performed many solo cabarets and one-woman shows during the last 20 years. Now that I have returned to New York, I look forward to finding new performance opportunities.

Jan Shapiro

I performed regularly for 30 years, but there are not the gigs there once were, and I do not perform every night as I did in my early career.

Jeannette LoVetri

I always sing on the first night of my training course in Somatic Voicework™ the LoVetri Method, Level I. I sing classical, music theatre, and jazz songs. About every other year I am a guest artist with the New York City Community Chorus. The rest is in the shower.

Dane Chalfin

I do a lot of public speaking, and I would argue that a public presentation is a performance. I do a little bit of studio work. I tend to get the jobs where they need eight voices but only have the budget for one. They need someone who can sound like different people. Even these gigs, I would rather pass on. I do not enjoy performing as much as I enjoy teaching these days.

I find teaching performance skills and teacher training is now much more rewarding. I think there is a real tendency for things in our industry to be very dull and very self-important, and I would rather impart simple information in a funny way that makes people remember it and have a decent time. I want someone to leave after two days of teacher training wondering how it flew by so fast, not looking at their watch.

I constantly demonstrate in my studio. I am a big stickler for other teachers doing this as well when I am mentoring. When I am training teachers, I tell them that you have to be able to do the stuff that you are saying. If you need to work on it, then practice. There is no excuse. Do not be too proud to keep having lessons. Teachers can easily forget how to be students which gets in the way of good teaching. I still take lessons with three different coaches for specific work because I want to improve my own singing, and because I learn a lot about teaching by being a student.

Wendy DeLeo LeBorgne

I do not perform as regularly as I would like any more. I will do one-off gigs here or there, but because of my job demands, I do not have the luxury of being able to perform very often these days.

Tracy Marie Bourne

I perform from time to time, but I teach many more hours than I perform. I have found the experience of performing has been a good reminder of the internal experiences that my students go through in preparing their voices and bodies for performance.

Marci Rosenberg

I perform fairly infrequently. When I do perform it is always musical theatre. I do think teachers should be able to demonstrate the appropriate sounds of the styles they specialize in.

Gillyanne Kayes

No, I do not perform at all nowadays.

Cate Frazier-Neely

I do not perform regularly any more. I began developing bi-lateral vocal fold paralysis in 2006, which was first misdiagnosed and then not properly diagnosed until 2013. I was told I probably would not sing again, and if I did, I would be lucky to recover about five pitches. Do not listen to the medical community when they give a prognosis. At this writing, I have not only recovered over two octaves and can illustrate most functional exercises well, but also have some of the beauty and strength of my voice present, and am recovering rhythmic ability. I turned towards my lifelong love of making things and am an abstract visual artist. I am a published composer with Arsis Press, and I just had my first book published called "Meditations to Feed Christmas", available on Amazon. It is a series of soul-searching reflections on the meaning of the winter holidays.

Kevin Wilson

I do not perform regularly any more. I consider teaching to be a full-time performing job and I am hopeful that our community will learn to embrace this idea. Teachers need to be committed to their students' development and focus on the studio. This is a big job with a lot of responsibility, and I find that performing often takes away from the students.

Matthew Edwards

I do not perform regularly. I made a choice many years ago to place 100% of my focus on my students and family. Teaching is infinitely more fulfilling to me than performing, and I would rather spend my time working on my pedagogical pursuits. I still practice and keep my voice in shape, but I rarely sing in public. Perhaps when I have an empty nest that will change, but for now, I feel fulfilled.

References and recommended reading

American Academy of Teachers of Singing. "Research and creative accomplishment in promotion and tenure: A realistic look at expectations for teachers of singing in academia." *Journal of Singing* 71, no. 2 (November/December 2014): 141–143.

Bartlett, Irene. "Reflections on contemporary commercial singing: An insider's perspective." *Voice and Speech Review* 8, no. 1 (2014): 27–35. doi.org/10.1080/23268263.2013.829711.

Cupido, Conroy. "Music performance anxiety, perfectionism and its manifestation in the lived experiences of Singer-Teachers." *Muziki: Journal of Music Research in Africa*, August 22, 2018. doi.org/10.1080/18125980.2018.1467367.

Finney, John and Felicity Laurence. "Teachers researching singing: Contexts, conundrums, and contributions." *Education 3-13: International Journal of Primary, Elementary and Early Years Education* 45, no. 6 (2017): 744–756. doi.org/10.108 0/03004279.2017.1342321.

Mills, Janet. "Working in music: Becoming a performer-teacher." *Music Education Research* 6, no. 3 (2004): 245–261. doi.org/10.1080/1461380042000281712.

Meyer, David and Matthew Edwards. "The future of collegiate voice pedagogy: SWOT analysis of current practice and implications for the next generation." *Journal of Singing* 70, no. 4 (March/April 2014): 437–444.

Parkes, Kelly A., Ryan Daniel, Tore West, and Helena Gaunt. "Applied music studio teachers in higher education: Exploring the impact of identification and talent on career satisfaction." *International Journal of Music Education* 33, no. 3 (2015): 372–385. doi.org/10.1177/0255761415581281.

Peeler, Karen. "Training the Artist-Teacher: Voice pedagogy at The Ohio State University." *Journal of Singing* 66, no. 2 (November/December 2009): 157–159.

Spivey, Norman. "Building bridges: Paths to a multifaceted career." *Journal of Singing* 72, no. 1 (September/October 2015): 1–5.

Triantafyllaki, Angeliki. "Performance teachers' identity and professional knowledge in advanced music teaching." *Music Education Research* 12, no. 1 (March 2010): 71–87. www.doi.org/10.1080/14613800903568254.

SECTION II:
Elements of Training

6

Posture and alignment

The singer's entire instrument is housed within the body, making optimal posture and alignment critical to the production of an efficient singing sound. The majority of pedagogues use an approach to posture and alignment that seeks to minimize tension (68%) and avoids prescribing any fixed "position" (52%). "Posture" itself is not an ideal word because it implies a static or fixed stance, which is anathema to the physical dynamics of free and expressive singing. The pedagogues point out that optimal posture and alignment cannot be maintained in real-life performance situations. It is one thing to understand the ideal and to execute it in a practice room or voice studio, but on stage, it may be impossible to maintain optimal alignment due to the intense physical demands of music theatre and CCM performance. A singer may be executing a triple pirouette or crawling on the ground. Their costume or hair design may impact physicality, such as wearing a corset, high heels, or a heavy wig. Performers may be playing an instrument at the same time, or hanging upside down from aerial silks with water pouring off their heads like P!nk singing "Glitter in the air" at the 2010 Grammy Awards[1]. None of these situations allow for optimal posture, so it is critical to train with varied movement and maintain flexibility; 40% of pedagogues integrate flexibility or stretches into their voice lessons.

Several bodywork methods aid in exploring optimal posture and alignment, such as The Alexander Technique or Feldenkrais Method®. More bodywork modalities may be found in the list below. Many of these may be applied within the context of studio voice lessons. Thirty-six percent of pedagogues report using these bodywork modalities in their teaching, or report referring students to seek further support from one of these modalities. Teachers also refer students with serious postural or alignment issues to a physical therapist, massage therapist, or chiropractor.

Thirty-two percent of pedagogues provide a checklist of how the singing body should be aligned from top to bottom or bottom to top. This minority number is likely due to the common desire to avoid "prescribing" a position, which could lead to excess tension. Some teachers advocate for a hands-off approach (8%), and only address posture and alignment if they are directly causing problems for the singer. If posture and alignment are not interfering with the singing, they do not intervene. Some point out that a "less than optimal" body alignment may be a symptom of a technical problem, and once the source of the problem has been addressed the body returns to a more optimal state on its own.

---

1   P!nk, "Live performance: Glitter in the air," accessed August 22, 2018, www.youtube.com/watch?v=6TRL-bz68vk.

The elements of highest priority in posture and alignment are summarized in the chart below.

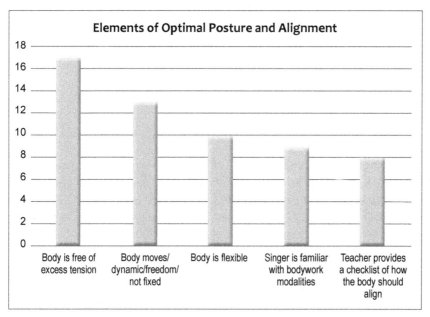

Bodywork modalities associated with singing:
The Alexander Technique: alexandertechnique.com/
Body Mapping: http://bodymap.org/main/
Feldenkrais Method®: www.feldenkrais.com/
Fitzmaurice Voicework®: www.fitzmauriceinstitute.org/
The Laban/Bartenieff Institute of Movement Studies, LIMS®: labaninstitute.org/
Lessac Kinesensic Training: lessacinstitute.org/
Linklater Voice: www.linklatervoice.com/linklater-voice/about-linklater-voice

Proprioception tools:
Balance boards
Yoga blocks
Exercise bands
Fit ball
Pilates ball

Self-reflection tools:
Mirror
Video recording

This chapter includes responses to the prompt "Please describe your approach to teaching posture and alignment". Every pedagogue addresses posture and alignment either directly or indirectly so therefore, the responses are presented in random order.

Jeannette LoVetri

The feet should be shoulder-width apart with the weight balanced over the feet such that movement is possible, and the body feels secure. Knees should be loose. The pelvic bone should be parallel to the floor and the spine should stretch and lengthen out of the pelvis. The lower abdominal muscles should work enough to allow the torso to lift (the ribcage to remain open) and the shoulders should be relaxed. The neck should be loose and long, with the head floating above it with the ears situated over the torso. The muscles of the neck should be relaxed and the face should be alert and alive, without strain. If all this was easy, we would all look fabulous, posturally speaking. These days, given how much we sit and how many things we carry on our shoulders and backs, such posture is rare to find in anyone. It takes conscious awareness and attention.

Kevin Wilson

With both rehabilitative and habilitative practice, the idea is to physically connect to the body through various stretches and physical awareness/grounding. Ideally, aligning should be in the standard ear/shoulder/hip/knee/ankle position, as the body will permit, without causing unnecessary tensions from over-correcting or "prescribed" posture. As voice teachers, we are correcting habitual issues. These changes should take time to re-shape and re-balance alignment for breath efficiency.

Irene Bartlett

My teaching has been greatly influenced by the Alexander Technique and in 2001 (from memory), I was fortunate to attend a NATS winter workshop where there were daily, intensive sessions in "Body Mapping" with Barbara Conable.[2] In keeping with the Body Mapping principles of tension-free movement, I encourage body awareness and flexibility through everyday movement activities such as walking (while singing), imagery of ball sports (especially the action of free movement of bouncing a ball or shooting hoops in basketball), and the use of proprioception tools such as balance boards and fit balls. My goal is to encourage students to find their own efficient dynamic alignment and balance as they work within the structures of their own bodies. I avoid using the word posture, noting that the dictionary definition of posture is "to fix or stake", as I believe that the word has strong connotations of effortful and rigid stance. In my experience, asking a student to engage a *posture* can create unnecessary tensions and an unnatural alignment. I ask them to find a balance over the arches of their feet by releasing the hip joints and activating the upper torso as if they are *really* interested in a conversation or are about to move quickly off the spot.

Edrie Means Weekly

A tension-free body is vital to all styles of singing. Demands of acting may interfere with body alignment and freedom. So, if a student has to slouch for the role, we work together to find ways to adjust and remain tension-free while producing healthy vocal function. Also, many

---

2   More information may be found at http://bodymap.org/main/.

commercial singers often play instruments while they sing and may adjust their bodies in a way that may develop torso tension. This will have a negative impact on the voice and can inhibit respiratory function. If needed, due to muscle tension or injury, I refer my clients to a physical therapist, massage therapist, or chiropractor.

Kimberly Steinhauer

We speak and sing on stage in many different postures. We learn to avoid constriction at the level of the vocal fold so that an actor/singer can choose to sing in any position.

Marcelle G. Gauvin

Posture and alignment are key factors in creating an efficient acoustical environment for singing. When assessing these points in a singer, I consider the following factors:
- Does the body's default alignment facilitate ease in phonation and free laryngeal function?
- Does the body have any obvious misalignments to the eye?
- Does the body have symmetry?
- Can a student maintain their singing posture with comfort and stability?
- Does a student have a history of injury, medical conditions or congenital issues that may impact their alignment?
- Does the student exercise regularly and if so, how?
- Does the student play an instrument while singing?
- Must a student deal with movement or choreography while singing?

I frequently recommend body work for students with compromised alignment, or suggest it as a prophylactic measure for singers who maintain a vigorous, highly demanding career. Massage therapy is very effective in correcting or minimizing stress-induced misalignments in my experience. For students who have postural issues due to trauma, inflammatory responses, and/or surgical procedures, myofascial release and craniosacral therapy can be extremely beneficial.

For all students, exercise executed with proper form and body work can improve posture and alignment as well as reduce stress levels.

Mark Baxter

In any genre of singing, the fundamentals listed in this question are confirmed by the quality of a voice and the visible efforts of a singer. So those are my two areas of focus. Rather than create a long list of reflexive behaviors to manage, I ask my students to create targets of the four aspects of sound: frequency, amplitude, timbre, and time. If one can comfortably produce a specific pitch at a specific volume with an intentional tonal color and rhythm, then all necessary physiological mechanisms are behaving properly. Form follows focus, so I suggest singers repeatedly ask their bodies to remain comfortable while they focus on desired sounds. This stimulates their brains to seek efficiency.

Since popular singing embraces a wide spectrum of timbres, I use non-behavioral adjectives like dark, bright, mellow, and edgy, to guide singers towards their intended sounds. My mantra is comfort and control. Comfort is encouraged by the release of restricting tensions as described below. I rely on the students' self-reporting and my observation of their physical efforts. Control is encouraged by asking students to produce a consistent volume and timbre within a two-octave range. If a student fails to do so, I suggest he or she does not "fix" the flaws by physical means (what can be felt) but rather, re-focus on the desired outcome: comfort and an intentional sound. What at first may seem like magical thinking – asking for a different outcome while repeating the same behavior – is actually encouraging micro adjustments to occur below proprioception. This approach allows each individual brain to seek the most efficient path to phonation, and each individual singer to retrain his or her unique artistic identity.

Kathryn Paradise

I often describe ideal posture for singing as "athletic ready" to engage the student's entire body in the activity of singing. Frequently, my students sing while accompanying themselves, so I coach them to "lift their upper body up out of their hip bones and engage their core", whether they are behind a piano, holding a guitar, sitting on a stool, or standing. The alignment of the head and neck has become a particular challenge in the age of smartphones and ceaseless hunching over laptops, so I bring this to their attention and often incorporate upper body stretches into the vocal warm up. Discussions of "lengthening the back of the neck" and "opening up the front of the body" are frequent in my studio.

Jan Shapiro

I have students look in the mirror, sometimes video record themselves while singing. I also stand next to the student and correct his or her stance/posture.

Tracy Marie Bourne

Posture is important, but it must be free and relaxed rather than rigid. I encourage singers to practice in front of a mirror from time to time so that they can see their physical habits and change them. The biggest problem that I have noticed in beginner singers is the tendency for them to push their head forward and their chin upward, especially when belting or singing loud sounds. I encourage them to notice this habit and then we will work to find a balanced alignment for their head – aiming for length in the back of their neck.

Lisa Popeil

I teach posture from the bottom up, beginning with: feet hip-width apart (what I call a "practice stance" which differs from various other "performance stances"); knees flexed (not bent and not locked back); lower belly soft (navel and below); upper belly soft (below sternum); sternum lifted as though being pulled up by a hook, resulting in a comfortably high chest; side and back ribs widened slightly to "singer's ribs" position with space between the shoulder blades; shoulders soft and forward (not pulled down or back); back of the neck long and soft (checking neck flexibility by moving head gently left and right); and imagining that the body is hanging from the crown of the head. Finally, I make sure that from a side-view, the shoulder is directly in line with the hip bone.

Mary Saunders Barton

Postural alignment is dynamic, never static. Actors are always "ready to move". Musical theatre performance integrates movement and acting as a primary part of technical training. It is useful to incorporate what students are learning about their bodies in expressive motion in order to bring a sense of that freedom and "relaxed readiness", even when they are absolutely still. Concentration/relaxation techniques they are learning in acting classes can be assimilated effectively in singing.

Independent studio teachers have to wear more hats. Most musical theatre performers starting careers after college will enter independent studios having already had significant body work. They will know where their most persistent tensions lie, and studio efforts will target release in those areas. If I feel they need extra help beyond what I can provide, I will refer them to Alexander, Fitzmaurice, Feldenkrais, Lessac, or other movement specialists.

Avocational singers are another matter. I once observed Joan Melton using laughter as a way to access core support and release tension. It is great fun to begin a lesson by inviting a student to start laughing. Full out, raucous laughter, until they have relinquished physical "control" (remember the telephone game?). It is very difficult to hang on to tension when you are in that state. The teacher has to be willing to fully invest in this too or it can never work. I have also found any of a variety of balance boards, inflatable discs, and balls sold at sports outlets, extremely helpful in releasing tension. For more information, please see my response under "Tension".

Dane Chalfin

My model as it stands today would start with stretch and release, particularly looking at muscles in and around the head, neck, back, and torso. Life in the 21st century brings a lot of bad body use due to driving, computer use, and cell phone neck. We know that when a muscle is in its most neutral condition, it has a freedom of movement that it does not have if it is carrying unnecessary tension. I will steal a quote from my colleague Dr Ron Morris (Griffith University, Queensland Conservatorium, Australia): "Singing is Movement". Everything has to move, and it does move, and it moves a lot. Rigidity through unnecessary tension is a problem.

I start with head/neck stretch, jaw, tongue, spine, shoulders. I would move then to active alignment. Good alignment is one thing. Perfect alignment does not exist. No one, except for the odd yoga master, has a really beautiful resting alignment. The singing instrument is already at a bit of a disadvantage because within our magic four inches of the vocal tract, we have an L-curve that really does not help us all that much. It is important that we set ourselves up with a decent alignment. For a lot of people, this does require effort. Alignment must be active to maintain ideal conditions until they become normalized. The head weighs about 14 pounds on average, and the muscles which are designed to hold it up against gravity live at the back of the neck. Because the vocal tract is so athletic and there are so many little muscles at the front trying to do intricate jobs, if those muscles in the back are not activated, the muscles at the front, which are supposed to be doing voice-jobs, are distracted with trying to hold up the head as well. It comes back to unnecessary tension which restricts movement.

The pelvis is another challenging element. Everyone wears high heels, particularly on stage. We have to have decent pelvis alignment, or we really compromise the natural reflexive relationship that we have to respiratory support. The entire trunk needs to be in a good position. When this is in place, then we have access to decent reflexive respiration.

Jeff Ramsey

I do not spend as much time on this, as I do not subscribe to any particular method such as Feldenkrais®, Body Mapping, or The Alexander Technique (more from lack of knowledge and not enough time invested in any of these modalities). What I try to do is make sure the student understands the concept of the lower body and overall posture by getting them to feel what it is like to sing with the body hunched over and then with their body upright, with a clenched stomach. They start to feel how uncomfortable both extremes can be. From there, we work on what is comfortable and gives them the most encouragement when breathing for singing.

Elisabeth Howard

I am a strong advocate of the Alexander Technique. I very often bring in an Alexander technician to work with a student in private lessons while the student sings exercises and repertoire so that the student can feel the proper body alignment and release unnecessary tensions. I cannot emphasize enough the importance of the Alexander technique for singers.

Kim Chandler

I favor a dynamic, flexible alignment with loose knees, pelvis, an open chest, and a long "noble" neck. I also encourage contemporary singers to move while vocalizing, as it is instinctive to do this and reinforces the movement required when performing.

Marci Rosenberg

In general I use a holistic approach, implementing exercises that address several aspects of voice production at the same time. I will typically incorporate voice into alignment work. As an example, I will look at all of the areas on the body that can be locked (knees, hips, ribcage, shoulders, neck, jaw). I look at how the ears align relative to the shoulders and what the singer's stance is regarding center of balance. If I notice an issue I will often take the singer to the extreme of that position and then have them sing and experience sound in an exaggerated version of what they naturally default to. Then I will go in the opposite direction and do the same. I may have them slowly move through these contrasting positions, both with and without voicing, allowing them to experience where their neutral setting is. I am also very much in favor of complimentary body work modalities, and I do not hesitate to recommend them when I think they are needed.

Matthew Edwards

I believe the body needs to be available to the performer, and that posture should not negatively impact the singing voice. This is tricky with commercial and musical theatre performers. Many commercial artists play an instrument and/or jump around the stage while singing. Musical theatre performers often dance while singing and must also adapt their performance to the director's vision, which will frequently require unusual physical positions.

I have many singers who come to me that have been taught a stance that includes a slightly tucked chin. This position is problematic for CCM singers as it can lower the larynx and keep it from rising when singing. A slightly elevated chin can be helpful but should not become habitual. The neck should never be rigid but rather, free to move. If a student needs major body work, I refer them to a specialist in that area. I think there is great value in all modalities of body work, but not everyone will respond well to every method. I think physical therapy is critical if there is a past injury. If tension is an issue, massage is a great starting place; meditation and yoga can also be very effective.

Trineice Robinson-Martin

Proper alignment should be maintained when singing in default mode. Proper alignment of the body consists of the weight of head balanced on the neck (i.e., head not too far forward, not too far back); shoulders back, and ribs lifted. To teach posture, I would simply ask the students to take the weight of their ribcage off their stomach, put shoulders down and forward, and align the top of the ears with the shoulders.

Posture and alignment should never keep a singer from being expressive in their body (movement as determined by cultural expectations).

Robert Edwin

I have created a catchy way of explaining the various component parts of the singing system. I call them the "tions" (pronounced "shuns") – **body position** (posture/alignment), **respiration** (breath management/support), **audiation** (hearing and reproducing pitch), **phonation** (vocal fold activity), **registration** (the "gears" of the vocal folds), **resonation** (amplifying and filtering the sound source using the three flexible resonators), **articulation** (shaping sound into understandable language), and **emotion** (the feelings that bring to life performed stories and songs).

Body position can be addressed via a simple movement. I have my students slowly put their arms over their heads. If they feel a measurable lift of their ribcage, then it's a sign that their posture is less than ideal. If nothing is moving other than their arms, then their body alignment is in a good place. I also delineate the difference between *tension* and *tenseness*. Muscles do two things – they tense and relax. In order for muscles, including singing system muscles, to do work, they must tense. The question then becomes "How much does a muscle need to tense in order to do the job it is asked to do?". Too little tension is *hypo* muscle activity. Too much tension is *hyper* muscle activity. I often use the Goldilocks porridge story as a teaching analogy: Is your voice technique "too hot," "too cold," or "just right"? Singers have to find a balance between hypo- and hyper-function to be their most efficient selves.

Audiation, which is a prephonatory listening event, is also a voice event. Students who come into my studio with difficulty matching pitch often have an unco-ordinated instrument that cannot accurately receive and reproduce the pitch signals from the brain. They may also have trouble discerning the pitch because of hearing/listening challenges. As they improve their overall voice technique, fine-motor movement, and listening skills, pitch issues usually diminish or disappear.

Seth Riggs and Margareta Svensson Riggs

Your spine contains your body's primary network of nerves – the spinal cord. The nerves for every limb and organ in your body are connected to your brain by this one network, which runs through the center of your spine. This main nerve cable branches out into smaller nerves, and then into still smaller nerves, until they reach out into every part of your body, including your larynx.

The function of your nerves is to pass along signals from your brain to other parts of your body. When your body is not aligned correctly, these signals become weakened or interrupted, because abnormal pressure is placed on your nerves as they pass through the openings in your spine. Poor posture inhibits not only the physical movement of your breathing muscles, which affects the air supply to your vocal cords, but also the nerve signals from your brain.

Your head, chest (always "comfortably high" so you can get a fuller and quicker supply of air) and pelvis should be supported by your spine in such a way that they align themselves, one under the other, with your shoulders back (no slouching) and with hips turned under. You should not stand rigidly, but comfortably prepared to sing. Your posture can work against you if you concentrate on it too much.

Modifications in your basic posture can be very effective in the performance of certain styles of music, helping you to create specific moods. However, until you have developed, and feel confident with, your basic vocal technique, you should avoid any type of extreme posture when you sing.

Wendy DeLeo LeBorgne

I technically and physiologically assess the parameters of alignment/posture, respiration, support, phonation, resonance, and artistry in the context of an artist's performance. This often happens outside of a lesson because, for my commercial artists, what they do in a lesson is often different than how they are performing in a live performance environment. I will have them bring me YouTube videos or live performance videos, and that is how I assess their posture. If they are playing a guitar, or if they are sitting on a stool, we start the posture conversation from where they are currently performing. My posture pedagogy, or corrective mechanism, becomes "How do we make you efficient in what you are doing? Whether it is sitting on a stool, or crawling on the floor, or hanging upside down on a barricade, what has altered your postural alignment (because you have to do those things)? But we also need to keep you artistically and vocally viable. So, what does that mean and do for the other subsystems of your voice?"

I use the same approach for all of the fundamental elements of voice, including breathing, support, registration, and belting.

Cate Frazier-Neely

The general idea is to lead a singer from any habitual static and stuck postural habits to an internal sense of fluidity and dynamic awareness. I encourage subtle changes in mindfulness and physical co-ordination through the use of props like yoga blocks, exercise bands, a Pilates ball, balance discs, or hands-on directives. Facetime lessons require a more verbal approach. I think "What specific non-singing exercises am I qualified to teach and monitor that will help this person start to substitute subtle, healthier muscle responses for current habits that are not serving them? This body part is pulled forward, so why is that happening? That area is collapsed, so what needs to pick up in muscle tone? This area is tight, so what needs to relax and strengthen to allow that area to free up? Which functional vocal exercises, based on vowel, pitch and intensity, do I co-ordinate with new alignment sensations to stimulate a motor sensory learning process rather than just completing a motor task?" The former results in lasting changes while the latter results in a quick fix that does not usually stay. However, I use quick fixes and band-aids when I am working in recording studios with singers whom I do not know, or with whom I have had no time before the recording sessions.

Cathrine Sadolin

I do not see the big need for correcting posture and alignment. I work with many professional singers, all of whom are healthy performers, and all of whom have no trouble singing. They can sing even if they are lying down. If you look at the needs of new productions, particularly in musical theatre, they have to do everything, even lie down with their hair hanging into the orchestra pit, and they might have to stab themselves, and scream, and sing. People want to see much more drama today than in the old time in opera. There you could just stand with hands folded and sing. Today, people are bored to death by this, and you will not be hired if you perform like this. You must be able to move around and perform all of the dramatic tasks that the director wants you to do. Ideal posture and alignment are not even possible.

Working on posture and alignment in a voice session is a waste of time, unless there is something wrong with the voice. Posture and alignment problems are very rare in my studio, perhaps one singer in a thousand has a true issue requiring correction. Even if I find a problem with posture and alignment, this is usually not the source of the problem. The main issue is technique, and I address that first. If the root issue is corrected, it will positively impact the entire system. Two times in my career, I have found that the main issue was posture and not technique. Usually I address technique and the posture corrects itself. Or, a singer may look like a hunchback but still sing beautifully. In that case, it is not my job to correct the posture. If they want correction for their posture I would refer them to a physiotherapist or specialist in this area.

Time in the recording studio should be spent on helping the singer to achieve their musical goals using the right technique, instead of time spent on correcting posture. Singers must be able to sit and stand in a million different positions, so I address technique rather than posture.

Gillyanne Kayes

Balance! Being able to find alignment without being fixed. I look for balance in the head-neck relationship; I pay attention to the feet and knees; I observe the spine and the pelvis. If I see nothing untoward, I do not intervene. If there are obvious postural imbalances, or negative patterns, then I will work with the singer to change these. However, sometimes a session with a physical therapist is more effective, and I will refer the singer to someone else for this.

References and recommended reading[3]

Adrian, Barbara. *Actor training the Laban way: An integrated approach to voice, speech, and movement.* New York, NY: Allworth Press, 2008.

Alexander, F. Matthias, and Edward Maisel. *The Alexander Technique: The Essential Writings of F Matthias Alexander.* London: Thames and Hudson, 1990.

Buchanan, Heather J. "Body mapping: Enhancing voice performance through somatic pedagogy." In *Teaching Singing in the 21st Century*, edited by Scott D. Harrison and Jessica O'Bryan, 143–174. Dordrecht: Springer, 2014.

Bunch Dayme, Meribeth. *The Dynamics of the Singing Voice.* 5th ed. New York, NY: Springer, 2009.

Carman, Judith E. *Yoga for Singing: A Developmental Tool for Technique and Performance.* New York: Oxford University Press, 2012.

Chapman, Janice L. *Singing and Teaching Singing: A Holistic Approach to Classical Voice.* 3rd ed. San Diego: Plural Publishing, 2016.

Conable, Barbara, and William Conable. *How to Learn the Alexander Technique: A Manual for Students.* Columbus, OH: Andover, 1995.

Conable, Barbara. *What Every Musician Needs to Know About the Body: The Application of Body Mapping to Making Music.* Revised. Portland: Andover Press, 2000.

de Alcantara, Pedro. *Indirect Procedures: A Musician's Guide to the Alexander Technique.* Oxford: Clarendon, 1997.

Dimon, Theodore and G. David Brown. *Anatomy of the Voice: An Illustrated Guide for Singers, Vocal Coaches, and Speech Therapists.* Berkeley: North Atlantic Books, 2018.

---

3   Additional bodywork resources are included in Chapter 17.

Feldenkrais, Moshe. *Awareness Through Movement: Easy-to-Do Health Exercises to Improve Your Posture, Vision, Imagination, and Personal Awareness.* New York: Harper One, 2009.

Friedlander, Claudia. *Complete Vocal Fitness: A Singer's Guide to Physical Training, Anatomy, and Biomechanics.* Lanham, MD: Rowman and Littlefield, 2018.

Gilman, Marina. *Body and Voice: Somatic Re-education.* San Diego: Plural Publishing, 2014.

Grant, Stephen J. "Vocal pedagogy and the Feldenkrais method." In *Teaching Singing in the 21st Century*, edited by Scott D. Harrison and Jessica O'Bryan, 175–185. Dordrecht: Springer, 2014.

Hackel, Erin. "Movement: Finding the perfect seasonings for each recipe." In *The Voice Teacher's Cookbook: Creative Recipes for Teachers of Singing* edited by Brian J. Winnie, 56–57. Delray Beach, FL: Meredith Music, 2018.

Heirich, Jane Ruby. *Voice and the Alexander Technique*, 2nd ed. Berkeley: Mornum Time Press, 2011.

Isley-Farmer, Christine. "Legs to sing on: A practical guide for singers and voice teachers." *Journal of Singing* 61, no. 3 (January/February 2005), 293–299.

Kind, Ethan. *An Alexander Technique Approach to Singing (Singers') Technique.* 2014. E-book.

Leigh-Post, Karen. *Mind-Body Awareness for Singers: Unleashing Optimal Performance.* San Diego: Plural Publishing, 2014.

Lessac, Arthur. *The Use and Training of the Human Voice: A Bio-Dynamic Approach to Vocal Life*, 3rd ed. Mountain View, CA: Mayfield, 1996.

Lieber, Richard L. *Skeletal Muscle Structure, Function, and Plasticity: The Physiological Basis of Rehabilitation.* 3rd ed. Baltimore: Lippincott, Williams & Wilkins, 2009.

Lister, Linda. *Yoga for Singers: Freeing Your Voice and Spirit through Yoga.* Raleigh: Lulu Press, 2011.

Lloyd, Adam, Bari Hoffman-Ruddy, Erin Silverman, and Jeffrey L. Lehman. "Vocal yoga: Applying yoga principles in voice therapy." *Journal of Singing* 73, no. 5 (May/June 2017): 511–518.

Lyle, Heather. "Stretching the dough: A Heather Lyle Vocal Yoga Method® singer's warm-up." In *The Voice Teacher's Cookbook: Creative Recipes for Teachers of Singing* edited by Brian J. Winnie, 71–72. Delray Beach, FL: Meredith Music, 2018.

Malde, Melissa, Mary Jean Allen, and Kurt-Alexander Zeller. *What Every Singer Needs to Know about the Body.* 3rd ed. San Diego: Plural Publishing, 2016.

Melton, Joan. *One Voice: Integrating Singing and Voice Techniques.* 2nd ed. Long Grove, IL: Waveland Press, 2011.

Morton, Jennie. "The integration of voice and dance techniques in musical theatre: Anatomical considerations." *Medical Problems of Performing Artists* 30, no. 2 (June 2015): 71–77.

Munro, Marth, Sean Turner, and Allan Munro. *Play With Purpose: Lessac Kinesensics in Action.* Lessac Training and Research Institute, 2017.

Neely, Dawn Wells. "A recipe for alignment." In *The Voice Teacher's Cookbook: Creative Recipes for Teachers of Singing* edited by Brian J. Winnie, 84–85. Delray Beach, FL: Meredith Music, 2018.

Nelson, Samuel H., and Elizabeth L. Blades. *Singing with Your Whole Self: A Singer's Guide to Feldenkrais Awareness Through Movement.* 2nd ed. Lanham, MD: Rowman & Littlefield, 2018.

Netter, Frank H. *Atlas of Human Anatomy.* 6th ed. Philadelphia: Saunders, 2014.

Peterson, Patti H. "Alexander or Feldenkrais: Which method is best?" *Choral Journal* 48, no. 11 (May 2008): 67–72.

Rollings, Amelia A. "The effects of heel height on head position, long-term average spectra, and perceptions of female singers." *Journal of Voice* 32, no. 1 (2018): 127.e15–127.e23. doi.org/10.1016/j.jvoice.2017.03.005.

Thurman, Leon and Graham Welch, eds. *Bodymind and Voice: Foundations of Voice Education.* 2nd ed. Iowa City: The Voice Care Network, 2000.

Wells Neely, Dawn. "Body consciousness and singers: Do voice teachers use mind-body methods with students and in their own practice?" *Journal of Singing* 73, no. 2 (November/December 2016), 137–147.

Wragg, Gerald. *Towards Vocal Freedom: Alexander Technique and the Use of the Singing Voice.* Austria: Mouritz, 2017.

7

Tension

In real-life performance situations, CCM singers do not often stand still in one place. They are dancing, moving, playing an instrument, or using physical gestures. Maintaining the physical freedom to move is critical for effective expression. Many pedagogues point out that zero tension is impossible to achieve. All muscle activity has some degree of inherent tension, all movement requires muscle engagement, and singing requires movement. As 52% of the pedagogues pointed out in Chapter 6, prescribing any "fixed" or "static" posture for the body can create unnecessary tension.

Also, 52% of the pedagogues point out that there can be both good and bad versions of tension in singing. Many pedagogues distinguish between "tension and tenseness". The former is desirable and necessary; the latter is not. Other pairings are "released tension patterns vs parasitic tension patterns", "contraction vs constriction", or "necessary constriction vs uncontrolled constriction".

The most commonly encountered negative tensions are detailed in the chart below. It will come as no surprise that laryngeal, jaw, and tongue tension are at the top of the list. Full body tension and breath tension are also common. Other types of tension mentioned by the pedagogues include emotional tension and stress, which can interfere with optimal vocal function. Creating an atmosphere of acceptance and honesty in the voice studio can go a long way toward helping a student release emotional tension and stress-related tension.

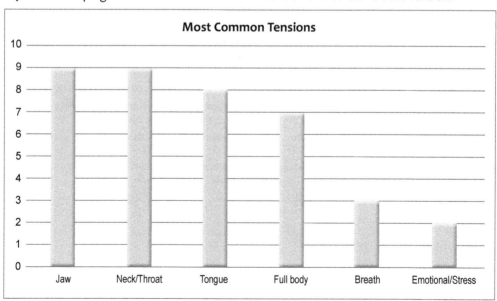

Several pedagogues note that compensatory tension may emerge as a symptom of a different problem, and the teacher must identify the source of the tension. Sometimes a lack of tension or muscle engagement in one area of the body can cause compensatory tension to manifest elsewhere. The teacher must directly or indirectly guide the student's instrument and body towards optimal function, meaning that that "right" level of tension is present in all the "right" places. The goal is to find an optimal balance of simultaneous "necessary tension" and "release" in singing. Telling a student in the imperative form to "RELAX the jaw!" was not recommended because that type of direct tactic could cause more jaw tension. The most commonly used direct tactic is a "hands-on" approach (26%). This manifests as the student massaging the area of tension, or simply placing hands on the area of tension, to encourage release. Some pedagogues report using a variety of external tools[1] to release tension and these are listed below.

Tools:
Corks (jaw and tongue)
Straw – SOVT (neck/larynx)
Straw – Tongue over straw (tongue)
Chopstick – Tongue over chopstick (tongue)
Mouth gauze to hold the tongue (tongue)
Balance boards (body)
Inflatable rings (body)
Myofascial release tools (targeted for any body part)

Several pedagogues describe using indirect approaches to provide an "opportunity" for the body to release compensatory tension on its own. Some of these indirect approaches include adjusting an element of vocal technique (52%), adjusting posture or alignment (35%), or moving the body while singing (30%). Some pedagogues use indirect but targeted vocalizes (30%), and some adjust vowels to release tension (30%). Several bodywork modalities detailed in Chapter 6 were referenced as excellent resources for movement, and these are listed again at the end of this chapter. Indirect and direct tactics to encourage a release of unnecessary tension are detailed in the chart below.

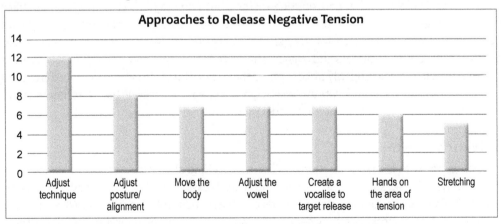

---

1   More information on "pedagadgets" may be found in Scott McCoy, "Pedagadgets," *Journal of Singing* 74, no. 5 (May/June 2018), 533–536.

This chapter includes responses to the prompt "Please describe your approach to teaching elimination of tension". It is clear from the responses that tension itself is not inherently bad, but the teacher must be able to identify the source of any negative tension and directly or indirectly evoke a release. Due to a large amount of consensus regarding the importance of releasing unnecessary tension, the responses are presented in random order.

Matthew Edwards

I cannot over-state the importance of releasing tension in a CCM singer's voice. I believe there are two major contributors to tension that are responsible for 80% of vocal problems. The first is trying to "place" the voice.

Placement is often used as a tool to fix problems related to registration. While this can work really well for some singers, for a lot of others, it is a recipe for disaster. Placement is something we experience when the vibrations created by the vocal folds travel through the vocal tract and vibrate the bone structure of our face. In order for this to happen, the vocal folds must produce strong harmonics. If the vocal folds are not doing their job, singers will often manipulate the vocal tract to squeeze their voice into the sound they want. For instance, let's say the student is trying to belt but the closed quotient is less than 50%, putting them on the heady side of mix. If the student tries to place the voice to improve the belt, they will be manipulating the vocal tract in an effort to amplify harmonics that are not present because the vocal folds are not closing firmly enough to produce them. In that instance, you must adjust the registration and as you do so, you will often see tensions release. If the student experiences a placement sensation when singing, I will use it, but I rarely suggest a placement myself. Instead, I give the student functional adjustments to elicit the sound we are seeking and allow them to define what they experience and label it for themselves.

The second cause of tension that I believe often leads to vocal problems is the incorrect formation of the vowel. I frequently work with singers who produce all of their vowels with some form of tongue retraction. When they pull the tongue back it dampens the sound, resulting in a warmer quality. If the student wants a bright quality, the only option is to constrict other parts of the vocal tract to produce a brighter sound. If we can reposition the tongue, jaw, and lips for a brighter vowel, the singer is less likely to use tension as a coping mechanism.

Of course, there are other contributing factors, but I find myself frequently coming back to moving singers away from a placement mindset and focusing on registration along with the correct formation of vowels for the genre they are performing. Tongue twisters are great tools for freeing the articulators and training the voice to be more agile. I don't usually address vibrato unless it is distracting. My philosophy is that when the voice is free and there is a good balance of transglottal airflow, vibrato will begin to appear naturally. When that happens, we can address any issues that surface as needed.

Gillyanne Kayes

It depends on what is meant by "tension". When we find the correct muscle balance for a vocal or physical task, suddenly it "flows" and feels "easy", even if it is energetic. That is my idea of eliminating tension. The rest depends on observation of the individual: What are their habitual tension patterns? Are they serving them or not? Could the sound still work for them if the habits were changed? Are they potentially dangerous?

Wendy DeLeo LeBorgne

First, you have to be able to identify where the tension is originating (posture, breath, laryngeal, jaw, etc.). After you identify where the tension pattern exists, then you find out why. For example, someone may have laryngeal tension, but it is actually coming from the fact that they are holding their breath. I would actually work on freeing the breath, which would in turn release the laryngeal tension. When I assess a singer, I look at where they are hyper-functional, and where they are hypo-functional. As much as I love to isolate the systems from one another, I really cannot because they are all interconnected. I do not always feel that the places that people hear/feel tensions directly correlate from the places from which the tension stems. It may often be stemming from one of the other sub-systems of voice.

Tracy Marie Bourne

Very important! Most of my teaching is about helping singers to identify unnecessary tension in their bodies. The jaw and tongue root are the biggest problems for most of my singers. Good alignment can resolve some of these issues, but it also requires some re-working of habitual mouth shapes. I often ask my singers to sing with their hands resting on the jaw joint at the side of the face to notice when they tighten these muscles. Sometimes I ask singers to hold their tongue while singing exercises (especially in their upper range) to notice when the tongue root pulls backward. I encourage them to feel as though they are about to bite an apple to find a free and open space in their mouth. Elimination of tension is a life-long project and requires constant monitoring in the lesson.

Jeannette LoVetri

Many CCM styles require a certain amount of tension in order to create the desired result. There is a difference, however, between tension and tenseness. Tension, or the ability to generate a high intensity sound, is necessary in rock, pop, country, gospel, and similar styles. When the vocal folds can close very firmly (increasing the closed quotient) and the air pressure level is high enough (when the ribs and abs are strong, and the inhalation is as full as possible), a great deal of sound can be comfortably produced. When the vocal production is coupled with the amplification of high frequencies so they are apparent in the acoustic spectrum, it is possible to create sounds that have a high decibel level without shouting or incurring vocal fatigue. The difficulty of accomplishing this task without also using the swallowing muscles (the constrictors) is significant, but possible. Those who do not develop independent responses in the throat (over time) by isolating both physical behaviors in the muscles that effect vocal production and clarifying the specific vocal quality necessary to the music, are often singing with unnecessary muscle strain or tenseness.

Sadly, individuals who have succeeded in having careers with very faulty vocal production or musculature that only moves in gross (large) movements, or is very constricted and effortful, have gone on to teach singing using manipulation and force as tools. They have only added to the confusion about what is and what is not vocal strain.

In the end, any unnecessary effort or tenseness in a sung sound should be eliminated through the use of appropriate vocal and breathing exercises. The idea that any kind of strong, forceful activity in the throat and body is harmful, is not correct. Much depends upon the kind of tension or tenseness taking place.

Kathryn Paradise

Tension reduction is a major focus in my work with most voice students. I speak to students about choosing when to use tension for a certain effect, and mitigating tension in most other cases. Main points of tension in my students tend to reside in the neck, tongue, and jaw. Reducing this tension involves a two-pronged attack, one to release the tension in the specific area and two, to replace that tension with effective breathing and postural alignment, and/or vowel modification. When you compare singing to an athletic activity, students immediately understand why tension is detrimental, and why it makes them prone to injury and inefficiency. Tongue and neck and jaw stretches are regular components of my students' warm-up and exercise routines. I also use chopsticks, corks, head shakes, "rag doll" postures, and gentle holding of the jaw, when appropriate.

Lisa Popeil

During my training, there was much emphasis on the importance of relaxation in good singing to the extent that many of my lessons focused on reducing tongue, jaw and neck tension using relaxation exercises. While I do think there is some benefit in becoming aware of body parts and what relaxation feels like, once I figured out more clearly how to support, I found that excessive tension, such as throat squeezing, choking, tongue bunching or swallowing, vocal fold pressing or jaw clenching, immediately lessened or even disappeared. At that point, I was struck by the idea that excessive tension in the local area of the neck and head was most likely compensatory tension, and that once I moved the necessary work of singing to my posture and support tasks, the compensatory tension could just let go.

Another element of the concept of work vs tension I would like to add is that I do not believe that relaxation is the key to easy singing. I prefer to think that every part of the body has a job; some parts are relaxed and others are working, even sometimes feeling quite a bit of effort. Knowing and practicing the tasks of the various parts of the body can empower a singer and aid in consistency. Sometimes, the technical problems that a singer exhibits result from not enough work or the wrong work. So, use of the word "tension" should not in itself be a bad thing; perhaps simply identifying incorrect, or even inadequate correct, work should be the focus in training.

Trineice Robinson-Martin

Unnecessary Tongue Tension (U.T.T). The tongue is one of the hardest muscles to keep relaxed, particularly in the back. While it is necessary for the tongue to contract to produce certain vowels and consonants (i.e., [e], [r], [I], [k], [s], [z], [n], etc.), singers must learn to control the amount of contraction when singing to avoid tongue tension. Tongue tension can affect your ability to change pitch, and even the speed of your vibrato.

Contraction vs Constriction. Singers have to learn the difference between contraction and constriction. There are many culturally viable and authentic sounds used in CCM that do require contraction in areas of the vocal tract. However, constriction occurs when singers become stuck in the contracted position. Singers have to be encouraged to maintain a free "default sound". They must know how to use contraction for effect only and not as their default.

I use a voice intensity chart to understand what different volume levels and emotional intensity levels feel like in the body as related to the sound that results.

All sounds have to be conditioned into the body so that their execution is done freely. This consists of exercises that take potentially pressurized sounds, either in terms of loud, high pitches, or problematic constant-vowel combinations sung in high tessitura ranges (such as "blessed", "you", "listen", "giving" etc.), and conditioning their execution through vocal modifications, or by gradually increasing the vocal range at a rate at which the singers are not straining.

Kevin Wilson

There is no such thing as tension-free singing. You breathe with tension, phonate with tension, etc. Negative tensions often times are habitual issues that do not allow us to have the expression we need due to imbalances. I do a great deal of physical exercises which I either made up or learned from Fitzmaurice, Lessac, and Linklater bodywork[2]. These exercises work the entire physical body towards "free" sound and the full body emotion. My students are taught to isolate the articulators and shapers of sound, the jaw, tongue, soft palate, and larynx, through physical movements, and by traditional and non-traditional vocal exercises such as wobbles, moans, fries, cries, sighs etc. I want my students to feel what the impulse to make sounds is versus a prescribed sound.

Marci Rosenberg

If warranted, I will use laryngeal massage to release tenacious laryngeal tension or areas of point tenderness, but not as a first intervention. Establishing good alignment is the first step to eliminating tension. Neck strap muscles are often problematic, and constant hovering over cellphones and computers has increased postural issues that impact good alignment. I use basic myofascial work on upper body, jaw, and tongue.[3] I find it is always fruitful to invest as much studio time and focus on eliminating tension as necessary, because it can be an exercise in futility to focus on only "singing" while ignoring the parasitic tension patterns that are impeding the sound production to begin with. I often work on tension patterns in isolation initially, but always add a singing component to ensure carry-over of the released tension pattern into singing. As stated in the chapter on posture and alignment, other somatic modalities are sometimes critical to address firmly established tension patterns.

Kimberly Steinhauer

Muscles only contract; therefore, there is "tension" in singing, especially singing those qualities with high acoustic output power. In Estill Voice Training®, we monitor for a low effort at the level of the true and false vocal fold (Most Comfortable Vocal Effort), knowing that effort in other parts of the body will be needed to make a quality seem "relaxed and effortless" at the level of the true vocal fold.

Cathrine Sadolin

It is important to define what we are talking about. Constriction around the vocal folds is necessary to form the desired sound. It is not inherently bad. We should not avoid constriction (because that would mean no sound); we should make sure we have the right constriction. If you relax everything, you cannot sing anything. Uncontrolled constriction should be avoided

---

2   A list of bodywork modality resources may be found at the end of this chapter.

3   More information may be found at www.myofascialrelease.com/.

because it can cause an undesired change of vocal mode. In order to avoid uncontrolled constriction, you must obey the rules of each CVT vocal mode (Neutral, Curbing, Overdrive, and Edge)[4]. For example, in Overdrive, you must use [ɛ] and [o] vowels, but not others. In Neutral, you can use many vowels, but [i] and [u] are the easiest. If volume or sound color are also not being executed according to the rules, it will cause uncontrolled constriction. Once you know the rules of each mode, you can sing whatever you like.

Any other constriction, such as neck or shoulder, does not usually have to do with the voice. You can move your body in strange tight ways and still sing beautifully. Of course, one would prefer to be comfortable in the body, but this does not have anything to do with singing.

Seth Riggs and Margareta Svensson Riggs

Generally, when you speak in a quiet, comfortable manner, the outer muscles do not interfere with the functioning of your larynx. That is because tone is not your concern, communication is. Your larynx is resting and functioning in a *speech-level* position. This is also the ideal vocal condition or posture with which to sing. Volume increase in both speech and singing is created with intensified support originating in the low abdomen, below your navel, and has nothing to do with the position of the larynx.

Mark Baxter

If a student is dramatically inhibited or withdrawn such that posture and breathing are unable to reflexively calibrate an alignment of a desired sound, I use movement to release the body and breath. Walking, knee bends, swinging arms, and shoulder rolls are all good options. These movements reward singing due to the muscle independence required for motion and the increased demand for oxygen. The released muscles and deeper inhalation allow emotionally restricted singers a momentary experience of effortless singing. At first, the vocal improvements feel like accidents, but with each successful repetition a direct neural pathway is established from the area of the brain involved with the planning, control and execution of voluntary movements (motor cortex) instead of the GABAergic signals (inhibition) I describe in Chapter 2. Once a singer trusts the floating sensation of balanced phonation, the elimination of tension can be summoned while standing still.

Cate Frazier-Neely

This is addressed indirectly through my approaches to posture, alignment and registration. It is addressed more directly in suggestions to the student to search for optimum strategies for their nutrition, hydration, life–work balance, and the effects of medications and environment on their central nervous system.

Edrie Means Weekly

I help singers to eliminate tension through laryngeal massage, body work, relaxation exercises and stretches, tongue and jaw dissociation, and breathing exercises. I also work on laryngeal flexibility/vocal agility through exercises, so the singer can alter shapes in the vocal tract to suit the style and sing the licks or riffs needed without tension or locked larynx.

---

4   More information on Complete Vocal Technique (CVT) may be found in the CVT App: completevocal.institute/app/.

Some of the vocal tract shaping exercises I use include: lift and flattening the soft palate, all sorts of tongue exercises, vowel shaping, vowel distortion shaping, along with *vocal stylisms*. These are the extra nuances added to a song for style effect, and are not usually written in the music. Some *vocal stylisms* are cry, fall-off, fall-ups, fry, bending the note, growl, pop-appoggiatura, waves, yodel, etc.

Some exercises I use to help a singer gain laryngeal flexibility have included the following:

1. Glides from low to high.
2. Y[æ]: Scale degree 1 (tonic) to 8va. Tonic in chest register – 8va in head register (with yodel or without) in a comfortable range.
3. [æ]: Start in chest and stay on note change to head. First as a quick yodel transition and then a slow non-yodel transition (starting A4 for women up to C5, D4 for men up to F4).
4. With a bright Y[æ]: 3, 2, 1 (mi, re, do) good for "tails" or "scream".
5. "Me": Scale degrees 5-6-5-4-5-4-3-4-3-2-3-2-1 (starting in the key of C - G4 for women, G3 men).
6. "Whoa": Pentatonic scale (C-D-E-G-A) in reverse with an added ½ step above; A-B♭-A-B♭-A-G-E-D-C. Use up and down the vocal range as feels comfortable in head, mix, and chest as well as different dynamics. This scale is common in rock music.
7. Blues Scale: C, E♭, F, F♯, G, B♭, C. Use ascending and descending with various melodies made up from the scale. Use up and down the vocal range as feels comfortable in head, mix and chest as well as different dynamics. This is great for learning to improvise. The blues scale is prevalent in the blues, R&B, gospel and rock.
8. "Guy-La" (without moving jaw): Scale degrees 5-4-3-2-1-2-3-4-5-4-3-2-1 (starting on G4 for women, G3 for men).
9. Nine tone scales to build flexibility and stamina.

Mary Saunders Barton

Physical tensions interrupt the flow of communication and endanger vocal health. I have a number of strategies to work on release in the studio. Engaging in familiar actions like shooting baskets or bowling or tennis, which require follow-through, can be useful. Many of the movement disciplines are helpful in this regard. I rely on the expertise of colleagues who specialize in the work of Moshe Feldenkrais, Catherine Fitzmaurice, Joseph Pilates, Arthur Lessac, Frederick Matthias Alexander, and Kristin Linklater[5] to help me with my students. I use balance boards and inflatable rings to focus attention on the abdominal core muscles and to encourage a released, energized stance. Any kind of torqued stance, as in yoga-based positions, is useful in accessing core muscles.

Problems with tongue retraction or jaw and neck tension can be tricky, and sometimes require minute-to-minute monitoring to identify and correct.

Marcelle G. Gauvin

Eliminating tension in singers is much like untangling a ball of yarn. It takes time and patience. Tension can be an overall generalized experience or an extremely localized one, but frequently it is both. Most singers I deal with enter their lessons in a highly stressed state due to academic or professional commitments. I attempt to help them decompress before we begin the lesson by keeping the tone in the studio light, relaxing

---

5   A list of bodywork modality resources may be found at the end of this chapter.

and welcoming. It is always understood that we will accept the voice as it is, in the present moment, and start from there. I usually get the student to focus and center during warm ups using semi-occluded vocal tract (SOVT) exercises or a very simple, familiar scale, and encourage them to move and stretch. Major scales, pentatonic scales, the blues scale, and natural minor are all good choices. As the warm up continues, localized areas of tension will present during phonation. At that time, I begin to integrate targeted exercises that encourage muscle unwinding and release.

As a rule, in dealing with tense tissue, I find two things to be true. Sometimes subtle, small adjustments can be more effective than assertive measures because they allow the involved muscles a chance to relax around an activity. Finding the exact exercise to address the issue does take some exploration but with patience, is well worth the effort. If the tension is severe, we may stop and do facial massage or McClosky relaxation exercises.[6] Other times, I may use lighter, quick moving exercises, over a greater range, that encourage the body to release through more active motion. The goal is always to meet the body where it is and allow it to unwind on its own terms by guiding it towards a healthy default. This requires time and trust in the idea that the body can and will take the lead given the proper stimulus. The body desires balance and free co-ordination. Releasing expectations and judgments about the process is helpful and facilitates a quicker response.

Elisabeth Howard

If you have the correct breathing and support, you have a big head start in not having tension in the first place. I make sure that the breathing and support are correct first. For those who come to me with jaw, neck, throat or tongue tension. I use a tongue release exercise that is specifically for releasing tension in the tongue, jaw, neck and throat.

Jeff Ramsey

The big culprits, we all know, are the jaw and the tongue. To that end, I go to methods I have learned from Mark Baxter and Jeanie LoVetri for eliminating tension. One of the things that helps my students along with practicing with an even volume is practicing with no emotion in their faces (for technical purposes only), as the face is one of the best indicators of any tension showing up. I use a mouth gauze for the students, having them hold their tongue gently while vocalizing. Other methods that come in handy to identify any tension are a straw under the tongue, or a wine cork in the mouth.

Jan Shapiro

I do not see the elimination of tension as a separate topic. Tension should not be part of a singer's performance. If the student concentrates on the co-ordination of breath and voice, there should never be tension. There are ways to help eliminate tension but in simple terms, all muscles must be relaxed everywhere.

Kim Chandler

I use a body stretch routine and continue to refine technical balance over time so that the minimum parts are working optimally.

---

6   David Blair McClosky, Your Voice at its Best (Boston: Little Brown and Co., 1972), www.mcclosky.org/.

Robert Edwin

I address tension as part of the body posi*tion* portion of the *"tions"* (pronounced "shuns") singing system. Please see my response under Posture/Alignment.

Dane Chalfin

Addressing tension is foundational to everything.

Bodywork modalities commonly associated with singing

- The Alexander Technique: alexandertechnique.com/
- Body Mapping: http://bodymap.org/main/
- Feldenkrais Method®: www.feldenkrais.com/
- Fitzmaurice Voicework®: www.fitzmauriceinstitute.org/
- The Laban/Bartenieff Institute of Movement Studies, LIMS®: labaninstitute.org/
- Lessac Kinesensic Training: lessacinstitute.org/
- Linklater Voice: www.linklatervoice.com/linklater-voice/about-linklater-voice

References and recommended reading

Barnes, John F. *Myofascial Release: The Search for Excellence.* 10th ed. Paoli, PA: Rehabilitative Services, 1990.

Burt, Diane and R. Russell Burt. "Temporomandibular dysfunction and the developing singer." *Journal of Singing* 71, no 1 (September/October 2014): 35–44.

Cookman, Starrlett and Katherine Verdolini. "Interrelation of mandibular laryngeal functions." *Journal of Voice* 13, no. 1 (March 1999): 11–24. doi.org/10.1016/S0892-1997(99)80057-5.

Deeter, Alissa. "Tennis ball massage to alleviate trigger point pain." *Journal of Singing* 70, no. 2 (November/December 2013): 157–163.

Duncan, Ruth. *Myofascial Release.* Champaign, IL: Human Kinetics, 2014.

Eller N., G. Skylv, E. Dahlin, P. Suadicini, F. Gyntelberg. "Health and lifestyle characteristics of professional singers and instrumentalists." *Occupational Medicine* 42, no. 2, 1 (January 1992): 89–92. doi.org/10.1093/occmed/42.2.89.

Kagan, Loraine Sydney and James T. Heaton. "The effectiveness of low-level light therapy in attenuating vocal fatigue." *Journal of Voice* 31, no. 3 (May 2017): 384.e15–384.e23. doi.org/10.1016/j.jvoice.2016.09.004.

Kochis-Jennings, Karen Ann, Eileen M. Finnegan, Henry T. Hoffman, Sanyukta Jaiswal. "Laryngeal muscle activity and vocal fold adduction during chest, chestmix, headmix, and head registers in females." *Journal of Voice* 26, no. 2, (March 2012): 182–193. doi.org/10.1016/j.jvoice.2010.11.002.

LeFevre, Carla. "Tongue management." *Journal of Singing* 68, no. 2 (November/December 2011): 157–162.

LeFevre, Carla. "Tongue management, part 2." *Journal of Singing* 74, no. 1 (September/October 2017): 51–55.

Lemon-McMahon, Belinda and Diane Hughes. "Toward defining 'vocal constriction': Practitioner perspectives." *Journal of Voice* 32, no. 1 (January 2018): 70–78. doi.org/10.1016/j.jvoice.2017.03.016.

Lombard, Lori E. and Kimberly M. Steinhauer. "A novel treatment for hypophonic voice: Twang therapy." *Journal of Voice* 21, no. 3 (May 2007): 294–299. doi.org/10.1016/j.jvoice.2005.12.006.

LoVetri, Jeannette, Susan Lesh, and Peak Woo. "Preliminary study on the ability of trained singers to control the intrinsic and extrinsic laryngeal musculature." *Journal of Voice* 13, no. 2 (June 1999): 219–226. doi.org/10.1016/S0892-1997(99)80024-1.

McClosky, David Blair. *Your Voice at its Best.* Boston: Little Brown and Co., 1972.

Scott McCoy, "Pedagadgets," *Journal of Singing* 74, no. 5 (May/June 2018), 533–536.

Phyland Debra J., Julie F. Pallant, Michael S. Benninger, Susan L. Thibeault, Ken M. Greenwood, Julian A. Smith, and Neil Vallance. "Development and preliminary validation of the EASE: A tool to measure perceived singing voice function." *Journal of Voice* 27, no. 4 (July 2013): 454–462. doi.org/10.1016/j.jvoice.2013.01.019.

Phyland Debra J., Susan L. Thibeault, Michael S. Benninger, Neil Vallance, Kenneth M. Greenwood, and Julian A. Smith. "Perspectives on the impact of vocal function of heavy vocal load among working professional music theater performers." *Journal of Voice* 27, no. 3 (May 2013): 390.e31–390.e39. doi.org/10.1016/j.jvoice.2012.12.003.

Phyland Debra J., Julie F. Pallant, Susan L. Thibeault, Michael S. Benninger, Neil Vallance, and Julian A. Smith. "Measuring vocal function in professional music theater singers: Construct validation of the Evaluation of the Ability to Sing Easily (EASE)." *Folia Phoniatrica et Logopaedica* 66, no. 3 (March 2015): 100–108. doi.org/10.1159/000366202.

Pettersen, Viggo, Kare Bjorkoy, Hans Torp, and Rolf Harald Westgaard. "Neck and shoulder muscle activity and thorax movement in singing and speaking tasks with variation in vocal loudness and pitch." *Journal of Voice* 19, no. 4 (December 2005): 623–634. doi.org/10.1016/j.jvoice.2004.08.007.

Solomon, Nancy Pearl. "Vocal fatigue and its relation to vocal hyperfunction." *International Journal of Speech-Language Pathology* 10, no. 4 (July 2009): 254–266. doi.org/10.1080/14417040701730990.

Steinhauer, Kimberly, Mary McDonald Klimek, and Jo Estill. *The Estill Voice Model: Theory and Translation.* Pittsburgh: Estill Voice International, 2018.

Sundberg, Johan and Margareta Thalén. "What is twang?" *Journal of Voice* 24, no. 6 (November 2010): 654–660. doi.org/10.1016/j.jvoice.2009.03.003.

Titze, Ingo. "Phonation threshold pressure: A measurement with promise but slow in development." *Journal of Singing* 67, no. 4 (March/April 2011): 425–426.

Titze, Ingo R., "Mechanical stress in phonation." *Journal of Voice* 8, no. 2 (June 1994): 99–105. doi.org/10.1016/S0892-1997(05)80302-9.

Titze, Ingo R., Christine C. Bergan, Eric Hunter, and Brad Story. "Source and filter adjustments affecting the perception of the vocal qualities twang and yawn." *Logopedics Phoniatrics Vocology* 28, no. 4 (December 2003): 147–155.

Titze, Ingo R., Jan G. Svec, Peter S. Popolo. "Vocal dose measures: Quantifying accumulated vibration exposure in vocal fold tissues." *Journal of Speech, Language, and Hearing Research* 46, no. 4 (August 2003): 919–932. doi.org/10.1044/1092-4388(2003/072).

Walker, Catherine A. "Let's talk about the tongue: A recipe for improved vocal ease and function." In *The Voice Teacher's Cookbook: Creative Recipes for Teachers of Singing* edited by Brian J. Winnie, 124–126. Delray Beach, FL: Meredith Music, 2018.

Walters Deeter, Alissa. "Overlooked and undermining: A look into some of the causes, effects, and preventatives to the dysfunctions generated by excessive tension." *Journal of Singing* 62, no. 1 (September/October 2005): 27–31.

Welham, Nathan V. and Margaret A. Maclagan. "Vocal fatigue: Current knowledge and future directions." *Journal of Voice* 17, no.1 (March 2003): 21–30. doi.org/10.1016/S0892-1997(03)00033-X.

Yanagisawa, Eiji, Jo Estill, Steven T. Kmucha, and Steven B. Leder. "The contribution of aryepiglottic constriction to 'ringing' voice quality: A videolaryngoscopic study with acoustic analysis." *Journal of Voice* 3, no. 4 (December 1989): 342–350. doi.org/10.1016/S0892-1997(89)80057-8.

8

Breath

Breathing is foundational to singing. However, in speech-centered singing styles (CCM), phrase lengths are often shorter than they would be in classical repertoire, or even in legit musical theatre repertoire. The large volume of air necessary to manage a lyric eight-bar phrase is not often necessary in CCM. Therefore, breathing for CCM singing can more closely resemble breathing in general. If the way a student is breathing is not causing any problems, some prefer to leave it alone. Some even believe that it is a waste of time to address it. Pedagogues state that breathing is an easy scapegoat for other technical problems and can quickly become an obsession for singers. Some caution that prescribing any one method or approach could cause additional and unnecessary tension.

The majority of pedagogues (65%) interpreted "breathing" as encompassing both inhalation and exhalation, but described the two stages differently. For 65% of the pedagogues, inhalation involves a rib expansion and a release of the abdominal muscles. The same number (65%) say that during exhalation, the abdominals contract while the ribcage remains expanded. This traditional approach to breathing closely resembles that of breathing for classical singing. The defining differences would be that a large volume of air is not necessarily inhaled due to the shorter phrase lengths in CCM material, and during exhalation, subglottal air pressure will vary widely according to volume and registrational choices.

Due to the differences in air volume, air pressure, and range of volume and registrational choices in CCM, 25% of pedagogues say that singers should know more than one way of breathing and that it should be customized for each person, circumstance, and style of singing. There is evidence that certain body types naturally breathe differently,[1] and would, therefore, experience varying levels of success using the traditional approach described above. It is recommended that teachers provide multiple strategies for breathing, especially for singing while dancing or playing an instrument. An approach to breath should be flexible enough to use in any physical situation, with any body type, in any style of music.

Several pedagogues pointed to the *Accent Method*[2] as a flexible model which allows for variation in breath volume suitable for CCM singing. This method is not well known in the U.S., but it is popular in the U.K. and Australia. Twenty percent of pedagogues advocate for the inhalation to happen as a recoil breath, allowing the natural vacuum to create a silent and efficient inhalation. Some pedagogues suggest connecting breath with the need to speak or express something. Cate Frazier-Neely poetically describes breathing as "an intoxicating and

---

1   Jennifer Griffith Cowgill, "Breathing for singers: A comparative analysis of body types and breathing tendencies," *Journal of Singing* 66, no. 2 (November/December 2009), 141–147.

2   More information may be found in Ron Morris and Linda Hutchison, *If in Doubt, Breathe out! Breathing and Support for Singing Based on the Accent Method*, (Oxford: Compton Publishing, 2016).

sensual act that precedes, and leads to, expression". Pedagogues recommend teaching as many approaches as possible, and allowing the student to select the best approach as needed.

Eight pedagogues (32%) view breathing and support as so intertwined that they responded to both prompts as one. In this chapter, one pedagogue refers to her response in the next chapter, under "support". In the next chapter on "support", seven pedagogues refer back to their response in this chapter, under "breathing". They are undeniably intertwined.

This chapter includes responses to the prompt "Please describe your approach to teaching breathing". The responses are presented in a loose order from those who describe a traditional approach to those who advocate for flexibility, multiple approaches, and customization.

Lisa Popeil

To begin with, I think it is absolutely crucial for teachers to separate the term "breathing" from the term "support". Though both terms relate to use of air, they are completely different tasks and generations of singers, including myself, have been confused by the intermingling of the two terms. For singing, I believe the term "breathing "should describe only the intake of air. This intake should be accomplished keeping certain goals in mind: breath should enter the body quietly, invisibly, and effortlessly. Towards that goal, I teach a step-by-step approach, beginning with a slightly open mouth, followed by an open throat (results in widening of the vocal folds), releasing the lower belly (navel and below), feeling air "fall" into the body, then imagining air filling up into the body to the "top of the head". This procedure can be practiced until the action becomes very rapid. Overall, this "lower belly breathing" approach minimizes chest lifting, gasping sounds, and prevents a high, constricted larynx resulting from clavicular breathing. I like to tell my students that we're now using the body's own natural vacuum effect to breathe, and should eliminate the troublesome word "inhale" from our vocabularies.

One of the old adages of some classical breathing pedagogies is that breathing through the nose is ideal. I have come to the conclusion that this action was in fact devised to help create the preferred resonator shaping for classical singing (low larynx, wide pharynx, raised soft palate and cheeks). A classical singer can easily create the desired resonator shape without thinking they have to sniff for every breath. When a singer takes air in through the mouth, air will also be coming into the nose. The only time I do breathe solely through my nose is in classical singing when I am waiting while a musical introduction or interlude is playing. The rest of the time, the only way to get enough air in quickly, quietly, and invisibly is through the mouth.

Marci Rosenberg

I think we can all agree that breathing is a very important part of efficient voice production, but I find that some teachers often "over blame" breathing for a multitude of voice issues, and singers are often pre-programmed to focus only on "lack of support" as the source of every voice production problem. I prefer to work on breathing in the context of actual sound production to maximize the specificity of the exercise. I do not typically address breathing independently of voice, and when I do it is because the singer has very little kinesthetic reference for an expanded breath, or is really demonstrating a very inefficient breathing pattern. If I do isolate breathing independent of voice production, it is to provide a tactile reference of the target movement. I have the student feel the ribs and what kinds of movements they make during the inhale and exhale. I will have them experience this in various different positions (i.e. sitting, leaning forward, standing, leaning forward on a wall etc.). I will always discuss expansion using the ribcage as a tactile reference. I do not focus on abdominal expansion as much because this can lead to an inaccurate somatic reference for what should be happening during inhalation. I frequently see a lot of "abdominal expansion" which is not resulting in actual efficient inhalation. I find that if the ribs are expanding all the way around to the back, then the diaphragm and abdomen are doing what they need to do. This becomes an important strategy for singers who are also very well-trained dancers, because they are taught to hold the abdominal musculature in as part of dance training. The breathing pattern typically needs to be different than that of a traditional classical inhalation with a released abdomen.

The exhale is equally important to the breathing cycle. There are two primary components I keep in mind regarding the exhale. First, the singer's ability to maintain a relatively open and expanded ribcage once the sound has been initiated. This can become challenging when dealing with a singer who is also dancing at a high level. The second component impacting the efficiency of the exhale has to do with the vocal folds. If a singer is not managing air efficiently and has a reduced ability to sustain a tone, the problem is often not a breathing issue, rather it is rooted in the vocal fold vibratory pattern, and inefficient valving of the airflow. In this case, the efficiency of vocal fold onset must be addressed or the perceived "breathing issue" will not resolve. This can take time depending on the age of the singer. If I feel an adequate amount of time has been spent on achieving clean efficient vocal fold closure and the breathiness remains, I never hesitate to have the student seen by a laryngologist to ensure the vocal fold structures are healthy.

Jeannette LoVetri

I teach intercostal/abdominal breathing: the postural muscles help a great deal during inhalation. The ribcage remains comfortably lifted and open regardless of inhalation or exhalation. The idea should be to draw breath into the lowest ribs (bottom of the lungs) without having the ribs expand further. The abdominal muscles move forward and out due to the action of the viscera (the internal organs), underneath the contracted diaphragm. As the organs of the viscera descend they also move forward and out, which pushes the abdominal wall forward and out as well. The student is encouraged to pay attention to areas of the body as they move, in whatever way they move, throughout the entire process.

Exhalation requires deliberate control over the ribcage and the abdominal muscles, such that the abdominals are contracting up towards the ribcage and in towards the spine during exhalation in phonation, or by expressing breath as a hiss while the ribs remain stable. For most people, keeping the ribs from collapsing during exhalation, as they are designed to do, is the hardest part to learn. Other muscles throughout the body can be recruited over time to make the process stronger and more secure.

Since everyone has a different awareness of and control over the body in various areas, the teacher must observe what is physically happening at all times and help the student/singer perceive what the body is doing in response to the intention of the instruction. The process is more complicated than it sounds, and it is a learned behavior for everyone. It has to do specifically with singing, and not with normal speech-based vocal use.

Seth Riggs and Margareta Svensson Riggs

You must let your stomach muscles all the way down below your navel drop out before contracting them, thus allowing the atmospheric pressure to facilitate the air rushing in and filling the lungs to a maximum. The air is then dispersed by pulling your muscles in and up, moving the air up against the damping vocal cords, which is the process that creates the sound; in other words, the phonation. You will notice a seesaw effect between the lower abdomen and the diaphragm: when one goes in, the other goes out, and at no time will you let your ribcage collapse. This is how you breathe when singing.

Breathing and support are essential. If you lift your chest and shoulders in order to breathe, your breath will be shallow and there is no air to create the support.

Equally, if you think you support by pushing the middle of your stomach down and out, your movement is the opposite of what needs to happen. You cannot support air to go up to your vocal cords by pushing down and out.

Jan Shapiro

There are so many ways to explain this important element of singing' and there are so many ways that voice teachers describe it! In my view, "breathing and support" are together – they are not separate. "Support" is just another way of saying "breathe low". I intentionally do not use the word "inhale" or "exhale" with students so much. In my mind "support" means both inhaling and exhaling – the action of breathing. In other words, "support" is the physical action of breathing. Believe it or not, sometimes students get fixated on "inhaling" and "exhaling" so that they actually become tenser!

I use several ways to help the student singer breath consistently lower. Sometimes he or she may lay on the floor or sit – relaxing, as in sleeping. I show students a picture of our anatomy – a diagram of the diaphragm, lungs, throat, abdominal muscles, etc. Although I know the names of all the muscles and their functions, I do not emphasize the names of each muscle but more how they function. My philosophy is that we already use the muscles in our body needed to sing – they already are within our body. We use the same muscles for living and talking. However, we need to make our breathing muscles stronger for our singing voices, which have more overtones and utilize a larger vocal range than in speaking. Essentially, we strengthen and co-ordinate our breathing muscles to work better for singing. It is the same for athletes who have natural physical ability but need further training to achieve finer co-ordination, endurance, and strength.

Tracy Marie Bourne

I teach all of my singers to breathe in with a relaxed abdomen and slightly widened ribs, and to support their sound with a "pulled in" abdomen during phonation. We spend time on breathing exercises that promote relaxation, including lying on the floor with knees bent to identify the feeling of relaxing the belly and back while breathing. I use exercises based on the "Accent Method" as well as core strengthening exercises to build support strength. A detailed explanation of this method as it relates to classical singing can be found in Janice Chapman's book[3], and a study on the effectiveness of this method in a tertiary classical context can be seen in Ron Morris's 2013 dissertation[4]. Recently, I have been using breathing exercises

---

3   Janice L. Chapman, *Singing and Teaching Singing: A Holistic Approach to Classical Voice*, 3rd ed. (San Diego: Plural Publishing, 2016).

4   Ron Morris, "The Effects of Accent Method Breathing on the Development of Young Classical Singers" (PhD diss. Griffith University, Brisbane, 2013), www120.secure.griffith.edu.au/rch/file/31c9fb59-1bd6-735b-be96-6f04fb955a52/1/Morris_2013_02Thesis.pdf.

from acting voice trainers, including Patsy Rodenberg, Kristin Linklater,[5] and Cicely Berry, to connect to breath and to build support. For an excellent and systematic book on voice training methods, see Carey and Carey's *Vocal Arts Workbook and Video: A practical course for developing the expressive range of your voice, Vol 1.*[6]

Dane Chalfin

I am a big fan of "Accent Method"[7] breathing. This is not terribly popular in North America, but it is popular almost everywhere else. It was designed as a speech therapy method to reconnect healthy abdominal support to phonation. You need to modify it a little to work with singers because we are dealing with larger volumes of air, or at times, significantly less air. The support system needs to be free to adapt to what is going on based on the sound we need.

About 10 years ago, it was mostly just the ladies who would hold in their tummies all the time. Now it is everyone. I blame *Men's Health* magazine, and Abercrombie & Fitch®. They have a lot to answer for! Very few singers who come into my studio can stand up or take a breath. These basic principles went very out of fashion in the last 20 years, particularly in Europe and Australia where looking at the larynx and vocal tract became very popular. We all got very excited because we could talk about the vocal tract, but I think that alignment and airflow sort of got thrown out like the baby with the bath water. Once alignment is in place, an Accent Method-style transversus abdominis-led out-breath is possible, followed by an abdominal wall release for the in-breath.

Robert Edwin

I teach respiration (breath management/support), as part of the *"tions"* (pronounced "shuns") singing system. Respiration is monitored by having my students place their hands on the lower part their ribcages with their thumbs on their backs and their fingers on their abdominal area. If they are breathing efficiently on inhalation, their hands will move outward. The breath should be 360 degrees rather than front- or back-loaded. On the exhalation phase of the breath, they should feel their hands gradually move inward as the air is expelled. While singing and speaking, they need to learn how to keep outward pressure on the ribs and abdominals (*appoggio*) to sustain breath management and prevent ribcage collapse. I instruct them to "hiss" while exhaling. This resistance to airflow allows them to experience that aforementioned outward pressure commonly referred to as support. They then, through repetitive exercises, carry that action into their speaking and singing technique.

Kim Chandler

I use the principles of the "Accent Method" (based on rhythmic accents, not spoken accents) by Danish phonetician and speech pathologist Svend Smith, applied to the singing voice. This method is particularly popular in Australia and the U.K., which is where I was introduced to it. This method started out many years ago as a rehabilitation method for disordered voices, but it has progressed over time to be equally beneficial for establishing good habits in healthy

---

5   More information may be found at www.linklatervoice.com/linklater-voice/about-linklater-voice.

6   David Carey and Rebecca Clark Carey, *Vocal Arts Workbook and Video: A practical course for developing the expressive range of your voice, Vol 1*, (London: Bloomsbury Methuen Drama, 2008).

7   Morris and Hutchison, *If in Doubt, Breathe out!*.

voices. I have found it to be highly effective for singers, de-mystifying and clarifying efficient breath flow and support based on a sound physiological foundation. It is also a "good fit" culturally for contemporary singers because the exercises are accompanied by a hand drum. I recommend the book *If in Doubt, Breathe Out!*[8]

Irene Bartlett

As speech quality and conversational phrasing (short length, strong consonant) are essential elements of all CCM styles, CCM singers require less breath volume (i.e., volume of breath in the lungs) than do classical singers. Regardless of genre or style, I believe that efficient breath flow is essential for free singing. I suggest to my singers that *breathing for singing* is not really different in action from *breathing for life*; however, exhalation is managed differently when singing. I encourage a passive inhalation through students' awareness of low abdominal and associated thoracic cylinder (rib) release. The *active* exhalation (I prefer to use *active* rather than *controlled*) used by singers requires sustained abdominal and thoracic muscle engagement for the continuous, balanced breath flow required for the length of any sung phrase as appropriate for the singer's style. A balanced breath flow requires low abdominal support (primarily a co-ordinated action of the pelvic floor, transverse abdominus, and internal oblique muscles) with a steady and reactive contraction of the abdominal wall. In my experience, a continuous breath flow (exhalation) minimizes habitual laryngeal tension. I find Accent Breathing[9] to be the most efficient method in marrying alignment, breath flow, and support.

Jeff Ramsey

There are so many methods, but I try to stick to the idea of ribcage expansion coupled with muscle engagement in the lower abdomen.

Elisabeth Howard

Ribs expand open on the intake of breath. Stomach is relaxed and not pushed out or in. Air is taken through the mouth. Air can be taken through the nose only if it can be inconspicuous.

Cathrine Sadolin

People breathe every day, so usually they are already pretty good at breathing. I believe that it is a waste of a singer's time to work on breathing because it is not usually the source of any problem. It is important to find the main issue and solve that problem first. Of course, sometimes you have to correct breathing, especially with someone with severe asthma. However, this is not typical.

Cate Frazier-Neely

What could I possibly add to what's already been understood and explained on this topic, especially because there are singers who sing well without "proper breathing and support"? Perhaps just this: the "natural" function of the thoracic diaphragm is related to the healthy

---

8   Ibid.
9   Ibid.

function of the other three diaphragms in the body. These are the cranial, cervical thoracic, thoracic and pelvic diaphragms, which together act as the body's pressure system to stabilize and control fluid distribution. When the action of one diaphragm in the body is compromised, so are the other diaphragms. This disrupts the cycle of the body's pressure system to "release" when we inhale and "engage" upon phonation. Then breath management becomes a frustrating obligation of "doing things" rather than an intoxicating and sensual act that precedes, and leads to, expression.

Many times, the dysfunction of a diaphragm comes from a place in the body other than the muscle itself. For example, we are just starting to understand the role of the psoas muscles in respiration, although sports' trainers and therapists know how important they are for whole body stabilization and movement.

A number of unrelated experiences can cause disruption of "the diaphragm dance" and are more common than many people realize. The effects of endocrine dysfunction, PTSD or chronic anxiety can have the same effects as abdominal surgery, tummy tucks, or physical and emotional abuse. There can be a neurological "freezing" of any of the domes, or even a "sucking up" as if they are retreating in defense. Cranial sacral therapy, Liz Koch's psoas work,[10] yoga, free dance, meditation and counseling can help a great deal.

Gillyanne Kayes

My approach is derived from the "Accent Method".[11] I find this is highly applicable to CCM singing because it allows for flexible breath use to suit varied phrase lengths and differing levels of subglottal pressure required by the genre.

Matthew Edwards

I believe respiratory strategies are very individual. The book *Respiratory Function in Singing*[12] by Thomas J. Hixon really opened my mind to the wide range of possibilities based on function. In the book, Hixon discusses a wide range of topics, including how a singer's perceptions about breath control are often incorrect, how vertebral alignment can affect respiration, mechanical differences between belly-in and belly-out, variations in movement of the thoracic and abdominal cavities, passive and active forces, how lung volume affects amplitude, along with many other topics. The book also provides exercises for practical application of the concepts.

In commercial styles, performers are always using a microphone. The large inhalation necessary to produce the amplitude required for classical singing is not necessarily beneficial for pop singers performing a breathy ballad. Because performance demands vary greatly among CCM singers, there is no one-size-fits-all approach.

I am always thinking of the interaction between the vocal folds and respiratory system: they must work together. If the vocal folds are in chest-dominant production, there will be a lot of subglottal pressure. Contracting the abdominal muscles will only increase that pressure and for a lot of young belters, it leads to pressed phonation and what those in the musical theatre industry call "screlting" (a mix of screaming and belting). At the same time, a soprano in head register, on the upper end of her range, will have more transglottal airflow because

---

10   More information may be found at http://coreawareness.com/.

11   Morris and Hutchison, *If in doubt, breathe out!.*

12   Thomas J. Hixon, *Respiratory Function in Singing: A Primer for Singers and Singing Teachers*, (San Diego: Plural Publishing, 2006).

there is a lower closed quotient. When more air is flowing through the folds, the pressure underneath will decrease more rapidly than when in chest voice. Therefore, abdominal contraction may help the singer maintain steady airflow. It is all very individual and we often need to think outside of the box when working with CCM performers.

Trineice Robinson-Martin

Breathing methods should be personalized per singer, with the caveat that a breathing method should NOT add pressure in the clavicle area and neck.

Constriction and Breathing: If you can hear the airflow when you breathe in, there is tension or obstruction in the throat (back of the mouth) and/or sinus cavity (in the nose).

"If it ain't broke, don't fix it": Breathing can sometimes be an obsession for voice teachers, and they often make students think there is more to it than there is. While efficient breath management is important, it isn't always necessary to start from scratch when learning a completely new breathing technique. Sometimes, all it takes is a little adjustment. When you understand the process, you can better determine if, and how much, adjustment you need to make in your own technique.

Kevin Wilson

There are many ways to breathe and I do not teach one specifically or in isolation. My students are taught to access breath through various movements and sensations in their body. I have discovered that bringing awareness to what can move and what we can control is very important. Finding expansion in the thoracic, epigastric, hypograstric, upper dorsal ribs, mid dorsal ribs, and lower back regions gives the student permission to access what they need for breathing and successful tone. Our inhalation and exhalation vary with emotional stimuli, which will require variation in our breathing. With my students, I clearly teach them the anatomy for inhalation and exhalation, and I have a sequence of breathing exercises that brings awareness to various muscles, including the transverse and internal/external oblique abdominals. In my years of teaching, I have found that students who are taught one type of breathing, or to isolate specific parts of their body i.e. ribs, abdomen, back, have unnecessary tensions and a lack of emotional connection to their singing. Awareness of the body is key! As Watson and Hixon wrote in 1985, "Psychological concepts are often in opposition to physiological systems."[13]

Mary Saunders Barton

Observing and interacting with classical colleagues over the years has greatly enhanced my ability to communicate this aspect of technical training. Teaching breathing for singing to dancers has been evolving to accept the notion of breathing *while* you move, and of allowing the breath to inform the movement. For ballet dancers who need to keep ribs closed in front, there is plenty of room for rib expansion in the back. For singing, it makes sense to link breathing ("inspiration") with the "need to say" because it makes a quick and effective connection to purposeful action. I encourage a full rib swing, making sure shoulders and arms are released while the abdominal muscles also release to facilitate the action of the diaphragm

---

13 Peter J. Watson and Thomas J. Hixon, "Respiratory kinematics in classical (opera singers)," *Journal of Speech, Language, and Hearing Research* 28 (March 1985), 104–122, www.doi.org/10.1044/jshr.2801.104.

as it descends. Some beginning students have difficulty isolating the external intercostals to achieve a full breath. A resistance breath strategy (place a finger over the lips to breathe in) may be all that is needed. A TheraBand tied around the ribs can be very helpful in drawing attention to the action of these muscles. Raising hands over the head and torqueing to the left and right, sustaining a yoga warrior pose, balancing on one foot, can also be helpful in stabilizing the rib swing while bringing awareness to the core abdominal muscles. For exhalation, I encourage students to sustain that rib swing (resist collapsing) and to notice the action of the transverse abdominal muscle, the oblique abdominal muscles, and the pelvic floor muscles, as they gradually return the diaphragm to its resting position. CCM singers may not need as much air as a Metropolitan Opera soprano to get through a phrase, but the importance of connecting body to sound is the same. How much air is used for a phrase is determined by the onset and breath control at the vocal fold level. As soon as this process is well understood, it is important to add voice, speaking and singing.

Edrie Means Weekly

I teach breath flow, pressure, and relaxation. Controlling the trans-glottal airflow or the amount of air that flows between the vocal folds, during phonation is known as breath management. The amount of air intake and subglottic air pressure (air pressure below the folds) depends on the style and dynamics of the song you are singing. Too much breath can lead to pressed phonation. If you fully inhale to capacity, the greater the breath pressure. If you inhale less air, the pressure will be less. The diaphragm extends downwards when you take a deep breath. Simultaneously, the external and internal intercostal muscles expand and raise the ribcage, and help in forced inhalation and forced expiration. A strong abdominal contraction results in a greater expiratory force and stronger subglottic air pressure. When the vocal folds are closed lightly, more air passes through the folds. When the vocal folds are pressed tightly together, then less air can pass through, creating a build-up of pressure below them.

A good rule of thumb is to take in enough breath needed for the phrase. A lot of vernacular singing styles are written with short quick phrases requiring less breath. Basically, the ideal amount of air to take in is the same as the amount of air you would need to speak loudly. It varies from singer to singer, and I recommend experimenting to find out what works physically well for the singer and the style of the music.

Different body types breathe differently, and different styles require different breathing approaches. Often, those with lean athletic bodies (particularly my strong dancer-singers) tend to engage in clavicular breathing. This upper lobar breathing results in shallow breaths. This may work for short phases found in pop/rock, but not for sustaining long phrases or a loud high belt note, which would need more subglottic air pressure.

Kathryn Paradise

Discussion of breathing should include both how you take in the air and how you use the air as it leaves you. In highly varied and improvisational commercial singing, it also includes an acknowledgement that how you breathe needs to be flexible and match the specific vocal demands of the musical moment. Since students come in all body types, and often bring a variety of athletic training and/or body image issues into the studio, I frequently teach as many methods of breathing as possible and challenge the students to find what works for them.

This exploration includes exercises that isolate the muscles in the back, core, and ribcage area, and exercises that vary the time of inhalation and exhalation/phonation, so that the student is able to confidently approach any musical challenge. I frequently coach classically trained singers to breathe more often and use their inhalation as a rhythmic device within commercial music. When speaking about using breath, I distinguish between "flow" and "resistance", and point out the appropriate uses of both (particularly when moving between less intense, low, speech-like passages, high sustained chest-mix and head voice).

Kimberly Steinhauer

Breath varies depending upon the anatomic/physiologic "mix" of the voice quality.

Wendy DeLeo LeBorgne

I technically and physiologically assess the parameters of alignment/posture, respiration, support, phonation, resonance, and artistry in the context of an artist's performance. This often happens outside of a lesson because, for my commercial artists, what they do in a lesson is often different from how they are performing in a live performance environment. I will have them bring me YouTube videos or live performance videos, and that is how I assess their breathing. If they are playing a guitar, or if they are sitting on a stool, we start the breathing conversation from where they are currently performing. My breathing pedagogy, or corrective mechanism, becomes "How do we make you efficient in what you are doing? Whether it is sitting on a stool, or crawling on the floor, or hanging upside down on a barricade, what has altered your breathing (because you have to do those things)? But we need to keep you artistically and vocally viable. So, what does that mean and do for the other subsystems of voice?" I use the same approach for all of the fundamental elements of voice, including breathing, support, registration, and belting.

Marcelle G. Gauvin

I address breath as part of support. Please see my response under "Support".

Mark Baxter

Please see my response under "Tension".

References and recommended reading

Bozeman, Kenneth. "Inspired inhalations." In *The Voice Teacher's Cookbook: Creative Recipes for Teachers of Singing* edited by Brian J. Winnie, 13–14. Delray Beach, FL: Meredith Music, 2018.

Carey, David and Rebecca Clark Carey. *Vocal Arts Workbook and Video: A practical course for developing the expressive range of your voice, Vol 1*. London: Bloomsbury Methuen Drama, 2008.

Chapman, Janice L. *Singing and Teaching Singing: A Holistic Approach to Classical Voice*, 3rd ed. San Diego: Plural Publishing, 2016.

Cleveland, Thomas F. "A comparison of breath management strategies of classical and nonclassical singers: Part 1" *Journal of Singing* 54, no. 5 (May/June 1998): 47–49.

Cleveland, Thomas F. "A comparison of breath management strategies of classical and nonclassical singers: Part 2" *Journal of Singing* 55, no. 1 (September/October 1998): 45–46.

Cleveland, Thomas F. "A comparison of breath management strategies of classical and nonclassical singers: Part 3" *Journal of Singing* 55, no. 2 (November/December 1998): 53–55.

Cowgill, Jennifer Griffith. "Breathing for singers: A comparative analysis of body types and breathing tendencies." *Journal of Singing* 66, no. 2 (November/December 2009): 141–147.

Hixon, Thomas J. *Respiratory Function in Singing: A Primer for Singers and Singing Teachers*. San Diego: Plural Publishing, 2006.

Hoit, Jeannette, Christie L. Jenks, Peter J. Watson, and Thomas F. Cleveland. "Respiratory function during speaking and singing in professional country singers." *Journal of Voice* 10, no. 1 (1996): 39–49. doi.org/10.1016/S0892-1997(96)80017-8.

Howell, Christina. "Breathing for singing." In *So You Want to Sing Rock'N'Roll: A Guide for Professionals* by Matthew Edwards, 247–256. Lanham, MD: Rowman & Littlefield, 2014.

Hudson, Barbara. "The effects of the Alexander Technique on the respiratory system of the singer/actor: Part I - F.M. Alexander and concepts of his technique that affect respiration in singer/actors." *Journal of Singing* 59, no. 1 (2002): 9–17.

Hudson, Barbara. "The effects of the Alexander Technique on the respiratory system of the singer/actor Part II: Implications for training respiration in singer/actors based on concepts of the Alexander Technique." *Journal of Singing* 59, no. 2 (2002): 105–110.

Gagné, Jeannie. "Cookin' with gas: Breathing facts, best practices, and helpful imagery." In *The Voice Teacher's Cookbook: Creative Recipes for Teachers of Singing* edited by Brian J. Winnie, 48-50. Delray Beach, FL: Meredith Music, 2018.

Leanderson, R., Johan Sundberg, and C. von Euler. "Breathing muscle activity and subglottal pressure dynamics in singing and speech." *Journal of Voice* 1, no. 3 (1987): 258–261. doi.org/10.1016/S0892-1997(87)80009-7

Leanderson, R. and Johan Sundberg. "Breathing for singing." *Journal of Voice* 2, no. 1 (1988): 2–12. doi.org/10.1016/S0892-1997(88)80051-1.

Lyle, Heather. *Vocal Yoga: The Joy of Breathing, Singing, and Sounding*. Pacific Palisades, CA: Bluecat Music and Publishing, 2010.

Lyle, Heather. "A historical look at breathing methods for singing." *Voice and Speech Review* 7, no. 1 (2011): 310–317. doi.org/10.1080/23268263.2011.10739560.

McCoy, Scott. "On breathing and support." *Journal of Singing* 70, no. 3 (2014): 321–324.

Mendes, Ana P., W.S. Brown, Christine Sapienza, and Howard B. Rothman. "Effects of vocal training on respiratory kinematics during singing tasks." *Folia Phoniatrica et Logopaedica* 58 (2006): 363–377. doi.org/10.1159/000094570.

Michael, Deirdre. "Dispelling Vocal Myths. Part I: 'Sing from your diaphragm!'" *Journal of Singing* 66, no. 5 (May/June 2010): 547–551.

Morris, Ron. "The Effects of Accent Method Breathing on the Development of Young Classical Singers." PhD diss. Griffith University, Brisbane, 2013. www120.secure.griffith.edu.au/rch/file/31c9fb59-1bd6-735b-be96-6f04fb955a52/1/Morris_2013_02Thesis.pdf.

Morris, Ron and Linda Hutchison. *If in Doubt, Breathe out! Breathing and Support for Singing Based on the Accent Method*. Oxford: Compton Publishing, 2016.

Petitt, Marcia. "Quiet breathing and breathing for singing: Anatomic and physiologic parameters." *Journal of Research in Singing and Applied Vocal Pedagogy* 18, no. 1 (1994): 21–40.

Pettersen, Viggo and Kare Bjorkoy. "Consequences from emotional stimulus on breathing for singing." *Journal of Voice* 23, no. 3 (May 2009): 295–303. doi.org/10.1016/j.jvoice.2007.08.006.

Sandage, Mary J., Nadine P. Connor, David D. Pascoe. "Voice function differences following resting breathing versus submaximal exercise." *Journal of Voice* 27, no. 5 (September 2013): 572–578. doi.org/10.1016/j.jvoice.2013.04.001.

Sliiden, Tommi, Sara Beck, and Ian MacDonald. "An evaluation of the breathing strategies and maximum phonation time in musical theater performers during controlled performance tasks." *Journal of Voice* 31, no. 2 (March 2017): 253. e1–253e.11. doi.org/10.1016/j.jvoice.2016.06.025.

Sundberg, Johan, Ninni Eilliot, Patricia Gramming, and Lennart Nord. "Short-term variation of subglottal pressure for expressive purposes in singing and stage speech: A preliminary investigation." *Journal of Voice* 7, no. 3 (September 1993): 227–234. doi.org/10.1016/S0892-1997(05)80331-5.

Sundberg, Johan and Margareta Thalén. "Respiratory and acoustical differences between belt and neutral style of singing." *Journal of Voice* 29, no. 4 (July 2015): 418–425. doi.org/10.1016/j.jvoice.2014.09.018.

Watson, Peter J., and Thomas J. Hixon. "Respiratory kinematics in classical (opera singers)." *Journal of Speech, Language, and Hearing Research* 28 (March 1985), 104–122. www.doi.org/10.1044/jshr.2801.104.

9

Support

"Support" can mean many different things in singing. Some use the term "support" interchangeably with "breath support", but the latter may also involve inhalation. "Support" is often conflated with breathing since it involves how air is exhaled. Sometimes it focuses solely on abdominal or intercostal muscle activity during phonation. It may also refer to emotional support. Scott McCoy defines support as "the dynamic interactions between the respiratory system, larynx, and vocal tract that enable singers to produce their desired sounds"[1]. McCoy maintains that support is "interdependent," "non-linear", and "variable",[2] meaning that it impacts and is impacted by several systems within the body, but not always in the same way. For purposes of this text, support is the regulation of airflow and air pressure during phonation (exhalation), processes which are controlled by muscles of the torso, the larynx, and the vocal tract. Tactics to achieve a "supported sound" will vary significantly based on unique physical anatomy of the performer and style of music, as well as registration, volume, and phrase length.

Because of the many different interpretations of the term "support", 20% of the pedagogues interviewed do not use the term. Instead, they use more specific terms such as breath pressure or breath flow (airflow). A few pedagogues mention that breath and support should be separated in training since very different activities take place during each phase. One pedagogue distinguishes between breath management (pressure) and breath control (flow). Eight pedagogues (32%) view breathing and support as so intertwined that they responded to both prompts as one. One such response appears in this chapter, and seven such responses appear in the previous chapter on breathing.

Like "breath", "support" is often over-blamed for any number of technical problems. Often, the perception is that *more* support is always better. However, with the short phrase lengths of CCM material, the frequent use of speech range, and the ubiquitous presence of audio technology amplification, support needs are often minimal. Belting is a low-breath flow and high-breath pressure activity due to the greater closed quotient.[3] By definition, the sustained belt (chest-dominant) "money notes" do not use as much air as the head-dominant "money notes" in legit musical theatre or operatic pop ("popera").[4]

---

1   Scott McCoy, "On breathing and support," *Journal of Singing* 70, no. 3 (January/February 2014), 323.

2   Ibid.

3   In chest-dominant sounds, the closed quotient is greater, see Nathalie Henrich, Christophe D'Allessandro, Boris Doval, and Michele Castellengo, "Glottal open quotient in singing: Measurements and correlation with laryngeal mechanisms, vocal intensity, and fundamental frequency," *The Journal of the Acoustical Society of America* 117, no. 3 (March 2005), 1417–1430, doi.org/10.1121/1.1850031.

4   Eva Björkner, "Musical theater and opera singing: Why so different? A study of subglottal pressure, voice source, and formant frequency characteristics," *Journal of Voice* 22, no. 5 (September 2008), 533–540, doi.org/10.1016/j.jvoice.2006.12.007.

Pedagogues point out that too much support (too high a rate of airflow or too much pressure) can lead to overly breathy phonation or pressed phonation. Neither extreme is desirable as a default sound but may be used for expressive purposes. In CCM repertoire, there are occasional long phrases or sustained high notes which require a truly deep breath, and extensive management of air pressure and flow during exhalation. However, these phrases are the exception, not the rule.

A flexible or efficient approach to "support" is preferred among 52% of the pedagogues. In live performances, CCM singers will need to produce an appropriately supported sound during a wide variety of physical activities. For expressive purposes, support may be varied to produce a breathy sound purposely or to yell healthily. Forty-four percent of pedagoguesdescribe a fairly traditional model of support, focusing on the muscle activity within the torso, but some also include breath flow and breath pressure activities within the larynx and vocal tract. An extensive reading list on support may be found at the end of this chapter, but readers should also refer to the reading list in the chapter on breath.

This chapter includes responses to the prompt "Please describe your approach to teaching support". Pedagogues were given the option of responding to breath and support as one topic, or addressing each term separately. Responses are presented in order from those who describe a traditional model of support, followed by those who advocate for a flexible and variable approach to support, followed by those who do not use the term "support", and ending with those who address "support" as part of breathing or another topic.

Dane Chalfin

In everyday tidal breathing, our support musculature is passive, on the in-breath and on the out-breath. Where singers mess up, in my opinion, is when they make a lot of muscular effort on the in-breath, and collapse on the out-breath. We have enough physiological information to say that that is probably the wrong way around. A reset of the abdominal musculature for an in-breath will give contemporary singers enough air to get through the vast majority of what they need. There are two exceptions: 1) sustained breathy singing, and 2) classical singing.

For the out-breath, this is where muscularity comes into place. We know we want to see the transverse abdominus engage first so that it compresses the abdomen to exert some pressure underneath the lungs. We want to see external and internal obliques come in towards the end of that cycle. Of course, we do not have much sensory perception of these muscles, so I do a lot of hands-on monitoring of the muscular junctions around the abdomen. If you palpate with your hands in what Janice Chapman would call the "diamond" of support,[5] you notice that there are muscular actions in the xiphoid process, in the lower abdominal pubic symphysis, and in and around the waist band. As the belly wall is being drawn in and up, you feel an outward kick in those junctions. This is the way we can monitor good support. When the hands are taken away, we should not really feel it anymore. It is governed by the desire to breathe out. I worry when singers say "I can really feel my support" because this usually indicates that there is unnecessary tension.

There is a great book called *If in Doubt, Breathe Out!*[6] by Ron Morris and Linda Hutchison, which is accent method breathing adapted for classical singing. You cannot completely crossover with contemporary singing, but the fundamentals are the same.

---

5   Janice L. Chapman, *Singing and Teaching Singing: A Holistic Approach to Classical Voice*, 3rd ed. (San Diego: Plural Publishing, 2016).

6   Ron Morris and Linda Hutchison, *If in Doubt, Breathe out!: Breathing and Support for Singing Based on the Accent Method* (Oxford: Compton Publishing, 2016).

Jeannette LoVetri

Support involves being able to regulate the duration and the pressure of the exhalation while balancing the ribcage against the abdominal muscles such that there is dynamic tension between those two structures, both on the outside of the body and within, indirectly, as well. The diaphragm, held in downward contraction by the action of the external intercostal muscles, is simultaneously being pushed by pressure from the viscera underneath, which in turn is generated by the contraction of the abdominal muscles. This chain reaction creates a tension between the external muscles (rectus abdominus and the obliques) and the viscera that allows pressure in the area of the mid-torso to keep the airflow strong even while it is being depleted over time. The longer the sound (or exhalation) lasts, the harder the abdominal muscles must contract. They push harder and harder on less and less air to keep the sound pressure level (volume) consistent. If this is not done, the sound would always get softer as the lungs were depleted. This gestalt is "support".

Seth Riggs and Margareta Svensson Riggs

Support is the amount of compressed air your vocal cords need to vibrate efficiently. As the larynx stays down during the breathing process, and the stomach muscles work from below the air from the very bottom below the navel, in and up, the damping of the vocal cords will begin to balance itself. A balanced voice is the same as singing evenly from bottom to top.

Breathing and support is a no more complicated law of physics than knowing how to carry a tray of food. The tray needs support from underneath in order to be moved. Once the tray rests on your palm, you automatically supply enough muscle power to carry it successfully.

Singers commonly use insufficient support, which will cause the throat to compensate by constricting. In turn, that not only leads to vocal problems but also results in strained and flat sounds.

Lisa Popeil

I think that support is the "make or break" ingredient in controlled and confident singing. Proper support gives the vocal folds the "oomph" they need to vibrate since, in my thinking, vocal folds need a steady stream of *pressurized* air to help them close without extraneous constriction. Support creates pressure in the equation. In fact, much of compensatory tension that singers experience in the tongue, jaw, and the front and back of the neck, can be directly attributed to inadequate thoracic and abdominal support. Having a precise method for support helps tremendously in building confidence that the voice will be steady, controlled, and consistent. Though it is possible to over-support (which creates its own set of problems, specifically, an audible stiffness in the vocal folds), most singers who have vocal instability, excessive compensatory tension, or lack of consistency, exhibit inadequate or incorrect action of the mechanism of abdominal breath support.

Some of the less effective support methods I have encountered include:
1. Do nothing, when properly closed, the vocal cords will take care of themselves.
2. Lift the chest high for breathing and push the chest up with shoulders back for singing.
3. Stick the sides of your neck outwards.
4. Pull the lower belly in and up.
5. Pull the lower belly in and bear down.

6. Push downwards into the perineum.
7. Push the side ribs and waist out.
8. Squeeze the upper belly in.
9. Push the back ribs out.
10. Push the lower belly out (this one creates the least attractive sound, particularly on high notes for many singers).

My favorite method of teaching support while singing is the "5 Jobs of Support":

1. Keep the chest comfortably high (but not overly hiked up) even when running out of air.
2. Keep the side and back ribs comfortably expanded, do not let them collapse.
3. Below the sternum, in the upper belly area, one can find a spot (or ridge or bump) which pushes out naturally when making a loud "sh" sound. I call this the "magic spot". Its job in singing and projected speech is to gently but firmly push OUT for every note, then relax it for breathing. Though it is not technically the diaphragm, this spot seems to help control diaphragmatic action and is the main pressure controller of the outgoing airstream. Many singers will find their "magic spot" an inch or two below the bottom of the sternum, but others, such as myself, may find this spot approximately 4 inches below the sternum.
4. The lower belly's job is to gradually pull straight in for singing and relax it completely for breathing. For classical singing, the lower belly need not relax completely for breathing, but for CCM, the best results can be obtained by relaxing the lower belly completely for breathing so that it has more range of motion, and speed of motion, particularly useful for hitting high belting notes. I call lower belly support "the high note helper" since pulling it in makes singing any high notes, whether in chest or head register, much easier and more beautiful.
5. The last main support job is waist support. For CCM, I teach pushing the waist out for singing and relaxing it for breathing; for classical it's fine to expand the waist for breathing and then push out for singing (meaning it never completely relaxes). Waist support is optional, depending on an individual's physical structure. Some singers can easily feel the narrowest part of their waist move when singing, others feel nothing. If a student cannot feel any movement in the waist, I tell them that it's not important and they should focus on the main four: chest, ribs, upper belly "magic spot", and lower belly.

This basic support method seems to work for men and women, young and old, in any genre, and can provide instant improvement in straight tone and vibrato control, reducing or eliminating compensatory tension in the usual suspects (tongue, jaw, neck), pitch regulation, power, easy high notes, and an overall sense of control and dependability.

Gillyanne Kayes

For me "support" is about 1) airflow, 2) subglottal pressure and vocal fold resistance, and 3) how these are managed physically by the singer by co-ordination of the muscles of the abdominal wall, including those at the back.

Elisabeth Howard

For support, I teach students to use the same muscles that they use for sneezing, coughing, and going to the bathroom, and to stay in that position until the end of the phrase. One must regulate the amount of air pressure according to high notes, low notes, louder notes, softer notes, crescendo, and decrescendo. I also use the concept of blowing up a balloon to feel muscular involvement.

Kimberly Steinhauer

Our Estill Voice Figures™ for Torso and Head/Neck are used to separate breath from support, and are practiced at every respiratory volume and voice quality. In Estill Voice Training®, the torso and head/neck may be anchored or relaxed but will most likely manifest as a continuum between these two extremes.

Cathrine Sadolin

It is very important that every singer who comes to an authorized Complete Vocal Technique (CVT) teacher is asked to describe how they support. They usually do not know exactly how or why they are supporting. It is a vague sensation. I want singers to leave the teaching studio knowing exactly how to support and why, otherwise we have not done our job. They may look at us like we are crazy, but that is because they have been singing for 20 years on a vague support technique. I make this claim because this challenges me to be specific, concrete, and precise. I ask them to make sure they understand support by the end of the session. This empowers the singer to make demands of their teachers, and also ensures that they are benefiting from each session in a concrete way and are able to reproduce the same sound when they are back home. You should be able to feel support in your body, and it is not difficult.

There are several points where you can feel the support working:
1. The area under the navel should move inward during singing/exhalation.
2. Put your hand at the solar plexus, under your sternum. When you inhale it comes out, and when you sing you should try to keep the solar plexus outward.
3. If you place your hands on your waist and cough, you will feel your hands being pushed outward; keep this movement during singing.
4. The lower ribs expand on inhalation, and we should try to keep the ribs out as long as possible when we sing.
5. You can also feel the ribs at the lower back expand when you inhale. Try to keep these out as long as possible when you sing.

The problem with support is that people often use too much energy, so they waste it before they really need it. We try to help them to control how much support they give and learn to use it only when necessary. I have them put their hands on the body in different places until they learn where their body moves and how. There are many ways to feel support, but it is important that it feels comfortable, with both the outward and inward sensations.

Trineice Robinson-Martin

An approach to support should be similar to an approach to the natural support that occurs during passionate and compelling communication. In other words, just as the body responds to an emotional situation and prepares for a response, as in when excited, angry, happy, or sad, the singer should replicate this.

The ability to produce and sustain a particular pitch and/or dynamic level is largely dependent upon breath management, i.e., the co-ordination of breath support (controlling breath pressure) and breath control (controlling the rate of expiration: how long it will take to run out of breath).

Muscles used for breath management include the rib muscles (intercostal muscles), abdominal muscles, low abdominal or pelvic floor muscles, and back muscles (particularly at the bottom of the ribcage).

A stable ribcage should be maintained to stabilize the execution of sung tones during active body movement as when dancing, rocking, or walking. If stability in the ribcage is not maintained during movement, it will be more difficult for singers to maintain a steady tone and breath flow, and they may fatigue more quickly.

Marcelle G. Gauvin

Stable support is an essential component of all excellent singing. It is best if the singer can remain natural and organic. However, as vocal demands increase, so do demands on breath management. It is extremely beneficial for students to gain an understanding of respiration and its role in phonation. That is why I always discuss anatomy and physiology in voice lessons. The goal for singers is to efficiently regulate airflow. The more athletic the singing, the more strength and stability is required in this process.

I do not use a "one-size-fits-all" approach to teaching breath support, as no two bodies are alike and different musical styles have unique requirements. I believe it's best to provide students with a number of strategies for support development, and then allow them to experiment with each until they achieve their desired result. Ideally, the body wants this co-ordination to be strong, dependable, and stress-free for optimum performance. In that light, the demands of an acoustic singer/songwriter will be very different from those of a rock and roll artist.

Edrie Means Weekly

I teach that the tone is supported by the amount of air that flows between the vocal folds (trans-glottal airflow) during phonation. The air force or speed in exhalation is supported/controlled by the amount of breath inhaled and activating the muscles of the ribs and abdomen. For example, if the client contracts their abs right after a deep breath, it will increase the pressure and flow at the level of the folds.

Wendy DeLeo LeBorgne

I technically and physiologically assess the parameters of alignment/posture, respiration, support, phonation, resonance, and artistry in the context of an artist's performance. This often happens outside of a lesson because, for my commercial artists, what they do in a lesson is often different from how they are performing in a live performance environment. I will have them bring me YouTube videos or live performance videos, and that is how I assess their support. If they are playing a guitar, or if they are sitting on a stool, we start the support conversation from where they are currently performing. My support pedagogy, or corrective mechanism, becomes "How do we make you efficient in what you are doing? Whether it is sitting on a stool, or crawling on the floor, or hanging upside down on a barricade, what has altered your support (because you have to do those things), and how do we keep you artistically and vocally viable? So, what does that mean and do for the other subsystems of voice?" I use the same approach for all of the fundamental elements of voice, including breathing, support, registration, and belting.

Jeff Ramsey

Support is another one of those funny words, as it means different things to different people. I like Mark Baxter's idea about making sure to dial in the right amount of air pressure proportionate to the task at hand. This comes through vocalizing.

Matthew Edwards

I do not use this word in my teaching unless it is a term that already resonates with the student. I remember singing in voice lessons while trying to lift the piano off the ground. I was instructed to engage my legs and abdominal muscles as I sang in order to improve my "support". While that approach may produce results for some, it has been my experience that for many others it produces a lot of tension and can lead to pressed phonation. The problem for me, at that point in my training, was that the mechanics of breath were not explained. I did not know if I was supposed to feel more pressure, let more air release, or something else. So, I just kept lifting until the teacher said it was right and hoped I could discover it on my own in the practice room.

If the term comes up, I compare it to emotional support. We emotionally support our friends by stepping in when they need us and backing off when they need space. I think we need to support our vocal folds by giving them what they need for any given situation and backing off when necessary. The approach will not be universal. If the vocal folds are closed firmly when the singer is belting, there is naturally going to be a lot of subglottal pressure. Contracting the abs will increase that pressure, which is not necessarily a good thing for a young singer. However, for more mature singers, the vocal folds may need a little extra breath pressure. Singers who are just learning to sing legit may not have enough airflow unless they lightly contract their abdominal wall. However, for others, contracting the abdominal wall in head or head-mix puts too much pressure on the vocal folds and the singer ends up with a breathy tone.

I also think we need to do more research on how aging affects the respiratory system. There are a few papers that talk about ossification of the costal cartilages and how that affects rib-cage expansion, how the elastic recoil of the alveoli reduces over time, and how overall lung capacity is reduced by nearly 50% by the time one reaches the late 50s to early 60s. We need more research to find out if these statistics from the general population translate to life-long singers. However, theoretically there could be major pedagogical implications. A 20-year-old female who has fully functioning lungs is likely to experience breath control in a completely different way from an older male teacher who is no longer performing on a regular basis. In my mind, when it comes to breath support, there are a lot of variables and no singular answer.

Kathryn Paradise

I generally avoid the term "support" because it is vague and non-specific. When I ask students with a history of vocal training how they breathe, they always use the term "support". However, when I inquire what this word means, they rarely know how to explain the concept. I DO talk to students about "bracing" for high notes or "suspending their ribcage" and/or "moving their air". I think these cues are related to the idea of "support" but are slightly more specific to the varied musical challenges commercial singers tend to encounter.

Kevin Wilson

I dislike the word support. I prefer to discuss and introduce the concept of flow and resistance to my students. Support for many students seems to equate to "holding" (different from sustaining), which is not really ideal. Flow and resistance discussions allow me to address tension in the body and the positive effect of tensions that are necessary for sustaining.

Marci Rosenberg

Support is a very non-specific term that I do not think has a true concrete meaning, and therefore I do not use it at all when teaching.

Mark Baxter

I find the lexicon of Bel Canto and Legit techniques to be an unintentional source of restricting behaviors for popular singers. These terms do not apply across all genres, as the timbres they encourage are not accepted in many sub-cultures of contemporary music. I particularly avoid the terms "support, register and belting" because they direct a singer's attention towards secondary muscle groups. Imagine you are standing on a beach and a friend points towards the water and shouts "I think that guy just beyond the breakers is drowning!". Instantly, you would squeeze your eyes and tense the back of your neck to "try" and focus on the swimmer. This added muscle behavior is simply an emotional response to let you "feel" like you're looking harder. If you continued to scrunch your face you would soon get a headache. This is why lifeguards focus their vision with their eyes – not their faces. In the same way, the ambiguity of many behavioral vocal commands causes singers to invent unnecessary muscle involvement so that he or she can "feel" the support, the register or the belt. This is not a productive way to encourage singers to trust their reflexes and employ the minimum effort required for each intended sound.

Jan Shapiro

In my view "breathing and support" are together – they are not separate. Please see my response under "Breath".

Robert Edwin

I teach respira*tion* (breath management/support), as part of the "*tions*" (pronounced "shuns") singing system. Please see my response under "Breath".

Cate Frazier-Neely

I address support as part of breathing. Please see my response under "Breath".

Mary Saunders Barton

I address support as part of breathing. Please see my response under "Breath".

Irene Bartlett

I address support as part of breathing. Please see my response under "Breath".

Kim Chandler

I address support as part of breathing. Please see my response under "Breath".

Tracy Marie Bourne

I address support as part of breathing. Please see my response under "Breath".

References and recommended reading

Björkner, Eva. "Musical theater and opera singing: Why so different? A study of subglottal pressure, voice source, and formant frequency characteristics." *Journal of Voice* 22, no. 5 (September 2008): 533–540. doi.org/10.1016/j.jvoice.2006.12.007.

Chapman, Janice L. *Singing and Teaching Singing: A Holistic Approach to Classical Voice*. 3rd ed. San Diego: Plural Publishing, 2016.

Cleveland, Thomas F., R.E. Stone, Johan Sundberg, and Jenny Iwarsson. "Estimated subglottal pressure in six professional country singers." *Journal of Voice* 11, no. 4 (December 1997): 403–409. doi.org/10.1016/S0892-1997(97)80035-5.

Griffin, Barbara, Peak Woo, Raymond Colton, Janina Casper, and David Brewer. "Physiological characteristics of the supported singing voice. A preliminary study." *Journal of Voice* 9, no. 1 (March 1995): 45–56. doi.org/10.1016/S0892-1997(05)80222-X.

Henrich, Nathalie, Nathalie Christophe D'Allessandro, Boris Doval, and Michele Castellengo. "Glottal open quotient in singing: Measurements and correlation with laryngeal mechanisms, vocal intensity, and fundamental frequency." *The Journal of the Acoustical Society of America* 117, no. 3 (March 2005), 1417–1430. doi.org/10.1121/1.1850031.

Herbst, Christian T. "A review of singing voice subsystem interactions: Toward an extended physiological model of 'support.'" *Journal of Voice* 31, no. 2 (March 2017): 249.e13–249.e19, doi.org/10.1016/j.jvoice.2016.07.019.

Indik, Lawrence. "The end of breath for singing: Exhalation and the control of breath at the end of the phrase." *Journal of Singing* 66, no. 2 (November/December 2009): 131–140.

Leanderson, R., Johan Sundberg, and C. von Euler. "Breathing muscle activity and subglottal pressure dynamics in singing and speech." *Journal of Voice* 1, no. 3 (1987): 258–261. doi.org/10.1016/S0892-1997(87)80009-7.

McCoy, Scott. *Your Voice: An Inside View*. 2nd ed. Delaware, OH: Inside View Press, 2012.

Michael, Deirdre. "Dispelling Vocal Myths. Part I: 'Sing from your diaphragm!'" *Journal of Singing* 66, no. 5 (May/June 2010): 547–551.

Morris, Ron and Linda Hutchison. *If in Doubt, Breathe Out!: Breathing and Support for Singing Based on the Accent Method*. Oxford: Compton Publishing, 2016.

Sand, Susanne and Johan Sundberg. "Reliability of the term "support" in singing." *Logopedics Phoniatrics Vocology* 30 (2005): 51–54. doi.org/10.1080/14015430510006712.

Sandage, Mary J., Nadine P. Connor, David D. Pascoe. "Voice function differences following resting breathing versus submaximal exercise." *Journal of Voice* 27, no. 5 (September 2013): 572–578. doi.org/10.1016/j.jvoice.2013.04.001.

Sonninen, A., A.-M. Laukkanen, K. Karma, and P. Hurme. "Evaluation of support in singing." *Journal of Voice* 19, no. 2 (June 2005): 223–237. doi.org/10.1016/j.jvoice.2004.08.003.

Steinhauer, Kimberly, Mary McDonald Klimek, and Jo Estill. *The Estill Voice Model: Theory and Translation*. Pittsburgh: Estill Voice International, 2018.

Sundberg, Johan and Margareta Thalén. "Respiratory and acoustical differences between belt and neutral style of singing." *Journal of Voice* 29, no. 4 (July 2015): 418–425. doi.org/10.1016/j.jvoice.2014.09.018.

Sundberg, Johan, R. Leanderson, C. von Euler, E. Knutsson. "Influence of body posture and lung volume on subglottal pressure control during singing." *Journal of Voice* 5, no. 4 (1991): 283–291. doi.org/10.1016/S0892-1997(05)80057-8.

Sundberg, Johan, Patricia Gramming, and Jeannette Lovetri. "Comparisons of pharynx, source, formant, and pressure characteristics in operatic and musical theatre singing." *Journal of Voice* 7, no. 4 (December 1993): 301–310. doi.org/10.1016/S0892-1997(05)80118-3.

Thalen, Margareta and Johan Sundberg. "Describing different styles of singing: A comparison of a female singer's voice source in 'Classical,' 'Pop,' 'Jazz,' and 'Blues.'" *Logopedics Phoniatrics Vocology* 26, no. 2 (2001): 82–93. doi.org/10.1080/140154301753207458.

Thorpe, C. William, Stephen J. Cala, Janice Chapman, and Pamela J. Davis. "Patterns of breath support in projection of the singing voice." *Journal of Voice* 15, no. 1 (March 2001): 86–104. doi.org/10.1016/S0892-1997(01)00009-1.

Titze, Ingo. "On flow phonation and airflow management." *Journal of Singing* 72, no. 1 (September/October 2015): 57–58.

10

Registration

Registration is a central issue to CCM voice training. The data indicate that there are two primary areas of focus which provide a framework for CCM voice training: registration (64%) and voice quality/vocal tract shaping (36%). These data are summarized in the chart below.

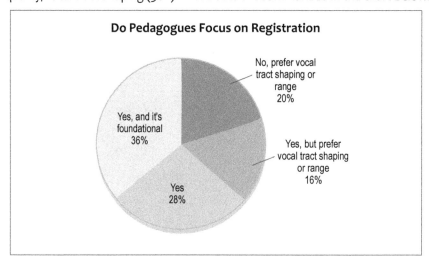

Of those who frame their voice training through registration, a majority state that registration work is central to their teaching and some of the most important work they do. Most describe registration as a vocal-fold-level (source) activity defined by thyroarytenoid (TA) and cricothyroid (CT) muscle engagement. Because singing is a non-linear process, registration can be impacted by activity in the vocal tract (filter), but no amount of vocal tract shaping can replace vocal fold muscle activity itself. The acoustic theory of voice production, or source-filter theory,[1] supports this view. Many reveal a strategy to isolate and strengthen two primary registers (M1[2]/chest/TA-dominant/modal and M2/head/CT-dominant/loft), and then work to blend, mix, or co-ordinate these registers to achieve a spectrum of expressive sounds.

"Mix" is a confusing term with several different interpretations. The majority of the pedagogues interviewed (71%) believe that mix is the predominant female singing sound that we hear most of the time, or any co-ordinated sound engaging both sets of TA and CT muscles. For many in the U.S., "mix" is a head-dominant sound whereas in the U.K., "mix" is

1   Introduced by Gunnar Fant in 1960, discussed in Alison Behrman, *Speech and Voice Science*, 2nd ed. (San Diego: Plural Publishing, 2013), 218–222.

2   M=Mechanism, M1=Mechanism 1 (TA-dominant register), M2=Mechanism 2 (CT-dominant register), described in Bernard Roubeau et al., "Laryngeal vibratory mechanisms: The notion of register revisited," *Journal of Voice* 23, no. 4 (July 2009), 425–438, doi.org/10.1016/j.jvoice.2007.10.014.

a chest-dominant sound (reported by Chalfin). Both forms of mix may shape the vocal tract with "twang" (epilaryngeal narrowing[3]), which makes them sound similar, but the vocal fold (source) activity is different. It is safe to say that "mix" is a spectrum of sounds that can range from chest-dominant (TA-dominant) to head-dominant (CT-dominant), depending on whom you ask.

A strong minority of pedagogues (36%) prefer to address the voice in terms of voice quality (vocal tract shaping), vocal mode[4], color, range, or even specific vocal fold condition, such as thick or thin. Those in this group argue that "registration" is a non-linear concept and the term can refer to several activities, including vocal fold muscle activity, pitch, vocal tract shaping, and volume (breath pressure). Some argue that these concepts should all be separated and addressed individually during technical training.

The terms "head" and "chest" have controversial roots but are nevertheless used by 73% of the pedagogues. Most pedagogues indicate a willingness and regular practice of adjusting terminology for each student. Teachers may have their own preferences but show a strong trend toward flexibility, in order to achieve faster results for the student. Terms used include CT or TA dominance, thin folds or thick folds, modal or loft, mechanism 1 (M1) or mechanism 2 (M2), light mechanism or heavy mechanism, high breath pressure or low breath pressure, and high range or low range. Those who argue against using the terms "chest" or "head" state that these terms are based on imagery and perception and are more useful when discussing resonance. Due to the prevalence of microphones, resonance does not play a large role in CCM training.

This chapter includes responses to the prompt "Please describe your approach to teaching registration". The responses are presented in order starting with those who prefer not to focus on registration or who do not use the term "registration," and proceed across the spectrum of preferences to end with those who state that registration work is central or foundational to their pedagogic approach.

Irene Bartlett

I do not focus students' attention on registration. I encourage them to practice across the full extent of their range using efficient breath flow and resonance to find a balanced vocal production. In my experience, once breath flow and vocal fold closure become balanced, the singer's natural tone and timbral qualities become established across their range. This balance can be achieved in many ways, but I favor semi-occluded vocal tract exercises such as Ingo Titze's *sing through a straw*, and vowels preceded by a gliding consonant such as *mmm* or y[j]. I suggest that singers begin with these exercises on a descending 5-note scale. Due to the necessity for CCM singers to maintain speech quality across their singing voice range, a *default neutral* to higher laryngeal setting is essential, as opposed to the stabilization of the larynx in a lower position for classical singers. CCM styles permit the singer freedom to

---

3   Also known as narrowing the pharynx/epilarynx or aryepiglottic sphincter. This is one of the ways to raise the F1 above and near the second harmonic (H2) as belters often do, described in Wendy D. LeBorgne and Marci Rosenberg, *The Vocal Athlete* (San Diego: Plural Publishing, 2014), 104. For more information on "twang" see Johan Sundberg and Margareta Thalén, "What is twang?" *Journal of Voice* 24, no. 6 (November 2010), 654–660, doi.org/10.1016/j.jvoice.2009.03.003, and Ingo Titze et al., "Source and filter adjustments affecting the perception of the vocal qualities twang and yawn" *Logopedics Phoniatrics Vocology* 28, no. 4 (December 2003), 147–155.

4   Mode, as referred to in Complete Vocal Technique. More information may be found at completevocal.institute/ or in the CVT app.

show uneven transitions (*passaggio* events) as a personal choice for emotional expression and style authenticity.

I avoid using the traditional terms of Chest/Head because I find that fact rather than imagery will reduce laryngeal tension and vertical note barriers for many singers. I believe that *chest* and *head* were useful images before advances in voice science proved that registration is primarily an activity of laryngeal muscle action, vocal fold vibratory patterns, and laryngeal positioning, particularly the antagonistic action of the cricothyroid and thyroarytenoid muscles in relation to the breath flow rate, sub-glottal pressure, and degree of low abdominal support. I do explain to my students that the terms *head* and *chest* are useful terms when used to describe the very real sensations of resonance (sympathetic vibrations that singers feel in the chest for low register notes, and, in the head for upper register notes. If students have questions about registration, I explain that audible or undesired shifts, such as a distinct change in tone/timbre or unintentional yodel (registration events) will occur if breath flow, support, and resonance are unbalanced. I have found that explaining the research on laryngeal "mechanisms"[5] is very empowering for students; that is, trusting the changing vibratory patterns of the vocal folds that occur naturally with efficient breath flow and support enhanced by style-appropriate resonance for the singer's desired tone. I choose not to use the term *mix* as factually, all heathy, prosodic vocal sounds are produced through the co-ordinated activity of the thyroarytenoid (TA) and cricothyroid (CT) muscles. I believe that "The Mix" has become a buzz term that adds even more confusion to the already complex activity we refer to as registration (e.g. head mix, chest mix, belt mix, etc.). I prefer to make students aware that they can employ a light or heavy registration in any of the mechanisms primarily through engagement with emotion, intention, and meaning.

Cathrine Sadolin

There is a lot of confusion on singing terminology in the singing world. People rarely agree on the meaning of the words. In Complete Vocal Technique, we don't use the word "register", "head voice" or "chest voice" because the terms mean different things to different people. This means that we when we try to talk together using these terms, it is causing confusion and the communication becomes polluted, and we do not understand each other. In CVT, we try to make terminology clearer. We avoid these ambiguous terms which may have many different meanings. In fact, we have a rule that every term must be clearly defined. Every sound must have only one term, and every term must mean only one thing. When we follow these guidelines, we create very clear terminology.

In my perception, "register" refers to pitch, volume, sound color, and character of the sound. In CVT, we simplify this by separating these different elements. When we talk about pitch, we use areas of the range, such as very high, high, middle, low, very low. Everyone understands these terms. When we talk about volume, we talk in terms of loud, medium, or quiet on a scale of 0 to 10. Quiet is 0–2, medium-quiet is 2–4, medium-loud is 4–7, and loud is 7–10. When we talk about sound color, we define the range of color such as darkest, darker, mid, lighter, lightest. The character of sound correlates to the vocal modes: Neutral, Curbing, Overdrive, and Edge. These are settings or gears of operation for the voice. The vocal modes comprise part of the definition of "register". However, a complete definition would also require information about pitch, volume, and sound color.

---

5   Roubeau et al., "Laryngeal vibratory mechanisms."

Jan Shapiro

"Registration" is a word I don't use very much when teaching. I simply use "your range."

I do not think singers should anticipate or overthink where they are singing in their high, middle, or low range. How do we develop a vocal range? We first learn to blend our voice regardless of whether we are singing low or high. This is essential in order to obtain consistency.

It's all a matter of breath coordination. I don't usually use the terms chest/head or mode 1/ mode 2. Instead, I refer to low, middle, or upper range.

When working with male students, I train the complete voice, including falsetto. I do not compare the female upper range with the male falsetto voice. Males have an upper range and a falsetto. "Head voice" in females is the upper range.

Mark Baxter

I find the lexicon of Bel Canto and Legit techniques to be an unintentional source of restricting behaviors for popular singers. These terms do not apply across all genres, as the timbres they encourage are not accepted in many sub-cultures of contemporary music. I particularly avoid the terms "support, register and belting" because they direct a singer's attention towards secondary muscle groups. For further explanation, please see my response under "Support".

Kimberly Steinhauer

Estill Voice Training® prefers the term "Voice Quality" and not "Register" because voice registers are pitch dependent. EVT explores singing every pitch in every voice quality, and always monitors for vocal health as a student takes a quality out of the natural, comfortable range. The six voice qualities in EVT are Speech, Sob, Twang, Opera, Falsetto, and Belt.

Dane Chalfin

Our terms stem from the classical idea that we should want a unified sound in an instrument that was not designed to do this. We think of the voice in sections related to pitch. This does not make sense for contemporary singers, nor for how the voice functions from birth, physiologically. Nathalie Henrich's model is well researched[6] and uses M0 (fry), M1 (vocal fold body and cover are vibrating), M2 (just vocal fold cover is vibrating), and M3 (whistle). There is no conclusive definition of M3 yet. This is one of those things that is interesting academically, but it is only used in opera. Mariah Carey used it a little, but it is unlikely to come back. Unless you are going above C6, which contemporary singers tend not to do, it is more of a party trick.

In the primal sounds model,[7] registration can vary, but it is most frequently found in certain patterns. For example, in sigh (breathy phonation) many people use a light incomplete closure M1, but fairly early in the range, it will change to M2. Some people will take M2 all the way down, until it is not possible anymore. Whimper is mostly M2 throughout, and as low as possible, then maybe a little bit of M1 at the bottom of the range. In whinge, it stays in M1 all the way up and all the way down. It is a bit like getting contemporary singers, male and female, to sing like classical tenors. The question is, is it a physical register, or is it a sensory perception register? Singers feel the vibration change its "placement" even though there is no mechanical change. We have a problem with registration where that is concerned. Perception

---

6   Ibid.

7   More information may be found at www.vocalrehabilitation.com/primal-voice-research.

of registers varies significantly from one singer to the next, and it depends on the size of the larynx. Even in contemporary singing, the size of the larynx matters. A bigger, thicker string is going to change what it is doing at different points. We can change the dimensions of the vocal tract in these gestures so that the acoustic phenomenon we are producing will change quite dramatically. We do not know how much of that has a backward effect on what the vocal folds and vocal tract are doing.

In yelling, optimal production is in M1 throughout the range. The vocal tract turns into a tiny tube and you can barely see the vocal folds. The middle constrictor, and the aryepiglottic structures narrow down to where you can barely see anything, but the singer feels that it is easy and open even though we see a very narrow space. Some people say, "You have to accept your registration transitions, or it is unsafe", but there are plenty of empirical data to refute that. There are people who belt, healthily, into their grave. It is about whether or not you can do it efficiently. And more importantly, whether you can release the laryngopharnageal gesture at the end of the sound. Singing is movement. If you get stuck anywhere you end up with problems. We see a lot of West-End girls, particularly in roles like Elphaba (*Wicked*), that end up in the clinic with a muscle tension disorder. This is often caused by spending so much time in a heightened gesture but not cooling down out of it, and not stretching in the opposite direction. If you are going to be in a high larynx, high pressure condition, you have to go back and do some stretching out in the opposite direction. I think that tailoring the warm-up to the singer is great, but the cool-down should also be tailored to counteract whatever they have to do eight shows a week.

There has not been enough research on contemporary singers. However, there is no evidence to suggest that you cannot stay in whatever register you want well outside of its comfort zone or normal use-area with training. There is no evidence that this would have a negative impact on the voice. If you are doing the gesture efficiently, if your perception of the vocal effort is very low, and you are not coughing or constricted, you are probably fine. Just do not get stuck in any one gesture. To me, this is using common sense and exercising reasonable limits.

From a "mixing" perspective, in the U.K. we tend to think of mix as a chest-based sound, an extension of chest, like crying out. Mix is not a reinforced head voice, as we sometimes see in North America. This is a much lighter, head or M2 set-up with a large amount of twang. This approach never has the intensity that is required for commercial singing. If mix is approached in this M1 way, there is no need for a register change (for men or women) because you can adopt that setting for the entire phonatory range. However, there is a perception of the internal vibration or "placement" changing. Often, when people start engaging more "cry", they feel the "placement" move up out of their chest/mouth towards the back of their head. Some people feel it, but where in the range depends on the size of the larynx.

The other problem with using registration as a way to balance a voice, or to focus on it too much, is that we are so poorly designed to hear ourselves. There is a lot of talk about what we would call an imaginary second *passaggio*, which for men is around A_4 and for ladies, around E_5 or F_5 on top. There is no mechanical change if you are in that mix or whinge sound, but your ear loses the ability to hear the lower frequencies in the sound. Up to that point, you can hear the fundamental frequency (the pitch), and you can hear all of the high and low harmonics relatively well. After that imaginary second *passaggio*, you lose the ability to hear the lower harmonics, so all of a sudden you feel that the voice goes into very treble-heavy territory. This feels really nice, but there is an internal-perceptual sound change. The singer has to trust that it still sounds OK to the audience and that they still hear the whole harmonic spectrum. Those who sing with a bright and edgy sound by default often do not even feel this change as they are so used to what that setting is like. I often see that singers are not quite accepting that acoustic change, so they start to add tongue root and jaw activity to give themselves an internally darker/thicker sound, which causes the external sound to get tight and not very vibrant.

Seth Riggs and Margareta Svensson Riggs

Registration is dependent on being able to sing through your bridges. What is a bridge? The Italian and classical term for bridge is *passaggio*. A passage. A bridge. The first bridge connects your chest voice and your head voice where there is a break naturally. Your voice reacts the same way in each bridge, and you have to therefore approach them the same way.

To register, or balance, the voice evenly through the full range requires the singer to accomplish the bridging process, which means that the singer sings evenly from bottom to top, in a connected voice, starting in chest voice (chest register,) and gradually increasing the amount of head voice as the pitch go up, with correspondingly less chest voice, but always keeping the anchor in the chest. This maintains the connection without flipping into falsetto. Both male and female singers are treated the same way, with the expectation of accomplishing at least three, sometimes four, octaves vocalizing

Each bridge works the same way. If a female singer is able to maintain a resting larynx on the speech level in the first bridge, which for her is A4, Bb4, B4 and C5 (this is a man's second bridge, his starts at E4, F4, F#4 and G4) she will be able to accomplish the second bridge with the same ease at E5, F5, F#5 and G5 (a man's third bridge). At that point, she is ready to go to the third bridge at A5, Bb5, B5 and C6 and then into the fourth.

However, if when she approaches the first bridge she begins to be extravagant and try to sing an A4 with a G4-stretch, meaning she doesn't increase the amount of head voice and correspondingly decrease the amount of chest voice in the mix that is required to go up evenly from G to A, but rather approaches A the same way she did G, her voice will become labored and restricted as the throat begins to close rather than remain open. Reaching during the transition in the first bridge will make it impossible to get to the second bridge.

In popular music and musical theatre it is all important because this is the range in which most of the repertoire lies. But if she does it properly, not only will she go through her whole range but also, the vowels will be pure and the lyrics easy to understand.

Kim Chandler

I am conversant in different systems and their labels for various voice qualities. I will use what is familiar to the client and introduce them to other concepts. I tend to favor terms that are used in the music industry, such as "Chest", "Head", "Falsetto", "Mix", and "Belt", but also those based on the "Primal Voice" work of a close colleague of mine, Dane Chalfin. These are "Sigh", "Whimper", "Whinge" ("Whining"), and "Yell" ("Calling") – terms that are everyday words, not technical terms that need to be defined. They are pre-set sounds that all human beings are capable of making and are a good fit stylistically for contemporary singing. "Because Primal Sounds are emotive and reflexive by nature, not only do they elicit immediate technical benefit, they are also emotionally and interpretively relevant to the songs ... " – Dane Chalfin. [8]

---

8   More information is available at www.vocalrehabilitation.com/primal-voice-research.

Elisabeth Howard

I isolate head/falsetto, chest, and then apply to the mix. Head register in female voices is the same physical sensation and produces the same sound as falsetto for male voices. I train all my students, every genre, and every age, in isolating the vocal folds for strengthening the head register-falsetto for men at every lesson. I give voice strengthening exercises in chest for men and non-classical female singers in CCM and music theatre. The mix for belting is a combination of chest and head register, which is why it is called the mix. The mix for high belting depends on a strong head register/falsetto since for the high belting mix, we use a combination of chest and head register to imitate the chest register by lowering the soft palate to add mask resonance, and by "leaning" the tone against the chest. The "chest lean" is my term for leaning the tone against the chest, which automatically lowers the larynx, giving more room in the vocal tract, thus adding more depth and richness to the tone quality. For various dynamics, we balance the vocal folds with the air pressure. For example, for *forte*/loud, the folds are stiffer, closer to the chest register, with more subglottal air pressure. For *piano*/soft singing, the vocal folds are more relaxed with less subglottal air pressure.

Vocal colors taught in the Vocal Power Method, chest, mouth, mask, and head, are used independently of dynamics. For example, you can sing high belt mix loud in chest, mouth or mask colors. Head color is reserved for soft singing. Special effects taught in the Vocal Power Method, i.e., the throat cry, throat laugh, creaky door, "back L" can be added for emotional impact. The lower mix is used to match head voice singing. It is a lighter chest mechanism. The singer must match the color of the preceding phrase or match the color to the next phrase. For example, in the song "I Feel Pretty" (*West Side Story*), the first two notes, "I feel" must be in lower mix for the purpose of 1) being heard above the accompaniment and 2) to match the word "pretty" which should be in head register.

I teach blending registers using a lower mix that blends with the soprano voice/head voice, and the mix for safe belting that blends with the chest voice.

Tracy Marie Bourne

I use registration exercises all the time with my singers. In musical theatre-style singing, it is vital that singers are able to consciously manage their register shifts. They need to be able to sing in a predominantly chest register sound (belt), and bring the chest register up to a relatively high pitch. They also need to be able to sing in a head register dominant sound (legit) and bring the head register relatively low in their range, although not as low as classical singers tend to do. Music theatre singers also need to be able to "disguise" the register shift when they sing in a "mix" quality. I define mix as a quality that perceptually blends the chest and head registers, although it should be noted that research suggests that the registers are not actually being mixed.[9] For more detail on mix, please see my response under "(In)consistency".

Wendy DeLeo LeBorgne

Registration will vary according to genre. As one example, for my jazz artists, we will use all different registrations, which becomes a stylistic choice. They might actually have breaks and

---

9   Michele Castellengo, Bertrand Chuberre, and Nathalie Henrich Bernardoni, "Is *voix mixte*, the vocal technique used to smooth the transition across the two main laryngeal mechanisms, an independent mechanism?" Proceedings of the International Symposium on Musical Acoustics, Nara, Japan, 2004. Michele Castellengo, S. Lamesch and Nathalie Henrich, "Vocal registers and laryngeal mechanisms, a case study: The French *Voix Mixte*," Ninth International Congress on Acoustics, Madrid, 2007.

cracks on purpose, and that is something we practice. Country artists also need to be able to yodel and crack. Instead of me imposing my terminology of chest, mix, head, on them, I ask them what they call the voice that they are using in a specific instance. Whatever terminology they are using, I will adapt to them, begin our registration conversation where they are, and expand their understanding and vocabulary about registration from that starting point.

Robert Edwin

I teach phona*tion* (vocal fold activity) and registra*tion* (the "gears" of the vocal folds) as parts of the *"tions"* (pronounced "shuns") singing system. Phona*tion*/registra*tion* occurs when the vocal folds adduct (close) and are set into motion. Since the human voice is gender neutral (physiologically, there is very little difference between a male and a female larynx), all of my students are required to use all of their voice from their lowest to their highest pitches. They vocalize in mode 1 ("chest voice") and mode 2 ("head/falsetto voice"), and also explore mode 0 ("vocal fry") and mode 3 ("whistle register"). All of this vocal fold activity is addressed through an ever-changing variety of major and minor scales, triads, and arpeggios using solfege, numbers, vowels and consonants, and, of course, words and phrases.

Edrie Means Weekly

Manuel Garcia II developed the scientific definition of registers that most voice pedagogues still used today: "A register is a series of homogeneous sounds produced by one mechanism, differing essentially from another series of equally homogeneous sounds produced by another mechanism."[10] Clifton Ware's definition is "A series of distinct, consecutive, homogeneous vocal tones that can be maintained in pitch and loudness throughout a certain range".[11] Basically, there are three parts to registration: a series of pitches, vocal fold vibratory patterns, and vocal timbre characteristics. How many registers there are is a constant debate among pedagogues.

I like to take the point of view there are two primary registers – chest and head. Both registers have a series of pitches (with a little overlapping), vibratory pattern, and vocal timbre characteristics. The vocal folds will be thicker in chest register or thinner in head register. Chest register (sometimes referred to as 'lower register') resonates in the upper chest and is the lower sounding quality associated with the male voice and the lower speaking voice in women. Chest register is thryroarytenoid (TA) muscle-dominant. Head register (sometimes referred to as "upper register') is the higher and lighter quality associated with the female voice. Head register is cricothyroid (CT) muscle-dominant. From those two registers, there is a combination – chest-mix, mix, head-mix – and adjusting the vibratory pattern of the folds for the tone the singer wishes to produce for the style. Mix is a balance of chest and head register, the blended voice connecting the two registers. The goal for most CCM singers is to sing in a mix throughout their range. It is important to have a solid mix to be able to belt. I consider falsetto in men and whistle tone in women extensions of their head register. I work on all these combinations and areas of the voice.

I work with each singer to isolate the primary registers with various exercises and then to blend the registers using glides and semi-occluded vocal tract exercises to smooth

---

10 Manuel Garcia, *Hints on Singing*, (London: E. Ascherberg, 1894), 8.

11 Clifton Ware, *Basics of Vocal Pedagogy: The Foundations and Process of Singing*, (New York: McGraw-Hill, 1998).

transitions. I use vowels: [a], [e], [i], [I], [o], [u], [æ], Y[æ], Y[o], on arpeggios, slides (whole note, 3rds, 5ths, octaves), triads, and 5- and 9-tone scales. The goal is to stabilize and co-ordinate vocal function.

Cate Frazier-Neely

I address registration as part of posture and alignment, and within laryngeal co-ordination and stability. Registers are isolated and combined by exercises that are based on small pitch patterns, specific vowels, and intensities of loud to soft. Within the same session, we move back and forth among a large variety of exercises, suited to the individual, that eventually allow the larynx to make smooth transitions of registration, up and down the scale, responding to the singer's communicative intent and the music's style. This manner of working comes from Cornelius Reid[12] and has been systemized and further developed by Jeannette LoVetri.[13] There is an informative dissertation by Jonathan Yarrington that explores the specifics of Reid's approach that is worth reading.[14]

This technical process takes time, patience, and regular practice to develop, and then the singer must understand that they need to keep rebalancing their registration as they perform over many years. In one case, I worked with an opera singer specializing in Baroque music who was also an old time Americana country singer, and who wanted to yodel and break as part of the style. She had trained the register transitions so masterfully with a fine teacher, but we had to design a way for her to let her muscles respond to her musical intent in the other style while continuing to sing Handel.

Wise and patient registration work as a foundation also has profound results for peri-menopause and menopausal singers, as well as those in voice therapy, outside of standard protocol.

Trineice Robinson-Martin

Head register/falsetto/head-dominant register/cricothyroid (CT)-dominant registration are all terms used to describe higher pitch ranges and/or lighter vocal qualities. This registration implies that thyroarytenoid (TA) muscle is less engaged/contracted, or even more passive, during the sound-making process; as a result the vocal folds are less dense and the CT muscle can easily dominate the function of the vocals by stretching and lengthening them at will. The more dominant the head register the thinner the vocal folds are when vibrating. When the head/falsetto register is developed, the singer will be able to sing softly with more ease, have more flexibility in the ability to change pitch resulting in a better intonation, and will be able to extend the overall vocal range to include higher pitches.

Chest register/chest-dominant register/thyroarytenoid (TA)-dominant registration is the registration associated with lower pitch ranges and/or heavier vocal qualities. This registration implies that the mass of the vocal fold, the TA muscle, is actively contracted even as the CT

---

12 Cornelius L. Reid, *The Free Voice: A Guide to Natural Singing,* (New York: Oxford University Press, 2018) and *Voice: Psyche and Soma,* (New York: Joseph Patelson Music House, 1975).

13 More information may be found at http://somaticvoicework.com/.

14 Jonathan S. Yarrington, "Voice Building Exercises from the Cornelius L. Reid Archive: An Introduction" (DMA diss., University of North Texas, 2014), digital.library.unt.edu/ark:/67531/metadc700053/m2/1/high_res_d/dissertation.pdf

muscle contracts to lengthen vocal folds when changing pitch. When the chest register is developed, the singer will be able to sing loudly with more ease, have greater stability and more fullness in the tone produced, and will extend the overall vocal range to include lower pitches.

Chest and head/falsetto register should be developed in isolation and then blended as determined by the parameters required in the chosen style of music. With the understanding that all sounds are physiologically some form of mixed registration, registers should be developed in their most dominant form (i.e. chest-dominant/thick folds or head-dominant/thin folds) starting the optimal ranges each registration. While the exact pitch is often individualized, generically speaking a female voice may start with developing a very dominant chest sound somewhere below middle C, and could start developing a very dominant head/falsetto around an octave above middle C, depending on the voice type. A male voice could develop the most dominant form of chest registration/thick folds at or around D below middle C, and falsetto somewhere around F above middle C, again depending on the voice type of the individual.

Flexibility of, and transition through, the various registrations (i.e. chest/thick, falsetto/thin, and everything in between) is encouraged at the natural points of transition areas first, then the voice is trained to gradually override these natural transition points in the desired level of mixed registration. For example, singers can gradually train the voice to maintain a chestier/thicker fold registration past the natural transition point, while managing the amount of thickness they wish to maintain for their desired sound (i.e. how much or how little head register they want to add in creating or sustaining the sound on any given pitch).

Kevin Wilson

All registers should be developed and balanced through variances and negotiations in breath pressure and resonance as necessary. I teach the standard fry, chest, mix, head, whistle registration terminology. However, I also discuss "lite mix" vs "heavy mix" and define the concept of modes, should they encounter that in the future.

Marci Rosenberg

I use registration terms when teaching and I approach singing from a registration perspective as a prominent component of my pedagogy. Put simply, I describe registration terms based on how we perceive them aurally, rather than as biomechanical behaviors. Chest register is perceived as speech-based in quality, head register is the lighter, non-speech-based quality, and mix is anything in between. Mix can also be divided perceptually into subcategories. A chest mix leans more toward a speech-like quality but is lighter than a pure chest register, and head mix is a lighter non-speech quality but it is not as light as pure head register. The extremes of chest voice and head voice do represent different biomechanical vocal behaviors, not unlike other paired structures in our body. If someone is having lower back pain, a physical therapist will not only provide exercises to stretch the back musculature, but also strengthen the antagonist muscles which are the abdominal muscles. This improves the efficiency of postural integrity. Similarly, though over simplified, I view registration, in part, as representative of the agonist/antagonist muscles associated with chest and head voice. I am a proponent of having balance and facility in both registers regardless of vocal style. Musical theatre singers must be able to belt, sing legit, and everything in between. Vocal training must take this into account and register balance is a critical skill for this. Sopranos must have strength in their chest voice and belters and men must have a well-developed head register. Teachers wanting exposure to a registration-based pedagogical approach should look at Somatic Voicework™ The LoVetri Method, which is a good starting point for teachers not familiar with this perspective. In addition to viewing registration in terms of agonist/antagonist muscle function, we cannot discount the role of acoustics and vocal tract shaping in voice production and perceived registration, and Ken Bozeman has written two very accessible books on vocal acoustics describing this.[15]

Lisa Popeil

Ah, the bucket of thorns! This topic has kept me up many nights (I may be exaggerating a bit here), and I reserve the right to change my mind about it in the future!

There seem to be two basic trains of thought about the meaning of a vocal register. The original definition of vocal registers (from Garcia) likened them to the different stops on an organ, meaning that a register is a series of notes with a similar sound. It turns out that this is actually a very good description and one that I have come to embrace. Another very useful, modern approach is to think of a vocal register as a unique vocal fold vibrational pattern. With this model, we can then denote four separate registers: Mode 0= vocal fry, Mode 1= chest, Mode 2= head, Mode 3= whistle. But then to complicate matters, voice scientist Ingo Titze has championed the concept that one cannot ignore vocal tract shaping differences when discussing vocal registers.[16]

All of these approaches are true, useful, and different views of an extremely complex issue that voice science is still investigating.

Then there is the messy topic of "mix". The main problem with this term, in my opinion, is that it means different things to different people. Some teachers use the term mix to mean a blend between chest and head voice; an actual third register. Others use mix to mean singing in a light, high chest voice, and is a term popular with CCM singers. Some singers use the term mix to mean a strong, low head voice. Very confusing!

After much experimentation and investigation, here are some of my current tenets of teaching vocal registers:

1. Singers can sing in EITHER their chest voice or their head voice.
2. Singers can learn to "feel" their vocal folds (particularly the sensation of the vocalis muscle contracting) and can also learn to feel vocal fold stretching, and vocal fold edge thinning and thickening – all useful in controlling the minute changes in registers.
3. Resonance characteristics (nasality, ring, brightness, vertical larynx heights, and pharyngeal widths) can be somewhat separated from registers at the vocal fold level, allowing singers to create resonance choices (like frosting) on top of chest or head voice (the cake).
4. Chest voice does not have to be loud and heavy. In my view, it is simply an unfortunately-named term based on a speaking or yelling sound. Likewise, head voice doesn't have to be fluty and light. Many CCM singers assume (most never having heard an operatic performance) that head voice is soft and breathy. Head voice can be many things, but it does not sound like one's speaking voice.

---

15 Kenneth Bozeman, *Practical Vocal Acoustics: Pedagogic Applications for Singers and Teachers* (Hillsdale, NY: Pendragon Press, 2014) and *Kinesthetic Voice Pedagogy: Motivating Acoustic Efficiency* (Gahannah, OH: Inside View Press, 2017).

16 Ingo Titze and Albert S. Worley, "Modeling source-filter interaction in belting and high-pitched operatic male singing," *The Journal of the Acoustical Society of America* 126, no. 3 (September 2009), 1530–1540, doi. org/10.1121/1.3160296.

5. Head voice and falsetto are interchangeable terms. I know that some teachers, especially men, consider head voice to be strong and falsetto to be weak and fluty, but I think that weak and fluty is just a variation of head voice.

6. Chest voice can be taken to the highest note of one's vocal range or at least, close to the top. Conversely, head voice can be taken down to one's lowest note or at least, a lot lower than expected. I can sing any note of my range in either register but did not know that until I tried!

7. High, light chest voice can be felt with vibration in the head, but that does not make it head voice! Where one feels vibration should not be the determining factor in registration. The differences can be easily felt in the vocal folds and larynx.

8. Register blending, or more precisely, the smooth transitioning between registers, is very important, but I think singers should know *which* register they are in when singing any note of a song, particularly in CCM. The only time I'm not sure which register I'm using is when doing sirens or rapid lip trills. Choosing registers is an important color choice as an expressive singer. When one thinks of singing in "mix", one might be missing out on an important opportunity to create a precise emotion, particularly in a delicate and transparent style like jazz.

9. Imagining a horizontal movement from the front to back of the vocal folds (adding more feeling in the front of the larynx as pitch lowers and more feeling in the back as the pitch rises) is, for most students, a revelation and allows them to add more vocalis ("front muscle" feeling) or less vocalis, more cricoid-thyroid ("back muscle" feeling), perhaps at will. Whether a student is in head or chest voice, this "feelable" model can not only provide a singer with a tool for smooth register transitions but also, allow one to thicken or thin the vocal fold edge on any note in either register. Radical, yes, but empowering.

10. Though I've been involved in research into vocal registers, both at the vocal fold level and in the vocal tract, I plan on doing quite a bit more, with a plan to look at glottal configurations using high speed videography, stroboscope, EGG, and direct EMG to compare head and chest registers throughout my 3 and ⅓ octave range. My particular interest for the future is the action of high chest voice and low head voice at the glottal level – so stay tuned!

Jeff Ramsey

Balancing the registers is key. I work on this by having students practice with an even volume, which helps to encourage a blending of registers. There are many methods for this. Some teachers work with the idea of isolating each register first before training them to mix/blend. I believe in getting them to understand the concept of chest and head coming together, regardless of what the initial response is from the vocal folds. It is not easy for many at first as it exposes the break (*passaggio*) for most; however, with diligence, they start to feel and hear a difference in how their voice operates when singing. They also start to feel how much less effort they have to make to get their voices moving. It definitely takes some practice. I know some colleagues may start from the top up, as it is easier. I do that as well but only so they get the concept of how the folds thin and lengthen. At some point, they have to learn how to ascend without taking all the weight of thicker folds up with them. Regardless of gender, I have both do the exact same exercises. The majority of students generally do not have as much access to the head voice; this is quite evident when they have to switch registers in order to keep the volume even at some point.

Gillyanne Kayes

My favorite topic! I think register management is essential to all singers and it is especially important to female singers of CCM, who spend far more time in modal (or chest) register than their classical counterparts. I subscribe to the notion of register categorization as follows: modal or M1 (with varying degrees of TA/CT "dominance"); falsetto or M2); I teach vocal fold fry mostly as an effect, but I also use it as a cooldown or for certain technical purposes.

As a teacher I tend to be multi-lexical; as a researcher I am more likely to pin my terminology down. So, for discussion of registers with my clients, I might use any of the following: M1, chest, speech-like; M2, head, falsetto; "mix" on M1 or M2; TA-dominant/CT-dominant. I do not regard "head voice" and "falsetto" as exactly interchangeable. I teach my clients that there are M1 versions of "head voice" and "falsetto" (M2) versions of "head voice". In my practice I refer to these as "head voice 1" and "head voice 2" (the latter being based on "falsetto" mechanism). It is a confusing area because register theory is largely based on the male voice and has been assessed mostly from classical singers, or classical singers compared with naïve singers.

We need much more data on CCM singers, especially females. Overall in my approach I consider it important for men to know how to access a "non-falsetto head voice", which in fact is based on M1, and sends it right away into a confusion of terminology, and for women to know that there are two types of "head voice" – one which will feel more "connected" (TA & CT to stretch and tension the folds) and one that is "looser" (TA lax). I recognize that what I am calling "connected head voice" in female singing might be identified as "middle register" or "mixed voice" in other labeling systems.

Jeannette LoVetri

Vocal registration is the primary ingredient in CCM styles. Singing a rock or pop song in a head-register-dominant vocal quality just makes the vocalist sound foolish. Not being able to hear and execute correct register function for any given CCM style is the single most typical problem that confounds both singers and singing teachers. Vocalists must address registration, particularly if they have not been trained to take the chest or lower register into higher pitches in a comfortable way, and this can't be done through breath support and resonance maneuvers. *Only work on registers is work on registers*, as this is work on the *source* of the sound. There is no substitute for balance of registration.

This implies that the vocalist has two well-developed vocal registers (high and low, light and heavy, cricothyroid (CT) or thyroarytenoid (TA), or chest and head – all the same things). The upper register (head or CT) is the weaker of the two in most adults. The emphasis on this register in a great deal of traditional classical vocal training helped to develop the ability to "sing in the mask." In CCM, we really don't need that and, in some styles, like jazz, such resonance is counter-productive. When both registers are strong in equal measure the middle range pitches of anyone's range will begin to "co-ordinate" or "blend". In CCM styles, the term for this quality is "mix". It's not the same as, but is related to, mid-range blend in classical singing, but the vowel sound configurations are usually different. This contributes to vowel sound "evenness" throughout the vocal range.

Kathryn Paradise

Registration is one of the first technical issues I tackle with a majority of my students. Commercial music requires a chest-dominant vocal sound and most students need assistance in achieving this in a healthy, sustainable way. I begin by confirming that they have a healthy, functioning low, chest voice, and high head voice/falsetto. After ensuring these elements are in place, giving exercises to shore up weak areas and clarifying terminology with the student, I explore "mix." I typically talk about mix as a fluid sound that can be either chest- or head-dominant. Depending on the voice type and already ingrained vocal habits, I will approach the mix sound with slides from either the top or bottom of the range on a bright vowel like [æ] (apple) or [e] (age). This is where vowel modification can become very helpful. I believe that using chest mix is the healthiest and most useful way to create what is commonly labeled a "belt" sound in commercial singing. I also believe that creating a perception of chest-dominant singing in the upper range of the voice is both a physical and acoustical phenomenon, and my teaching reflects this. In my experience, it is important to recognize each student's unique voice type, vocal health history, and stylistic needs when expanding the range of chest mix upward.

When exploring new ways of approaching and understanding registration in different areas of the voice, students typically feel like their voice is out of control or "weak" and introduce tension into the mechanism to "fix" what they don't like. To avoid this, I aim to create exercises and choose repertoire that sets the student up to succeed and gradually work outward into more challenging tasks. I also explain to students that the process takes time and encourage them to pick repertoire that highlights their strengths in regard to registration and range.

Mary Saunders Barton

The essence of the *bel canto can belto* pedagogy lies in the subtle balancing of bass and treble functions throughout the entire singing range on a *mixed continuum*. Singers should always be in some form of mix. Like many of my colleagues, I currently identify registers by muscular function and refer to fry, chest, head, and flute (sometimes called whistle) as four distinct modes (0-3). Young women can usually access all four modes and male singers at least three. The balancing of modes 1 (chest, thyroarytenoid [TA] function, thick folds) and 2 (head, falsetto, cricothyroid [CT] function, thin folds) is the most critical technique in musical theatre. It gives the singer access to added range and commercial viability in an industry where casting is determined by *character*, not *voice type*. The starting point in training musical theatre singers will be determined by where their weak points are. If the CT component is undeveloped, and it frequently is in young singers, we will have to address that first in order to prevent the TA muscle from overpowering the instrument. As they mature, that second *passaggio* into "lofty" head voice and the upper belt extension around Eb5 can often be an area of weakness for women that requires careful attention to balanced technique.

For women and men, one of the most common challenges in contemporary chest-dominant singing for musical theatre is tracking the vowels in each word throughout the range of a given song while maintaining a consistently balanced (un-pressed) phonation. It is often those closed vowels in speech ([i] and [u]) that want to migrate or flip when they feel too pressurized. If a woman is new to belting, it can be a challenge to access that trumpet like AH on the word "high", for example, on a Bb4. If she feels too much subglottal pressure, it is normal to experience a "fight or flight" response and flip to head (CT) on the diphthong. There are many playful ways to address this middle voice issue for women. Alternating abruptly between TA- (chest) and CT-(head-)dominant qualities in speech on different vowels can help promote co-ordination between Bb4 and D5, then *slowly* speaking the words of a sung phrase. Take the lyric "All you need is love" by the Beatles, for example. Have the student speak through every syllable on a Bb4 encouraging an energized elevated delivery. Then have her sing the phrase on the same note. The option of a belt can occur quite naturally on the word "love". Many women will be surprised at how effortlessly that mixed belt emerges once speaking elements are balanced.

A few good examples of the middle voice or "standard" belt resonance are Sutton Foster on the final "love" in "Gimme Gimme" from *Thoroughly Modern Millie*, or Barbra Streisand on the final "parade" in "Don't Rain on My Parade" from *Funny Girl*, or Idina Menzel on the final "I" at the end of "The Wizard and I" from *Wicked*. Women are vowel choreographers in the middle voice where the belt resonance should be seen as an optional color. To be sure, a degree of modification of the vowel is required as the pitch rises, but without sacrificing the intelligibility of the lyric. For women, the acoustic variations possible in chest-dominant repertoire diminish above Eb5 where the vowel resonance becomes uniform in that tenor-like high belt range.

Male musical theatre singers encounter the same resonance options in their high mixed range above the second *passaggio* at approximately F4.

Although the use of electronic enhancement obviates the need for the kind of self-amplification required of classical singers, the most effective training for musical theatre singers should take place in an acoustic setting in my view. This ensures an accurate aural perception of the sounds they are making. We are conditioning muscles after all and, as in any physical activity, vocal longevity will depend on even wear to avoid repetitive strain.

Matthew Edwards

It is easiest to write about registration in black and white but the truth is, there are many shades of grey. I like to think of the voice as consisting of chest and head on the extreme ends of the spectrum, and variations of mix in the middle, which can be divided into chest-mix and head-mix. However, not all singers feel like they have four options; some feel only chest and head, others feel chest, head, and a single quality of mix. Therefore, I am very flexible with my terminology when working one-on-one with singers.

The terms head and chest are controversial because they were originally associated with sensations of placement and not actual vocal fold function. However, they are terms that are widely understood and accepted, and I do not see a need to replace them. Current research indicates it is actually a physiological and acoustic event, meaning that the vocal folds and vocal tract must work together. However, when teaching, I think it is essential to address each component separately before thinking about the interactions of the whole system.

In relation to the action of the vocal folds, I think of registration as having two components: the thickness of the folds and the amount of medial compression. It is possible to sing in chest voice (thick vocal folds/high closed quotient) with very little airflow (pressed phonation) or with more airflow (flow phonation). Both variations should be available to students who sing CCM styles.

I train the extremes first, then develop the middle, and eventually work with my students to find as many variations as possible. As co-ordination at the vocal fold level improves, I begin working with variations of bright and dark vowels, along with everything in the middle. Addressing registration is one of the most important things a CCM teacher does.

Marcelle G. Gauvin

The development of balanced registration is fundamental to me in vocal training. An instrument is at its healthiest when head and chest register are open, free, balanced, and blended. This process increases an artist's range and therefore an artist's options. Then the vocalist has a blank canvas on which to create freely. Frequently, professional demands will pull an artist more to one side of the registration scale than another. My job is to re-balance the instrument without sabotaging the artist's needed professional default. For contemporary styles, the ability to mix registers is becoming a greater necessity. As industry demands on singers continue to rise, the ability to mix can add longevity to an artist's career by decreasing strain and increasing choices. It also allows for greater sophistication in musical interpretation by facilitating subtle register adjustments, especially in the mid-voice area. Every artist appreciates options.

References and recommended reading

Austin, Stephen F. "Treasure 'chest:' A physiological and pedagogical review of the low mechanism." *Journal of Singing* 61, no. 3 (January/February 2005): 241–252.

Barlow, Christopher and Jeannette LoVetri. "Closed quotient and spectral measures of female adolescent singers in different singing styles." *Journal of Voice* 24, no. 3 (May 2010): 314–318. doi.org/10.1016/j.jvoice.2008.10.003.

Behrman, Alison. *Speech and Voice Science.* 2nd ed. San Diego: Plural Publishing, 2013.

Björkner, Eva, Johan Sundberg, Tom Cleveland, and Ed Stone. "Voice source differences between registers in female musical theater singers." *Journal of Voice* 20, no. 2 (June 2006): 187–197. doi.org/10.1016/j.jvoice.2005.01.008.

Bourne, Tracy and Dianna Kenny. "Vocal qualities in music theater voice: Perceptions of expert pedagogues." *Journal of Voice* 30, no. 1 (January 2016): 128.e1–128.e12. doi.org/10.1016/j.jvoice.2015.03.008.

Bozeman, Kenneth W. *Kinesthetic Voice Pedagogy: Motivating Acoustic Efficiency.* Gahannah, OH: Inside View Press, 2017.

Bozeman, Kenneth W. *Practical Vocal Acoustics: Pedagogic Applications for Singers and Teachers.* Hillsdale, NY: Pendragon Press, 2014.

Castellengo, Michele, Bertrand Chuberre and Nathalie Henrich Bernardoni. "Is *voix mixte*, the vocal technique used to smooth the transition across the two main laryngeal mechanisms, an independent mechanism?" Proceedings of the International Symposium on Musical Acoustics, Nara, Japan, 2004.

Castellengo, Michele, S. Lamesch and Nathalie Henrich. "Vocal registers and laryngeal mechanisms, a case study: The French *Voix Mixte*." Ninth International Congress on Acoustics, Madrid, 2007.

Cowley, Rowena. "Knowledge and skill in teaching registers: A reflection on practice." In *Perspectives on Teaching Singing: Australian Vocal Pedagogues Sing their Stories* edited by Scott D. Harrison, 122–140. Bowen Hills, Qld.: Australian Academic Press, 2010.

Duncan, Kate. "The plain cookie: Overcoming the myth of the female vocal 'break.'" In *The Voice Teacher's Cookbook: Creative Recipes for Teachers of Singing* edited by Brian J. Winnie, 31-32. Delray Beach, FL: Meredith Music, 2018.

Echternach, Matthias, Lisa Popeil, Louisa Traser, Sascha Wienhausen, Bernhard Richter. "Vocal tract shapes in different singing functions used in musical theater singing: A pilot study." Journal of Voice 28, no. 5 (September 2014): 653. e1–653.e7. doi.org/10.1016/j.jvoice.2014.01.011.

Frizzell, J.D. "Transitioning from dinner to dessert: *Passaggio* in contemporary singing." In *The Voice Teacher's Cookbook: Creative Recipes for Teachers of Singing* edited by Brian J. Winnie, 46-47. Delray Beach, FL: Meredith Music, 2018.

Garcia, Manuel. *Hints on Singing.* London: E. Ascherberg, 1894. Scholar's Choice edition, 2015.

Hall, Karen. *So You Want to Sing Music Theatre: A Guide for Professionals.* Lanham, MD: Rowman & Littlefield, 2014.

Henrich, Nathalie, Christophe D'Allessandro, Boris Doval, and Michele Castellengo. "Glottal open quotient in singing: Measurements and correlation with laryngeal mechanisms, vocal intensity, and fundamental frequency." *The Journal of the Acoustical Society of America* 117, no. 3 (March 2005): 1417–1430. doi.org/10.1121/1.1850031.

Herbst, Christian T. and Jan G. Svec. "Adjustment of glottal configurations in singing." *Journal of Singing* 70, no. 3 (January/February 2014): 301–308.

Hollien, Harry. "Vocal fold dynamics for frequency change." *Journal of Voice* 28, no. 4 (July 2014): 395–405. doi. org/10.1016/j.jvoice.2013.12.005.

Howard, David M. "Variation of electrolaryngographically derived closed quotient for trained and untrained adult female singers." *Journal of Voice* 9, no. 2 (June 1995): 163–172. doi.org/10.1016/S0892-1997(05)80250-4.

Howard, David M. "Electrolaryngographically revealed aspects of the voice source in singing." *Logopedics Phoniatrics Vocology* 35, no. 2 (April 2010): 81–89. www.doi.org/10.3109/14015439.2010.482863.

Section II: Elements of Training *Registration*

Kiesgen, Paul. "Registration." *Journal of Singing* 62, no. 5 (May/June 2006): 537–539.

Kochis-Jennings, Karen Ann, Eileen M. Finnegan, Henry T. Hoffman, Sanyukta Jaiswal. "Laryngeal muscle activity and vocal fold adduction during chest, chestmix, headmix, and head registers in females." *Journal of Voice* 26, no. 2, (March 2012): 182–193. doi.org/10.1016/j.jvoice.2010.11.002.

Kochis-Jennings, Karen Ann, Eileen M. Finnegan, Henry T. Hoffman, Sanyukta Jaiswal, and Darcey Hull. "Cricothyroid muscle and thyroarytenoid muscle dominance in vocal register control: Preliminary results." *Journal of Voice* 28, no. 5 (September 2014): 652.e21–652.e29. doi.org/10.1016/j.jvoice.2014.01.017.

LeBorgne, Wendy D. and Marci Rosenberg. *The Vocal Athlete*. San Diego: Plural Publishing, 2014.

LoVetri, Jeannette. "Female chest voice." *Journal of Singing* 60, no. 2 (November/December 2003): 161-164.

LoVetri, Jeannette, Susan Lesh, and Peak Woo. "Preliminary study on the ability of trained singers to control the intrinsic and extrinsic laryngeal musculature." *Journal of Voice* 13, no. 2 (June 1999): 219–226. doi.org/10.1016/S0892-1997(99)80024-1.

Miller, Donald Gray. "Registers defined through visual feedback." In *Teaching Singing in the 21st Century*, edited by Scott D. Harrison and Jessica O'Bryan, 133–141. Dordrecht: Springer, 2014.

Miller, Donald G. and Harm K. Schutte. "Mixing the registers: Glottal source or vocal tract?" *Folia Phoniatrica et Logopaedica* 57 (2005): 278–291. doi.org/10.1159/000087081.

Neumann, Katrin, Patrick Schunda, Sebastian Hoth, and Harald A. Euler. "The interplay between glottis and vocal tract during the male *passaggio*." *Folia Phoniatrica et Logopaedica* 57 (2005): 308–327. doi.org/10.1159/000087084.

Reid, Cornelius L. *The Free Voice: A Guide to Natural Singing*. New York: Oxford University Press, 2018.

Reid, Cornelius L. *Voice: Psyche and Soma*. New York: Joseph Patelson Music House, 1975.

Roubeau, Bernard, Nathalie Henrich, and Michele Castellengo. "Laryngeal vibratory mechanisms: The notion of register revisited." *Journal of Voice* 23, no. 4 (July 2009): 425–438. doi.org/10.1016/j.jvoice.2007.10.014.

Sadolin, Cathrine. *Complete Vocal Technique Application*: completevocal.institute/app/.

Salomao, Gláucia Lais and Johan Sundberg. "What do male singers mean by modal and falsetto register? An investigation of the glottal voice source." *Logopedics Phoniatrics Vocology* 34, no. 2 (June 2009): 73–83. www.doi.org/10.1080/14015430902879918.

Steinhauer, Kimberly. "Everything is a mix: It depends on your recipe!" In *The Voice Teacher's Cookbook: Creative Recipes for Teachers of Singing* edited by Brian J. Winnie, 116–118. Delray Beach, FL: Meredith Music, 2018.

Steinhauer, Kimberly, Judith Preston Grayhack, Ann L. Smiley-Oyen, Susan Shaiman, and Malcom R. McNeil. "The relationship among voice onset, voice quality, and fundamental frequency: A dynamic perspective." *Journal of Voice* 18, no. 4 (December 2004): 432–442. doi.org/10.1016/j.jvoice.2004.01.006.

Stone, R.E., Thomas F. Cleveland, and Johan Sundberg. "Formant frequencies in country singers' speech and singing." *Journal of Voice* 13, no. 2 (June 1999): 161–167. doi.org/10.1016/S0892-1997(99)80020-4.

Story, Brad, Ingo R. Titze, and Eric A. Hoffman. "The relationship of vocal tract shape to three voice qualities." *The Journal of the Acoustical Society of America* 109, no. 4 (April 2001): 1651–1667. doi.org/10.1121/1.1352085.

Sundberg, Johan and Margareta Thalén. "What is twang?" *Journal of Voice* 24, no. 6 (November 2010): 654–660. doi.org/10.1016/j.jvoice.2009.03.003.

Svec, Jan G., Johan Sundberg, and Stellan Hertegard. "Three registers in an untrained female singer analyzed by videokymography, strobolaryngoscopy and sound spectrography." *Journal of the Acoustical Society of America* 123, no. 1 (January 2008): 347–353. www.doi.org/10.1121/1.2804939.

Tan, Kendrich Graemer Ong. "Contact quotient of female singers singing four pitches for five vowels in normal and pressed phonations." *Journal of Voice* 31, no. 5 (September 2017): 645.e15–645.e22. doi.org/10.1016/j.jvoice.2017.02.014.

Thalen, Margareta and Johan Sundberg. "Describing different styles of singing: A comparison of a female singer's voice source in 'Classical,' 'Pop,' 'Jazz,' and 'Blues.'" *Logopedics Phoniatrics Vocology* 26, no. 2 (2001): 82–93. doi.org/10.1080/140154301753207458.

Thuesen, Mathias Aaen, Julian McGlashan, and Cathrine Sadolin. "Investigating laryngeal 'tilt' on same-pitch phonation: Preliminary findings of vocal mode metal and density parameters as alternatives to cricothyroid-thyroarytenoid 'Mix.'" *Journal of Voice*, in press. doi.org/10.1016/j.jvoice.2018.02.023.

Titze, Ingo and Albert S. Worley. "Modeling source-filter interaction in belting and high-pitched operatic male singing." *The Journal of the Acoustical Society of America* 126, no. 3 (September 2009): 1530–1540. doi.org/10.1121/1.3160296.

Titze, Ingo R., Christine C. Bergan, Eric Hunter, and Brad Story. "Source and filter adjustments affecting the perception of the vocal qualities twang and yawn." *Logopedics Phoniatrics Vocology* 28, no. 4 (December 2003): 147–155.

Titze, Ingo. "Formant frequency shifts for classical and theater belt vowel modification." *Journal of Singing* 67, no. 3 (January/February 2011): 311–312.

Titze, Ingo R. *Principles of Voice Production*. Iowa City, IA: The National Center for Voice and Speech, 2000.

Willis, Elizabeth. "Registration in young voices: A balancing act." In *Perspectives on Teaching Singing: Australian Vocal Pedagogues Sing their Stories*, edited by Scott D. Harrison, 141–154. Bowen Hills, Qld.: Australian Academic Press, 2010.

Yarrington, Jonathan S. "Voice Building Exercises from the Cornelius L. Reid Archive: An Introduction." DMA diss., University of North Texas, 2014. digital.library.unt.edu/ark:/67531/metadc700053/m2/1/high_res_d/dissertation.pdf.

Zangger Borch, D. and Johan Sundberg. "Some phonatory and resonatory characteristics of the rock, pop, soul, and Swedish dance band styles of singing." *Journal of Voice* 25, no. 5 (September 2011): 532–537. doi.org/10.1016/j.jvoice.2010.07.014.

11

(In)Consistency

Many pedagogues believe that one of the most essential tasks in voice training is to connect the two primary vocal registers, creating "mix". However, 52% of pedagogues point out that an imperceptibly smooth transition between registers is not always desirable in CCM genres, and it is important to preserve the ability to abruptly change register if desired. Yodels and flips are used in bluegrass, country, gospel, pop, and R&B genres. Being able to sing with a variety of sounds and registrational choices provides a broad expressive palette and allows music theatre performers to sound authentic in many different sub-genres.

Training "consistency" in the range refers to a registrational activity, specifically, disguising the shift between M1/chest register and M2/head register. For some teachers, this also involves adjustments in pitch, volume, control, and effort. A seamless transition is desirable in legit music theatre and operetta, and 43% of pedagogues report training towards consistency between registers. However, some styles will require the voice to sound "untrained" or "natural". In some genres, a voice that plays with the registrational break can make a more interesting and expressive sound. What may have once been considered a "fault" in classical singing can be a distinctive and marketable component of the CCM voice, so long as it is healthy.

Pedagogues report using targeted vocal conditioning across registers to work consistency. Music theatre singers work on consistency and inconsistency simultaneously, by carefully selecting repertoire to keep both skills active; 52% of pedagogues report training both consistency and inconsistency between the registers, as desired.

This chapter includes responses to the prompt "Please describe your approach to teaching consistency through the range". However, because half of the responses pointed out that consistency was not necessarily the goal, the prompt was changed to "Please describe your approach to teaching consistency or inconsistency, as desired". The responses are presented in order beginning with those who describe training consistency, followed by those who train both consistency *and* inconsistency, and ending with those who prefer not to teach consistency, or address the topic as part of another chapter.

Kim Chandler

I generally use semi-occluded sounds and favorable vowels on customized *portamenti* exercises (sirens) to help achieve smooth "gear changes" (*passaggi*) and tonal consistency.

Some level of vocal agility (flexibility, dexterity) is beneficial for a balanced vocal technique and therefore I advocate that all singers include speed exercises based on scales, modes, arpeggios, intervals, melodic fragments in their routine practice. Instrumentalists spend time slowly building up dexterity on their instrument; vocalists should not be exempted from this process. Besides which, many styles of pop music, e.g., soul, gospel, pop, R&B, country, require agility and fluency in order to achieve the riffs and runs that feature in these styles.

Kevin Wilson

A voice must be flexible and agile for consistency. This flexibility is in the big movers I call "the variables": jaw, tongue, soft palate, and larynx. I use vowel modification, breath balancing, and resonance adjustments throughout the staff depending on the needs of the repertoire. I work for my students to have one sound top to bottom without audible registration changes.

Elisabeth Howard

The mix is used for consistency of tonal quality throughout the range. I teach co-ordinating and balancing the breath flow with the correct amount of vocal fold tension/stiffness, and using the colors taught in the Vocal Power Method[1] (chest, mouth, mask, and head), especially chest and nasal, to match the chest register.

Tracy Marie Bourne

I teach all of my singers to sing through all of their range. We aim for a free sound in the highest and lowest pitches, and in chest and head registers. When singing in "mix" I encourage my singers to notice the difference between the feel of chest and head registers, then we work through exercises that promote brightness (or twang) in the sound. Research on vocal fold behavior underlying vocal registers suggests that the vocal folds function in a distinct and autonomous fashion for chest (also described as laryngeal mechanism 1) and for head registers (also described as laryngeal mechanism 2).[2] When aiming for a blended sound (i.e. mix), the vocal folds may adjust, but can still be identified as either laryngeal mechanism 1 or laryngeal mechanism 2. In order to achieve a perceptually blended sound, singers learn to adjust the vocal tract so that any "break" between the laryngeal mechanisms is disguised. In a study I did with Dr Maëva Garnier of three female music theatre singers producing music theatre vocal qualities, we found that the singers each had different strategies to produce the mix sound in the middle of their range.[3]

Robert Edwin

As part of the Phonation/registration component of the "*tions*" (pronounced "shuns") singing system, both my male and female students work to execute smooth mode 1 and 2 register transitions (*passaggi*) to be able have a co-ordinated and seamless sound when needed.

I teach resonation (amplifying and filtering the sound source using the three flexible resonators) as part of the "*tions*" singing system. Resonation exercises show my students the almost unlimited tonal colors possible in the human voice. Since our three flexible resonators (throat-mouth-nose) can change shape, my students journey from nasality to throaty, from brassy belt to "pear-shaped" classical, from high *chiaro* to low *oscuro* vowel and consonant modification, and everything in between. They find the sounds that fit many different styles and genres, and use them in both vocalises and repertoire. My music theatre students really appreciate the variety of sounds they can make, which increases their chances for

---

1   More information on the colors taught in the Vocal Power Method may be found in Elisabeth Howard, *Sing! The Vocal Power Method* (New York: Alfred Music, 2006).

2   Bernard Roubeau, Nathalie Henrich, and Michele Castellengo, "Laryngeal vibratory mechanisms: The notion of register revisited," *Journal of Voice* 23, no. 4 (July 2009), 425–438, doi.org/10.1016/j.jvoice.2007.10.014.

3   Tracy Bourne and Maëva Garnier, "Physiological and acoustic considerations of the female music theater voice," *The Journal of the Acoustical Society of America* 131, no. 2 (February 2012), 1586–1594, doi.org/10.1121/1.3675010.

employment. Even my specialists in opera, pop, rock, folk, R&B, and jazz come to realize that working the whole voice creates balance and vocal health in their singing systems. I like to call it a complete workout in the vocal gym.

Marci Rosenberg

Semi-Occluded Vocal Tract (SOVT) exercises are wonderful for developing consistency throughout the range. There are many variations of SOVTs, from straw phonation in water to cup phonation and many more. I also find glides to be very useful here too. Consistency throughout the vocal range stems from having a balanced instrument. In order to maintain consistency, the singer must maintain a balanced instrument. This includes effective warm up and cool down, and regular vocal balancing.

Mark Baxter

Developing consistency throughout the range is the bedrock of my approach. I establish objective, observable targets with students before they vocalize. I am constantly re-focusing their behavior by asking "What pitch, what volume, what timbre and what duration or rhythm are you asking for?" Brains develop better co-ordination when focused on intentional targets.

Cate Frazier-Neely

Developing consistency throughout the range is addressed through breath, breath management, register co-ordination, and vocal tract adjustments and sensations, often working vowel to vowel, syllable by syllable, phrase by phrase.

Seth Riggs and Margareta Svensson Riggs

To sing consistently through the singer's full range is not unlike string instrumentalists who play their instruments by fretting and damping the strings at various lengths, thereby creating specific notes. The more the string is damped, the less of the string is vibrating and the higher the pitch.

Similarly, it can be helpful to think of the vocal cords working in the same way. As a singer goes up a scale connected, the vocal cords zip up, making the vibrating part shorter and shorter and the pitch higher and higher. When the singer is narrowing the vowels in the bridges (*passaggi*), it allows for the damping of the cords and the bridging process to complete. Again, when singing, regardless of pitch, allow your larynx to rest in the general, low area where you speak, have knowledge of the bridges, and treat them in the same manner, narrow the vowels, and use proper breath support.

Lisa Popeil

There are only two instances where I speak of consistency through the range: 1) evenness in registration between chest and head voice and 2) the ability to maintain a legato line in any style by connecting vowels and continuing to "blow" steady air through the phrase, even if one is running out of air.

Wendy DeLeo LeBorgne

Jazz and country artists might not want consistency through the range. For those that do, I work on balancing bottom up and top down, depending on where the student is starting. Most of my artists these days tend to have a bottom-heavy dominance in their voice. We work a lot from top down to keep it balanced. I encourage a lot of cross-training from head voice to chest voice so that the mix becomes even. The student comes to understand what a top down note feels like and what a bottom up note feels like, in the same pitch range which provides them with options for singing the same note with several different vocal effort levels.

Kimberly Steinhauer

A tenet of Estill Voice Training® is to be consistent or inconsistent through the range of your choice.[4]

Cathrine Sadolin

In CVT, within each vocal mode (Neutral, Edge, Overdrive, and Curbing[5]), the sound should be consistent through the range. Some modes are limited by range, such as Overdrive. It's not physiologically possible to take Overdrive very high in the range. If we say that "throughout the range", that means two or so octaves of useable sound. Trouble with consistency often comes with changing modes. If you don't want to change the sound, keep the mode the same. To teach a yodel, I would teach a conscious and abrupt change of mode between Overdrive and Neutral. When you know the modes, then you can learn technically to yodel in 10 minutes.

Jeannette LoVetri

Depending upon the age and background of the singer, expanded range is a desirable goal towards efficient vocal function in healthy singing. Pop vocalists, however, do not have to have the same kind of consistency of vocal production as do classical or music theatre vocalists. Equalization of vowel sound characteristics is an ingredient of classical vocal training, but CCM makes no such demands. Therefore, consistency in someone's range depends on a number of things. The goal is to teach someone to have a full, free, unfettered vocal instrument and then to offer the option of training towards the style or styles the vocalist wishes to sing. With that in mind, the amount of consistency can vary from just a bit to quite a lot.

Kathryn Paradise

If a student's registration is "well organized" and his/her vowels are relatively stable, consistency of range is typically present. This can be worked on directly with wide ranging exercises when necessary. I encourage my students to be able to both demonstrate unity and evenness in their voices, as well as uniqueness and variety, depending on the musical situation. Typically, consistency and function are the focus of voice exercises while intentional variation is a focus of the repertoire work.

---

4   More information may be found in Kimberly Steinhauer, Mary McDonald Klimek, and Jo Estill, *The Estill Voice Model: Theory and Translation* (Pittsburgh: Estill Voice International, 2018).

5   More information on the vocal modes in Complete Vocal Technique may be found at completevocal.institute/complete-vocal-technique/, or within the CVT app.

Marcelle G. Gauvin

Traditional vocal pedagogy would certainly state that consistency through the range is imperative for a well-trained voice and I am in complete agreement. If I am training singers who plan on having versatile careers, an instrument that exhibits connection and continuity in registration, vowel, and resonance throughout its range will certainly increase their chances for success. The exception to this, however, is the vocal stylist. This singer actually develops a signature sound by working around these range inconsistencies in a unique way. As long as the voice production is healthy, I feel it is my obligation to preserve these idiosyncrasies if they contribute to the singer's artistic identity. As a rule, however, I will attempt to guide the singer into a more consistent co-ordination with the understanding that we are merely exploring options, not correcting a fault.

Trineice Robinson-Martin

For CCM styles in general, the voice should be trained to maintain a speech or spoken quality throughout registration. However, the voice should maintain the ability to change vocal textures at will for stylistic purposes. While having a seamless voice (or the ability to maintain one vocal texture) from the bottom of a singer's range to the top has its benefits, not being able to change textures has its limitation. It is the difference between having an extensive color palette of all pastel colors, versus having a color palette that has primary colors, pastels, and neon colors. Having choices would be the ideal training, and most importantly, consistency in terms of stability and dependability of notes throughout a singer's range is a primary goal. In gospel and soul singing, a chest-dominant sound is used throughout the range. However, one often finds instances in which a singer will want to intentionally flip into a head-dominant sound to enhance a stylistic effect.

Edrie Means Weekly

I work with each singer to isolate the primary registers with various exercises and then to blend the registers using glides and semi-occluded vocal tract exercises to smooth transitions. Those who struggle through the "break" I encourage to take their time going through the transition and accept the instability while letting go of their fear. I work with them on blending that specific area of their voice. I have the singer glide, carrying the lower register higher than usual and then descending, bringing the upper register lower than usual.

Next, we work on transitioning in and out of chest and head register. This is done by asking the singer to transition a bit earlier than they normally would using a heavier or lighter quality. Together we explore the transition and take the time it needs to smooth out and stabilize.

Sometimes certain styles such as bluegrass, country, gospel, pop, R&B, will use breaks in the voice. These types of flips or yodels are important to the authenticity of the style and cannot be left out. In order to assure the singer is true to the needs of the style, we work with these stylistic nuances while working on blending the registers. I believe that consistency, flexibility, and balance throughout the range is important. I also consider pitch accuracy, being in the center of the pitch, to be part of training consistency. I train singers to be consistent in pitch, volume, and effort throughout the range.

Gillyanne Kayes

Consistency throughout the range is not really a requirement in CCM singing, although in Musical Theatre singing, a more consistent tonal quality may be required. Flexibility of range is far more important than consistency, i.e., being able to move between regions of range with ease. I train both to preserve and disguise the transition between M1 and M2 because I work with different genre types in my studio. I do think that ability to smooth across the M1/M2 transition is a useful skill and many of my singers will need it; especially the women. For men it's less important in CCM genres at least. I never use the term "break" as it carries a pejorative. I talk about "transition/shift/gear-change/hand-over", or any of these.

Mary Saunders Barton

For musical theatre and CCM styles, tonal variety is the spice of life. A single measure of music might invite a number of register/resonance balances dictated by the lyric.

The "mixed voice" of musical theatre singers allows sopranos to be mezzos and baritones to be tenors. The goal is to bridge all transitions seamlessly, creating a continuum by balancing the action of the thyroarytenoid and cricothyroid muscles so the voice has equivalent power in all ranges.

Technological advances in acoustic enhancement allow musical theatre and CCM performers more dynamic latitude, and can help protect them from blowing out their voices when singing in loud environments.

Matthew Edwards

In a lot of commercial styles, consistency is not desirable. In fact, if you have a student who likes the breaks in their voice, you can do more harm than good by trying to eliminate the break. If the motor system gets fine-tuned for consistency, it can be very difficult for the singer to go back to a raw approach to registration shifts. That is in part why I do not work on classical vocal literature with commercial or musical theatre singers.

When working with a student who is locked into a consistent sound, I spend a lot of time with onset and release exercises, vowel morphing, and riffing. I will have them do a lot of active listening exercises as well. My favorite is to have them get a lead sheet for a song that has been covered by multiple artists. I have them sit down with a pack of colored pencils and create their own notation system for the style tags each artist uses in their interpretation. After the student has notated each artist's interpretation, I have them imitate the different renditions to get the style tags into their voice. Then I have them go through and pick and choose which style tags they want to keep for their own performance. The process usually opens the student's eyes to how small differences can have a huge impact on the delivery of a song. By getting them to experiment and think outside of the box, they let go and have more fun.

In musical theatre, students must learn to sing consistently and then learn how to break the rules to imitate pop/rock styles. This is not an easy task. I like to begin with speech-like songs and work on getting the articulators free while helping the student understand registration. When they are doing well with their speech-like songs, I begin moving them towards contemporary ballads and then eventually Golden-Age ballads. My philosophy is that it is easiest for the motor system to learn new patterns if we begin with sounds that are similar to what they use in everyday speech. As the body adapts to singing, it is easier to refine their speech and give their vowels additional acoustic energy for older styles of musical theatre. As we work on refining, I also jump back and forth between pop/rock tunes to keep them from getting locked into any singular vocal quality.

Dane Chalfin

I want to work every singer in the widest variety of gestures I can get them in, through as much of their range as I can keep them in the gesture. This is the ultimate flexibility. The idea of one sound from top to bottom is so limiting. This is like having one color in your crayon box. It is boring, and you are not going to get a gig singing like that. I want to hear every sound working throughout as much of the range as possible.

Irene Bartlett

As CCM singers are expected to sound vocally genuine (that is, true to their spoken voice qualities), consistency of tone or timbre is not a consideration for either the singer or their audience. I believe that any technical work must be appropriate to the singer's vocal range, voice weight, stamina, and tessitura, whilst also addressing the specific elements/effects inherent in any given CCM style. The exception to this rule is in the performance of *legit* repertoire for music theatre performance where consistency throughout the singer's range *is* style-relevant.

Jan Shapiro

The idea is to sing freely throughout your vocal range. Please see my response under "registration".

Jeff Ramsey

I address (in)consistency as part of registration. Please see my response under "Registration".

References and recommended reading

Blyskal, Elena. "The female *primo passaggio*: A survey of its physiology, psychology, and pedagogy." *Journal of Singing* 69, no. 1 (September/October 2012): 11–19.

Bourne, Tracy and Dianna Kenny. "Vocal qualities in music theater voice: Perceptions of expert pedagogues." *Journal of Voice* 30, no. 1 (January 2016): 128.e1–128.e12. doi.org/10.1016/j.jvoice.2015.03.008.

Bourne, Tracy and Maëva Garnier. "Physiological and acoustic considerations of the female music theater voice." *The Journal of the Acoustical Society of America* 131, no. 2 (February 2012): 1586–1594. doi.org/10.1121/1.3675010.

Bourne, Tracy, Maëva Garnier, and Adeline Samson. "Physiological and acoustic characteristics of the male music theatre voice." *The Journal of the Acoustical Society of America* 140, no. 1 (July 2016): 610–621. doi.org/10.1121/1.4954751.

Bourne, Tracy, Maeva Garnier, and Diana Kenny. "Music Theater Voice: Production, Physiology and Pedagogy." *Journal of Singing* 67, no. 4 (March/April 2011): 437–444.

Bozeman, Kenneth Wood. "Acoustic *passaggio* pedagogy for the male voice." *Logopedics Phoniatrics Vocology* 38, no. 2 (July 2013): 64–69. doi.org/10.3109/1401439.2012.679967.

Duncan, Kate. "The plain cookie: Overcoming the myth of the female vocal 'break.'" In *The Voice Teacher's Cookbook: Creative Recipes for Teachers of Singing* edited by Brian J. Winnie, 31–32. Delray Beach, FL: Meredith Music, 2018.

Echternach, Matthias, Johan Sundberg, Susan Arndt, Michael Markl, Martin Schumacher, and Bernhard Richter. "Vocal tract in female registers: A dynamic real-time MRI study." *Journal of Voice* 24, no. 2 (March 2010): 133–139. doi.org/10.1016/j.jvoice.2008.06.004.

Frizzell, J.D. "Transitioning from dinner to dessert: *Passaggio* in contemporary singing." In *The Voice Teacher's Cookbook: Creative Recipes for Teachers of Singing* edited by Brian J. Winnie, 46–47. Delray Beach, FL: Meredith Music, 2018.

Henrich, Nathalie, Christophe D'Allessandro, Boris Doval, and Michele Castellengo. "Glottal open quotient in singing: Measurements and correlation with laryngeal mechanisms, vocal intensity, and fundamental frequency." *The Journal of the Acoustical Society of America* 117, no. 3 (March 2005): 1417–1430. doi.org/10.1121/1.1850031.

Herbst, Christian T. and Jan G. Svec. "Adjustment of glottal configurations in singing." *Journal of Singing* 70, no. 3 (January/February 2014): 301–308.

Hollien, Harry. "Vocal fold dynamics for frequency change." *Journal of Voice* 28, no. 4 (July 2014): 395–405. doi.org/10.1016/j.jvoice.2013.12.005.

Howard, Elisabeth. *Sing! The Vocal Power Method.* New York: Alfred Music, 2006.

Kochis-Jennings, Karen Ann, Eileen M. Finnegan, Henry T. Hoffman, Sanyukta Jaiswal. "Laryngeal muscle activity and vocal fold adduction during chest, chestmix, headmix, and head registers in females." *Journal of Voice* 26, no. 2, (March 2012): 182–193. doi.org/10.1016/j.jvoice.2010.11.002.

Kochis-Jennings, Karen Ann, Eileen M. Finnegan, Henry T. Hoffman, Sanyukta Jaiswal, and Darcey Hull. "Cricothyroid muscle and thyroarytenoid muscle dominance in vocal register control: Preliminary results." *Journal of Voice* 28, no. 5 (September 2014): 652.e21–652.e29. doi.org/10.1016/j.jvoice.2014.01.017.

LoVetri, Jeannette, Susan Lesh, and Peak Woo. "Preliminary study on the ability of trained singers to control the intrinsic and extrinsic laryngeal musculature." *Journal of Voice* 13, no. 2 (June 1999): 219–226. doi.org/10.1016/S0892-1997(99)80024-1.

Means Weekly, Edrie. "Hearty country jam with vocal stylisms." In *The Voice Teacher's Cookbook: Creative Recipes for Teachers of Singing* edited by Brian J. Winnie, 127–129. Delray Beach, FL: Meredith Music, 2018.

Miller, Donald G. and Harm K. Schutte. "Mixing" the registers: glottal source or vocal tract? *Folia Phoniatrica et Logopaedica* 57 (2005): 278–291. doi.org/10.1159/000087081.

Miller, Donald G., Jan G. Svec, and Harm K. Schutte. "Measurement of characteristic leap interval between chest and falsetto registers." *Journal of Voice* 16, no. 1 (March 2002): 8–19. doi.org/10.1016/S0892-1997(02)00066-8.

Neumann, Katrin, Patrick Schunda, Sebastian Hoth, and Harald A. Euler. "The interplay between glottis and vocal tract during the male passaggio." *Folia Phoniatrica et Logopaedica* 57 (2005): 308–327. doi.org/10.1159/000087084.

Patel, Sona, Anjli Lodhavia, Saul Frankford, Oleg Korzyukov, and Charles R. Larson. "Vocal and neural responses to unexpected changes in voice pitch auditory feedback during register transitions." *Journal of Voice* 30, no. 6 (November 2016): 772.e33–772.e40. doi.org/10.1016/j.jvoice.2015.11.012.

Roubeau, Bernard, Nathalie Henrich, and Michele Castellengo. "Laryngeal vibratory mechanisms: The notion of register revisited." *Journal of Voice* 23, no. 4 (July 2009): 425–438, doi.org/10.1016/j.jvoice.2007.10.014.

Sadolin, Cathrine. *Complete Vocal Technique Application*: completevocal.institute/app/.

Schutte, Harm K. and Donald G. Miller. "Belting and pop, nonclassical approaches to the female middle voice: Some preliminary considerations." *Journal of Voice* 7, no. 2 (June 1993): 142–150. doi.org/10.1016/S0892-1997(05)80344-3.

Spivey, Norman and Mary Saunders Barton. *Cross-Training in the Voice Studio: A Balancing Act.* San Diego: Plural Publishing, 2018.

Steinhauer, Kimberly, Mary McDonald Klimek, and Jo Estill, *The Estill Voice Model: Theory and Translation.* Pittsburgh: Estill Voice International, 2018.

Steinhauer, Kimberly. "Everything is a mix: It depends on your recipe!" In *The Voice Teacher's Cookbook: Creative Recipes for Teachers of Singing* edited by Brian J. Winnie, 116–118. Delray Beach, FL: Meredith Music, 2018.

Thalen, Margareta and Johan Sundberg. "Describing different styles of singing: A comparison of a female singer's voice source in 'Classical,' 'Pop,' 'Jazz,' and 'Blues.'" *Logopedics Phoniatrics Vocology* 26, no. 2 (2001): 82–93. doi.org/10.1080/140154301753207458.

Thuesen, Mathias Aaen, Julian McGlashan, and Cathrine Sadolin. "Investigating laryngeal 'Tilt' on same-pitch phonation: Preliminary findings of vocal mode metal and density parameters as alternatives to cricothyroid-thyroarytenoid 'Mix.'" *Journal of Voice*, in press. doi.org/10.1016/j.jvoice.2018.02.023.

Titze, Ingo R. "Mixed registration." *Journal of Singing* 75, no. 1 (September/October 2018): 49–50.

Titze, Ingo R. "Bi-stable vocal fold adduction: A mechanism of modal-falsetto register shifts and mixed registration." *The Journal of the Acoustical Society of America* 135, no. 4 (2014): 2091–2101. http://www.doi.org/10.1121/1.4868355.

12

Belt

Belting is perhaps the most controversial topic in the field of voice pedagogy, yet it is also one of the most thoroughly investigated and discussed. For some classical pedagogues, belt is a proverbial four-letter word. The warning was, "If you belt, you will ruin your voice". There are countless lifelong careers which dispel this myth, including Aretha Franklin, Stevie Wonder, Idina Menzel, Barbra Streisand, Liza Minelli, and so many more. Tastes have changed in popular music, and belting is now a requirement for all voice types in musical theatre. Some voices are built for it. Others have to learn how to do it.

In *The Vocal Athlete*, LeBorgne and Rosenberg present a chapter[1] on the pioneers of belting pedagogy: Jo Estill, Jan Sullivan, Larra Henderson, Jeannette LoVetri, Robert Edwin, Seth Riggs, Lisa Popeil, and Mary Saunders Barton. Among these perspectives, the definition of belt varies widely. Sullivan asserts that belting is not the same as chest voice but is related to speech.[2] Henderson argues that belting is a mix of chest and head voice with a frontal focused tone.[3] Edwin explains that belting is chest-voice-dominant vocal quality but is not the same as chest voice.[4] Popeil maintains that belting is speech-like or yell-like, but there are many different kinds of belting (heavy, ringy, brassy, nasal, and speech-like).[5] These definitions are brief, but also contradictory. It is clear that no two pedagogues agree, even among the few pioneers. LeBorgne and Rosenberg note that within the pioneering generation, CCM pedagogy relies on "conventional wisdom and empirical observation combined with the research that does exist" which must be perpetually refined.[6] As more research has been conducted and more pedagogues have joined the pioneers in developing approaches to teach belting, more refinement has occurred. After gathering data for this text, there are still many different points of view, but there are a number of elements upon which a majority of pedagogues agree.

When asked to describe their approach to belting, 88% of pedagogues reported that they use the term "belt", and 76% of pedagogues provided a definition of belting. As expected, these definitions varied widely, and some contained contradictory descriptions. Within the narrative of their responses ($n = 17$), 94% of pedagogues indicated that belting is more than

---

1   Wendy D. LeBorgne and Marci Rosenberg, "Belting pedagogy: An overview of perspectives," in *The Vocal Athlete* (San Diego: Plural Publishing, 2014), 217–226.

2   Ibid., 219-221 and in Jan Sullivan, "How to teach the belt/pop voice," *Journal of Research in Singing and Applied Vocal Pedagogy* 13, no. 1 (1989), 41–56.

3   Ibid., 221 and in Laura Browning Henderson, *How to Train Singers*, 2nd ed. (West Nyack, NY: Parker Publishing, 1991).

4   Ibid., 222-223 and in Robert Edwin, "Belting 101. Part 1," *Journal of Singing* 55, no. 1 (September/October 1998), 53–55 and "Belting 101. Part 2," *Journal of Singing* 55, no. 2 (November/December 1998), 61–62.

5   Ibid., 223-224 and in Lisa Popeil, "The Multiplicity of Belting," *Journal of Singing* 64, no. 1 (September/October 2007), 77–80.

6   Ibid., 225.

one sound. With more than one kind of belting identified by 94% of responses, the search for a singular definition of "belt" is more futile than ever. However, the most common defining characteristics used to describe belt are summarized in the chart below. According to these data, a definition of belting with the highest level of pedagogical consensus is a loud, speech-like, intense sound that is carried into the high range, and is registrationally both full chest voice/mechanism 1 *and* chest-dominant mix. While this definition contains an apparent contradiction (how can registration be both full chest and chest-dominant mix?), the answers below support more nuanced definitions containing pitch parameters. In these responses, "belt" registration is defined as full chest/mechanism 1 up to a maximum high point in the range (around F4 for men and C5 for women). Beyond that point, belt is registrationally defined as a chest-dominant mix.

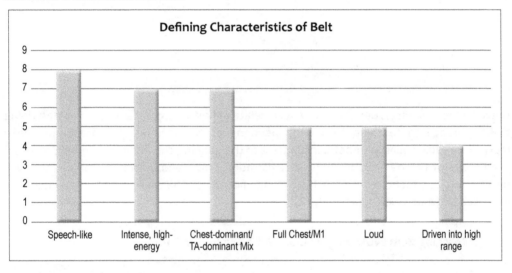

The data indicate that there is some consensus on some defining characteristics of belting:
- 94% believe that belting is not just one sound, but many different sounds within a particular aesthetic.
- 79% believe that "belt" is not interchangeable with "mix" (the term "mix" should not be confused with "chest-dominant mix" which is supported by other data below).
- 64% believe that belting is always loud.
- 53% believe that belting is a registrational event (as opposed to voice quality/vocal tract shaping).
- 40% believe that belting is speech-like.
- 35% believe that belting is intense, high-energy, passionate, or exciting.
- 35% believe that belting involves "chest-dominant/TA-dominant/M1-dominant mix."

Further analysis of the responses that include a definition of belting reveal three primary points of view on the definition of belting: it is either a registrational activity (vocal fold behavior), a voice quality (vocal tract behavior), or both. Most of the pedagogues ($n = 19$) respond to this question, revealing a majority (53%) that views belting as a registrational activity. A minority (21%) view it as a voice quality or activity defined by vocal tract shaping. Five pedagogues (26%) view belting as *both* a registrational event and a voice quality (vocal tract shaping event), and this group includes both pioneers and newer teachers.

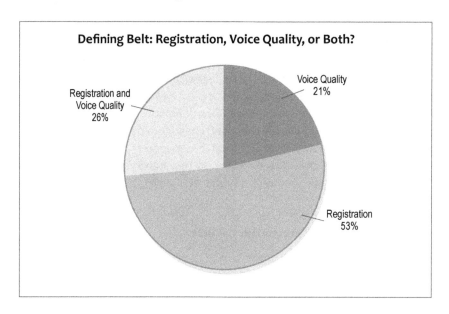

However, how belting is defined does not correlate to how belting is taught. When describing their approach to teaching belting, 13 pedagogues reported using prompts to evoke registration, voice quality, or both. In contrast to the defining characteristics of belt, an equal percentage of teachers reported using registration (46%), and *both* registration and voice quality (46%), as tactics to train belting. A significantly smaller percentage of teachers use exercises to evoke voice quality only (8%).

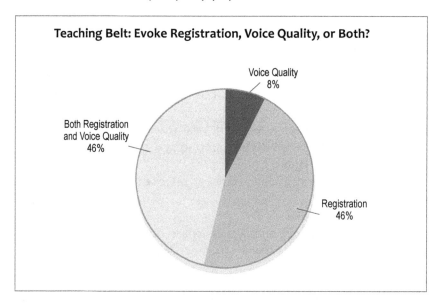

When asked to describe how they teach belting, 48% of pedagogues provided details on their approach. Specific registrational-strengthening or voice-quality evocation tactics were revealed. The most common strategies for teaching belt are summarized in the chart below.

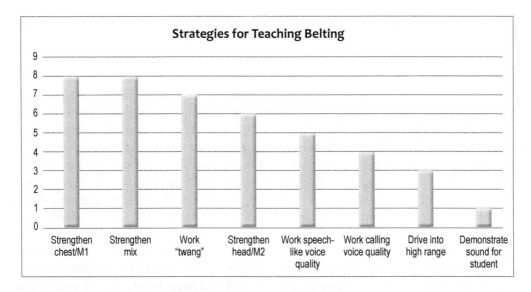

The data indicate that there is some consensus on some approaches to teaching belt:
- 67% of pedagogues work to strengthen chest voice/M1 singing.
- 67% of the pedagogues work to strengthen some type of "mix".
- 58% of the pedagogues work on "twang".[7]
- 50% of the pedagogues work to strengthen head voice/M2 singing.
- 42% work on a speech-like voice quality.

Some teachers do not use the word "belting" at all (*n* = 3), mostly due to its highly variable definition. Precautions are offered in many of the responses (69%). The two most common warnings are: to be mindful of excess tension; and to avoid hyper-functional pressing of the vocal folds during belting. Several responses emphasize that the goal is an easy, efficient, and flexible sound.

Further study of how belting is being taught is certainly called for. The data presented here were processed from open-ended responses to a single prompt, and they may not represent the pedagogues' comprehensive views on belting. A survey format would yield more consistent and concrete results. However, these data provide a preliminary indication of some consensus on several defining and practical elements of training belting. This text celebrates and applauds the many different approaches to CCM singing pedagogy. The goal is not to determine which approach is best but rather, to shed light on the many possible approaches, and to guide readers to explore specific elements of these varied approaches. Readers are also encouraged to dive into the plethora of research published on the topics of belting science and pedagogy, some of which are listed at the end of this chapter.

This chapter includes responses to the prompt "Please describe your approach to teaching belting". Responses are presented in a loose order from those who do not use the term

---

7   In this instance, "twang" refers to aryepiglottic (or epilarynx) narrowing, which often results in a strengthened singer's formant. More information on "twang" may be found in Johan Sundberg and Margareta Thalén, "What is twang?" *Journal of Voice* 24, no. 6 (November 2010), 654–660, doi.org/10.1016/j.jvoice.2009.03.003, Ingo R. Titze, Christine C. Bergan, Eric Hunter, and Brad Story, "Source and filter adjustments affecting the perception of the vocal qualities twang and yawn," *Logopedics Phoniatrics Vocology* 28, no. 4 (December 2003), 147–155, and Eiji Yanagisawa, Jo Estill, Steven T. Kmucha, and Steven B. Leder, "The contribution of aryepiglottic constriction to 'ringing' voice quality: A videolaryngoscopic study with acoustic analysis," *Journal of Voice* 3, no. 4 (December 1989), 342–350, doi.org/10.1016/S0892-1997(89)80057-8.

"belting", followed by those who do use the term, and end with those who provide detailed pedagogical strategies.

Cathrine Sadolin

"Belting" is also one of those words where the meaning has been polluted. Everyone has a different definition of this sound. We do not talk about belting in Complete Vocal Technique, as it would cover many different sounds and vocal modes: Neutral, Curbing, Overdrive, and Edge. We have to identify which kind of belting sound we are talking about or choose a different language. In an article published in 2017, we used Overdrive and Edge as refiners of the concept of "belting" through measuring audio perception, laryngostroboscopic imaging, acoustics, long-term average spectrum (LTAS), and electroglottography (EGG).[8] We have defined each term so that everyone knows what we are talking about, both practically, and scientifically.

To teach each mode, we start with the foundation of three overall principles: 1) you must have support; 2) you must have necessary twang; and 3) you should avoid protruding the jaw and tightening the lips. Observing these principles will ensure that you are singing in a healthy way. Then we choose the vocal mode and obey the rules for that mode. Next, we choose the desired sound color on a spectrum of light to dark. If desired, we then choose the effect such as distortion or ornamentation. We work with a student to arrange the vocal tract in the best way, have them make the sound, then check to see if they are happy with the sound. Then we have them repeat it many times and correct them according to the desired sound and according to how it feels to the singer. If it's not comfortable, then something is wrong. We continue to adjust until the singer is absolutely satisfied with the sound itself and the ease of production. We have the singer describe exactly what they are doing, how it feels and how it sounds so that they can reproduce the sound when they get back home.

Kathryn Paradise

People often use the term "belt" when they are referring to a chest-dominant mix or speech-like/calling out quality used in a high range. In popular music, chest-mix is a more appropriate term because this part of the range needs to be flexible in its timbre and use. Additionally, to me, belting implies a chest-dominant sound that is solely reliant on the muscular function in the vocal mechanism, rather than the acoustical perception of the vocal tone. Therefore, I try to avoid using the term belt. I have this discussion with my students, so they are aware that people mean different things when they use this word and they are prepared for how to technically produce a sound that pleases, no matter the audience, producer, or circumstance.

Mark Baxter

I avoid using the term "belting". For further explanation, please see my response under "Support".

---

8   McGlashan et al., "Overdrive and Edge as refiners of 'belting?' An empirical study qualifying and categorizing 'belting' based on audio perecption, laryngostroboscopic imaging, acoustics, LTAS, and EGG," *Journal of Voice* 31, no. 3 (2017), 385.e11–385e.22, doi.org/10.1016/j.jvoice.2016.09.006.

Gillyanne Kayes

I used to be influenced by the Estill approach to belting, but more recently I find that this approach is too complicated. I think that studies by the following researchers can enlighten us as to the phonatory and resonatory strategies for belting: Titze "Belting and a High Larynx Position",[9] and Lebowitz and Baken "Correlates of the belt voice: A broader examination"[10]. I also find Ken Bozeman's description of "open timbre" and "yell coupling" in *Practical Vocal Acoustics* accessible and practical.[11]

Wendy DeLeo LeBorgne

The majority of my artists are already belting at a professional level. Therefore, I'm not often training emerging belters but rather, refining an artist's current belt sound or belt choices for a given role. We talk about efficiency, when they are going to stylistically choose to use the belt, and how heavy, or light, or bright, or dark will it be in the particular song they are working on.

Jeannette LoVetri

This term refers to a kind of vocal quality found primarily in vocal music. In some styles, it refers to a kind of music written to be sung in a belt quality (a belt song), and also to someone who sings in this vocal quality – a belter. There is no other comparable word in other styles of singing. (You cannot be a *classicaler*, *classicalizing* a classical song, but you can be a *belter*, *belting* out a belt song.)

This quality can be found all over the world in many styles of music: flamenco, mariachi, African music from many countries, Middle-Eastern music, and traditional music from the Balkans. In the United States, it was found in gospel music that may have its roots in spirituals sung by slaves in the field. It can be heard in country music and in the CCM styles that were born here such as rock, R&B, and pop music. Belt has been a staple on Broadway from its earliest days in Vaudeville because the sound had to carry to the back of the theatre on human lung-power alone. Those who could make a trumpet-like sound (called brassy then and now) were able to bring an audience to its feet or its knees. Al Jolson and Ethel Merman both had strong, clear voices that easily carried in unamplified theatres and had long, important careers as belters in Vaudeville, on Broadway, on radio, in film, in theatre and later, on TV.

Rock and roll has had an increasingly important influence on vocal sound and, with the addition of louder and louder amplification, the vocal quality we typically hear has been driven to extreme proportions. Those who specialize in rock or pop belting are like athletes who specialize in a particular sport and only that sport. It is rare, if not impossible, to find a vocalist who sings extremely loud high belted notes and also does another style easily. In music theatre, many singers are expected to sing in at least three vocal qualities: chest (belt), mix and "legit", or a classical sound. The training that allows for such "crossover" is specific and unique. In no other genre is such specific vocal production expected or required. The vocalists who do such crossover singing (generally) do not also specialize in high belting.

---

9   Ingo Titze, "Belting and a high larynx position," *Journal of Singing* 63, no. 5 (May/June 2007), 557–558.

10   Amy Lebowitz and R.J. Baken, "Correlates of the belt voice: A broader examination," *Journal of Voice* 25, no. 2 (March 2011),159–165, doi.org/10.1016/j.jvoice.2009.10.014.

11   Kenneth W. Bozeman, *Practical Vocal Acoustics: Pedagogic Applications for Teachers and Singers* (Hillsdale: Pendragon Press, 2013), 20–31.

Cate Frazier-Neely

There are as many varieties of belting as there are singers, which Lisa Popeil calls a "multiplicity of belting".[12] It comes out of very deep emotional expression and cannot be taken separately from the environment and culture in which a singer grows. Belting effectively is dependent on a person's anatomical structure, personality, and tonal perception. It can be developed but it takes time and patience.

We used to have "record development deals" where a record company would invest a few years in developing a promising singer before launching them. We don't have that anymore, but the development is still needed to do the work.

We need to be on "pressed vocalization alert" due to a fine line between belting and hyperfunction of throat muscles which can cause fold dysfunction or muscle tension dysphonia. High-level belting increases tension on the vocalis muscle, so part of my work is guiding singers towards how and when to use a lighter vocal mechanism. This gets down to specific pages of a score or parts of a song, phrases, words, and even single pitches and syllables. It's called "making music".

The Art of Pacing is lost on some teachers and coaches, and this is why I think it is important for teachers of CCM to have experience touring as a singer in pop or rock, or performing lead roles on stage, outside of academia, in less than ideal conditions. One has to be taught, and then experience, how to snatch areas of rest and re-balance within performing. Great belters display variation when singing all the time, not only because it is musical and expressive, but because it re-balances the registration in wise ways.

Mary Saunders Barton

The *can belto* part of this approach continues to be fraught with misunderstanding, possibly stemming from the word itself, with synonyms like slamming, bashing, battering, and bludgeoning. It is no wonder teachers recoil from such an image. My own evolving definition is gender-neutral and range-specific. In a speech(TA-, mechanism 1-)-dominant mix above the F4 *passaggio* for both men and women, it is possible to create a floated "call". This "belt" color can occur on open vowels (such as [a] as in "hot" (in American speech), [ɛ] as in "met," or [æ] as in "hat") as an optional resonance in that G4 to D5 range, co-ordinating treble and bass. The resonance is mixed so it carries dynamic flexibility. It is not always loud. If it is only possible to sing loudly, then it is not technically well produced or healthy. Think of the remarkably sweet belt sound Barbra Streisand was able to make back in the 70s in a song like "People" from *Funny Girl*.

The laryngeal height in musical theatre is variable. For the middle voice belt, it is at a comfortable speaking level. The mouth is "biting an apple". The tongue is high and forward. This is the posture of a spoken call.

In my experience, it is possible for women to carry an open belt or call as high as D5 before it closes back into a speech mix and converges with the closed vowels ([i] as in "meet" and [u] as in "you") in the high mixed belt of Elphaba's witches' siren "defying gravity" from *Wicked*.

Obviously, for men, the belt quality is in a considerably higher part of their range relatively, although the pitches are the same (above the F4 *passaggio*) but I am hearing some phenomenal mixed singing these days and there is no telling what technical feats we will be hearing in the future from male singers.

---

12 Lisa Popeil, "The Multiplicity of Belting," *Journal of Singing* 64, no. 1 (September/October 2007), 77–80.

Trineice Robinson-Martin

I think of belting as more of a quality than a registration. There are many types of belt qualities, as belt sound merely exaggerates the sound of loud, passionate, energized speech. Just as there are variations found in the quality of a person's speaking voice – which can vary based on voice type, regional dialects, and cultural influences – there are also varying qualities of belt found in singing styles. In its most general sense, a belt quality can be described as loud, brassy, edgy, and sometimes perceived as twangy (very bright and forward, almost nasal in quality). These textures are perceived as "belt" when executed above the *primo passaggio* at E4 and in response to emotionally charged musical contexts.

Physiologically speaking, a belt quality maintains a chest-dominant registration between E4 and D5/Eb5 (i.e., "chest belt"), and gradually releases towards a more head-dominant registration above C5 while still maintaining a bright, edgy, high-powered, speech-quality sound. The belt quality above Eb5 is usually maintained using head/falsetto-dominant registration with the mouth and tongue positioned to exaggerate a bright, whinny, speech-quality sound. I refer to this as a "top-down belt" because while it more effectively maintains a belt quality when used above Eb5, below Eb5 it must employ more chest voice in order to maintain edge and fullness.

Teaching belt comprises conditioning the voice to maintain consistency through the range. Please see my response under "(In)Consistency".

Lisa Popeil

Traditionally, belting has been a word that described loud, resonant, high-pitched chest voice singing, primarily used by females in musical theatre. The term has also been used to describe similar vocal sounds in other genres such as gospel or rock. Interestingly, belting can be used to describe both a style *and* a technique. As a teacher, I am most interested in the "how" of belting, what are the techniques. Frankly, over time, I have had to believe in a broader definition of what belting is. Though I concede that the traditional definition (loud, high, nasal) is still the most widely accepted, there has been, for at least a decade, an ever-continuing increase in the use of rock and pop music in contemporary musical theatre. I believe this increase has expanded the palette of vocal colors singers can utilize, thereby requiring an update on the traditional view of what belting should sound like.

With this in mind, as a pedagogue, I define "belting" to mean any high-pitched chest voice singing. Though belting is usually loud and nasal, it can now include other sounds which are heard as an extension of one's speaking voice.

I believe that equating belting with nasality diminishes the possible colors available to a singing actor. There are many high, chest voice sounds which may emphasize ring (2800 –3400 Hz) over nasality, and it is even possible to create a duller, less resonant sound in high chest voice. In musical theatre, the greater one's control of various resonances, the better. Resonance choices should be based on the needs of the character rather than on the limitations of the singer.

As a technique used in rock, pop, R&B, country, and gospel, belting is used frequently with each genre having its own pre-determined resonance conventions.

To raise chest voice (and again, by this term I mean any vocal sound that is based on speech or yelling), implementing certain mechanisms can provide safety, consistency, and reliability in this often-demanding vocal technique.

Here are some pointers which will help:

1. Posture is important; the chest must be held comfortably high.
2. By increasing the outward firming of the upper belly "magic spot" while singing, the vocal folds will receive increased sub-glottal pressure in the airstream, allowing them to hold a thicker edge and longer closed phase, both required for healthy chest voice production.
3. Head angle for belting; many professional singers use a "tipped up" head posture. The back of the neck should still be lengthened, and the head should still be in line with the body. But when the chin and head are tipped up slightly compared to classical singing, one can more easily implement "belter's bite".
4. In "belter's bite" the masseter muscle is more active than in classical singing. This firming action naturally protrudes the jaw and chin and allows an easier forward movement of the hyoid bone. The jaw will now be firmer, but not tense, and must be able to move quickly up and down. I call this jaw action "firm but flexible".
5. "Laryngeal Lean"; when the hyoid bone pulls forward as the pitch ascends in chest voice, it can be felt as a though the larynx is leaning forward, hence the name. Adding "lean" reduces over-lifting of the larynx and helps to produce an unpressed vocal fold sound when belting as the pitch rises.
6. A sense of breath-holding; since the closed phase is longer and speed of closure is faster in the glottal configuration of chest voice compared to head voice, the subjective sense of breath-holding while belting aids in the ease of production.
7. Vocal fold pressing must be avoided in belting. Over-squeezing of vocal fold tissue, specifically at high amplitude, increases the risk of damage to the vocal fold mucosa.

Irene Bartlett

My approach to teaching *belt* is based in my years of listening to CCM singers, my own performance experience, and my study of voice physiology and anatomy. Belt is employed to some degree by CCM singers to express heightened emotion and to produce specific vocal effects that define each individual style. Belt is an intense vocal sound pitched mostly in the singer's natural speech range. The tone can be heavy or light, but a sustainable belt has to be produced on a free breath flow not pressed phonation (excessive laryngeal muscle tension). CCM style authenticity demands speech vowels and articulated diphthongs (not Italianate vowels as in classical singing) because the shape of the word and how it is spoken is intrinsic to creating a genuine speech/conversational quality. Resonance appears to be brighter and more intense than is acceptable in classical singing styles, even to the point of sometimes seeming to be nasal, but *it should not be nasal* unless driven by regional accents or particular style effects.

I teach belt singers that it is essential to *warm-up* across their entire vocal range with exercises into the upper register to build flexibility and strength in the CT musculature. The main difficulty for CCM singers is that although Belt singing is TA-dominant, CT muscles must be trained to naturally increase activity as the voice ascends in pitch, while the TA maintains a strong antagonistic engagement to maintain mass on the vocal folds and resultant speech production. To develop this co-ordination, I suggest that students employ voice function exercises like calling out (not shouting) on commonly used words such as: Yeah, Hey, Yoo-Hoo, Yip-ee, etc.

I believe that there are "degrees" of belt. The *degree* is dependent on style elements and the singer's stage of vocal development, vocal strength, and stamina. I train my singers to belt through the development of a dynamic relationship of consistent airflow rate with glottal adduction and vocal fold lengthening, appropriate for the particular CCM style and the desired characteristic effects. I strongly encourage a connection with innate primal sound (emotion, intention, feelings) and effort levels focused primarily in the body – not in the larynx.

In short, my model for teaching belt is:
- Build a foundation of good alignment and low abdominal support.
- Employ speech quality with twang (forward resonance).
- DON'T sing with a low larynx and/or wide pharynx into the upper register.
- Set-up for speech phrasing.
- DON'T take in more air than is needed (especially before upper register notes) as Belt needs less breath volume than other style-based techniques.
- Be physical – involve the whole body – DON'T focus tension in the upper torso or the larynx.
- Adjust keys to suit your tessitura.
- DON'T try to fill the room with sound.
- Learn to use amplification.

Dane Chalfin

Belting varies depending on whom you ask and what research you look at. To an audience, all that "belting" means is loud. If you look at the Estill Model™, it is very much a yell-based setting. When you look at the acoustics, there is a really specific set of circumstances, which the pop world of vocal coaches would agree is a belt. It is like being yelled at but in a really exciting way. That mix, or crying posture, in which pop artists probably sing 70–80% of their lives, we would not consider to be "belting." When you hear Whitney Houston, sing the bridge of "Didn't We Almost Have It All" most listeners feel that they are being yelled at. If you hear Deborah Cox sing "Nobody's Supposed to Be Here" you can hear the cry in everything.

This is again why I like primal sound,[13] because if I ask someone to cry versus yell, they know exactly what that is. It is a vernacular approach which is also emotionally relevant to the text being sung. Vocal technique is only there to serve communication. The lyric and intention of the song is "King". The voice needs to match it. This is why when you hear someone sing a song which is really tough, or angry, or joyous, and they go into that light "mix", it just does not quite cut it. When I work with clients on the West End, this is the difference between getting a standing ovation and not. The real belters always get people on their feet because of the primal excitement in the sound.

We are learning about this phenomenon called parasympathetic response now. This is way above my pay grade, but what the science is telling me is that when someone makes a sound, for example, two versions of "belt", 1) a crying gesture and 2) a yelling gesture, our bodies automatically respond to those sounds on an instinctive level. The fight or flight response we have to yelling makes the audience want to jump to its feet. This is also why some of us get a lump in the throat when someone is in a crying gesture. This is fascinating to me because it takes primal sound into a whole new category of being audience-focused. This is about using the sounds to guarantee that your audience feels the way you want them to feel.

For a new belter, I would start by having them call out to me in a very non-excited way. You start with that everyday calling voice that feels really easy. It should not feel big or "overly-

---

13 More information on Primal Sound may be found at www.vocalrehabilitation.com/primal-voice-research.

supported". In nature, our everyday yelling gesture is actually a very small gesture. There is a small feeling at the level of the source, but it comes out really loud. A common pitfall in belting is when singers try to make what is loud even louder. They do not realize that the room does all the work. This is where I start with almost any sound. If the gesture we are looking for is not easily accessible, we take it back to everyday use.

If people cannot find their "mix" I ask them to do it again while whining and complaining. I demonstrate this sound for them. If they cannot find breathy singing, such as classical singers who want to switch over into pop, we imitate Keanu Reeves in *The Matrix*, or use "late-night phone voice". We play around until the singer recognizes the feeling, and then we start to assign pitch. I always do the same stuff, five-tone scales, fifth sirens, octave sirens, very simple stuff. We need to give the singer a few minutes of proprioception. Their body has to get used to how it feels. Once they can latch onto that feeling, we can get more pitch-specific and vowel-specific.

Seth Riggs and Margareta Svensson Riggs

Traditionally, "belting" is the Broadway term for singing in mainly chest voice, as opposed to "legit", which is the Broadway term for singing in mainly head voice, resembling classical singing.

Today, belting has become synonymous with the sound of musical theatre, and when done right, it is very appealing. Even in revivals of musicals from the "legit era" of the 40s, 50s, and early 60s, a belt-mix is usually the preferred choice, and the style of music gives the perception of "legit." The resembling of classical singing is replaced with a chest quality with head voice mixed in. When going up, the bridges (*passaggi*) are acknowledged as they should be in every style of singing.

In belting, just as in other music genres that resonate beginning in chest, it is vital to use mix when approaching the bridges, keeping the larynx down and allowing for the higher pitches in a healthy and attractive way. If not, belting becomes yelling in and above the first bridge, and very tiring and damaging for the vocal cords.

It might be worthwhile to mention that the way the term "belting" is used in general today, is as a specific sound within one genre of music, not a specific vocal technique. It differs from other popular music genres, where each singer's unique sound, style, and quality is what makes them the artists they are, and it is of paramount importance to not take their individuality away from them. But just like musical theatre differs from other popular music genres by not allowing for individual musical choices or improvisation, belting is a more uniform sound where the singer's personal characteristics are toned down in favor of the overall sound.

Our approach to belting technically has the same principles as our approach to all genres of music. However, the genre is a stylistic choice rather than a technical choice.

You would not for instance, refer to the singer Adele as belting, although so far she sings mainly in chest voice. However, to use the term belting to describe her singing is inappropriate as she has a characteristic sound. Belting is usually nowadays isolated to describe Broadway, or musical theatre type singing sung mainly in chest voice, where the singers' individual characteristics are not necessarily easy to tell apart. The goal for someone who wants to be regarded as "belting" is to sound like a usual Broadway belter. Any two Broadway belters may sound very similar to one another, and one belter can be replaced by another belter. In "pop" it is more desirable to sound unique with distinctive vocal characteristics; no two voices are interchangeable.

Matthew Edwards

If you want to work in musical theatre today, you must belt; it is no longer an option. The confusion seems to be around what exactly it means to belt. There is no codified definition that is universally accepted. However, I see a pattern among casting directors, agents, and pedagogues – if it is speech-like, on the chesty-side of mix, but sung only at a moderate volume, it is mix. When that same quality is louder, more exciting, and driven into the upper part of the singer's range, it is belt. The belt quality is primarily found at or above A4 in women and F4 in men. However, it is subjective. Until the 1980s, women were rarely asked to belt above D5. As microphones became common on the musical theatre stage in the 1980s, and composers began to draw inspiration from Top 40 radio, vocal range expectations increased. Today it is common for composers to ask female performers to belt up to F♯5 with some riffs reaching as high as A5.

In commercial styles, there are no standards. I think we tend to see more chest in commercial belting than in musical theatre. However, you must remember commercial artists are singing into a microphone and the signal is processed by the sound board. Adjustments to compression and equalization settings can make a voice seem chestier than it actually is. That is why I keep a microphone in my studio to help students find a healthy commercial belt that incorporates amplification.

When I am teaching a female to belt, who has never done so before, I begin by teaching her to sing like she speaks. The goal is to establish a solid speech-like mix in the middle of her range. I then begin strengthening her pure chest voice, slowly working it up to around A4. At the same time, I work on strengthening her head-mix, bringing it down to around C4. As the two extremes develop, I begin to show the student how she can blend the two in the middle. We spend time bringing the head-mix down and crescendoing into chest-mix. We then switch to beginning in chest voice and decrescendoing into chest-mix on an ascending five-note scale. I use a lot of McClosky[14] tongue twisters as I carry the chesty-mix up to help students avoid tension. The process is very individual. Everyone has different issues; some find it easy to add chest to their mix, for others it is a struggle. You also have to take into consideration the natural weight of the voice and allow the student to find their own way of belting that fits their type and the dramatic circumstances of the song they are singing. For men, the process is similar. However, most of the focus is on lightening registration around E4 to F4 and above, while modifying to brighter vowels.

Marcelle G. Gauvin

Once a student has both a well-developed chest register and a stable support system, the option to belt in a healthy manner becomes more available. Belting is defined as bringing chest voice up high and loud, so it can be quite rigorous to train and sustain. I prefer establishing a healthy blend/mix technique first before strengthening belt, to make sure the mid voice remains balanced and flexible. Then I strengthen the chest register, slowly establishing it in the lower range before carrying it up. Frequently, when done well, belt can incorporate some mix in its production. When learning to belt, it is necessary to work the upper chest range assertively. Therefore, I limit the amount of time I spend working this area of the voice and frequently switch to different vocal functions during a lesson. Because students co-ordinate

---

14   These may be found in David Blair McClosky, *Your Voice at its Best* (Boston: Little Brown and Co., 1972), 42–57.

muscle systems differently, I draw upon several different methodologies to approach this task until I find the best one for a student's body type – one that generates the desired result with efficiency and effectiveness. An important reminder to students when addressing belting is that voices are not genetically identical – some are more predisposed to carrying up vocal weight ("natural belters") than others. With proper vocal exercise, however, the ability to belt can be trained for most in a healthy way.

Marci Rosenberg

I describe belting perceptually as chest register-based, high volume singing that extends higher than the traditional chest range. There are many shades of belting from a heavy chest-dominant quality to a lighter chest mix quality. The instrument must be balanced on both ends before I address belting. I will use different approaches depending on the skill of the singer and the instrument I am working with. I tend to start from a speech-based place and will use simple conversational phrases on an arpeggio using belt-friendly vowels. Mary Saunders Barton has some nice belt-friendly phrases she uses in her *Bel Canto Can Belto* workshops. As the voice becomes more consistent, I will work it up into higher registers and start sustaining the higher part of the arpeggio. I also use glides on a 1-3-1 and 1-5-1 throughout the first *passaggio*, working on consistency and stability. It is important that the singer not muscle through the first *passaggio* and that they allow the voice to "wiggle" around as it finds the right co-ordination. Patience is key. I also carefully monitor a singer's perceived level of vocal effort throughout so that they have an internal gauge of how things should feel. Belting should not cause fatigue, hoarseness or pain. I often will use a pre- and post-singing example with the student so that they can feel and hear the difference between hyperfunctional belting and efficient belting. Going back to my earlier comment about agonist/antagonist muscle pairs, extensive work in a heavier chest register must be balanced by the working in the opposite register. This helps minimize the risk of getting vocally stuck.

Elisabeth Howard

Belting could be anywhere in the voice, but most often refers to the mid and higher ranges. For women, chest voice can go as high as a C above middle C and higher, but I would not recommend taking the full chest higher than a B-flat. This is where the mix serves its purpose in imitating chest from about a B-flat above middle C to the F or G above that. Oddly enough, I have found this the same for tenors. Mix starts at about B-flat above middle C and can go as high as the F or G above that. For baritones, the mix starts on a G or A above middle C and can also go up to an F above that. Because we are using the head voice/falsetto to access the mix, I find that the mix can go almost as high as the head/falsetto.

Here is an easy exercise for learning how to belt safely in the mix. I begin in chest register on a comfortable note and work up in half steps, gradually decreasing vocal fold stiffness as we approach the head register range but maintaining nasal resonance and some degree of chest register. On a descending arpeggio 8-5-3-1 (C-G-E-C) I use a detached arpeggio on the sound "Ow!" as if you were pinched and exclaimed, "Ow!". I use that sound because it needs to be a nasal resonance to help get the tone into the mask:

1. Descending detached "Ow! Ow! Ow! Ow!"
2. Then the same descending arpeggio sung legato on "ay" as in the word, "day". [ε]----------------[i]!". The sustaining vowel sound is the first sound in the diphthong, [εi], as in "day, way, say, may".

3. Then again legato, using four pulses of vibrato on each note on the first vowel sound of the diphthong, [ɛ]; the last note would be five pulses for a sense of ending. An advanced student can do eight pulses of vibrato on each note and the last note would be nine pulses.

I describe the feeling as "Anchor in the mask, lean into the chest", thereby achieving a mask sound that has richness. When you use the "chest lean" the larynx automatically lowers, allowing more space in the vocal tract. It's like turning a violin into a cello or a flute into a bassoon.

The term, "Belting", usually refers to middle range and high mix notes for dramatic effect. I would not consider the term low belting to be the norm, although I can see that in the maid's song "Hold On" (*The Secret Garden*) for example, she uses a full, strong low voice on "When you see a storm is coming". But I would not consider that mix, it is solid chest register. I capitalize MIX sometimes to bring attention to the fact that we use head and chest registers in combination to effect a blending of registers. It is an important word in teaching CCM.

Edrie Means Weekly

Belting is thryroarytenoid (TA) muscle-dominant, produced with high sub-glottic pressure, volume, and a longer closed phase. It is part of chest register. It is a loud, exciting, and brassy ring with high energy. It can be bright or dark depending on whether the vowel is dark or bright. The vocal folds are pressed tightly together, and the larynx is often raised. Sometimes there is no ring and the closed phase is longer. I approach belting carefully with beginners and younger voices. Singers should have a solid mix before they can belt. When they have accomplished that, we begin by adding a little more chest to their mix through various vocalizes and exercises, including speaking lower in a male voice, calling etc. I work on extending chest register through exercises that include glides. Once this becomes more stable, we move on to building stamina by sustaining the belt note and co-ordinating the abs and ribs for steady airflow and pressure. There are several exercises I use to build stamina.

Kevin Wilson

I teach both open (standard) and closed (mixed) belting to my students. I work first to develop the speech flexibility up to A4/Bb4. I work on invoking twang above that speech placement mixed or chest register. (Yes, it is called twang by science and is the result of the aryepiglottic sphincter narrowing. Not calling it what it is causes too much confusion in our community.) I work the mix belt through G5, and open standard belt to D5 in the full chest.

Kim Chandler

My belt "recipe" is:
- High level of support (i.e. gentle transversus abdominis elevation on voicing that continues steadily throughout the phrase).
- Low airflow.
- Dynamic posture.
- High energy level.
- Open chest position.
- Long neck with ears positioned over shoulders.
- Slightly elevated head position ("singing to the gallery").

- Raised soft palate.
- Wide vowels.
- Lots of "twang"(i.e. an energy-efficient acoustic boost in the higher frequency range, created in the epilarynx, that provides "cut" to the voice).
- Percussive initial consonants.

Kimberly Steinhauer

Belting is produced by crying babies, gospel singers, classical tenors, and American musical theatre singers. In Estill Voice Training®, targeted exercises using 13 anatomic structures are called Figures for Voice™. EVT operationalizes a specific Belt quality and then provides Figure options for a variety of belt qualities (mixes) in any genre of music.[15]

Jeff Ramsey

Let's face it. We know in today's contemporary singing world the use of chest voice is vital, particularly when going for a loud volume up high. This does not mean never using head voice. As a matter of fact, in order to belt well, one should have access to both chest and head voice. Working with the same method of practicing with an even volume, I have the students turn up the volume each time so that they are aware of the changes that happen, given the volume, the pitch, and the vowel, as these elements also dictate register changes. Once again, the key is to ask for the sound they want and let the vocal folds decide how it will give them it (headier mix, chestier mix, etc.).

Robert Edwin

I teach belting as part of the Phona*tion*/registra*tion* component part of the "*tions*" singing system. Belting is mechanism 1- or chest voice-dominant singing by both males and females that is much more speech-based than in classical singing. The vowels are produced in an "east-west" mouth position rather than the "north-south" position for classical and legit singing. It is usually bright, loud, and often brassy and straight-toned. I tell my students that soft belt is an oxymoron. Soft belt is a mix! We also explore the extremes of breathy and pressed phonation, both as danger zones and as occasional and usable stylistic effects.

Tracy Marie Bourne

Music theatre singers must be able to belt in a consistent and healthy manner. I teach it as a sound that is similar to speech, but on pitch. It requires a good deal of energy, and a bright sound. Research has shown that typically, this sound is produced with a high tongue and larynx and high lung pressures[16], although there appear to be exceptions in individual singers.[17] Singers tend to produce the sound with a more open mouth shape for belt than for

---

15 More information is available in Kimberly Steinhauer, Mary McDonald Klimek, and Jo Estill, *The Estill Voice Model: Theory and Translation* (Pittsburgh: Estill Voice International, 2018).

16 Van Lawrence, "Laryngological Observations on Belting," *Journal of Research in Singing* 2, (1979), 26–28. Beth Miles and Harry Hollien, "Whither belting?" *Journal of Voice* 4, no.1 (1990), 64–70, doi.org/10.1016/S0892-1997(05)80083-9.

17 Jeannette LoVetri et al., "Preliminary Study on the Ability of Trained Singers to Control the Intrinsic and Extrinsic Laryngeal Musculature," *Journal of Voice* 13, no. 2 (1999), 219–226, doi.org/10.1016/S0892-1997(99)80024-1.

classical singing,[18] and vocal folds are thicker and more adducted, with more activity in the thyro-arytenoid (vocalis) muscles than for classical singing.[19]

I generally encourage singers to make this sound with "fullness" rather than "loudness" so that they don't get too "pushy" with the sound. We use exercises such as speaking on pitch or calling over a distance to get singers comfortable with the feeling of this sound.

I have found that singers usually find the sound easily, provided they are comfortable with high energy performance. I have also found that I haven't needed to worry too much about breathing techniques for this quality, although the higher pitches usually need a relatively strong level of support. The vocal folds do not need too much air to produce a belt, and I have found that a breath that is too low can relax the vocal folds. However, if singers aim to breathe high, they may become very tense in the neck. Recent studies on breathing techniques for music theatre singing have shown that singers tend to breathe similarly for belt and "neutral" styles of singing.[20] More detail in regard to breathing patterns for belt may be found in Monika Hein's dissertation in German.[21]

Jan Shapiro

Quite a hot topic among voice teachers! To "belt" without tension is the goal. Teaching healthy belting is something that takes time and, in my view, cannot be achieved until the singer has mastered good technique. The singer needs to develop a blend of registers first and foremost. Sound production comes from good technique and breath management. There is also the element of articulation that helps to bring the voice forward and away from the throat. The most common pitfall for belting is forcing the voice to be louder than the individual voice capability. I think the strength of the belt voice comes with time.

References and recommended reading

Bestebreurtje, Martine E. and Harm K. Schutte. "Resonance strategies for the belting style: Results of a single female subject study." *Journal of Voice* 14, no. 2 (June 2000): 194–204. doi.org/10.1016/S0892-1997(00)80027-2.

Berg, Gregory. "Bel canto-can belto: teaching women to sing, musical theatre: Mary Saunders-Barton on belting and the mixed middle voice." *Journal of Singing* 67, no. 3 (January/February 2011): 373–375.

---

18 Johan Sundberg et al., "Comparisons of pharynx, source, formant, and pressure characteristics in operatic and musical theatre singing," *Journal of Voice* 7, no. 4 (December 1993), 301–310, doi.org/10.1016/S0892-1997(05)80118-3. Ingo Titze and Albert S. Worley, "Modeling source-filter interaction in belting and high-pitched operatic male singing," *The Journal of the Acoustical Society of America* 126, no. 3 (September 2009), 1530–1540, doi.org/10.1121/1.3160296.

19 Jo Estill, "Observations about the quality called belting," in *The Ninth Symposium, Care of the Professional Voice*, ed. B. Weinberg & V. Lawrence (The Juilliard School, New York City: Voice Foundation, 1980), 82–88. Johan Sundberg et al., "Comparisons of pharynx, source, formant, and pressure characteristics in operatic and musical theatre singing."
Eva Björkner et al., "Voice source differences between registers in female musical theatre singers," *Journal of Voice* 20, no. 2 (June 2006), 187–197, doi.org/10.1016/j.jvoice.2005.01.008.
Tracy Bourne and Maëva Garnier, "Physiological and acoustic considerations of the female music theater voice," *The Journal of the Acoustical Society of America* 131, no. 2 (February 2012), 1586–1594, doi.org/10.1121/1.3675010.
Tracy Bourne et al., "Physiological and acoustic characteristics of the male music theatre voice," *The Journal of the Acoustical Society of America* 140, no. 1 (July 2016): 610–621, doi.org/10.1121/1.4954751.

20 Johan Sundberg and Margareta Thalén, "Respiratory and Acoustical Differences Between Belt and Neutral Styles of Singing," *Journal of Voice* 29, no. 4 (July 2015), 418–425, doi.org/10.1016/j.jvoice.2014.09.018.

21 Monika Hein, "Die Gesangtechnik des Beltings: Eine Studie über Atemdruck, Lungenvolumen und Atembewegungen" (Ph.D. diss., Universität Hamburg, 2010), http://ediss.sub.uni-hamburg.de/volltexte/2010/4556/pdf/DissMonikaHeinBelting.pdf.

Bergan, Christine C., Ingo R. Titze, and Brad Story. "The perception of two vocal qualities in a synthesized vocal utterance: Ring and pressed voice." *Journal of Voice* 18, no. 3 (September 2004): 305–317. doi.org/10.1016/j.jvoice.2003.09.004.

Björkner, Eva, Johan Sundberg, Tom Cleveland, and Ed Stone. "Voice source differences between registers in female musical theatre singers." *Journal of Voice* 20, no. 2 (June 2006):187–197. doi.org/10.1016/j.jvoice.2005.01.008.

Björkner, Eva. "Musical theatre and opera singing—Why so different? A study of subglottal pressure, voice source, and formant frequency characteristics." *Journal of Voice* 22, no. 5 (September 2008): 533–540. doi.org/10.1016/j.jvoice.2006.12.007.

Bourne, Tracy and Maëva Garnier. "Physiological and acoustic considerations of the female music theater voice." *The Journal of the Acoustical Society of America* 131, no. 2 (February 2012): 1586–1594. doi.org/10.1121/1.3675010.

Bourne, Tracy, Maëva Garnier, and Adeline Samson. "Physiological and acoustic characteristics of the male music theatre voice." *The Journal of the Acoustical Society of America* 140, no. 1 (July 2016): 610–621. doi.org/10.1121/1.4954751.

Bourne, Tracy, Maëva Garnier, and Dianna Kenny. "Music theatre voice: Production, physiology and pedagogy." In *Perspectives on Teaching Singing: Australian Vocal Pedagogues Sing their Stories*, edited by Scott D. Harrison, 170–182. Bowen Hills, Qld.: Australian Academic Press, 2010.

Bourne, Tracy, Maëva Garnier, and Diana Kenny. "Musical theatre voice: production, physiology and pedagogy." *Journal of Singing* 67, no. 4 (March/April 2011): 437–444.

Bourne, Tracy and Dianna Kenny. "Vocal Qualities in Music Theater Voice: Perceptions of Expert Pedagogues." *Journal of Voice* 30, no. 1 (January 2016): 128.e1–128.e12. doi.org/10.1016/j.jvoice.2015.03.008.

Bozeman, Kenneth W., *Practical Vocal Acoustics: Pedagogic Applications for Teachers and Singers*. Hillsdale: Pendragon Press, 2013.

Edwards, Matthew. *So You Want to Sing Rock 'N' Roll: A Guide for Performers*. Lanham, MD: Rowman & Littlefield, 2014.

Edwin, Robert. "Apples and oranges: Belting revisited." *Journal of Singing* 57, no. 2 (November 2000): 43–44.

Edwin, Robert. "Belt yourself." *Journal of Singing* 60, no. 3 (January/February 2004): 285–288.

Edwin, Robert. "Belting 101. Part 1." *Journal of Singing* 55, no. 1 (September/October 1998): 53–55.

Edwin, Robert. "Belting 101. Part 2." *Journal of Singing* 55, no. 2 (November/December 1998): 61–62.

Edwin, Robert. "Belting: Bel canto or brutto canto?" *Journal of Singing* 59, no. 1 (September/October 2002): 67–68.

Edwin, Robert. "A broader Broadway." *Journal of Singing* 59, no. 5 (May 2003): 431–432.

Edwin, Robert. "Contemporary music theater: Louder than words." *Journal of Singing* 61, no. 3 (January 2005): 291–292.

Edwin, Robert. "Belt is legit." *Journal of Singing* 64, no. 2 (November/December 2007): 213–215.

Estill, Jo. "Belting and classic voice quality: Some physiological differences." *Medical Problems of Performing Artists*, 3 (1988): 37–43.

Estill, Jo. "Observations about the quality called belting." In *The Ninth Symposium, Care of the Professional Voice*, ed. B. Weinberg & V. Lawrence, 82–88. New York City: Voice Foundation, 1980.

Estill, Jo, O. Fujimura, M. Sawada, and K. Beechler. "Temporal perturbation and voice qualities." In *Vocal Fold Physiology: Controlling Complexity and Chaos* edited by Pamela J. Davis and Neville H. Fletcher, 237–252. Singular Publishing, 1996.

Echternach, Matthias, Lisa Popeil, Louisa Traser, Sascha Wienhausen, and Bernhard Richter. "Vocal tract shapes in different singing functions used in musical theater singing: A pilot study." *Journal of Voice* 28, no. 5 (September 2014): 653.e1–653.e7. doi.org/10.1016/j.jvoice.2014.01.011.

Fantini, Marco, Franco Fussi, Erika Crosetti, and Giovanni Succo. "Estill voice training and voice quality control in contemporary commercial singing: An exploratory study." *Logopedics Phoniatrics Vocology* 42, no. 4 (December 2017): 146–152.

Garner, Kelly K. "Cooking up popular styles and a healthy belt voice." In *The Voice Teacher's Cookbook: Creative Recipes for Teachers of Singing* edited by Brian J. Winnie, 51–52. Delray Beach, FL: Meredith Music, 2018.

Garner, Kelly K. *So You Want to Sing Country: A Guide for Performers*. Lanham, MD: Rowman & Littlefield, 2017.

Green, Kathryn. "Cross training ingredients for the female belt and classical voice." In *The Voice Teacher's Cookbook: Creative Recipes for Teachers of Singing* edited by Brian J. Winnie, 53–55. Delray Beach, FL: Meredith Music, 2018.

Green, Kathryn, Warren Freeman, Matthew Edwards, and David Meyer. "Trends in musical theatre voice: An analysis of audition requirements for singers." *Journal of Voice* 28, no. 3 (May 2014): 324–327.

Hall, Karen. *So You Want to Sing Music Theater: A Guide for Performers*. Lanham, MD: Rowman & Littlefield, 2014.

Henderson, Laura Browning. *How to Train Singers*. 2nd ed. West Nyack, NY: Parker Publishing, 1991.

Herbst, Christian T. and Jan G. Svec. "Adjustment of glottal configurations in singing." *Journal of Singing* 70, no. 3 (January/February 2014): 301–308.

Howard, David M. "Electrolaryngographically revealed aspects of the voice source in singing." *Logopedics Phoniatrics Vocology* 35, no. 2 (April 2010): 81–89. www.doi.org/10.3109/14015439.2010.482863.

Miles, Beth and Harry Hollien. "Whither belting?" *Journal of Voice* 4, no.1 (1990): 64–70. doi.org/10.1016/S0892-1997(05)80083-9.

Mindel, Valerie. *So You Want to Sing Folk Music: A Guide for Performers*. Lanham, MD: Rowman & Littlefield, 2017.

Latimerlo, Gina and Lisa Popeil. *Sing Anything: Mastering Vocal Styles*. G. Latimerlo and L. Popeil, 2012.

LeBorgne, Wendy Lynn DeLeo. "Defining the belt voice: Perceptual judgments and objective measures." (Ph.D. diss., University of Cincinnati, 2001).

LeBorgne, Wendy, Linda Lee, Joseph C. Stemple, and Heather Bush. "Perceptual findings on the Broadway belt voice." *Journal of Voice* 24, no. 6 (November 2010): 678–689. doi.org/10.1016/j.jvoice.2009.02.004.

LeBorgne, Wendy D. and Marci Rosenberg. *The Vocal Athlete*. San Diego: Plural Publishing, 2014.

Lebowitz, Amy and R.J. Baken. "Correlates of the belt voice: A broader examination." *Journal Voice* 25, no 2 (March 2011): 159–165. doi.org/10.1016/j.jvoice.2009.10.014.

Lombard, Lori E. and Kimberly M. Steinhauer. "A novel treatment for hypophonic voice: Twang therapy." *Journal of Voice* 21, no. 3 (May 2007): 294–299. doi.org/10.1016/j.jvoice.2005.12.006.

LoVetri, Jeannette, Susan Lesh, and Peak Woo. "Preliminary Study on the Ability of Trained Singers to Control the Intrinsic and Extrinsic Laryngeal Musculature." *Journal of Voice* 13, no. 2 (1999): 219–. doi.org/10.1016/S0892-1997(99)80024-1.

LoVetri, Jeannette. "Contemporary commercial music." *Journal of Voice* 22, no. 3 (May 2008): 260–262. doi.org/10.1016/j.jvoice.2006.11.002.

LoVetri, Jeannette L. and Edrie Means Weekly. "Contemporary commercial music (CCM) survey: Who's teaching what in nonclassical music." *Journal of Voice* 17, no. 2 (June 2003): 207–215. doi.org/10.1016/S0892-1997(03)00004-3.

LoVetri, Jeannette. "Contemporary commercial music: More than one way to use the vocal tract." *Journal of Singing* 58, no. 3 (January 2002): 249–52.

LoVetri, Jeannette. "Female chest voice." *Journal of Singing* 60, no. 2 (November/December 2003): 161–164.

LoVetri, Jeannette. "The confusion about belting: A personal observation." *VoicePrints Journal of the New York Singing Teachers' Association* (September/October 2012): 4–7.

Maxfield, Lynn and Brian Manternach. "Perceptual differences between novice and professional music theater singers." *Journal of Voice* 32, no. 5 (September 2018): 572–577. doi.org/10.1016/j.jvoice.2017.08.007.

McCoy, Scott. "A Classical Pedagogue Explores Belting." *Journal of Singing* 63, no. 5 (May/June 2007): 545–549.

McCoy, Scott. "Why I don't teach belting." *Journal of Singing* 70, no. 2 (November/December 2013): 181–182.

McCoy, Scott. "The old dog learns a new trick or (Why I now teach belting)." *Journal of Singing* 73, no. 1 (September/October 2016): 45–46.

McGlashan, Julian, Mathias Aaen Thuesen, and Cathrine Sadolin. "Overdrive and Edge as refiners of 'belting?' An empirical study qualifying and categorizing 'belting' based on audio perception, laryngostroboscopic imaging, acoustics, LTAS, and EGG." *Journal of Voice* 31, no. 3 (May 2017): 385.e11–385.e22. doi.org/10.1016/j.jvoice.2016.09.006.

Miller, D.G., Schutte, H.K. "Mixing" the registers: glottal source or vocal tract? *Folia Phoniatrica et Logopaedica* 57 (2005): 278–291. doi.org/10.1159/000087081.

Popeil, Lisa. "Comparing Belt and Classical Techniques Using MRU and Video Fluoroscopy." *Journal of Singing* 56, no. 2 (November/December 1999): 27–29.

Popeil, Lisa. "The Multiplicity of Belting." *Journal of Singing* 64, no. 1 (September/October 2007): 77–80.

Popeil, Lisa. "Baking a great belting sound." In *The Voice Teacher's Cookbook: Creative Recipes for Teachers of Singing* edited by Brian J. Winnie, 90–92. Delray Beach, FL: Meredith Music, 2018.

Robinson-Martin, Trineice. *So You Want to Sing Gospel: A Guide for Performers*. Lanham, MD: Rowman & Littlefield, 2017.

Roll, Christianne. "The evolution of the female Broadway belt voice: Implications for teachers and singers." *Journal of Voice* 30, no. 5 (September 2016): 639.e1–639.e9. doi.org/10.1016/j.jvoice.2015.07.008.

Saunders Barton, M. *Bel canto/can belto: Teaching women to sing musical theatre*. DVD. University Park, PA: Penn State Media Sales, 2007.

Saunders Barton, M. *Bel canto/can belto: What about the boys? Teaching men to sing musical theatre*. DVD. University Park, PA: Self Published, 2014.

Schutte, Harm K. and Donald G. Miller. "Belting and pop, nonclassical approaches to the femalemiddle voice: Some preliminary considerations." *Journal of Voice* 7, no. 2 (June 1993): 142–150. doi.org/10.1016/S0892-1997(05)80344-3.

Schutte, Harm K., James A. Stark, and Donald G. Miller. "Change in singing production, objectively measured." *Journal of Voice* 17, no 4 (December 2003): 495–501. doi.org/10.1067/S0892-1997(03)00009-2.

Shapiro, Jan. *So You Want to Sing Jazz: A Guide for Performers.* Lanham, MD: Rowman & Littlefield, 2016.

Spivey, Norman. "Music theatre singing ... let's talk. Part 1: The Relationship of Speech and Singing." *Journal of Singing* 64, no. 4 (March/April 2008): 483–489.

Spivey, Norman. "Music theater singing...let's talk. Part 2: Examining the debate on belting." *Journal of Singing* 64, no. 5 (May/June 2008): 607–614.

Steinhauer, Kimberly, Mary McDonald Klimek, and Jo Estill. *The Estill Voice Model: Theory and Translation.* Pittsburgh: Estill Voice International, 2018.

Story, Brad, Ingo R. Titze, and Eric A. Hoffman. "The relationship of vocal tract shape to three voice qualities." *The Journal of the Acoustical Society of America* 109, no. 4 (April 2001): 1651–1667. doi.org/10.1121/1.1352085.

Sullivan, Jan. "How to teach the belt/pop voice." *Journal of Research in Singing and Applied Vocal Pedagogy* 13, no. 1 (1989): 41–56.

Sundberg, Johan and Margareta Thalén. "What is twang?" *Journal of Voice* 24, no. 6 (November 2010): 654–660. doi.org/10.1016/j.jvoice.2009.03.003.

Sundberg, Johan and Margareta Thalén. "Respiratory and Acoustical Differences Between Belt and Neutral Styles of Singing." *Journal of Voice* 29, no. 4 (July 2015): 418–425. doi.org/10.1016/j.jvoice.2014.09.018.

Sundberg, Johan, Margareta Thalén, and Lisa Popeil. "Substyles of belting: Phonatory and resonatory characteristics." *Journal of Voice* 26, no. 2 (January 2012): 44–50. doi.org/10.1016/j.jvoice.2010.10.007.

Sundberg, Johan, Patricia Gramming, and Jeannette Lovetri. "Comparisons of pharynx, source, formant, and pressure characteristics in operatic and musical theatre singing." *Journal of Voice* 7, no. 4 (December 1993): 301–310. doi.org/10.1016/S0892-1997(05)80118-3.

Thalen, Margareta and Johan Sundberg. "Describing different styles of singing: A comparison of a female singer's voice source in 'Classical,' 'Pop,' 'Jazz,' and 'Blues.'" *Logopedics Phoniatrics Vocology* 26, no. 2 (2001): 82–93. doi.org/10.1080/140154301753207458.

Thuesen, Mathias Aaen, Julian McGlashan, and Cathrine Sadolin. "Investigating laryngeal 'Tilt' on same-pitch phonation: Preliminary findings of vocal mode metal and density parameters as alternatives to cricothyroid-thyroarytenoid 'Mix.'" *Journal of Voice*, in press. doi.org/10.1016/j.jvoice.2018.02.023.

Titze, Ingo and Albert S. Worley. "Modeling source-filter interaction in belting and high-pitched operatic male singing." *The Journal of the Acoustical Society of America* 126, no. 3 (September 2009): 1530–1540. doi.org/10.1121/1.3160296.

Titze, Ingo R., Christine C. Bergan, Eric Hunter, and Brad Story. "Source and filter adjustments affecting the perception of the vocal qualities twang and yawn." *Logopedics Phoniatrics Vocology* 28, no. 4 (December 2003):147–155.

Titze, Ingo. "Formant frequency shifts for classical and theater belt vowel modification." *Journal of Singing* 67, no. 3 (January/February 2011): 311–312.

Titze, Ingo. "Can a belt or call timbre be achieved without a large closed quotient?" *Journal of Singing* 72, no. 5 (May/June 2016): 587–588.

Titze, Ingo. "The case of the missing or depressed fundamental: Belting and trumpeting." *Journal of Singing* 73, no. 1 (September/October 2016): 53–54.

Titze, Ingo. "Belting and a high larynx position." *Journal of Singing* 63, no. 5 (May/June 2007): 557–558.

Yanagisawa, Eiji, Jo Estill, Steven T. Kmucha, and Steven B. Leder. "The contribution of aryepiglottic constriction to 'ringing' voice quality: A videolaryngoscopic study with acoustic analysis." *Journal of Voice* 3, no. 4 (December 1989): 342–350. doi.org/10.1016/S0892-1997(89)80057-8.

Yamin, Eli. *So You Want to Sing the Blues: A Guide for Performers.* Lanham, MD: Rowman & Littlefield, 2018.

Zangger Borch, D. and Johan Sundberg. "Some phonatory and resonatory characteristics of the rock, pop, soul, and Swedish dance band styles of singing." *Journal of Voice* 25, no. 5 (September 2011): 532–537. doi.org/10.1016/j.jvoice.2010.07.014.

13

Vowels

The majority of pedagogues agree that in CCM styles, vowel modification is minimal. Most of the time, the language should sound unaffected and speech-like. However, the pedagogues assert that some intentional vowel modification may serve technical or stylistic goals, or both. The chart below shows the breakdown of pedagogues who use vowel modification for technical purposes (46%), stylistic purposes (21%), or both (33%).

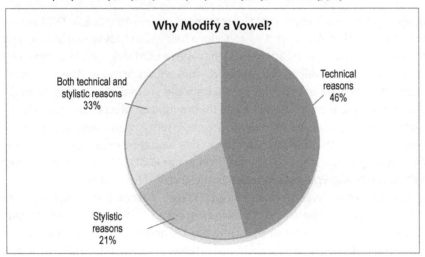

In technique, vowel modification is most commonly used to maintain vocal health at the extremes of range and when belting. Many pedagogues assert that certain vowels lend themselves to a particular register and can be used to aid or delay register transitions. On the stylistic side, a dialect may be called for in music theatre or in certain CCM genres, such as country or indie rock.[1] Several pedagogues note that when made with conscious intent, vowel modifications may also serve as potent expressive tools due to their influence on timbre. A detailed breakdown of the most common reasons for vowel modification is presented in the chart below.

---

1   For an ironic tutorial on vowel modification in Indie rock music, see Madeline Roberts' "How to hip-sing" video, posted on November 19, 2013. www.youtube.com/watch?v=e-0K77ccAOU, accessed on August 22, 2018.

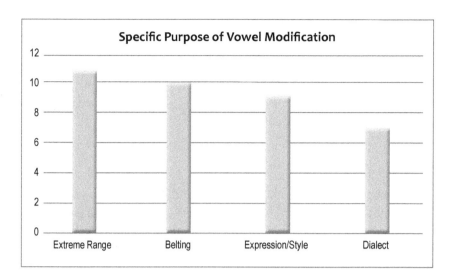

Several pedagogues point out how important the treatment of consonants is in CCM genres due to the prominence of rhythm. An interesting topic for a follow-up study would be the more general prompt "please describe the treatment of language in CCM singing", encompassing both consonants and vowels, as well as the role of rhythm within prosody. The percussive elements of consonants can drive the rhythm or maintain the groove of the song. In music theatre, the goal is to make the words clear but make them sound unaffected (unless a dialect is required). However, some changes to articulation are necessary to move between different sub-styles of music theatre. Neither vowels nor consonants would be executed in the same fashion in "If I loved you" (*Carousel*) and "St. Jimmy" (*American Idiot*). A list of recommended reading on both consonants and vowels is included at the end of this chapter.

This chapter contains responses to the prompt "Please describe your approach to teaching vowel modification". The responses are presented in a loose order starting with those who use vowel modification primarily for technical purposes, then those who use it primarily for stylistic purposes, and finally, those who use it for both technical and stylistic purposes.

Trineice Robinson-Martin

Vowels should be modified to create the freest sound on any given pitch.

Jan Shapiro

I do not much like the term "vowel modification" because it sounds like we are altering vowels. To me, it is about how we articulate vowels and consonants. Anyone who does public speaking, acting, or teaching needs to know how to project and be understood without over-using the voice or becoming hoarse. This is no different to me than someone who is training for a marathon, learning how to gain body strength, or swimming. Singers need to pay attention to keeping vowels more open because often we are sustaining a note/holding on to vowel. In order for the vowel to be understood and yet free, we need to open our mouths more than when we speak. In general, the shape of the mouth will be different, at least momentarily when singing a vowel sound.

Cate Frazier-Neely

Vowel modifications as pitch ascends can be explained as 1) subtle adjustments with the articulators to allow for the acoustical changes needed for most voices to function with ease 2) a very gradual vowel substitution like [I] for [i], or 3) moving the mouth into a rectangle shape which will help vowels move towards [a], [ʌ], or [æ] (as in the word "cat") to stay in a desired TA-dominant registration. Singers need developmental time, or have unusually fine instincts, to become reflexive to pitch and vowels.

All vowel modification is only as effective as the co-ordination of the laryngeal muscles and cartilages.

There is more variation of vowel integrity accepted throughout the variety of styles found in CCM than in the various forms of classical singing. "Destroyed vowels" are a problem only if they contribute to vocal fold dysfunction. Some sectors of the music industry advise clients to not change their "natural" way of pronouncing or they will sound "trained", meaning inaccessible to the listener. But subtle changes for vocal health reasons can be encouraged through sustained pitches and melancholic songs or ballads of all genres.

Music reflects the language of the culture in which it develops, and when there are changes in the way a language is spoken, or the emotional state of a culture, it is reflected in the way the music is sung. So, singing "legato vowels" is not always a desired outcome in many current styles. Think of the legato of Joni Mitchell or Ella Fitzgerald versus Fiona Apple or Connie Rae Bailey.

Robert Edwin

I teach articula*tion* (shaping sound into understandable language) as part of the *"tions"* (pronounced "shuns") singing system. Articula*tion*, the shaping of sound into stylistically-appropriate and understandable language, is a major point of focus in my pedagogy. No matter what the genre, if words are being used, I believe the singer has the responsibility to pronounce them so that an audience can follow the storyline. My rock singers are as guilty as my opera singers in getting sloppy with diction. I teach my students to respect the lyricist as well as the composer. To that end, we do an exercise that highlights each articulator. We start with the jaw and do a five-note scale, singing a "yah" on each note. We address the lips with a "bah" followed by a "tah" for the teeth, a "lah" for the tongue, a "nah" for the soft palate, and a "hah" for the throat. We then reverse the order and come back out to where we started with the jaw. Whether one is singing classical or CCM styles, the laws of nature force us to modify vowels and consonants, especially as melodies ascend to the higher ranges of the human voice. For example, singing the words "me" or "you" in a high belt or a high soprano requires the actor to concede a bit to the singer in terms of intelligibility and tonal quality.

Jeannette LoVetri

In CCM styles the vowels do not modify in the same way they do in classical singing. The goal for musical theatre singing is to have the lyrics be clearly delivered, so the vowels remain as close to correct speech as possible. In high belting (such as would be found in rock or gospel styles), the vowels are modified because the larynx rises, changing the shape of the vocal tract. The two kinds of vowel modification are quite different, as one is for the purpose of enhancing resonance (acoustic efficiency) and the other is for allowing the vocal quality to remain unchanged, as it is based upon loud speech-based production.

Elisabeth Howard

Pronunciation of vowels depends on the genre of music. For the higher pitches, the vowel must be modified, including adjusting the jaw space, tongue position, and lip shape, but not to the point of being misunderstood by your audience or looking unnatural. Composers are usually pretty wise and do not write vowels impossible to be understood on extremely high notes.

Wendy DeLeo LeBorgne

I only teach vowel modification if the lyricist has written an inappropriate vowel on an inappropriate pitch, something that becomes almost physiologically impossible to do based on vowel acoustics. We would work on "cheating" the vowel as opposed to "modifying" because we still have to understand the word/text as whatever the lyricist has written/ intended. This tends to happen on high belt, oftentimes for higher sopranos, or even with tenors and bari-tenors. It is only necessary when there is a frequency vowel that is not actually possible to sing as is where written, so, we "cheat" the vowel a little bit.

Lisa Popeil

I teach the modification of the [i] vowel in both pop and classical techniques as pitch ascends *if* the vowel is overly shrill. Otherwise, regarding vowel work, I only teach correct pronunciation of vowels according to the dialect requirements of a particular genre (e.g. [aI] instead of [ai] for for R&B). An example would be the word "night", which normally would be pronounced [nait] and in a more colloquial dialect, [naIt]. Also, I occasionally may "fix" a vowel sound if a singer has an idiosyncratic way of making that sound.

In the classical world, there seem to be two schools of thought regarding the action of the mouth, tongue, and jaw in the making of vowel sounds: one school focuses on a somewhat unmoving jaw with vowels made mostly inside the mouth using the tongue; the other, of which I am a member, is that changing the mouth shape for each vowel is more visually interesting and aids in intelligibility of the text.

Seth Riggs and Margareta Svensson Riggs

As the damping (phonation) process begins, the singer must narrow the vowels to complete the bridging process and successfully go up the full range. This will also make the vowels sound pure and the lyrics easy to understand. In other words, if you do not narrow the vowels in your bridges (*passaggi*), not only will you not make it through your bridges, but contrary to what you might believe, you will also distort the vowels of the words you are singing. Distorted vowels are a sure sign of external musculature activity you do not want, and is a sure sign of the larynx rising.

For instance, for the word "love" to come out as the emotion the singer wants to sing about, we spell it "L-U-V" [lʌv]. The vowel stays pure, the larynx stays low, and we understand the word for what it is.

If on the other hand the singer sings "L-O-V-E" in the middle of the first bridge, the vowel is now wide, it brings up the larynx, the singer is all of a sudden reaching, and the word comes out as [læv], which means "bathroom" in English slang and not the emotion that it was meant to be. Most importantly, it will cause the singer to pull up the chest to where the throat will eventually close off and force the singer to flip to falsetto. In our experience, pulled-up chest is the main reason for nodule formation. If the damping is not done properly, the beginnings of a nodule will have started.

We use specific exercises that contribute to the release of purity in the vowel, with the larynx remaining low, as the bridging is accomplished with no pushing.

Cathrine Sadolin

In Complete Vocal Technique, we use four different vocal modes, like four gears in a car: Neutral, Curbing, Overdrive, and Edge. Certain vowels can only be executed in certain vocal modes. There are similar limitations to pitch and volume. There are many advantages and disadvantages to each vocal mode. If you know your vocal mode, you will understand the limitations of vowel choices within each mode. In Edge, for instance, you do not sing an [u] vowel. Immediately, it will feel difficult, and by trying to do it you could hurt your voice. The vowels must be changed in order to get or sustain the vocal mode desired. These limitations are based on acoustic rules, so the audience does not perceive the vowel modification. Céline Dion often modifies her [u] vowel to [œ] if she is singing in Edge with a lot of power.

Kim Chandler

I suggest judicious, tasteful vowel modification, such as the "morphing" of [u] towards [ɔ] and [i] towards [ɛ] in high intensity singing, such as belting.

An important part of CCM style is the treatment of consonants, or articulation. Because pop music is rhythmically oriented, the percussive element in the lyric often provides an essential part of the rhythmic fabric of a song. The primary articulators – the tongue and lips – need co-ordination work as a routine part of a practice regime in order to achieve percussive "tightness" in a similar way to drummers and percussionists who use their hands. Fast, consonant-based exercises are recommended and can include basic beat-boxing for the more adventurous. Fortunately, there are also many examples of fast lyric patterns found in repertoire in a range of classic and contemporary pop music that can add relevance to practice.

In 2014, I wrote that "a delicate balance between over and under articulation is required. My general suggestion is that the initial consonants of lyrically and rhythmically significant words be emphasized in order to create drive and intensity. Conversely, the consonants at the ends of words are generally de-emphasized. Fortunately, the right amount of consonant pressure is also technically efficient."[2]

Kathryn Paradise

In the commercial music context, vowel modification can mean many different things. Instead of seeking the most efficient acoustical resonance and projection, as is often the case in un-amplified, non-commercial styles, I use vowel modification to achieve both relaxed vocal production, and timbre variety. As it relates to registration, I also teach students that vowel modification can be helpful when trying to gain control over either delaying or expediting the transition from one part of the voice to another. For example, I may have the student work on an ascending melodic passage by comparing what happens when they modify their vowel towards a feeling of "snarl" versus a feeling of "dopiness". When doing so, I ask the

---

2   Kim Chandler, "Teaching popular music styles," in *Teaching Singing in the 21st Century* edited by Scott D. Harrison and Jessica O'Bryan, (Dordrecht: Springer, 2014), 41.

student to observe what timbre and registration feels most natural to the voice. We can then transition these vowel modification markers into repertoire depending on what color and weight the student wants to sing a certain passage.

In speech-like singing, vowel modification also comes up as an issue when migrating the natural tensions and interferences caused by colloquial American English, particularly in the country music genre. Here, I can help the student make determinations about when altering the vowel away from the sound of speech is advantageous, and when it sounds fraudulent to the style.

Kevin Wilson

I teach vowel modification for negotiating *passaggi* specific to genre. For musical theatre, in contemporary belt where the mix is taken above D5, I teach females to sing modified "closed" vowels through the first *passaggio* such as [e], all influenced with [æ], which allows for the tongue, larynx, and soft palate to adjust, the aryepiglottic folds to narrow (twang, if you call it that), and the registration to negotiate towards more cricothyroid dominance. For standard belt where the student is not traditionally belting above D5, I teach open vowels such as [a] and [ɛ] to keep the thyroarytenoids dominant through the *passaggio*. In legit musical theatre I teach regional dialect "pure" vowels on the staff, negotiating the first *passaggio* towards head voice at D4/E4.

Matthew Edwards

There are no standards in commercial styles. If you want proof that sloppy diction can be successful for some singers, Google "misheard song lyrics"; the results will give you a good laugh. I approach each song individually and work on adjusting the articulators as necessary to improve pronunciation (if appropriate) and/or make it easier to sing extreme notes. When you are belting, everything tends to go towards an open vowel with a trumpet mouth shape. It is very difficult to sing a pure [i] or [u] in that position, so modification on those and closely related vowels is a must. In commercial music, I stick with the singer's goals. If they want to have a southern accent, or want their vowels to sound nasal and whiny, I go with it. In musical theatre, there is a standard expectation that the end result will have no apparent accent unless specifically called for by the script. Therefore, I find myself addressing diction issues in musical theatre more frequently than in commercial styles.

Tracy Marie Bourne

I only use a little vowel modification in music theatre teaching because the words must sound as close to speech as possible. Obviously, character work does involve different regional accents. In Australia, we are often working with North American accents when performing musical theatre repertoire. I have found that "forward", bright, twangy vowels [ɛ] as in "yeah", [æ] as in "cat", are important for belt and for belt-mix singing, whereas more "back" vowels such as [u] as in "who", and [ɔ] as in "poor", are more relevant to legit-style singing.

Gillyanne Kayes

I teach vowel modification as a choice. In my experience, the type of vowel modification required depends on 1) the singer's vocal tract morphology and 2) the music they are singing –

style and pitch range. I do not use the same approach to vowel modification with each singer: strategies for resonance tuning necessarily differ between the genres, also between genders and – perhaps most importantly – can be customized to the individual voice. My guess is that this is due to morphological differences between individual singers.

Edrie Means Weekly

I only teach vowel modification on extreme high notes, if necessary, to cause less strain and more comfort for the singer. In the majority of the range, I encourage speech-like vowels in the style of vernacular speech. I use diphthongs and triphthongs, depending on style and dialect.

Marci Rosenberg

I train singers to sing vowels the way that they speak them until they are higher in their tessitura and modification is required to maintain acoustic integrity. This is particularly true for musical theatre and other CCM singers where the text takes precedence over a legato vocal line. It is not uncommon to see a singer, particularly if they have had a lot of ensemble choral singing, not to be able to sing a pure, unmodified vowel, particularly [i]. This tells me that the mechanism is somewhat stuck in a certain position. If needed, I will use myofascial and stretching techniques to release the tongue, and suprahyoid muscles to increase flexibility and release holding patterns that are distorting vowel production. I am of the mindset that any type of vocal tract modification or vowel distortion is fine if it is an aesthetic choice appropriate for a specific genre or character, as long as you do not get stuck in that setting and you can always find a neutral position.

Irene Bartlett

In general, I believe that vowel modification is unnecessary in CCM singing styles, except perhaps at the extremes of a singer's voice production (for example, high belt singing or extreme vocal effects). However, modification may be necessary for character-based or regional accents, and some specific style-related CCM vocal effects.

Kimberly Steinhauer

Diction is dependent on the language, musical style/genre, and dialect. In Estill Voice Training®, we do not modify vowels to achieve a voice quality. We practice every vowel and consonant in every voice quality.

Marcelle G. Gauvin

As a contemporary-styles teacher, vowel modification and morphing come with the territory. The sky is the limit for all possibilities of vowel color and combinations, and much depends on the musical style being sung. Vowels can be modified for stylistic ornamentation, expression of cultural regionalism, dynamic build, and/or increased resonance. I will train a singer to first identify the types of vowels they use in a musical style, then work to make sure those vowel types are carried throughout their range freely. From that point, we expand the singer's options by working on a different vowel color palette and eventually morph one color to another throughout the range. Singers find this type of exploration very rewarding because it opens up their artistic tool box.

Mary Saunders Barton

Communicating a composer's lyric intelligibly is a primary obligation for musical theatre performers. The story must be clear. The diction should not "call attention to itself" or to any technical effort on the part of the singer to create a certain resonance or perceived "desirable" tone quality. It should seem organic and truthful. Ernest Newman, author and critic for the *London Sunday Times*, wrote these words a week after the death of the legendary John McCormack in 1938 – "He was a supreme example of the art that conceals art, and sheer hard work that becomes manifest only in its results, not in the revolving of the machinery that has produced them".[3]

There are stylistic exceptions in pop and rock genres where extreme vowel modifications are an essential ingredient of authentic style. In rock songs, for example, intelligibility often takes a back seat to style as in the phrase "See Rock Citay" from the musical by the same name (*See Rock City*) or "Charlaayayay" in "The History of Wrong Guys" from *Kinky Boots*.

Mark Baxter

I prefer that singers explore volume modification before vowel modification. Maintaining a consistent volume as one extends the range of the voice prevents the increase of subglottic pressure. This allows the thyroarytenoid muscles to remain pliable and present less resistance to the cricothyroid muscles. This affords singers greater control over the open/close quotient of their laryngeal mechanisms, so they achieve their desired intensity with a minimum of strain on the structure. This approach is unique to contemporary singing due to the use of microphones. Without the need to project the voice over an orchestra, the popular singer is free to utilize conversational timbres. Therefore, vowel modification tends to be a hallmark of style rather than necessity. Unless of course the singer's fundamental frequency is higher than the formants of a vowel.

Jeff Ramsey

I teach from a "color" perspective as opposed to a functional perspective. In other words, I want the singer to be able to figure out why they modify and how, in most cases, the problem stems from air pressure. Once they understand that, they can modify as they need to for the color and not necessarily to solve any tension they may have. This is particularly the case with popular music as we do not necessarily modify vowels in the same way as, say, someone who is singing opera.

References and recommended reading

Barlow, Christopher and Jeannette LoVetri. "Closed quotient and spectral measures of female adolescent singers in different singing styles." *Journal of Voice* 24, no. 3 (May 2010): 314–318.

Behrman, Alison. *Speech and Voice Science*. 2nd ed. San Diego: Plural Publishing, 2013.

Bestebreurtje, Martine E. and Harm K. Schutte. "Resonance strategies for the belting style: Results of a single female subject study." *Journal of Voice* 14, no. 2 (2000): 194–204.

Chandler, Kim. "Teaching popular music styles." In *Teaching Singing in the 21st Century* edited by Scott D. Harrison and Jessica O'Bryan, 35–51. Dordrecht: Springer, 2014.

---

3   Ernest Newman, quoted in "John McCormack: A Centenary Tribute," program, presented by the Dublin Grand Opera Society, Olympia Theatre, Dublin, spring 1984.

Chicurel-Stein, Steven R. "A consommé of consonants." In *The Voice Teacher's Cookbook: Creative Recipes for Teachers of Singing* edited by Brian J. Winnie, 20–21. Delray Beach, FL: Meredith Music, 2018.

Lain, LaToya. "Delectable diction and dialect in the negro spiritual." In *The Voice Teacher's Cookbook: Creative Recipes for Teachers of Singing* edited by Brian J. Winnie, 67–68. Delray Beach, FL: Meredith Music, 2018.

Lamesch, Sylvain, Boris Doval, and Michele Castellengo. "Toward a more informative voice range profile: The role of laryngeal vibratory mechanisms on vowels dynamic range." *Journal of Voice* 26, no. 5 (September 2012): 672.e9–672. e18. doi.org/10.1016/j.jvoice.2012.01.005.

Lebon, Rachel. "Utilizing the natural prosody of speech in cooking up hot jazz, pop, and 'patter' tunes." In *The Voice Teacher's Cookbook: Creative Recipes for Teachers of Singing* edited by Brian J. Winnie, 69–70. Delray Beach, FL: Meredith Music, 2018.

LoVetri, Jeannette, Mary Saunders Barton, and Edrie Means Weekly. "A brief overview of approaches to teaching the music theatre song." In *Teaching Singing in the 21st Century.* Edited by Scott D. Harrison and Jessica O'Bryan, 53-66. Dordrecht: Springer, 2014.

Nix, John. "Vowel modification revisited." *Journal of Singing* 61, no. 2 (November/December 2004): 173–176.

Ophaug, Wencke. "The diminished vowel space in classical singing and the tug of war between 'speech-true' and modified vowels." *Journal of Singing* 73, no. 3 (January/February 2017): 293–303.

Roberts, Madeline. "How to hip-sing." Posted on November 19, 2013, accessed on August 22, 2018. www.youtube.com/watch?v=e-0K77ccAOU.

Robinson-Martin, Trineice. "Performance styles and music characteristics of black gospel music." *Journal of Singing* 65, no. 5 (May/June 2009): 595–599.

Stone, R. E., Thomas F. Cleveland, P.Johan Sundberg, and Jan Prokop. "Aerodynamic and acoustical measures of speech, operatic, and Broadway vocal styles in a professional female singer." *Journal of Voice* 17, no. 3 (September 2003): 283–297. doi.org/10.1067/S0892-1997(03)00074-2.

Story, Brad, Ingo R. Titze, and Eric A. Hoffman. "The relationship of vocal tract shape to three voice qualities." *The Journal of the Acoustical Society of America* 109, no. 4 (April 2001): 1651–1667. doi.org/10.1121/1.1352085.

Story, Brad H. "Synergistic modes of vocal tract articulation for American English vowels." *Journal of the Acoustical Society of America* 118, no. 6 (December 2005): 3834–3859.

Titze, Ingo R. "Introducing a music notation scheme for pitch-vowel interaction." *Journal of Singing* 68, no. 1 (September/October 2011): 49–50.

Titze, Ingo R. "Can a singer's personalized formant frequency space be helpful in performing multiple styles?" *Journal of Singing* 72, no. 3 (January/February 2016): 331-332.

Titze, Ingo. "Falsetto register and vowels." *Journal of Singing* 63, no. 4 (March/April 2007): 441–442.

14

Expression

In 2017, global revenue from the recorded music industry totaled 17.3 billion dollars (U.S.).[1] If people are willing to spend billions of dollars, year after year, just to listen to music, it must be providing something that they cannot find anywhere else. Music provides an emotional experience, a transformative journey, or a catharsis. Music is part of every social event, wedding, funeral, road trip, break-up, and make-up. It is woven into the fabric of every culture around the world. Popular music both shapes and reflects cultural development.

Initially, this question was placed at the end of the list of interview prompts. However, it quickly became clear that the majority of these pedagogues view technique as inseparable from expression in CCM singing; 67% made the point that technique exists to serve expression or to make expression possible, or that perfect technique without expression is unacceptable. In other words, the entire purpose of developing technique is to expand the expressive palette. The role of expression is one of the defining differences between classical training and CCM training. In *Cross-Training in the Voice Studio*, Spivey and Saunders Barton state that opera is "...music first and musical theatre is words first..."[2]. Those "words" provide the platform for expression. In CCM, expression is paramount, and several pedagogues point out that imperfect technique is forgiven (if not celebrated) as part of telling an authentic human story. Moving an audience through raw emotion and bringing them on a journey matters infinitely more than making a "flawless" sound. Opera is certainly dramatic and expressive, but vocal imperfections can be distracting in opera, and can diminish the power of expression. The pedagogues maintain that this is not the case in CCM singing.

In academia, the classical model marginalizes acting training. Operatic superstar Renée Fleming explains that when she was studying at Juilliard "there was a strict separation between the music and drama departments. You couldn't take classes in acting and movement".[3] In fact, lower standards are still in place for university opera programs accredited by the National Association of Schools of Music (NASM). As of 2018, NASM only requires "basic"[4] development of skills in acting for opera programs, while they require "thorough"[5] development of skills in acting for music theatre programs. Acting/storytelling does not appear to be valued as much in opera as it is in musical theatre.

---

1   Statista, "Global recorded music revenue from 1999 to 2017 (in billion U.S. dollars)," accessed on August 23, 2018, www.statista.com/statistics/272305/global-revenue-of-the-music-industry/.

2   Norman Spivey and Mary Saunders Barton, *Cross-Training in the Voice Studio: A Balancing Act* (San Diego: Plural Publishing, 2018), 26.

3   Renée Fleming, quoted in Christopher Isherwood, "Operatic acting? Oxymoron no more," *New York Times*, September 9, 2007, accessed on August 12, 2018, www.nytimes.com/2007/09/09/arts/music/09char.html.

4   National Association of Schools of Music, *NASM Handbook 2017-2018* (Reston, VA: National Association of Schools of Music, 2017), appendix I.B., 162.

5   Ibid., 163, 164.

When training musical theatre singers, the pedagogues report that university programs provide acting coursework to support the development of this skill in their voice students. However, acting exercises are also commonly used within the voice studio, with 25% of the pedagogues reporting that they use specific acting or story-telling techniques within voice lessons to help their students engage in expressive singing. An extensive list of acting resources may be found at the end of this chapter.

Popular music, rather than utilizing traditional theatrical acting methods, evokes and expresses emotions. It can serve as a vehicle for social change or as a platform from which to present a point of view on a controversial or delicate topic, such as gender fluidity or female sexual pleasure. It can also be used for religious expression or worship, as in "praise and worship" music, which has significantly grown in popularity over the past few decades. As of a 2018 survey by Statista, 19% of respondents believe that Contemporary Christian music is representative of modern America.[6]

In CCM genres, the pedagogues report that authentic, unique, and emotional performance is valued even more highly than technique. A majority of the pedagogues (67%) report using techniques in voice lessons to evoke an "emotional" connection to the material. A large number (42%) also emphasize the importance of authentic expression in performance. The addition of emotion into singing can have a significant impact on the voice itself, and readers are encouraged to explore the research in this area, some of which is listed at the end of the chapter. Recommended reading on the connections between popular vocal music, religious expression, and social change are also included at the end of this chapter.

This chapter includes responses to the prompt "How do you help a student integrate technique and expressivity?". Because of the strong level of consensus on the high value of expression in CCM singing, the responses are presented in random order.

Mary Saunders Barton

Putting song and story together is a fundamental part of the musical theatre training process. However, as a voice teacher I do not have to go it alone. I can share the responsibility with teachers who specialize in the training of actors. My job is to make sure my students do not leave that training behind when they sing. It is important for voice teachers who teach college-age actors to be conversant with the language used in their acting classes in order to support the development of this critical skill.

When I was starting my own career in NYC, one of my first acting teachers was Michael Shurtleff, the influential casting director, playwright, and author of the perennially popular book *Audition: Everything an Actor Needs to Know to get the Part*.[7] In that book, he lists 12 Guideposts for actors, very simple and direct, and easily aligned with any method-based approach. I would certainly recommend them as helpful prompts when students get stuck in voice technique land. The second of these guideposts, "What are you fighting for?", is a very immediate way to re-focus a student's attention on the lyrics.

---

6   Statista, "Public opinion on the music genres which are representative of America today in the United States as of May 2018," accessed on August 23, 2018, www.statista.com/statistics/864602/music-genre-modern-america/.

7   Michael Shurtleff, *Audition: Everything an Actor Needs to Know to get the Part* (New York: Bantam, 1980).

Marcelle G. Gauvin

I help a student to integrate technique and expressivity:

1. By utilizing registration choices that change throughout the song.
2. By changing the rhythmic feel of scales, drills, and repertoire.
3. By focusing on the physical embodiment of lyrics.
4. By incorporating acting technique in song interpretation to varying degrees depending on the style being sung.
5. By singing the same song/exercise at different tempos.
6. By encouraging students to compose original material.
7. By improvising. If a student can freely create a musical idea in the moment with clarity and musicality, then the marriage between technique and expressivity is successful.
8. By call and response. I lead them into technical challenges as well as expressive ideas that happen simultaneously. I also set certain improvisation parameters such as "only in head voice", "end your phrase in chesty mix", etc. It has proven to be a very effective method for integrating these two ideas.

Trineice Robinson-Martin

Style conditioning exercises are designed to help bridge the connection between technique and expressivity. Therefore, all exercises are constructed in the context that resembles an emotional response. Whether it is an exercise that uses an elongated sigh or a definitive statement, style conditioning exercises allow singers to practice emotional expression and vocal stability at the same time.

Mark Baxter

I often refer to the balancing of emotions and physical skills when singing as "surfing" the song. The difference is that singers have to make their own waves. Feelings rise and fall inside us, creating surges of energy to be harnessed. Like surfers heading for the ocean, performers drive to gigs or the studio hoping the swells will be plentiful. Sometimes, the waves are too big, causing beginners to lose control and wipe out. Calling up tears in a performance is one thing, crying is another. Tapping into anger certainly creates waves, but what good are huge swells if your board gets trashed on the very first run? Too often, though, it is a singer's fear of falling that reduces the power of the surf, making the songs safe and uneventful. It takes skill and courage to conjure up an appropriate wave of emotion from placid waters.

Some people are good at making waves. When working with emotionally unrestricted singers, my focus is on minimizing their efforts. It is easy to mistake push for passion. When working with inhibited singers, I remind them that a wave is a wave. One does not have to specifically feel anger, happiness, loneliness or love to express them in song. The listener simply needs to hear an emotional sound. Pain is often substituted as pleasure in films. In 1978, 12-year-old Brooke Shields played a child prostitute in the movie *Pretty Baby*. To create the appearance of pleasure during her love scene, director Louis Malle stood just outside of the shot and dug his fingernails into Brooke's foot. The result was so convincing the movie was banned in some provinces of Canada and earned an X rating in the U.K. In the same way, it is unreasonable to expect a singer to re-live the emotions that inspired a song after performing it a thousand times.

Once a wave has been created the dance begins. This is the point where singer and surfer alike rely on their physical skills. Subtle, reflexive, muscle activity constantly adjusts to changing conditions. It is impossible to think fast enough; the technique must be unconscious. I instruct all my students that they only need to rise to their potential – not to someone else's. Popular audiences are known to celebrate the unique qualities of singers, making it both a welcoming and intimidating art form. There is no particular skill-set required for connecting with listeners, and no guarantee that superb technique will bring acceptance. I encourage students to strip away imitations and pretense in order to discover their authentic selves. Ironically, it is flaws and inabilities that define a contemporary singer's style, and if he or she is courageous enough to sing from that vulnerable truth, expressivity flows like a conversation with a best friend. That is exactly what popular audiences seek: to bond with the person singing.

Kevin Wilson

To help a student integrate technique and expressivity, I use emotional flash cards that I created from a chart of emotions, ranking standard emotions like happy, sad, angry, afraid, and ashamed from high to low intensity of feelings. I have breathing assignments to help students develop relationships with these emotions, to bring awareness to their bodies during these emotions and/or physical reactions. In my opinion, technique is what allows you to tell the story that YOU want or need to tell.

Tracy Marie Bourne

I spend the first half of each lesson on technical exercises; the second half of the lesson is about applying these technical concepts in repertoire. Once a singer has memorized the song, we work on it as an acting piece. I encourage them to move beyond "listening" to their sound and to focus more on being "present" and using the text to tell a story. We use acting techniques including text analysis, gesture work, and improvisation.

Kim Chandler

This is a very individual journey with each client so it's difficult to generalize. However, I find that the "Primal Sounds"[8] work of Dane Chalfin is highly effective in integrating technique and expressivity. The primal sounds used in singing are often technically efficient already, and become "hard wired" with the requisite emotion (thanks to their connection to the limbic system) – it is a great "package deal". We work through the lyric, discuss the emotional journey of the song, and use this as a template for deciding which primal sounds would best express these emotions.

Marci Rosenberg

These two components (technique and expressivity) represent the yin and yang of vocal performance. They must exist symbiotically, working to enhance not diminish the performance. The mechanical technique achieved in the studio serves the singer in that he/she does not need to focus on mechanics at all while performing. The emotional connection to the song further enhances the mechanics of voice production, and sometimes can provide the freedom and release that may have been elusive in the voice studio. To me, perfectly technical singing

---

8   More information on Primal Sounds may be found at www.vocalrehabilitation.com/primal-voice-research.

without any expressivity or emotional connection leaves me unsatisfied. I would prefer to hear a technically flawed performance that is expressive and connected to the singer.

Matthew Edwards

Commercial and musical theatre performers are professional story tellers. I believe you can use many of the same tools with both. The major difference is that commercial artists are telling their own story, while musical theatre artists are telling the character's story. Yes, they may use their own life experiences as tools, but at the end of the day they are not singing about the details of their own lives.

I use many different tools, but my go-to is a simplified version of Chekhov's psychological gesture work.[9] I teach students six primary gestures: push, pull, throw, tear, lift, and crush. We then think about each phrase and make a choice of which gesture is the best fit. I have the student perform the phrase with the gesture several times in a row, and then have them drop the gestures and perform the song while feeling that same urge to act within themselves. The goal is to have the physical action stir an emotional response that the singer can use during performance. It helps students connect to the song without over-intellectualizing the process.

Commercial singers can easily identify with primal urges to do something to someone else, and quickly realize that tapping into their desire to physically move will help bring their performance to life. Musical theatre performers usually quickly grasp this approach and are able to integrate it into whatever other training they have.

Cate Frazier-Neely

There is a point where emotion and technique meet and become one thing. You begin to not be able to discern one from the other. The technique becomes the expression, and the expression is the technique. Functional training eventually frees a musical soul and allows the magical experience of this connection. I love helping someone come to an understanding of the difference between emoting or imitating, and feeling how music is released when the throat and body are working together. Character, subtext and plot development are important but in well-written music, all of these elements are contained in the music. It is up to us as singers to have developed an instrument capable of expressing the highs and lows of human emotion and everything in between. This is why repertoire choice is so important for a singer of any age. While the heart may be capable of understanding the emotion, the body may not be able to sustain its expression.

We do not grow as singers and as teachers solely in voice lessons, degree programs, or in the virtual or brick and mortar classroom. We learn mostly in the space between lessons and workshops, and during our own curious play with our voices. We learn by working for many years with other musicians, and by learning to share our most vulnerable places by not giving a hoot what people think of us or what our critics say.

Jeff Ramsey

One thing I have learned over the years is that the student needs to practice technique so that the habits of practicing show up in their singing. When a student is performing, that is not the time to think about anything other than expressing the lyrical sentiment of a song, not how

---

9   Found in Richard Brestoff, *The Great Acting Teachers and Their Methods* (Hanover, NH: Smith & Kraus, 1996).

much air to take in or whether or not you created enough acoustical space. This is something I have learned myself from experience as it would jam my voice up, thinking about everything else but the words of the song, and how to convey them emotionally.

Gillyanne Kayes

I have a range of things that I do to help a student integrate technique and expressivity. The majority of my work is with musical theatre singers, so we work on text, subtext and characterization. I also use devices such as emotional "cue cards" and story time-lines with movement between the different time zones in the song. I love to unravel text and meaning in a song for my singers. The other area I will focus on is how to deliver the song material from a vocal perspective – how does THIS voice sing this song and make it their own? How does the singer best deliver the words and song message or feel? I will talk about song landscape (highs and lows) and finding the "essence" of the song for that singer (emotional cue cards can be used by any singer type).

Jeannette LoVetri

If the instrument is freely produced, strong and responsive, consistent and variable, honest and recognizable, and if the student has a clear idea of what he/she wants to communicate through the words and music, the expressiveness often just shows up. If it does not, the student needs to (separately) work on either story-telling or acting until it does. It is remarkable that even very high-level professional artists do not really do any deep investigation into the material they sing; they do not personalize it and they do not know what they want the audience to understand in their performance. Being "who you are" is all that matters when you sing, but it takes work to know how to locate that "true you" and bring that person forward without self-consciousness or undue pride.

Edrie Means Weekly

In my teaching, the goal is for the singer to sing a commercial or musical theatre song authentically. It is more than singing the notes and lyrics in the written score; acting cannot be left out of the voice. Authenticity includes the style, expression, emotion, and storytelling used so that the audience is invited into the character's world through song. The story line is expressed vocally through the choice of style such as country, jazz, pop, rap, rhythm and blues (R&B), and rock, with variations in vocal quality ranging from legit, mix, and belt.

I cross-train my clients'/students' vocal production muscles so they have consistency throughout their range, and use vocalises to gain laryngeal flexibility while maintaining healthy vocal function.

I teach vocal expression by teaching the various *vocal stylisms* used in the different styles they are singing. These are the extra nuances added to a song for style effect and are most often not written in the music. *Vocal stylisms* is the term I gave to all these added nuances years ago; some use the phrase "pop" *stylism*, "tags", or other terms for commercial music nuances. I use the term *vocal stylisms* because in musical theatre character roles, the singer can use *stylisms* from pop, country, R&B, jazz, or rock in the song for emphasis of particular words or action taking place, although the song itself may be written in a traditional musical theatre style. Some *vocal stylisms* are cry, fall-off, fall-ups, fry, bending the note, growl, pop-appoggiatura, waves, yodel, and different kinds of onsets and releases.

Emotion and expression are also created vocally by varying the dynamics, coloring the tone, varying the use of vowels and consonants, using alliterations (repetitions of a particular sound), and by using *vocal stylisms* such as bending the pitch (sliding into it from above or below), sliding from one pitch to another, crying, growling, and using vocal fry or a kind of *creaky* sound. The singer can also shorten the vowel and emphasize a particular consonant, or use word painting to color lyrics by creatively singing onomatopoetic words such as chirp, drip, bang, knock, zip, and click, as if to make them sound like the things the words represent. On words such as fall and drool, it's also possible to seem to *fall off* the pitch by gliding down to the next note, which adds more color and emphasis to the meaning of the words. With all new songs, I have the vocalist learn the song as written, both the rhythms and the melody, so they can later include authentic stylistic choices, such as back-phrasing, vocal *stylisms*, and improvisational aspects.

I have a character/song report sheet for my musical theatre singers to use as a guide to connect technique to expression.

Some of the questions include:
1. How does your diction reflect your character? Is there an accent? What does the character's speaking voice sound like?
2. How do the dynamic and possible modulation changes affect the vocal quality? Does it cause you to sing in chest register, head register or mix?
3. Are there emotions behind the dynamic changes?
4. How does tempo change affect the mood of your character and your voice?
5. Are there any repeats of phrases? Words? If so, how are you going to express these repeats?

Wendy DeLeo LeBorgne

From a song standpoint, we break it down like you would break down a scene. Where are the beats? What is the emotional subtext? How would you speak it if you were talking to somebody? Who are you talking to? We break it down very much like how you would have a conversation.

Students need to have a really strong sense of technique before they can be overly expressive. For my commercial artists, I talk about it like a dancer going to the gym, or a gymnast who performs floor exercises. You have to have strength and stamina first, and it has to be fairly well-ingrained so that you don't have to think about your technique when you go out and perform as an artist. When you go out and artistically connect, I don't want you thinking "How am I breathing?" or "What is my posture like?". That needs to be a day to day activity that we incorporate into your lessons and your technical training, so that when you perform it's an inherent part of who you are. You can just go out and sing.

Lisa Popeil

I always start with solving technical problems first before tackling the details of expressivity. Technique first, expressivity second. When I struggled with my technique, full of questions about how to sing well, and battling with my tone, my vibrato, my air, in fact everything, I found myself unable to make artistic choices. Though I am aware and have experienced that expressiveness can sometimes *help* one's technique, that good technique, since it is accidental, is less likely to be dependable.

Having said that, there are some hyper-technical people who are disabled technically by worry. For that rare group, we'll go right into singing for joy and I will show them the many tricks of the trade regarding exhibiting emotion (e.g. making a mental movie, who-what-when-why-how, pronunciation, dynamic choices, resonance, and airflow changes), all in an attempt to have the singing create emotion in the listener.

For most singers though, better control of the basic skills is a pre-requisite to learning *stylisms* and expressive devices which can really sell a song. One of my favorite formulas is what I call "The Three Cs": control, consistency, confidence. In that order. Confident singers are then able to move to the next level of creating magical art with their voices.

Seth Riggs and Margareta Svensson Riggs

Technique does not stand on its own. It is there to assist an artist to be the best they can be. Without musicality and artistic expression, there is nothing of substance to assist.

It is important to recognize the individual quality that sets an artist apart. In pop genres, it is all important not to take that quality away, but to direct the singer to a healthier and more extensive use of the voice while at the same time maintaining individuality.

For an artist who lacks technique, the expression will suffer along with the voice in the areas where it is crucial, just as if there is no expression, it does not matter how good the technique is.

Starting with the technical aspects of a song, once the student has an understanding of what needs to happen, we address expression, much like an actor approaches a text. To focus on what the words of the song actually mean not only helps the emotional impact on the audience, but also helps the technical aspects for the singer, as the singer emphasizes communication rather than sound.

Robert Edwin

Emo*tion* is the umbrella that covers all the other *"tions."* I believe there should be some emotional connection to almost every vocal activity a singer does. If the goal of technique is to provide a singer with a consistent and predictable foundation for vocal performance, then emotion should always be included in technical training. How can vocalizing with blank minds and blank faces prepare one for performing songs? Dull and boring singers do not entertainers make! My singers tell stories in their technique ("I'd LOVE to sing a major diatonic scale using solfege!" or, "Watch how much I enjoy demonstrating good breath management!" or, "I HATE the articulation exercise, so I'll overdo it in a mocking way just to show my displeasure!"), which allows them to segue smoothly into their repertoire as the actor/singers they are supposed to be.

Technique and expressivity need not be mutually exclusive. Emotion can and should be a part of most technical work. Why can't a solfege scale become important and engaging to the singer? Why can't work on the *passaggio* include an expressive context? Who said voice technique has to be robotic and boring? It's like you're throwing a party for all the *"tions"* except emo*tion*. Then later, after the party is already in progress, you decide to invite emo*tion* in. That *"tion"* should be there at the start of the party! It makes sublime sense to me that an emotionally-connected singer will segue from technique into repertoire more easily and effectively than someone who has shut down or ignored perhaps the most important element in singing, which is human communication.

Cathrine Sadolin

This depends on what the singer wants. If they are asking me to help them improve expression in a particular part of a song, I would ask them to describe the problem. We would discuss the goal and try to apply changes to the sound. It is constantly the singer who is leading where we go. This is true for everything: technique, rhythm, ornamentation, expression, and songwriting. In everything we do, it is the singer who knows how it should sound, not me, not the teachers. We are just servants to help them achieve their goals.

Dane Chalfin

I would tell students the truth about integrating technique and expression. It is a really big problem with college students, particularly in the first few years of training, but I also see it in some professionals. They are caught up in trying to prove themselves and find themselves. They are always showing off. I get really tired of being slapped in the face by a big voice or over-riffing. Getting them to trust that their point of view is valid, and that they can back off and do what the song dictates, is the hardest thing. I will tell them: "No, I do not believe you. It is too big. Go back to the lyric. What does the lyric say? In real life, if you said that, how would you feel? What would that sound like? Just do that. What is the underlying emotion?". It has to be emotionally relevant, or it does not make any sense.

As teachers, we really need to consider expressivity to be part of technique. The old idea that we first get technically solid, and then we think about interpretation, is backward. We know that emotional neurology is hard-wired to the vocal mechanism. We are taking a lot of instruction from the emotional part of our brain. I think we need to keep interpretation at the heart of all technique, particularly in contemporary singing. This is the singing of the people; the vernacular singing. It has got to be real. That is why we like it. Do what you need and do what the audience needs.

A lot of people mistake sheer brute force for emotion, especially men. You just have to tell them "This is not a larynx-measuring contest. This is not about your ego; it is about the song." It is a lot of "Calm down dear; just do what is appropriate". I do not care how many records someone has sold. I will say that to them just as often as I would to someone auditioning for college. I will say "Wow, stop waving that thing in my face". Conversely, sometimes I wonder why some singers will not actually use their voices. Some are stuck in the fear of hurting themselves. This is sometimes taught and sometimes a personal thing. For me, the bottom line is always about setting up a body to be free, flexible, and able to respond to the interpretive needs of the song in a way that is healthy and sustainable and dripping with truth.

Jan Shapiro

If a singer has good technique, expression and style will come together naturally. However, I do believe there are gifted vocalists who are naturally expressive the moment they sing. Not every singer possesses this. This is why even vocalists with smaller voices (i.e. Billie Holiday and Edith Piaf) captured audiences around the world. When these vocalists sang, they made the audience feel the words of the song.

Kimberly Steinhauer

After careful, explicit training of the voice at the "voice gym" we do not separate technique from expressivity. Before learning a song, the student has to research the context of the piece and then decide on the vocal delivery. If it is a theatrical piece, the student must be strong in the voice of the character, and practice speaking dialogue before singing the music.

Kathryn Paradise

Integrating technique and expressivity depends highly on the student and his/her goals. Generally, I try to isolate technical, functional voice training into a regular regime of exercises that become integrated into muscle memory, so that the performance of repertoire can be geared towards creativity and expression. However, in the typical academic cycle of preparing repertoire for juries and recitals, this is not always possible. I have had a lot of success when a technical concept can be tied to the emotion being expressed. For example, by soliciting a breathy, speech-like timbre in the verse of a pop song by highlighting the introspective nature of the lyric, or by invoking strong posture and an open mouth for a high, chest-dominant note on a bridge by connecting it to the growth in conviction to the message of the song as we head to the final chorus. In this way, technical issues can be addressed without being a distraction from the emotion and expression required for the performance.

Elisabeth Howard

I believe a solid technique is the key to artistic expression, i.e., flexibility in range and the ability to control all the aspects of vocal technique including, but not limited to, vibrato, resonances, blending registers, head voice, chest voice, and the MIX. Stage presence and communicating with an audience is just as important as solid technique and style. A top performer has to love people and love sharing their talent with them. A top performer must be vulnerable and likeable. A top performer knows how to LET IT SHINE!

References and recommended reading

Acting and authenticity

Adler, Stella. *The Art of Acting*. Edited by Howard Kissel. New York: Applause Books, 2000.

Brestoff, Richard. *The Great Acting Teachers and Their Methods*. Hanover, NH: Smith & Kraus, 1996.

Brestoff, Richard. *The Great Acting Teachers and Their Methods Volume 2*. Hanover, NH: Smith & Kraus, 2010.

Brunetti, David. *Acting Songs*. North Charleston, SC: BookSurge, 2006.

Chekhov, Michael. *On the Technique of Acting*. New York: Harper, 1993.

Deer, Joe and Rocco Dal Vera. *Acting in musical theater: A comprehensive course*. 2nd ed. New York: Routledge, 2015.

Esper, William and Damon DiMarco. *The Actor's Art and Craft: William Esper Teachers the Meisner Technique*. New York: Anchor Books, 2008.

Guskin, Harold. *How to Stop Acting*. New York: Farrar, Straus and Giroux, 2003.

Hall, Karen. *So You Want to Sing Music Theatre: A Guide for Professionals*. Lanham, MD: Rowman & Littlefield, 2014.

Hagen, Uta. *Respect for Acting*. 2nd ed. New York: Wiley, 2008.

Isbell, Tom. *Lessons: The Craft of Acting – Truthful Behavior on Stage or Screen*. Colorado Springs: Meriwether Publishing, 2006.

Isherwood, Charles. "Operatic acting? Oxymoron no more." *New York Times*. September 9, 2007. Accessed on August 12, 2018. www.nytimes.com/2007/09/09/arts/music/09char.html.

Kayes, Gillyanne. *Singing and the Actor*. 2nd ed. New York: Routledge, 2004.

Meisner, Sanford, and Dennis Longwell. *Sanford Meisner on Acting*. New York: Vintage Books, 1987.

Moore, Tracey, and Allison Bergman. *Acting the Song: Performance Skills for Musical Theatre*. New York: Allworth Press, 2008.

National Association of Schools of Music. *NASM Handbook 2017-2018*. Reston, VA: National Association of Schools of Music, 2017.

Ostwald, David F. *Acting for Singers: Creating Believable Singing Characters*. New York: Oxford University Press, 2005.

Schreiber, Terry. *Acting: Advanced Techniques for the Actor, Director, and Teacher*. New York: Allworth Press, 2005.

Spivey, Norman and Mary Saunders Barton. *Cross-Training in the Voice Studio: A Balancing Act*. San Diego: Plural Publishing, 2018.

Shurtleff, Michael. *Audition: Everything an Actor Needs to Know to get the Part*. New York: Bantam, 1980.

Stanislavski, Constantin. *An Actor Prepares*. Translated by Elizabeth Reynolds Hapgood. New York: Routledge, 1989.

Emotion

Bicknell, Jeannette. "Just a song? Exploring the aesthetics of popular song performance." *Journal of Aesthetics and Art Criticism* 63, no. 3 (Summer 2005): 261–270. www.doi.org/10.1111/j.0021-8529.2005.00206.x.

Chalfin, Dane. "From 'me' to 'we': Audience-focused practical tools for interpretation and performance." In *The Singer-Songwriter Handbook*, edited by Justin A. Williams and Katherine Williams. New York: Bloomsbury Academic, 2017.

Cooper, Gloria. "Once more with feeling: The crossover artist's first steps in making an emotional connection with a popular or jazz song." *Journal of Singing* 60, no. 2 (November/December 2003): 153–157.

de Boise, Sam. *Men, Masculinity, Music and Emotions*. Basingstoke: Palgrave Macmillian, 2015.

Dibben, Nicola. "Vocal performance and the projection of emotional intimacy." In *The Ashgate Research Companion to Popular Musicology*, edited by Derek B. Scott, 317–333. London: Routledge, 2009.

Dibben, Nicola. "Subjectivity and the construction of emotion in the music of Björk." *Music Analysis* 25, no. 1-2 (March 2006): 171–197. www.doi.org/10.1111/j.1468-2249.2006.00237.x.

Dukes, Richard L., Tara M. Bisel, Karoline N. Borega, Eligio A. Lobato, and Matthew D. Owens. "Expressions of love, sex, and hurt in popular songs: A content analysis of all-time greatest hits." *Social Science Journal* 40, no. 4 (October 2003): 643–650. http://www.doi.org/10.1016/S0362-3319(03)00075-2.

Gellel, Adrian-Mario. "Traces of spirituality in the Lady Gaga phenomenon." *International Journal of Children's Spirituality* 18, no. 2 (May 2013): 214–226. www.doi.org/10.1080/1364436X.2013.796309.

Green, Andrew. "Rage Against the Machine, Zapatismo, and the aesthetics of anger." *Popular Music* 34, no. 3 (October 2015): 390–407. www.doi.org/10.1017/S0261143015000331.

Hakanpää, Tua, Teja Waaramaa, and Anne-Maria Laukkanen. "Emotion recognition from singing voices using contemporary commercial music and classical styles." *Journal of Voice*, In press. doi.org/10.1016/j.jvoice.2018.01.012.

Izdebski, Krzysztof, ed. *Emotions in the Human Voice: Volume I Foundations*. San Diego: Plural Publishing, 2007.

Izdebski, Krzysztof, ed. *Emotions in the Human Voice: Volume II Clinical Evidence*. San Diego: Plural Publishing, 2008.

Izdebski, Krzysztof, ed. *Emotions in the Human Voice: Volume III Culture and Perception*. San Diego: Plural Publishing, 2008.

Monti, Elisa, David C. Kidd, Linda M. Carroll, and Emanuele Castano. "What's in a singer's voice: The effect of attachment, emotions and trauma." *Logopedics, Phoniatrics, Vocology* 42, no. 2 (July 2017): 62–72. www.doi.org/10.3109/14015439.2016.1166394.

Moore, Allan. "Authenticity as authentication." *Popular Music* 21, no. 2 (May 2002): 209–223. doi.org/10.1017/S0261143002002131.

Negus, Keith. "Authorship and the popular song." *Music & Letters* 92, no. 4 (November 2011): 607–629. doi.org/10.1017/S0261143002002131.

Neto, Leon. "Contemporary Christian music and the 'Praise and Worship' style." *Journal of Singing* 67, no. 2 (November/December 2010): 195–200.

Reinhert, Kat. "Original recipes: Application of vocal technique to address artistic choices in original music." In *The Voice Teacher's Cookbook: Creative Recipes for Teachers of Singing* edited by Brian J. Winnie, 97–98. Delray Beach, FL: Meredith Music, 2018.

Robinson-Martin, Trineice. "Performance styles and music characteristics of black Gospel music." *Journal of Singing* 65, no. 5 (May/June 2009): 595–599.

Robinson, Daniel K. "Voice in worship: The contemporary worship singer." In *Teaching Singing in the 21st Century* edited by Scott D. Harrison and Jessica O'Bryan, 319–334. Dordrecht: Springer, 2014.

Robinson-Martin, Trineice. "Take my hand: Teaching the Gospel singer in the applied voice studio." In *Teaching Singing in the 21st Century* edited by Scott D. Harrison and Jessica O'Bryan, 335–352. Dordrecht: Springer, 2014.

Schellenberg, E. Glenn, and Christian von Scheve. "Emotional Cues in American Popular Music: Five Decades of the Top 40." *Psychology of Aesthetics, Creativity & the Arts* 6, no. 3 (August 2012): 196–203. www.doi.org/10.1037/a0028024.

Shumway, David R. "The emergence of the singer-songwriter." In *The Cambridge Companion to the Singer-songwriter*, edited by Katherine Williams and Justin A. Williams, 11–20. Cambridge: Cambridge University Press, 2016. doi. org/10.1017/CCO9781316569207.

Statista. "Global recorded music revenue from 1999 to 2017 (in billion U.S. dollars)." Accessed on August 23, 2018. www.statista.com/statistics/272305/global-revenue-of-the-music-industry/.

Steinhauer, Kimberly M. and Jo Estill. "The Estill Voice Model: Physiology of emotion." In *Emotions in the Human Voice: Volume II Clinical Evidence*, edited by Krysztof Izdebski, 86–99. San Diego: Plural Publishing, 2008.

Thompson, Paula and Victoria S. Jaque. "Holding a mirror up to nature: Psychological vulnerability in actors." *Psychology of Aesthetics, Creativity & the Arts* 6, no. 4 (November 2012): 361–369. www.doi.org/10.1037/a0028911.

Till, Rupert. "Singer-songwriter authenticity, the unconscious and emotions (feat. Adele's 'Someone Like You')." In *The Cambridge Companion to the Singer-songwriter*, edited by Katherine Williams and Justin A. Williams, 291–306. Cambridge: Cambridge University Press, 2016. doi.org/10.1017/CCO9781316569207.

Tyrangiel, Josh. "Emotional rescue." *Time* 159, no. 21 (May 27, 2002): 59–60.

Walker, Gwendolyn and Cody Commander. "The emotionally prepared singer." *Journal of Singing* 73, no. 3 (January/February 2017): 261–268.

van den Tol, Annemieke J.M., "The appeal of sad music: A brief overview of current directions in research on motivations for listening to sad music." *Arts in Psychotherapy* 49 (July 2016): 44–49. www.doi.org/10.1016/j.aip.2016.05.008.

Williams, Katherine and Justin A. Williams, eds. *The Cambridge Companion to the Singer-songwriter*. Cambridge: Cambridge University Press, 2016.

Popular song and social change

Aoki, Andrew L., and Valerie Martinez-Ebers. "Notes from the Underground: Popular Music and African American empowerment." *Conference Papers: American Political Science Association* (January 2011): 1–26.

Bartkowiak, Matthew J. *The MC5 and Social Change: A Study in Rock and Revolution*. Jefferson, NC: McFarland, 2009.

Brackett, David. "(In search of) musical meaning: genres, categories and crossover." in *Popular Music Studies*, edited by David Hesmondhalgh and Keith Negus, 65–83. London: Arnold, New York: Oxford University Press, 2002.

Burke, Patrick. "Rock, race, and radicalism in the 1960s: The Rolling Stones, Black Power, and Godard's One Plus One." *Journal of Musicological Research* 29, no. 4 (October 2010): 275–294. www.doi.org/10.1080/01411896.2010.513322.

DeWall, C. Nathan, Richard S. Pond, Jean M. Twenge, and Keith W. Campbell. "Tuning in to psychological change: Linguistic markers of psychological traits and emotions over time in popular U.S. song lyrics." *Psychology of Aesthetics, Creativity & The Arts* 5, no. 3 (August 2011): 200–207. www.doi.org/10.1037/a0023195.

Edwards, Leigh H. *Dolly Parton, Gender and Country Music*. Bloomington: Indiana University Press, 2018.

Geidel, Molly. "Supermaxes, stripmines, and Hip-Hop." *Journal of Popular Music Studies (Wiley-Blackwell)* 17, no. 1 (April 2005): 67–76. www.doi.org/10.1111/j.1524-2226.2005.00034.x.

Glen, Patrick. "'Oh you pretty thing!': How David Bowie 'Unlocked everybody's inner queen' in spite of the music press." *Contemporary British History* 31, no. 3 (September 2017): 407–429. www.doi.org/10.1080/13619462.2016.1261696.

Gracyk, Theodore. *I Wanna Be Me: Rock Music and the Politics of Identity*. Philadelphia: Temple University Press, 2001.

Jarman-Ivens, Freya, ed. *Oh Boy! Masculinities and Popular Music*. New York: Routledge, 2007.

Jackson, Mark Allan. "Electric chair blues: Black expression and execution in the era of Jim Crow." *Journal of Popular Music Studies (Wiley-Blackwell)* 29, no. 4 (December 2017): n/a. www.doi.org/10.1111/jpms.12245.

Kearney, Mary Celeste. *Gender and Rock*. New York: Oxford University Press, 2017.

Orejuela, Fernando. *Rap and Hip Hop Culture*. New York: Oxford University Press, 2015.

Pach, Chester. "'Rock 'n' Roll is Here to Stay': Using Popular Music to Teach About Dating and Youth Culture from Elvis to the Beatles." *OAH Magazine of History* 18, no. 4 (July 2004): 44–47.

Papayanis, Marilyn Adler. "Feeling free and female sexuality: The aesthetics of Joni Mitchell." *Popular Music & Society* 33, no. 5 (December 2010): 641–655. www.doi.org/10.1080/03007766.2010.510919.

Phillips-Hutton, Ariana. "Private words, public emotions: Performing confession in indie music." *Popular Music* 37, no. 3 (October 2018): 329–350. www.doi.org/10.1017/S0261143018000387.

Pruitt, Lesley. "Real men kill and a lady never talks back: Gender goes to war in Country Music." *International Journal on World Peace* 24, no. 4 (December 2007): 85–106.

Rabaka, Reiland. *Civil Rights Music: The Soundtracks of the Civil Rights Movement*. Lanham, MD: Lexington Books, 2016.

Rabaka, Reiland. *The Hip Hop Movement: From R&B and the Civil Rights Movement to Rap and the Hip Hop Generation*. Lanham, MD: Lexington Books, 2013.

Shonekan, Stephanie. *Soul, Country, and the USA: Race and Identity in American Music Culture*. New York: Palgrave Macmillan, 2015.

Statista. "Public opinion on the music genres which are representative of America today in the United States as of May 2018." Accessed on August 23, 2018. www.statista.com/statistics/864602/music-genre-modern-america/.

Stephens, Vincent. "Crooning on the fault lines: Theorizing Jazz and Pop vocal singing discourse in the Rock Era, 1955-1978." *American Music* 26, no. 2 (Summer 2008): 156–195.

Szatmary, David P. *A Time to Rock: A Social History of Rock and Roll*. 3rd ed. New York: Schirmer, 1996.

Whiteley, Sheila. *Women and Popular Music: Sexuality, Identity, and Subjectivity*. New York: Routledge, 2000.

Williams, Sherri. "Cardi B: Love & Hip Hop's unlikely feminist hero." *Feminist Media Studies* 17, no. 6 (December 2017): 1114–1117. www.doi.org/10.1080/14680777.2017.1380431.

Wrathall, Mark A., ed. *U2 and Philosophy: How to Decipher an Atomic Band*. Chicago: Open Court Press, 2006.

SECTION III:
Special Demands from the Industry

15

Audio technology

The impact of audio technology on voice use in general and studio voice training in particular, is a large topic worthy of dedicated research. This chapter merely represents the tip of the iceberg on what should be a deep dive of research for any teacher of CCM singing.

Amplification is an inherent part of musical theatre and CCM singing. In musical theatre, sensitive head-mounted condenser microphones allow the singer to perform at low effort levels yet still achieve a satisfying range of expression. In CCM singing, teachers describe the microphone as an extension of the voice and an essential and expressive tool. It takes training and practice to expertly wield a hand-held microphone in live performance. Not all of the pedagogues use a PA (public address) system in their studios, but nearly all agree that it is essential for singers to understand how audio technology impacts their voices.

At a minimum, singers should understand how the different varieties of both dynamic and condenser microphones impact pick-up patterns and sensitivity levels. When pedagogues refer to "microphone technique" they are speaking of a variety of practical and stylistic applications for using this tool. Microphone technique includes how to hold a microphone, how to modify volume, diction, or *stylisms* for an optimal sound, and how to move the microphone or adjust the way it is held to achieve a desired vocal effect.

According to Matthew Edwards, it is critical for teachers and singers to understand some basics of signal processing, including equalization (EQ), compression, reverberation (reverb), and auto-tune, because these effects can significantly alter the resulting sound.[1] Edwards has published several book chapters on what singers and voice teachers should know about audio technology, and he has produced an excellent YouTube video demonstrating the sound of each signal processing effect listed above in back-to-back comparisons of the same audio excerpt.[2] Beyond signal processing, it is helpful for singers and teachers to understand what a mixer does, the difference between a monitor and a speaker, and some basics of digital voice processors. Teachers report that students are often self-motivated to seek information on how all of this technology works, but teachers may be less so. Edwards's articles are a great starting point, and an extensive recommended reading list may be found at the end of this chapter.

---

1 Matthew Edwards, "The art of perfection: What every singer and voice teacher should know about audio technology," in *The Vocal Athlete* by Wendy D. Leborgne and Marci Rosenberg (San Diego: Plural Publishing, 2014), 271–294 and Matthew Edwards, "I love it loud! Using audio enhancement technology," in *So You Want to Sing Rock 'N' Roll* (Lanham, MD: Rowman & Littlefield, 2014) 167–191.

2 Matthew Edwards, producer, "Back-to-back comparisson [sic] of vocal effects," accessed September 12, 2018, www.youtube.com/watch?v=a4GofSN6J4w. More information may be found at http://www.edwardsvoice.com/.

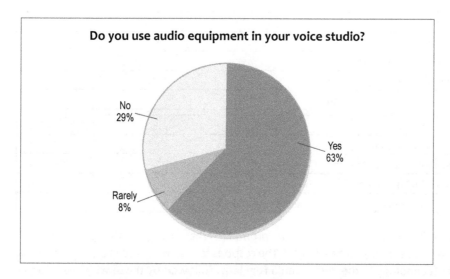

The 37% of teachers who do not use audio technology in their studios regularly prefer to keep the focus of study on vocal production at the source. Pedagogues report that singers can hear themselves best when they are un-amplified, and they can develop kinesthetic awareness that they will rely upon if they are in a performance situation where they cannot control how they hear themselves.

It is important to note that in musical theatre singing, sound engineering and sound design are rarely within the control of the singer. There are experts on the production team who do that work for them. However, if a singer understands the basic concepts and vocabulary used by the sound team, they can communicate their needs and desires more effectively. With the standard eight-show week, savvy singers can prevent fatigue by leaning on the support of the sound system.

In a typical live concert or recording studio, a singer may have more control over how their voice is processed through the sound system. Emerging professionals may need to provide their own audio equipment or produce their own recordings. At a minimum, they must be able to request or provide their preferred microphone, and it is important for them to know which microphones work best for their voices. In a recording setting, an astute singer will be able to listen back and request adjustments to achieve the best result.

The majority of pedagogues (63%) use microphones and a PA in their studios, but they usually keep the components simple: a few different microphones, an amplifier, and speakers. They use the most common dynamic hand-held microphone, the Shure SM-58, with perhaps a few additional options. Some teachers ask their students to bring their own microphones of choice for consistency. Teachers report that they often start the lesson un-amplified during technical work and utilize the PA in repertoire work. They do not typically use a mixer or any processing effects within the studio, unless a student specifically requests it. Universities can offer supporting coursework in the area of audio technology for CCM singers, and it is a required component of most collegiate programs in CCM singing. Because the internet is forever, even students should aim to produce the best-sounding material possible if they plan to share content online. Some of the most common audio equipment brands and software programs used by the pedagogues are listed below.

Sound equipment
Sweetwater, www.sweetwater.com/
TC-Helicon, www.tc-helicon.com/
Shure, http://www.shure.com/americas
Bose, www.bose.com/en_us/index.html

Software
Audacity, www.audacityteam.org/
VoceVista, http://www.vocevista.com/
Sing & See, www.singandsee.com/
Estill Voiceprint™, www.estillvoice.com/pages/clinical-software

This chapter includes responses to the prompt "What are your thoughts on audio technology? Do you use it in your teaching?". The responses are presented in order from those who use audio technology in the voice studio regularly, followed by those who use it rarely, and ending with those who do not use it.

Kimberly Steinhauer

I use audio technology daily in teaching.[3] Every form of feedback is embraced and used in athletic training. I use the appropriate technology for my vocal athletes.

Irene Bartlett

Given the extent of engagement that our students have with online technologies, I believe that today's CCM studio teacher has to be conversant with digital platforms such as backing track sites, music writing programs, repertoire sites, recording programs, and the function and application of amplification equipment (live sound reinforcement).

As CCM singers rarely perform in superior acoustic spaces (such as concert halls and cathedrals), they are reliant on live sound reinforcement for both artistic expression (conversational and intimate style interpretation) and performance longevity (vocal health). In fact, the PA is a direct and essential extension of the singer's voice. As an industry "insider" I can report that rather than being the focus of attention, most CCM performances occur in environments where live music is used primarily to create ambiance and atmosphere for a venue. The CCM singer has to produce and maintain their vocal production against a background of white noise (the loud speaking of audiences and the clatter of glasses, plates etc.), while competing with loud, electronic instruments and/or recorded backing music. After many years of personal experience singing in such acoustically-inferior venues, and in an effort to reduce vocal loading and associated vocal fatigue, I consider the training of students in the operation and use of live sound reinforcement as a vital component of my teaching practice. Beyond offering information on *best fit-to-task* PA systems, I advise singers on selection of the most appropriate microphone to voice type. A PA is set up permanently in my studio and while technical work is trained *off mic*, all performance practice is undertaken with full PA. If my students are working professionally, or are considering a professional career in CCM, I can

---

3   A central tool to the Estill Voice Training® model is the real-time spectral analysis program Voiceprint™ that can record, analyze, and play-back the voice. More information may be found at www.estillvoice.com/.

offer them a basic working knowledge of equalization and mixing of amplified sound to suit their specific performance environments.

I find acoustic analysis programs to be a useful studio tool, especially for students with strong visual learning modes. I have been using VoceVista[4] and Sing&See[5] software since they became commercially available. My interactions and communications with students through internet sites such as YouTube, Skype, and Zoom are commonplace. However, I do not choose to teach using these platforms unless the student has previously studied with me in face-to-face lessons.

Dane Chalfin

Yes, I have an audio set-up in my studio. If I am working with people who are regularly performing on-mic, we have to work on-mic, or at least alternate between on- and off-mic because the microphone and any live effects and processing they are using changes how they are going to approach what they are doing. For a contemporary singer, using a microphone needs to become an extension of their instrument. Microphone technique is really important. I have a full PA system in all of my studios. For tour preparation, my students bring in their entire set-up, running a laptop, floor pedals, playing guitar, etc. No matter how exhaustive it is to bring it all in and set it up, all of those components are needed to evaluate the situation.

I had a five-piece band, in which four of them sang really tight harmonies with a huge amount of live processing. They are all also playing instruments and running their own processing. On day one of tour preparation, we decided to move about 50% of their live work onto the track because they could not accomplish all of it live. We could do it in the studio, but not live. With the advent of TC-Helicon products in particular, people have so much live tuning and effects just at the touch of a button. If they are using effects in performance, I want them to use them in the studio too. They need to learn how much they can use them, and how much they can depend on them. This also helps them to develop taste because the pre-sets are often too harsh and dramatic, and they start to understand some of the nuances.

Kim Chandler

I have a Bose PA system (speakers and small mixing desk) and microphone permanently set up in my teaching studio. I generally do not use amplification for vocal exercises, but I do use it when working on repertoire because pop singers always use microphones in performance. Good mic technique needs to become second nature. If a singer also expresses interest in understanding the sound system, (e.g. how to set it up, basic equalization etc.), then I will include this.

Matthew Edwards

I have a Bose Tower with a Bose ToneMatch mixer that I keep in my studio. The ToneMatch has equalization, reverb/delay, and compression, and creates a great final product. Commercial singers are always performing on-mic, so it is important to show them how to make the microphone part of their instrument and technique. In the recording studio, you just want the

---

4   More information may be found at http://www.vocevista.com/.

5   More information may be found at www.singandsee.com/.

artist to sing their heart out, but on tour they have to have strategies to conserve their voice over multi-hour gigs. If they learn how to use the mic and listen to themselves in the monitors, they will do much better.

Now of course there is a big difference in working with an established professional and an aspiring professional. Established pros have a full sound team working for them and they do not have to think about the details. However, aspiring pros will often perform in venues where they will have to provide their own sound equipment, or they will have a sound guy who does not understand the voice. In those instances, having knowledge of how sound equipment works, and what to ask for in terms of adjustments, is critical.

Robert Edwin

Other than my exclusively classical singers who are required to be acoustic and self-amplified, the rest of my students have to know something about microphone technique as well as the tools for the alteration of pitch and tone quality. To that end, my studio is equipped with microphones and a wonderful Bose amplification system, as well as recording equipment. New CCM singers need to realize that almost all of the singing they hear on recordings and in public performances is altered by audio technology. The unaltered acoustic voice is what we train, but it can end up sounding very different when processed through current technology. Young singers trying to copy the altered voices they hear can get themselves into vocal trouble very quickly.

Cate Frazier-Neely

There is an emerging body of scholarship that explores the relationship between developments in popular music, digital culture and the creative process.[6] To pretend that CCM and technology are not intertwined is akin to burying one's head in the sand, or sticking your fingers in your ears while singing "La, la, la....". It also does not help prepare a singer for the fact that all their hard work will go up in smoke without the co-operation and skill of sound engineers or band leaders who know what they are doing, or effective sound equipment. Readers may find my article, "Live vs. Recorded: Comparing Apples and Oranges to Get Fruit Salad" to be of use on this topic.[7]

I have a basic Beta 58-A Shure microphone and amplifier and use my computer or iPhone with speakers as a resource, but I have given up on pretending to know anything about how to record or edit. I emphasize that monitors, sound systems, and the performing space all affect a CCM singer, and frequently ask questions about the environment in which a singer will be performing so they can become aware of what may affect them and use visualization to prepare. I do not pretend to know a thing about how to set up and monitor sound systems, but I do try to help students take charge of what they need and learn to communicate with other musicians and technicians.

A whole fascinating history of musicals and the use of microphones has come out of developments in the recording industry and the influence of pop and rock genres on theatre. This means that contemporary musical theatre is written to be sung with

6   Robert Strachan, *Sonic Technologies: Popular Music, Digital Culture and the Creative Process*, (London: Bloomsbury Publishing, 2017).

7   Cate Frazier-Neely, "The Independent Teacher--Live Vs. Recorded: Comparing Apples to Oranges to Get Fruit Salad," *Journal of Singing* 69, no. 5 (2013), 593–596.

microphones and a whole sound system. In the area where I live, there is a local "pre-professional" company that does contemporary musicals and takes great pride in insisting that their singers perform without microphones in order to learn to project. I think this is a form of vocal abuse.

Marcelle G. Gauvin

Audio technology is important and inseparable from today's contemporary vocal pedagogy. My students sing through a sound system comprised of microphones, a mixing board equipped with equalization, and powered speakers. Students need to explore microphone technique while incorporating dynamics and vocal colors before they perform publicly. They learn about the basics of live sound equalization and begin to understand the unique role microphones play in each CCM style. It is important for students to understand the unique characteristics and pick-up patterns of each microphone. The ultimate goal is to utilize a microphone naturally, as if it were merely an extension of the voice.

Elisabeth Howard

To teach CCM, it is necessary to provide at lessons the equipment necessary to emulate the commercial sounds that we hear on recordings. Contemporary commercial singing is never produced without a microphone. For this reason, I have a boom-stand microphone at the piano for me and a stand-up microphone for the student when we work on a song, which is the last half of the lesson. I used to use a "Singing Machine" to play CDs of various prominent singers singing their songs, and had a huge collection of CDs, most of which I gave away, due to new technology. I use YouTube recordings on my iPad, or the student brings in a song on their phone. We hook up my iPad (or their phone) to Blue Tooth and pair it with a small and very inexpensive ($20) speaker that can be placed anywhere in the room. It amplifies the sound as if the performer were right there with you.

At each lesson, we either continue working on the same song, or the student brings in another song. I usually choose songs when a student has an audition for a particular style of singing, such as a music theatre audition that needs for example, a blues or rock feel. I use recordings of top singers. From these recordings, I take the student phrase by phrase through the song slowly and methodically, analyzing and copying every nuance, from type of vibrato, to coloration, use of registers, head, chest, mix, phrasing, pronunciation, dynamics, "licks" and "runs", and the use of the vocal tract to enhance the emotional outpouring of the music such as "throat cry," throat laugh," "Creaky door," "Back L".[8] Basically, all the components typical of that style. My method of teaching style is to have the student use their ear to copy, phrase-by-phrase, what they hear. This is the method that instrumentalists use to play in specific styles. I guide the students as we go through the song, sometimes only working on a few phrases at a time.

Wendy DeLeo LeBorgne

Today, everyone needs to have a very good sense of audio technology. They need to understand how microphones and acoustics can influence the voice, in and out of the studio. I do use audio technology in the studio with my commercial artists, but not with classical

---

8   For more information, see Elisabeth Howard, *Sing! The Vocal Power Method* (New York: Alfred, 2006).

artists unless they are learning to cross-over. I have sound equipment in my studio, including a soundboard and 6-8 microphones, which are a mix of condenser and dynamic. A lot of my artists bring their own microphone to their lessons. We may test out some others to see which one they like the best with their voice. After we choose one, then that is what we use for lessons, because that is what they are using all the time.

I teach a commercial vocal pedagogy class to Doctor of Musical Arts (DMA) classical artists at the University of Cincinnati, College - Conservatory of Music. Within the course, the students learn they have to be able to set up a soundboard, and microphone, amplifier, and demonstrate an understanding of how increasing specific frequencies with specific voices make a difference (help or hindrance). They must understand that different microphones make different voices sound differently. They also need to know what compression and amplification are, and basic terminology related to audio acoustics. I recommend some additional readings by Matt Edwards[9] on this topic as well.

Seth Riggs and Margareta Svensson Riggs

Audio technology is constantly evolving. We have gotten used to recordings that are manipulated to perfection, and for some the goal is even a processed sound. In a concert, we don't know if we hear someone actually sing live anymore. Some do, and some of those bravely, and it can be a rough experience for a listener used to the recordings. Even rougher for the singer. But then there are those artists who sing great.

As a singer, you want to master your singing to the best of your ability, and that is what we teach. The extent of our audio technology in a regular lesson includes microphones that we run through a PA. Just as in any live situation, it is easy to start to compete with the musicians and the crowd for power, and there is nothing gained by risking the singer starting to yell simply because they can't hear themselves well enough. Allowing the microphone to do the work instead is a given.

Trineice Robinson-Martin

I use audio technology in my teaching a lot, particularly in terms of backing tracks for warm-ups and songs. I use an application called iReal Pro™[10] which I play through the sound system in my studio. I produce many of my functional and style conditioning exercises using this application, as it helps students to make a direct connection between the training and stylistic context. Singers are encouraged to use a microphone during style conditioning exercises and song interpretation coaching. In terms of equipment, I use a Shure SM58 microphone (typical for most venues), or the students bring their own microphone, and I have a small 8-channel mixer with effects and PA in my studio. I teach all of my students how to use a sound system, and what a proper and inadequate EQ for their voice sounds like.

Edrie Means Weekly

I think it is important for the student to understand the basics of audio technology. I use it in my teaching. I have my students use the microphone in their commercial songs, and show them how the microphone can work for them by using less voice for expression and certain vocal *stylisms*. I

---

9   Edwards, "The art of perfection."

10 More information may be found at irealpro.com/.

have a TC-Helicon VoiceLive[11] with a Shure PG48 microphone and Behringer speaker in my studio. VoiceLive has equalization and effects in a floor pedal, with the vocal processor and 200 select presets for genre or voice effects type. There is also a harmonizing effect and a looper.

Kathryn Paradise

Audio technology is an essential tool in the commercial voice studio. I frequently make use of both live performance and studio recording technology when teaching. My students perform regularly on microphone and get feedback on their use of the technology, including tips on how to use monitors and effectively EQ their own voice. I make regular use of a digital audio workstation (DAW), audio interface and studio condenser microphone, to produce for the vocalists in the lesson and on their own tracks and originals, demonstrating studio techniques and methods for "comping a vocal".[12] Most of my students receive some training in music technology as part of their degree program at Belmont University, but even those who do not, avidly pursue the knowledge on their own. There are many resources and tutorials online for students interested in recording and producing their own music, and this is fast becoming a required skill for those pursuing a career in commercial music.

Cathrine Sadolin

If the singer is comfortable working on microphones, then we use them. If the singer prefers not to use the PA system, then we do not use it. This is completely up to the singer.

If the singer wants to use the sound system, then we use a simple PA system. We keep the equalization (EQ) the way the singer wants it. It the singer doesn't have a preferred EQ, we keep the EQ to a minimum so that he/she can hear what they are doing. We usually set it up in the configuration that the singer wants, using their preferred microphone.

Lisa Popeil

I love using audio technology for my CCM students and so do they. I have a recording studio set up: the student is the "artist" and I act as the "producer." I have the student sing with a karaoke track or I will create one for them, then show them how the multi-track recording process is done. If I need to record piano or add background vocals, I will even teach the student to run the recording process themselves.

My students find that singing with headphones into a good microphone improves their skills more quickly than singing in the room. I often hear from them "I can really hear myself!". Then, of course, I will tune their pitch digitally in my recording program and provide a finished recording with a perfected version of their singing. The process is exciting and addictive, and the singers can improve quite quickly.

Jan Shapiro

I generally do not use a microphone and PA system in my private lesson studio. However, when I taught performance classes and ensembles, I used a PA system and taught microphone

---

11 Footswitch controlled mic preamp and vocal harmony effects processor. More information may be found at www.sweetwater.com/

12 "Comping" or "compiling" the best vocal performance from multiple takes is a common editing task for DAW users.

technique. If a private student needs practice in microphone technique, I do use a microphone and PA set-up to work solely on how to sing with the microphone in my studio. I use a mixer amplifier, speakers, and microphone.

Tracy Marie Bourne

When I taught music theatre students, there was a component of their course that included microphone technique as part of a cabaret project. Otherwise, I do not tend to do much microphone work or other sound technology work with my singers. Almost all of my singers are interested in music theatre singing, and this style of performance rarely uses technology that is controlled by the singers. In a professional theatre context, an external audio technician will amplify and adjust the sound, but the singer will rarely have any say or any control over it.

Gillyanne Kayes

Personally, I do not teach microphone technique. My clients either already know how to work the microphone or are used to being amplified in stage performances as they are all working singers. I like to see the music my clients are singing if I possibly can, but quite a few of them work with backing tracks and I have become used to this as well. The internet is a wonderful thing!

Jeff Ramsey

I believe anything that can further the concepts and ideals for a student is always something to consider. I, however, have not used it in my studio as of this writing, but we do have classes here at Berklee for the students to learn more about microphone technique, for instance, classes where they work with instrumentalists and have to use microphones in order to be heard.

Marci Rosenberg

I do not happen to use audio technology when teaching, because I do not see a large number of pop/rock singers. However, I think this is essential if you are working with a lot of singers who focus on any type of pop/rock style.

Kevin Wilson

I do not teach microphone techniques in the studio. I encourage my students to use their voice naturally and allow for the professional sound engineers to do their job.

Mark Baxter

I do not use microphones in my teaching studios. I want singers to form intimate relationships with their voices and develop deep motor skills. This way they are not dependent on technology and can better guide a sound engineer as to how they prefer to be recorded or amplified. Too often, singers become intimidated when surrounded by equipment in a recording studio or live venue. I remind them that every dial, every switch, every flashing light is there to augment their performance. The gear is there to serve the singer – not the other way around. Sound technicians often forget this! It is helpful, but not necessary, to learn the vernacular of sound engineering. Ultimately, singers are responsible for knowing their voices, and if the amplified or recorded result of a performance does not meet their expectations they must speak up.

"Warmer, brighter, too harsh, not enough edge" is all a technician needs as guidance. It is remarkable how digital technology has changed the recording process and altered the culture of contemporary music. But what has not changed is the listener's connection to the identity of a singer and the sentiment of a song.

Jeannette LoVetri

I keep an acoustic studio, and even though I do have electronic equipment there, I rarely dig it out. Learning how to use a microphone is essential in all CCM styles, and being knowledgeable about how a sound system works so the vocalist can either run that system on his/her own or know how to talk to a sound engineer in terms of what is desired, is necessary. All vocalists who sing with bands or alone with piano in a club or cafe should understand how to choose a good microphone, have a personal monitor, and how to get them to work optimally. I do not teach any of that. Students have to find someone else to help them, but the information and the people who teach it is not difficult to locate.

Mary Saunders Barton

I work acoustically in my studio because I am interested in voice building and that is difficult to assess with amplification. I do think singers should seek out opportunities to interact with experienced sound engineers in order to increase their understanding of microphone techniques. Although I can see the value in audio feedback devices like VoceVista for resonance adjustments, I have not used them in my studio.

References and recommended reading

Björkner, Eva. "Musical theater and opera singing - Why so different? A study of subglottal pressure, voice source, and formant frequency characteristics." *Journal of Voice* 22, no. 5 (September 2008): 533–540. doi.org/10.1016/j.jvoice.2006.12.007.

Bos, Nancy. "Microphone technique: Cooking up complex vocals." In *The Voice Teacher's Cookbook: Creative Recipes for Teachers of Singing* edited by Brian J. Winnie, 11–12. Delray Beach, FL: Meredith Music, 2018.

Corbett, Ian. *Mic it! Microphones, microphone technique, and their impact on the final mix.* Burlington, MA: Focal Press, 2015.

Daugherty, James F. "Too much noise in the kitchen." In *The Voice Teacher's Cookbook: Creative Recipes for Teachers of Singing* edited by Brian J. Winnie, 24–25. Delray Beach, FL: Meredith Music, 2018.

Dittmar, Tim. *Audio Engineering 101: A Beginner's Guide to Music Production.* Burlington, MA: Focal Press, 2011.

Edwards, Matthew. "The art of perfection: What every singer and voice teacher should know about audio technology." In *The Vocal Athlete* by Wendy D. LeBorgne and Marci Rosenberg, 271–294. San Diego: Plural Publishing, 2014.

Edwards, Matthew. "I love it loud! Using audio enhancement technology," in *So You Want to Sing Rock 'N' Roll*, 167-101. Lanham, MD: Rowman & Littlefield, 2014.

Federman, Jeremy and Todd Ricketts. "Preferred and minimum acceptable listening levels for musicians while using floor and in-ear monitors." *Journal of Speech, Language, and Hearing Research*, 51, no. 1 (February 2008): 147–159.

Frazier-Neely, Cathryn. "Live vs. recorded: Comparing apples to oranges to get fruit salad." *Journal of Singing* 69, no. 5 (May/June 2013): 593–596.

Gibson, Bill. *Vol. 1: Microphones and Mixers.* Milwaukee: Hal Leonard, 2007.

Horning, Susan Schmidt. "Engineering the performance: Recording engineers, tacit knowledge and the art of controlling sound." *Social Studies of Science* 34, no 5 (October 2004): 703–731. doi.org/10.1177/0306312704047536.

Howard, David M. and Damian T. Murphy. *Voice Science, Acoustics and Recording.* San Diego, CA: Plural Publishing, 2008.

Huber, David Miles and Robert E. Runstein. *Modern Recording Techniques.* 9th ed. New York: Routledge, 2018.

Morange, Séverine, Daniele Dubois, and Jean-Marc Fontaine. "Perception of recorded singing voice quality and expertise: Cognitive linguistics and acoustic approaches." *Journal of Voice* 24, no. 4 (July 2010): 450–457. doi.org/10.1016/j.jvoice.2008.08.006.

Petrescu, Nicolae. "Loud music listening." *McGill Journal of Medicine* 11, no. 2 (November 2008): 169–176.

Rudolph, Thomas and Vincent Leonard. *The iPad in the Music Studio: Connecting Your iPad to Mics, Mixers, Instruments, Computers, and More!* Milwaukee: Hal Leonard, 2014.

Strachan, Robert. *Sonic Technologies: Popular Music, Digital Culture and the Creative Process.* New York: Bloomsbury Publishing, 2017.

Tyrangiel, Josh. "Auto-tune: Why pop music sounds perfect." *Time*, February 5, 2009. Accessed September 10, 2018, http://content.time.com/time/magazine/article/0,9171,1877372,00.html.

Welch, Graham F., David M. Howard, Evangelos Himonides, and Jude Brereton. "Real-time feedback in the singing studio: An innovatory action-research project using new voice technology." *Music Education Research* 7, no. 2 (July 2005): 225–249. doi.org/10.1080/14613800500169779.

16

Improvisation

Improvisation is highly complex and style-specific, requiring an aural understanding of harmony and scales, and a trusting spirit of spontaneity. However, it is possible to learn to improvise by ear without understanding any of the music theory, harmonic progressions, or scales used. A student can have a natural flair for improvisation and execute it brilliantly without knowledge of music theory. Approaches like "Call & Response or Circle Singing"[1] can make improvisation accessible to every level of musician. However, one should be an advanced musician with a detailed understanding of theory in order to *teach* improvisation.

The majority of pedagogues (76%) teach musical improvisation as part of CCM voice training. Pedagogues who specialize in jazz and R&B must teach improvisation due to the inherent demands of these genres. To help a student develop mastery most approaches rely on a sense of spontaneous play in combination with a thorough understanding of theory and alternative scales, including major pentatonic, minor pentatonic, modal, whole-tone, blues, or minor scales. Some suggest using these scales in vocal warm-ups or conditioning so that the students become as deeply acquainted with them as they are with the major scale.

Of the 24% of teachers who say they do not teach improvisation, most are specialists in music theatre singing which does not often require improvisation. Some pedagogues only offer an introduction to improvisation, and then refer out to specialists who can work at a more advanced level. This reflects a growing trend of collaborative teaching, wherein a singing teacher is part of a larger team of educators who contribute to a student's overall growth as a musician by specializing in different areas. Having a team of educators is a common design in university programs. However, some independent teachers also report a regular practice of referring students to a more qualified expert in improvisation if needed.

---

1   An improvised process of community-singing, wherein singers stand in a circle around one person who leads the group by introducing different musical motives to create a multi-part harmonic obbligato, and then improvises a solo or invites others to improvise a solo over the harmonic obbligato.

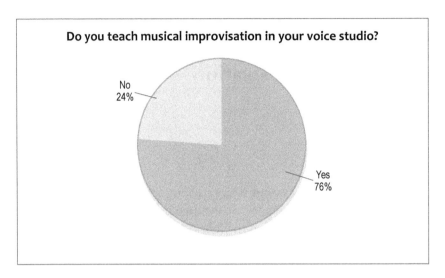

Do you teach musical improvisation in your voice studio?

No
24%

Yes
76%

This chapter includes responses to the prompt "Do you teach improvisation? If so, how do you teach it?". Responses are presented beginning with those who teach improvisation and offer specific techniques or resources on how they do this, and end with those who do not teach musical improvisation. Three pedagogues responded with a single declining statement: "No, I do not teach improvisation". These responses were included in the data analysis presented above, but they are not printed among the narratives below.

Cate Frazier-Neely

If a singer has not enjoyed or established a routine of listening, listening, listening to master improvisers or those skilled with singing historically accurate ornaments in classical music, we start with a listening journal and specific recommendations. It is something I try to do consistently for the length of time someone works with me. This is coupled with recommendations for practice on riffs, runs, and ornaments.

For those new to improvising, I start with simple call and response, changing a tune by one pitch or using a series of simple improv games I have learned over the years from vocal jazz educators. It depends on what they want to do. A great place to learn to improvise is in Circle Singing, made popular by Bobby McFerrin, which is a lot like learning to play Celtic music by consistently sitting in on a jam session. You learn by doing, and I try to encourage people to attend these kinds of things. Many singers can imitate improv or specific ornaments off jazz or classical recordings, but it is in listening to the harmonic structure underneath and understanding the connection to that is missing. Working with pitch relationships, harmony and theory become really important.

For advanced-intermediate jazz singers, they will either have their own resources for furthering improvisation or learning to riff cleanly (there are several good ones on the web) or I will send them to one of my students who teach vocal jazz at the college level and are working as jazz, gospel or R&B singers.

Kathryn Paradise

Improvisation is a complex and highly specialized craft, which can be difficult to fully explore in the context of a voice lesson. However, it is a necessary skill for commercial singers. In lessons, I incorporate improvising over common chord progressions into regular warm-ups. I also require students to transcribe melismatic runs and improvisations applicable to their genre of specialization, and practice improvisation over the chord changes of every song in their repertoire. In commercial singing (versus jazz singing), improvisation is typically applied when the singer changes the melody and phrasing of a song. To this end, I spend a significant amount of time helping students make cover songs unique and different through melodic and rhythmic variation and re-arrangement. Singers do best with an approach that combines both theoretical and "by ear" exploration of improvisation.

Kim Chandler

Ad libbing is a standard feature of a lot of pop music, so those who sing the styles that require it need to work on it and practice it, if it's not something that comes naturally. Regarding technique, I suggest they optimize their range, agility, and pitch accuracy. Musically, I suggest they build the foundational patterns by practicing relevant scales and modes, particularly the major and minor pentatonic scales, as these are the scales of choice used in most *ad libs*. I also recommend practicing generic licks and riffs from real songs, and jamming along to different grooves and chord sequences. The creative brain used in improvising needs as much exercise as anything else so that the ideas flow fluently and confidently.

Some level of vocal agility (flexibility, dexterity) is beneficial for a balanced vocal technique and therefore, I advocate that all singers include speed exercises based on scales, modes, arpeggios, intervals, and melodic fragments in their routine practice. Instrumentalists spend time slowly building up dexterity on their instrument; vocalists should not be exempted from this process. Besides which, many styles of pop music, e.g. soul, gospel, pop R&B, country, require agility and fluency in order to achieve the riffs and runs that feature in these styles.

Lisa Popeil

I teach improvisation for both jazz and R&B and use imitation as the primary tool. For instance, I will play a chord progression, or loop a portion of a karaoke track, to demonstrate vocal riffs, beginning with an easy two- or three-note riff before trying more complex lines. Using this call and response method (I sing, they repeat), I can assess their skill level and may back-track to simpler concepts like legato, decrescendos, and vibrato choices. For R&B, I also teach a method which involves cutting long riffs into "chunks", then describing the number and direction of notes within each chunk. I also use a computer program to loop and slow down a riff, so we can really discern the chunks and patterns.

For jazz improvisation, I will pick a section from a jazz song and create improvisations based on a familiar melody. I start, they repeat. Each succeeding phrase is made a little longer, rangier, or difficult, hoping to give the student not only new ideas, but to develop their courage to create their own melodic variations.

Kimberly Steinhauer

I teach very basic improvisation with some singers using a combination of solfege/music theory and practicing the skill of "covering" exactly (voice quality, phrasing, pitches, rhythms, diction, etc.) sections of songs from the top improvisers in their chosen style of music.

Trineice Robinson-Martin

I teach improvisation during style conditioning sessions, using the iReal Pro™ application.[2] Depending on the style of music I am teaching at the time, I adjust which chord changes I use and my approach. For example, jazz singers should at minimum be familiar with the blues form and I-vi-ii-V chord progression. Therefore, jazz exercises tend to use those chord progressions. Gospel/soul singers should be familiar with I-IV-V at a minimum, and their exercise will use those chord changes. Improvisation exercises for jazz singers will focus on rhythmic variations, and chord and scale relationship, melodic development, and phrasing. Improvisation for gospel/soul singers will focus on the expansion of melodic sequence and textual improvisation and phrasing.

Robert Edwin

Like any learning experience, judicious copying is usually a good place to start. I encourage my singers to listen to and try to duplicate improvisational melismas, riffs, and runs in the genre of their choosing. However, my favorite tool for teaching CCM improvisation is the twelve-bar blues. I use it as an exercise with almost all of my students, including my classical singers. We use the traditional pattern of four bars (measures) of the one chord (in the key of C, that would be the C-chord), two bars of the four chord (that would be the F-chord), two bars of the one chord, one bar of the five chord (that would be the G-chord), one bar of the four chord, one bar of the one chord; and finally, one bar of the turnaround-and-do-it-all-over-again five chord. Any key works and any lyric content is acceptable, from "do wah" scats to extended narratives. I go into greater detail about this in my *Journal of Singing* column, "Singin' the Blues: A Pedagogic Tool".[3] What's fun and even liberating about this exercise is that students create the melody and lyric. Even if it's the most basic of creations, it's *their* creation. Patience with beginners is required, especially opera singers who are trying to cross over "Jordan" into the CCM "campground".

Mark Baxter

My approach to training improvisation is to first un-train the blocks that prevent the flow of ideas from inspiration to phonation. A belief that one's behavior is outside the cultural norms causes dissonance between the emotional center of the brain (the limbic system) and its executive functions located in the prefrontal cortex. I explain the cognitive neuroscience, if there is a scarcity of ideas, and then encourage students to silence their internal critiques by replacing a song's lyrics with gibberish. Creating nonsensical sounds requires the brain to abandon its normal motor program for singing. In doing so, restricting judgments are greatly reduced and an opportunity for melodic creativity presents itself. Once singers are emotionally liberated, exploring various modes and scales like major and minor pentatonic, Lydian, and the use of the ubiquitous blue notes in contemporary music, become an endless menu of possibilities. Freedom before rules.

---

2   iReal Pro™ application for phone, tablet, and Mac. Creates a real-sounding band to accompany you as you practice and collects chord charts. More information may be found at irealpro.com/.

3   Robert Edwin, "Singin' the Blues: A Pedagogic Tool," *Journal of Singing* 71, no. 5 (May/June 2015), 613–615.

Marcelle G. Gauvin

I use the following approaches to teach improvisation:

1. Jamming with students – trading 4s/8s, call & response.
2. Student learns harmonic motion by singing roots, then 3rds, then 7ths.
3. Student sings scales behind the chords.
4. Transcriptions of great improvisers.
5. Ornamenting melody lines.
6. Student sings a motif over chord changes.
7. Student writes a blues or short solo.
8. Circle singing.
9. Assigned listening to great improvisers such as Ella Fitzgerald, Louis Armstrong, Jon Hendricks, Betty Carter, Bobby McFerrin, Kurt Elling, Sheila Jordan, Sarah Vaughan, Carmen McRae, Nancy King, to name but a few.

Edrie Means Weekly

I teach improvisation through exercises I use in warm-ups. Depending on learning style, I will teach basic ornamentation because most improvisations can be traced back to Baroque ornamentation. I use jazz educator Bob Stoloff's book, *Scat! Vocal Improvisation Techniques*[4], because it has a lot of good exercises. Those who are visual learners need to see it written down, so we write it out. Most of the time a client who is a strong belter has trouble moving the voice for improvisation. In these cases, I will work on agility through different lick/riff patterns in head or head/mix first before adding a strong mix to the improvisation.

Elisabeth Howard

I have my students practice the blues and pentatonic scales first. Then we do a back-and-forth imitation of licks and runs. I accompany on the piano. First, I make up a phrase and they imitate what I do and gradually when they feel secure, they are left on their own to improvise what they feel.

Jeff Ramsey

I am working on my own book with regards to improvisation as it relates to R&B, blues, and gospel music. The big thing to get them active in a particular genre is to give them exercises in the style of music they sing. In R&B, blues, and gospel styles, the riffs are largely formed from the pentatonic and blues scales, so why not use those as another option to the most commonly used five-note scale?

Wendy DeLeo LeBorgne

I teach improvisation with my jazz artists and some of my music theatre students. We will learn scat and riffing through improvisation. I will give them parameters to stay within a note range. When I teach the commercial vocal pedagogy class, I will have the students transcribe riffs from recorded artists. It is particularly valuable for classical artists to understand what happens with riffing both rhythmically and vocally.

---

4   Bob Stoloff, *Scat! Vocal Improvisation Techniques* (Brooklyn: Gerard and Sarzin, 1996).

For improvisation, I will play a series of jazz chords, any standard jazz chord progression, and I will have them warm-up their voice by practicing vocal improvisation. I saw this exercise in a workshop with Robert Edwin at a Voice Foundation Symposium[5] many years ago and loved it. He would play chord progressions and have his artists improvise in mid-voice, high, scat, and so on. It was a great vocal warm-up and fun for the artists.

Jan Shapiro

I teach improvisation within the voice lesson depending upon the student. I teach improv according to a specific vocal style. Improvisation in jazz is a different approach than say, R&B. I also think that some voices naturally have faster vocal agility than other voices. I may sing an example to a student and then ask them to sing it back, or I may play a "riff" on the piano and ask them to sing it back. Or we will discuss several vocalists and his or her approach to improvisation.

Seth Riggs and Margareta Svensson Riggs

We often include improvisation as part of singing songs, since the singer needs to make the song his or her own in various ways. That goes for both the meaning of the words as well as musically.

When it comes to the music, we may sing a passage that the singer mimics, we may do call and response, or take turns in singing the melody with very minor changes each time - really just any ongoing singing over the chords that encourages creativity that the singer latches on to and can start to build on.

Part of being a performer is to be free musically to do whatever you want and be confident doing it, to have so much control over the music and your musical ability that you can make it fresh is part of the live experience. Therefore, it is essential to be able to improvise.

Cathrine Sadolin

In Complete Vocal Technique, we teach everything that has to do with singing. We have techniques for improvisation, phrasing, rhythmic improvisation, and melodic improvisation. We also teach song-writing. When teaching improvisation, we start with practical application rather than theoretical study. Using a learn-by-ear approach, a singer can develop improvisation by simple means. Every singer can do this, even if they do not understand music theory or scales. If people want call and response, we offer that too. We show them how to make chords and how to practice. We always pay attention to what the singer wants. We help them find their own way to improvisation, what works best for them. This preserves their uniqueness.

Irene Bartlett

I teach improvisation as needed for the style. When working with jazz voice students, I teach conversational phrasing through rhythm, articulation (both music and diction), and personal story sharing. This involves assisting the student to connect to the lyrics of the song through a memory of some personal event. This elicits a degree of vulnerability that conveys honesty and genuine emotional connection to their audience. Their musicianship is developed through

---

5   The Voice Foundation is an organization dedicated to voice research, medicine, science, and education, with an annual symposium in Philadelphia. More information may be found at: voicefoundation.org/.

jazz scales and modes to inform their ability to hear the chord progression and harmonic structure. First though, I insist that they learn the actually written melody of the song. I also coach pop, rock, and R&B improvisation using the style-appropriate basic licks and melisma. However, once I have trained the basic style effects on a secure, efficient technique, I refer students who are serious about learning these styles to a colleague who is expert in the particular style elements and effects of the music.

Kevin Wilson

I have students create stories in their songs and change the intention. Sometimes I will write in the five stages of grief, or random emotions out of context, to see how that will affect the story and create a new discovery. For tone variation or "riffing", I try to introduce musical modes to my students to help inform their choices, but riffing should be used sparingly for strong emotional choices in performance, and only when appropriate to the style of music.

Matthew Edwards

I introduce students to improvisation but usually refer out for those who want to work at an advanced level. I teach students the pentatonic and blues scales, and create vocal exercises based on those scales to help them become familiar with the language. At the same time, I get them started singing over the chord changes in simple songs, so they can develop an understanding of chord tones and how to use them as landing places along the way. We also play around with rhythm, so they get the idea of how to use back phrasing, anticipations, and syncopations to vary a melody. Beyond that, they really need to work with a specialist.

Jeannette LoVetri

I used to teach workshops using movement and sound, focusing on improvisation in a free manner. I do not teach that now except on rare occasions. I do not have the skills to teach improvisation as a jazz singer would use it, creating new melodies over chord progressions. The idea that someone can sing freely, moving away from the melody and rhythm, for the sake of expression, is helpful, but in music theatre one is restricted to small changes, and in classical repertoire one must sing what is written unless, perhaps, one is performing an *acapella cadenza*.

Dane Chalfin

I do not teach improvisation. I am not the greatest musician. If I need a style coach, I have two of the best on this planet on my speed dial and I will hand students over to them. Kim Chandler[6] (U.K. vocal coach and singer) and I have evolved a sort of partnership by accident. She is one of the only people I can team-teach with. We do a lot of client-sharing, because it is about what is best for the singer. She is Ms Funky, and I am Mr Functional. I can be a decent style coach, but if I know that they need a better one, I send them straight to Kim.

---

6   More information may be found at http://www.kimchandler.com/.

Tracy Marie Bourne

I do not teach musical improvisation. We will sometimes use theatre improvisation when working on a character, or the acting details in a song. For example, I might ask the singers to act the lyrics out, as if they were a monologue, or I may ask them to identify and develop physical shapes (including posture and gestures) for their character. We often talk about objectives, and actions for the song, and how this influences their emotional energy and musical choices.

References and recommended reading

Agrell, Jeffrey and Patrice Ward-Steinman. *Vocal Improvisation Games: For Singers and Choral Groups*. Chicago: GIA Publishing, 2014.

Azzara, Christopher D., Richard F. Grunow, and Edwin Gordon. *Creativity in Improvisation*. Chicago: GIA Publications, 1997.

Bell, Dylan. "What Do They Need? Exploring the Art of Teaching Vocal Jazz Improvisation." *Canadian Music Educator / Musicien Educateur Au Canada* 55, no. 2 (Winter 2013): 38–42.

Berliner, Paul. *Thinking in Jazz: The Infinite Art of Improvisation*. Chicago: University of Chicago Press, 1994.

Caldwell, Timothy. *Expressive Singing: Dalcroze Eurhythmics for Voice*. Englewood Cliffs, NJ: Prentice Hall, 1995.

Chandler, Kim. *Funky 'n' Fun Vocal Training Series, vol. 1–4*. CDs or MP3 file downloads. http://www.funkynfun.com/.

Cox, Nancy. "Advocacy for Jazz Pedagogy: Where to Find Resources and Quality Teaching Tools." *Choral Journal* 47, no. 3 (September 2006): 47–51.

Dayme, Meribeth and Cynthia Vaughn. *The Singing Book*, 3rd ed. New York: Norton, 2014.

Edwin, Robert. "Singin' the Blues: A Pedagogic Tool." *Journal of Singing* 71, no. 5 (May/June 2015): 613–615.

Goodman, Gabrielle. *Vocal Improvisation: Techniques in Jazz, R&B, and Gospel Improvisation*. West Roxbury, MA: Goodness Music, 2009.

Hargreaves, Wendy. "Pathways for teaching vocal jazz improvisation." In *Teaching Singing in the 21st Century*, edited by Scott D. Harrison and Jessica O'Bryan, 303–317. Dordrecht: Springer, 2014.

Hargreaves, Wendy. "Jazz improvisation: The voice teacher's challenge." In *Perspectives on Teaching Singing: Australian Vocal Pedagogues Sing their Stories*, edited by Scott D. Harrison, 259–275. Bowen Hills, Qld.: Australian Academic Press, 2010.

Legg, Andrew, and Philpott, Carolyn. "An analysis of performance practices in African American gospel music: rhythm, lyric treatment and structures in improvisation and accompaniment." *Popular Music* 34, no. 2 (May 2015): 197–225. www.doi.org/10.1017/S0261143015000264.

Madura Ward-Steinman, Patrice. *Getting Started with Vocal Improvisation*. Reston, VA: MENC, 1999.

McFerrin, Bobby and Roger Treece. *Circlesongs*. DVD. Freiburg: Hochschule für Musik, 2011.

McGuinness, Pete. "Scat Singing." *Downbeat* 81, no. 1 (January 2014): 102–103.

Peckham, Anne. "Vocalise patterns for the contemporary singer." *Journal of Singing* 59, no. 3 (January/February 2003): 215–220.

Rhiannon. *Vocal River: The Skill and Spirit of Improvisation*. Hakalau, HI: Rhiannon Music, 2013.

Rutherford, Paris. *The Vocal Jazz Ensemble*. Milwaukee: Hal Leonard Corporation, 2008.

Robinson-Martin, Trineice. "Gospel styles, performance practices, and improvisation tools." In *So You Want to Sing Gospel: A Guide for Professionals*, 123–157. Lanham, MD: Rowman & Littlefield, 2017.

Shapiro, Jan. "Scat and interpretation." In *So You Want to Sing Jazz: A Guide for Professionals*, 129–148. Lanham, MD: Rowman & Littlefield, 2016.

Sharon, Deke. "Soup to nuts: Using your voice as many different sounds." In *The Voice Teacher's Cookbook: Creative Recipes for Teachers of Singing* edited by Brian J. Winnie, 107–108. Delray Beach, FL: Meredith Music, 2018.

Sichivitsa, Veronica. "Audacity in vocal improvisation." *Teaching Music* 14, no. 4 (February 2007): 48–51.

Stoloff, Bob, *Scat! Vocal Improvisation Techniques*. Brooklyn: Gerard and Sarzin, 1996.

Stoloff, Bob. *Blues Scatitudes: Vocal Improvisations on the Blues*. Brooklyn: Gerard and Sarzin, 2003.

Stoloff, Bob. *Vocal Improvisation: An Instru-Vocal Approach for Soloists, Groups, and Choirs*. Boston: Berklee Press, 2012.

Treece, Roger. *Circlesongs: The Method – Musical Fluency through Circlesinging.* Ober-Mörlen: Edition Ferrimontana, 2015.

Ward-Steinman, Patrice Madura. "Vocal improvisation and creative thinking by Australian and American university Jazz singers." *Journal Of Research In Music Education* 56, no. 1 (Spring 2008): 5–17.

Ward-Steinman, Patrice Madura. "Developing improvisation skill and the confidence to teach it." *Choral Journal* 55, no. 1 (August 2014): 59–61.

Weir, Michelle. *Jazz Singers Handbook: The Artistry and Mastery of Singing Jazz.* Van Nuys: Alfred Publishing, 2005.

Weir, Michelle, John Clayton, Joe LaBarbera, Darmon Meader and Don Shelton. *Vocal Improvisation.* Rottenburg N., Germany: Advance Music, 2001.

Zavalloni, Cristina. "On improvisation." *Contemporary Music Review* 25, no. 5/6 (October/December 2006): 539–540. doi.org/10.1080/07494460600990638.

17

Beyond the voice studio

Beyond just singing well, previous chapters have emphasized the need for CCM singers to be familiar with bodywork modalities, as well as expressive tactics from acting to emotional authenticity. This chapter discusses what training CCM voice teachers believe that their students should seek outside of the voice studio. Specifically, what do they need that they will not be able to get from their voice teachers? What other skills and knowledge will benefit CCM singers in particular?

According to the pedagogues, the most important secondary training is dance, with 54% of teachers listing this as a necessary skill which must be honed outside the voice studio. Considering the importance of dance in musical theatre and the prevalence of dance in pop/rock concerts, it is clear that advanced dance skills will make a singer more employable. Many novelty fad dances achieved iconic stature because they were made famous by a singer: James Brown and the mashed potato; Michael Jackson and the moonwalk; MC Hammer and the running man; and in contemporary times, twerking, whip, and nae-nae.

Acting training was also highly recommended (50%), especially for work in music theatre performance. Many pedagogues recommend training to play an instrument, such as piano or guitar (33%), and learning how to write songs (25%). Other important topics include knowledge of recording equipment and audio technology (25%) so that students can record demo tapes. Many pedagogues recommended vocal cross-training (25%), such as singing in a genre outside your specialization, working on repertoire in the register opposite to that which you regularly use, or keeping the entire instrument healthy by regularly conditioning the entire range. Knowledge of music theory (21%) and aural skills (17%) was also recommended. Some pedagogues noted that these skills may not be as critical as others in CCM singing but would nevertheless benefit any singer. In musical theatre work, the study of speech and dialect was recommended (17%). Other recommendations from 8% of the pedagogues are healthy eating/maintaining good general health, knowledge of accounting, knowledge of marketing, and knowledge of vocal pedagogy.

The most important aspects of training beyond the voice studio are summarized in the chart below.

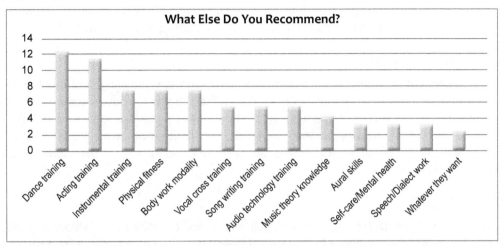

Self-care and maintenance of mental health were strongly emphasized by 17% of the pedagogues. This is an increasing area of concern in college training programs. Since 2010, college students from 93 U.S. universities have reported a consistent increase in depression, generalized anxiety, and social anxiety.[1] These troubling data are particularly relevant to training singers and singing actors, since this type of work is extremely personal and authenticity is an essential ingredient to effective performance. It is not uncommon for a student to break down in a voice lesson because of the nature of the work. While voice teachers can offer compassion, mental health treatment is beyond the scope of a singing lesson. Teachers should refer a student to a licensed therapist or counseling center.

The performing industry itself has performance anxiety, uncertainty, and rejection built into its very structure, which can be an additional source of stress for performers. Even when performers work regularly, a *successful* workload may demand as much as eight musical theatre performances each week, or a year-long performing tour. Performers often suffer from vocal or physical fatigue and need to understand how to cope with both. The industry remains extremely critical throughout the entire career of a performer, and one under-energized performance or cancelled concert can have drastic implications. It is necessary to find strategies to remain physically healthy and to deliver high-energy performances over a long-term career. Some pedagogues suggested practicing meditation (8%), practicing humility (4%), and maintaining a healthy sense of humor (4%), all of which may help singers to cope with the lifestyle of a performer.

In line with the trend of increasing flexibility among teachers, 13% recommend training outside the voice studio in "anything the student wants or needs". These pedagogues emphasized that they are in service to the student and should, therefore, work as efficiently as possible to help their students achieve their individual tailored goals. Students will make faster progress when supported by a team of specialists.

---

1   Center for Collegiate Mental Health (CCMH), "2015 Annual Report (Publication No. STA 15-108)," (State College, PA: Penn State, 2016), 6. Accessed on August 12, 2018, sites.psu.edu/ccmh/files/2017/10/2015_CCMH_Report_1-18-2015-yq3vik.pdf

This chapter includes responses to the prompt "What sort of additional training do you recommend to students?". The prompt occasionally called for clarification, and was modified to "What additional training is beneficial for singers, beyond the voice studio?". Responses are presented in a loose order, according to the specific training recommended.

Marcelle G. Gauvin

My recommendations depend on the musical style they are pursuing. Musical theatre students need dance and acting training. Pop singers benefit from dance and studio production training. Any contemporary artist should have some proficiency on guitar or piano. Songwriting classes are extremely beneficial to all commercial styles. Vocal pedagogy classes are also beneficial, so that artists can teach in order to sustain themselves while developing their careers.

Mark Baxter

It is extremely beneficial for singers to play guitar or piano. It solidifies their relationship with music and expands the number of cortical areas devoted to producing and assessing sound.

Trineice Robinson-Martin

I recommend additional training in composition, ear training, and audio sound technology.

Seth Riggs and Margareta Svensson Riggs

Singing is of course a way of making music. Therefore, basic musicianship should begin as soon as possible. Any music training is encouraged, at least so that one can have the same reference points as fellow musicians.

We highly recommend learning an instrument. Nobody would question that playing the piano, guitar, flute, or violin well requires ongoing learning and practice, and that an understanding of melody, harmony, rhythm, theory, and composition, as well as involvement in reading music, are all part of being a musician. As a singer, you are a musician too, and this knowledge is equally important to you. The more music you know, the more interesting choices you will be able to make.

We also recommend dancing and acting training. Just as singing is a way of rhythmical artistic expression through music, so is dance. We recommend acting because regardless of genre, singing is acting on pitch. You have to communicate the words of your songs in a believable way, provoking an emotional response in your audience.

In addition, depending on what the goals are, training in songwriting and being able to record your own tracks, is very useful.

Most of all, go out there and work any gig you can get. There is no better training than actually doing it.

Irene Bartlett

First and foremost, I encourage my singers to understand their instrument in the same physical way that players of man-made instruments do. I instruct them on how to listen to and sing across a wide range of music styles and genres. Initially, I listen with my students to help them to recognize the voice elements/effects that outline and describe the style. I encourage all students to sing repertoire outside of their comfort zone. For example, I encourage rock singers to practice folk or jazz standards; conversely, I ask jazz singers to sing pop and country styles. For training purposes, all of my students (female and male) are expected to sing some repertoire that *lives* in their upper register. For CCM singers I have found that the most aesthetically palatable and vocally accessible repertoire is to be found in the library of Broadway *legit* music theatre. This activity is necessary to fully develop the singer's potential vocal range while it simultaneously builds stamina and flexibility of the laryngeal, breathing, and support muscles.

While not absolutely necessary for CCM singers, I do suggest that basic theory and aural skills are extremely helpful, as is learning to play an instrument (other than voice), if only at a basic level.

Kathryn Paradise

I recommend yoga, acting, stage movement/dance, piano and/or guitar lessons, music technology lessons/classes, anything related to musicianship (theory, ensemble experience, composition/arranging, etc.), music business and entrepreneurship classes, and guided meditation/mindfulness.

Jan Shapiro

For many of my students, I do not recommend anything. It depends upon the individual. I may recommend other voice teachers, meditation, yoga, or some other physical exercise, if there is lots of tension.

Dane Chalfin

For undergraduates, I recommend that they get a job pouring frozen yogurt into a cup or work behind a counter selling jeans. They should clean people's houses. I encourage them to get a job that is not fun, not creative, and not well paid. This allows them to appreciate how lucky they are to get to do the job that they do as musicians. This prevents future feelings of entitlement. Undergraduates have changed a lot in the last 20 years. I think everyone should spend a lot of time doing the hard yards and paying their dues. I do not like how instantly available everything is these days. I think it is de-valuing the time it takes to get good at anything.

Physical fitness cannot be stressed enough. I recommend training in everything that has to do with flexible core stability: Yoga, swimming, boxing (pads, not contact), and hiking out in the woods and mountains. Many performers have never even run for a bus. I work with a lot of groups who tour, and there is a big stage to fill. If the performer is not used to moving while singing, this will be challenging. Work with a trainer who understands that you cannot put a lot of strain on the neck when working out. We also need to avoid anything that makes the abdomen feel "locked". Working with health and fitness people who understand the singer's needs is critical. Flexibility is key. The secret to a long career is to keep your body moving.

I also recommend meditation, or any version of self-care. It is difficult for most performers to learn this because they are in a business that constantly demands more from them. These increasing demands are often attached to a pay check that the performer needs. They are often being asked to do impossible things, like sing Elphaba (*Wicked*) eight shows per week. It is not an easy gig, so the performers have got to look after themselves. I see a lot of performers playing Judas (*Jesus Christ Superstar*) or Elphaba or similar roles in the voice clinic,

I have worked on tours for these kinds of shows because these roles are almost inhuman to sing. Very few people have the natural chops to maintain this pace. Self-care and staying healthy are both so important.

I am very "Zen" these days. I would like for everyone to have fun, love, and not take things too seriously. You get up and make strange noises at people for a living. You do not actually have to do much work for this. It is taxing, strenuous, emotionally draining, and it is work in and of itself, but no one is in a stone quarry digging by hand. It may feel like the world is crashing down because the second half of the second 45-minute set felt a little bit tricky, but it is important to maintain some perspective. Humor is critical. I think voice teaching has to be playful. It cannot be too regimented or methodical because we are trying to tap into reflexive gestures which stem from the limbic system. That emotional motor system is crucial to easy singing. Singing is about feeling and sharing those emotions. If you are treating singing like math, you are in the wrong gig.

Mary Saunders Barton

Musical theatre performers are required to integrate many skills as they train. Singing teachers are only part of the picture. In today's elite Bachelor of Fine Arts (BFA) musical theatre programs, the collaboration among dance, singing voice, speech, movement, and acting faculty is a given in the training process. Independent studio voice teachers encountering beginning or early-career performers will need to encourage these students to be pro-active in pursuing other aspects of their training on their own. We can be helpful in many ways, but we are not enough.

Jeannette LoVetri

A great deal depends on age, natural abilities, and what the student might want to sing. A youngster or a teen needs to learn basic vocal function and be exposed to their entire voice in a healthy manner. Unless the child has a natural aptitude for belting, I don't recommend that as a goal for beginners, regardless of their age. "Traditional training" implies "classical training", as that is all there was in days past. These days, any number of approaches are possible but the training for vocal function should remain *separate from literature* (repertoire). Classical music is wonderful, but it does not have to have anything whatsoever to do with vocal function. The voice can be trained well without relying upon classical music in any way.

Just because someone has a degree in voice – a master's or a doctorate – even if it is from a prestigious music conservatory or university, it does not mean they sing well or can teach singing effectively, particularly in styles they have not sung or studied. Singing teachers all have their own ideas about what is "correct" or "best", but few of them understand how to use vocal exercises, coupled with physical awareness, to elicit a response from the throat in singing other than one they may do themselves or the one that a student typically has through habit.

Students are in a very vulnerable position when they begin training in a profession that has no set vocal standards, no consistent guidelines, no vetting for teaching standards, or qualifications aside from those established at individual universities, which maintain their own criteria. It is wise to have several investigative sessions when beginning to study with any teacher or school.

Wendy DeLeo LeBorgne

Students who want to become professional performers in commercial music need to get in the mindset of being a vocal athlete. This includes eating healthily, being in a good psychological mindset, going to the gym regularly in addition to vocal, acting, and dance training. I feel strongly that they need to train like an athlete and they need to start doing this at a young age to be able to perform professionally. This work is done outside of the studio.

For those who want to teach commercial music, if they come from a classical background, I encourage them to listen to artists who are currently commercially viable, whether or not they like the sound. Sometimes, classical singers gravitate towards listening to only legit musical theatre, or crossover opera artists singing musical theatre. These may be viable artists, but these sounds are not all that are getting hired on Broadway or in the commercial markets. Classical singers tend to not always like all of the sounds that they hear in the commercial world (which is OK, we all have different aesthetic tastes!), but they may shy away from listening to this broad range of singing as a result. This is completely understandable. However, if they want to understand what is being hired in the market, which is ultimately what they need to help their students train in a healthy way, they need to listen to the artists who are winning Tony awards, Grammy awards, and Country Music awards, whether or not they like the sound. This trains their ears, and then they need to work to understand how that sound is produced in the most healthy and efficient way possible, realizing that not everything we sing, classical or commercial, is vocally healthy. I have never seen beautiful, perfect feet in professional ballerinas. This is not because they are doing anything wrong, but because they are using their feet at their maximum physiologic extreme, and they get blisters and calluses and deformities.

Lisa Popeil

Some students are interested in all aspects of music and performance, others just want to sing better. If a student is interested in learning how to read music, I am thrilled to teach them how to sight-sing, how to read piano notes, rhythm reading, intervals, scales, all the way to chord progressions and 7th chords. But I never push it. I try to think of my relationship with my students as one of service... asking myself "How can I be of service to *their* goals?".

For my private musical theatre students, I recommend dance classes. For the actors, of course, there is a multitude of acting classes available in Los Angeles, and for others I recommend taking piano lessons (with me or someone else) and/or guitar lessons. For those interested in song-writing, I expose them to the skills of pop song-writing, and how to use a multi-track program, such as Logic Pro X,[2] on a computer as we create and record musical and vocal tracks to flesh out their original songs.

Kimberly Steinhauer

I recommend any training in which they acquire extra skills for their chosen artistic fields.

Cathrine Sadolin

My recommendations vary depending on what the singer wants. If someone wants to be the kind of rock singer who plays the guitar, they should learn how to play guitar. If they want to

---

2   More information may be found at www.apple.com/logic-pro/.

be the kind of rock singer that jumps around while singing, they should go to the gym. If they want to be a very calm and theatrical performer, they should practice that. Whatever it is that they want to do, that is what they should study.

Tracy Marie Bourne

If singers are serious about music theatre, they need to learn how to act. They also need dancing skills – jazz, ballet, and tap. I encourage my child singers to learn music theory.

Marci Rosenberg

I am a huge proponent of various somatic modalities such as Feldenkrais™, myofascial work, and Alexander Technique™. I think this kind of work is essential for healthy sound production and longevity as a singer and is often overlooked as part of a voice training paradigm. I also think it is critical for any type of singer to be physically fit as a performing career can be very physically demanding and taxing on the body. Most musical theatre performers are also dancers and therefore, they also need to attend to those physical demands and needs in addition to their vocal health.

Matthew Edwards

Commercial singers must be business minded. I recommend they learn about accounting, marketing, and how to manage their social media like a professional. I also think it is beneficial for them to learn how to run recording software, even if only to help them with their song-writing.

Musical theatre performers must learn how to dance. They need to take ballet and jazz religiously. They also need to find a good acting teacher and take classes regularly. When they are in New York, they need to take classes with casting directors and agents. It is one of the best ways for them to learn how the industry sees them and how to audition for the jobs they want.

Elisabeth Howard

The "Triple Threat" is to be taken seriously. To be competitive, singers should take acting classes, dance classes, speech classes, and Alexander Technique. I also recommend yoga for physical and mental well-being.

Robert Edwin

A well-rounded performer should be able to sing, act, and dance. Therefore, training in all three disciplines should be a requirement for the serious and ambitious artist. Also, it helps if a performer is somewhat literate in those areas as well. In today's competitive world, it is a good thing to be able to actually read music, words, and choreography.

Gillyanne Kayes

I recommend physical training so that students keep fit and flexible, and performance workshops, including workshops with other trainers. I would include in this category Feldenkrais™ rather than Alexander, Yoga, or Pilates (with the proviso that singers need to relax the transversus abdominis to breathe in).

Jeff Ramsey

I have not recommended much outside of vocal training, but I have mentioned Feldenkrais®, body mapping, yoga, and The Alexander Technique. These are subjects that I am interested in working with as well and incorporating into lessons.

Kevin Wilson

I recommend various voice and speech methods for actors, acting, movement, and dance.

Kim Chandler

I recommend physical exercise: cardio, core strength, and flexibility. A fit, healthy body is a good foundation on which to build a fit, healthy singing voice with robust technique and sufficient stamina.

Edrie Means Weekly

I highly recommend additional training in dancing, acting/dialects, body work, and piano/music-reading skills.

References and recommended reading

Arneson, Christopher. "Performance anxiety: A twenty-first century perspective." *Journal of Singing* 66, no. 5 (May/June 2010): 537–546.

Barefield, Robert. "Fear of singing: Identifying and assisting singers with chronic anxiety issues." *Music Educators Journal* 98, no. 3 (March 2012): 60–63. www.doi.org/10.1177/0027432111434588.

Bartlett, Irene and Pat H. Wilson. "Working 9-5: Causal relationships between singers' 'day jobs' and their performance work, with implications for vocal health." *Journal of Voice* 31, no. 2 (March 2017): 243.e27–243.e34. doi.org/10.1016/j.jvoice.2016.04.003.

Beeman, Shellie. "A recipe for relaxation and fighting vocal fatigue." In *The Voice Teacher's Cookbook: Creative Recipes for Teachers of Singing* edited by Brian J. Winnie, 5–6. Delray Beach, FL: Meredith Music, 2018.

Bennett, Dawn, ed. *Life in the Real World: How to Make Music Graduates Employable*. Champaign, IL: Common Ground Publishing, 2012.

Blumenfeld, Robert. *Teach Yourself Accents: Europe – A Handbook for Young Actors and Speakers*. Milwaukee: Limelight, 2014.

Blumenfeld, Robert. *Teach Yourself Accents: The British Isles – A Handbook for Young Actors and Speakers*. Milwaukee: Limelight, 2013.

Blumenfeld, Robert. *Teach Yourself Accents: North America – A Handbook for Young Actors and Speakers*. Milwaukee: Limelight, 2013.

Blumenfeld, Robert. *Accents: A Manual for Actors*, rev. New York: Limelight, 2002.

Boyle, V.P. *Audition Freedom: The Irreverent Wellness Guide for Theatre People*. New York: MaxTheatrix, 2008.

Bunch Dayme, Meribeth. "An argument for whole body and holistic approaches to research in singing." *Journal of Singing* 63, no. 1 (September/October 2006): 59–64.

Center for Collegiate Mental Health (CCMH). "2015 Annual Report (Publication No. STA 15-108)." State College, PA: Penn State, 2016. Accessed on August 12, 2018, sites.psu.edu/ccmh/files/2017/10/2015_CCMH_Report_1-18-2015-yq3vik.pdf.

Colier, Nancy. *Getting Out of Your Own Way: Unlocking Your True Performance Potential*, 2nd ed. New York: Book Case Engine, 2014. Kindle.

Diaz, Frank M. "Relationships among meditation, perfectionism, mindfulness, and performance anxiety among collegiate music students." *Journal of Research in Music Education* 66, no. 2 (July 2018): 150–167. doi.org/10.1177/0022429418765447.

Edwards, Matthew. *So You Want to Sing Rock 'N' Roll: A Guide for Professionals*. Lanham, MD: Rowman & Littlefield, 2014.

Edwin, Robert. "Cross training for the voice." *Journal of Singing* 65, no. 1 (September/October 2008): 73–76.

Elliott, Martha. "Singing and mindfulness." *Journal of Singing* 67, no. 1 (September/October 2010): 35–40.

Feller, Allison. "Saut de chat meet fa-la-las: Conquer the physicality of singing while dancing." *Dance Magazine* 92, no. 5 (May 2018): 52–53.

Farrar, Ann. "A call for wellness curricula in the Arts." *Teaching Artist Journal* 15, no. 1 (January 2017): 28–32. http://www.doi.org/10.1080/15411796.2017.1297616.

Feinstein, David, Donna Eden, and Gary Craig. *The Promise of Energy Psychology: Revolutionary Tools for Dramatic Personal Change.* New York: Jeremy P. Tarcher/Penguin, 2005.

Flom, Jonathan. *Act like it's your business: Branding and marketing strategies for actors.* Lanham, MD: Scarecrow Press, 2013.

Friedlander, Claudia. *Complete Vocal Fitness: A Singer's Guide to Physical Training, Anatomy, and Biomechanics.* Lanham, MD: Rowman and Littlefield, 2018.

Garner, Kelly K. *So You Want to Sing Country: A Guide for Performers.* Lanham, MD: Rowman & Littlefield, 2016.

Glasheen, Kate. "Negotiating the contrary craft of the triple-threat." *Voice and Speech Review* 11, no. 1 (2017): 20–39. doi.org/10.1080/23268263.2017.1370833.

Haas, Aaron. "Creativity through silence: Exploring the use of meditation in musical performance." *Journal of Singing* 74, no. 5 (May/June 2018): 563–570.

Hague, Daydrie and Mary J. Sandage. "Evaluating the effects of stress reduction techniques and Fitzmaurice Voicework® on physiologic markers and mental states related to performance anxiety in student actors." *Voice and Speech Review* 10, no. 2-3 (2016): 121–130. www.doi.org/10.1080/23268263.2016.1355518.

Hakanpää, Tua, Teja Waaramaa, and Anne-Maria Laukkanen. "Emotion recognition from singing voices using contemporary commercial music and classical styles." *Journal of Voice*, In press. doi.org/10.1016/j.jvoice.2018.01.012.

Hall, Karen. *So You Want to Sing Music Theatre: A Guide for Professionals.* Lanham, MD: Rowman & Littlefield, 2014.

Heirich, Jane Ruby. *Voice and the Alexander Technique,* 2nd ed. Berkeley: Mornum Time Press, 2011.

Helding, Lynn. "Mindful voice: Music performance anxiety." *Journal of Singing* 73, no. 1 (September/October 2016): 83–90.

Holmes, Shannon. "Autoethnography and voicework: Autobiographical narrative and self-reflection as a means towards free vocal expression." *Voice and Speech Review* 10, no. 2-3 (2016): 190–202. doi.org/10.1080/23268263.2016.1337552.

Jimenez, Belinda Paige. "The effects of 'performance adrenaline' on the performing singer." *Voice and Speech Review* 9, no. 2-3 (2015): 149–167. doi.org/10.1080/23268263.2016.1159432.

Klickstein, Gerald. *The Musician's Way: A Guide to Practice, Performance, and Wellness.* New York: Oxford University Press, 2009.

Kopf, Ginny. *The Dialect Handbook: Learning, Researching, and Performing a Dialect Role.* Orlando: Voiceprint, 2003.

Larrouy-Maestri, Pauline and Dominique Morsomme. "The effects of stress on singing voice accuracy." *Journal of Voice* 28, no. 1 (January 2014): 52–58. doi.org/10.1016/j.jvoice.2013.07.008.

Leborgne, Wendy D. and Marci Rosenberg. *The Vocal Athlete.* San Diego: Plural Publishing, 2014.

Lightfoot, J. Timothy and Jennie Morton. "The physiology of dancing and singing at the same time." *Voice and Speech Review* 8, no. 3 (2014): 280–287. doi.org/10.1080/23268263.2014.942585.

Manternach, Brian. "Vocal exercise: Using the correct ingredients in the correct order." In *The Voice Teacher's Cookbook: Creative Recipes for Teachers of Singing* edited by Brian J. Winnie, 75–76. Delray Beach, FL: Meredith Music, 2018.

Meier, Paul. *Accents and Dialects for Stage and Screen: An Instruction Manual for 24 Accents and Dialects Commonly Used by English-Speaking Actors,* 22nd ed. Lawrence, KS: Paul Meier Dialect Services, 2012.

Meizel, Katherine. "A powerful voice: Investigating vocality and identity." *Voice and Speech Review* 7, no. 1 (2011): 267–274. doi.org/10.1080/23268263.2011.10739551.

Melton, Joan. *Dancing with Voice: A Collaborative Journey Across Disciplines.* Create Space Independent Publishing, 2015.

Melton, Joan. "Integrative links: Voice and dance in performance." *Voice and Speech Review* 8, no. 2 (2014): 199–206. doi.org/10.1080/23268263.2014.887242.

Mindel, Valerie. *So You Want to Sing Folk Music: A Guide for Performers.* Lanham, MD: Rowman & Littlefield, 2017.

Monti, Elisa, David C. Kidd, Linda M. Carroll, and Emanuele Castano. "What's in a singer's voice: The effect of attachment, emotions and trauma." *Logopedics, Phoniatrics, Vocology* 42, no. 2 (July 2017): 62–72. www.doi.org/10.3109/14015439.2016.1166394.

Morton, Jennie. "Voice and dance technique integration: Triple threat or double trouble?" *Voice and Speech Review* 8, no.

2 (2014): 212–216. doi.org/10.1080/23268263.2014.887243.

Morton, Jennie. *The Authentic Performer: Wearing a Mask and the Effect on Health*. Oxford: Compton Publishing, 2015.

Nelson, Samuel H., and Elizabeth L. Blades. *Singing with Your Whole Self: A Singer's Guide to Feldenkrais Awareness Through Movement*. 2nd ed. Lanham, MD: Rowman & Littlefield, 2018.

Perdomo-Guevara, Elsa. "Is music performance anxiety just an individual problem? Exploring the impact of musical environments on performers' approaches to performance and emotions." *Psychomusicology: Music, Mind & Brain* 24, no. 1 (March 2014): 66–74. www.doi.org/10.1037/pmu0000028.

Robinson-Martin, Trineice. *So You Want to Sing Gospel: A Guide for Performers*. Lanham, MD: Rowman & Littlefield, 2017.

Rosenberg, Marci. "Staple pantry ingredients: Applying exercise physiology principles when training the vocal athlete." In *The Voice Teacher's Cookbook: Creative Recipes for Teachers of Singing* edited by Brian J. Winnie, 102–104. Delray Beach, FL: Meredith Music, 2018.

Schneider, Erin and K. Chesky. Social support and performance anxiety of college music students. *Medical Problems of Performing Artists*, 26, no. 3 (2011): 157–163.

Shapiro, Jan, *So You Want to Sing Jazz: A Guide for Professionals*. Lanham, MD: Rowman & Littlefield, 2016.

Spivey, Norman and Mary Saunders Barton. *Cross-Training in the Voice Studio: A Balancing Act*. San Diego, CA: Plural Publishing, 2018.

Stanton, Harry E. "Reduction of performance anxiety in music students." *Australian Psychologist* 29, no. 2 (1994): 124–127. www.doi.org/10.1080/00050069408257335.

Thomson, Paula and Victoria S. Jaque. "Holding a Mirror Up to Nature: Psychological Vulnerability in Actors." *Psychology of Aesthetics, Creativity, and the Arts* 6, no. 4 (November 2012): 361–369. www.doi.org/10.1037/a0028911.

Walker, Gwendolyn and Cody Commander. "The emotionally prepared singer." *Journal of Singing* 73, no. 3 (January/ February 2017): 261–268.

Yamin, Eli. *So You Want to Sing the Blues: A Guide for Performers*. Lanham, MD: Rowman & Littlefield, 2018.

18

Voice science

The application of voice science into pedagogical practice has been the subject of some debate within the pedagogical community. These pedagogues agree that the voice operates according to scientific principles, and that a knowledge of voice science is not just advantageous, but critical for a teacher of CCM singing. A substantial majority of pedagogues say that they use voice science with students to some degree (96%). Many use it as a regular practice (60%), and these respondents are mostly university teachers. The majority of voice science use manifests as fact-based anatomy and physiology (89%), and to a lesser extent, as helping students understand the principles of acoustics (21%). Many pedagogues point to the benefits of establishing a common scientific vocabulary which will be useful over a long course of study, and perhaps even transfer to another teacher in future years. Several pedagogues underline the correlation between understanding vocal function and the development of kinesthetic awareness of the instrument. Surprisingly, only one pedagogue pointed to vocal health as an application of voice science in the studio.

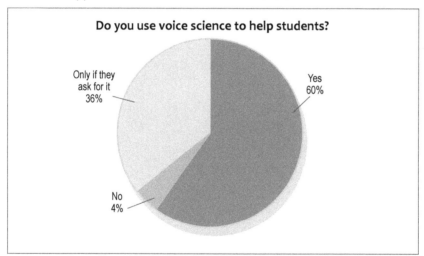

Some pedagogues use voice science in the studio only if the student requests it (36%), or not at all (4%). These respondents are mostly independent studio practitioners, often working on acute issues with students that they may not see regularly. When there is a professional-level singer in the studio who needs a quick solution to a problem, there is no time for an anatomy and physiology lesson. This preference is practical, but it also represents a dilemma: science and artistry are sometimes at odds. Understanding how things work will not automatically guarantee better singing. The connection between science and artistry is an exciting area in singing research and professional development, but also an area which needs significant further study. Again, most pedagogues state that knowledge of voice science is advantageous for the teacher, but it need not be explained to the student in order to achieve a desired result. If requested, many pedagogues offer additional scientific instruction through resources, tools, [1] and digital applications which may be explored outside the voice studio. Many of these resources are also listed in other technically specific chapters.

Tools:
Models/Illustrations
Charts/Diagrams (Blue Tree Publishing[2])
Paper model of the larynx (Vocal Process[3])
Videos/Animations
Photos
Customized PowerPoint Presentation/Handouts
Straws
Duck call
Hands-on/palpation
Mirror
Looking into the mouth with a flashlight
Rubber bands
Articles/Books

Applications:
Essential Anatomy
Human Anatomy Atlas
Complete Anatomy
Vocal Folds ID
SpectrumView

Spectrographic Software:
Estill Voiceprint Plus ™
Spek (Freeware)
VoceVista

This chapter includes responses to the prompt "Do you use voice science to help students? If so, how do you explain this to students?". The responses are listed in order from those who use voice science in voice lessons regularly, to those who only use it upon request or not at all.

---

1 An interesting discussion of pedagogical tools may be found in Scott McCoy, "Pedagadgets," *Journal of Singing* 74, no. 5 (May/June 2018), 533–536.

2 Blue Tree Publishing provides software, active media, printed media, models and crystal art to enhance teaching and learning. See http://www.bluetreepublishing.com/.

3 Download the free Vocal Process Tilting Larynx PDF Template: vocalprocess.co.uk/build-your-own-tilting-larynx/.

Kathryn Paradise

All of my students receive some level of scientific understanding of the "Three R's" (respiration, registration, and resonation). They also get a thorough overview of vocal health, including how to monitor their vocal load, avoid environmental and behavioral causes of vocal damage, and make use of semi-occluded vocal tract exercises. How I explain voice science to students depends on their existing skill level and their specific goals. For example, the first time I address a scientific topic I will stay fairly general and try to make the concept easy to remember by pairing it with a physical, visual, or aural cue. The second time the same topic comes up, I will give a more detailed explanation that includes more technical terms and a lengthier exploration into the "grey area" surrounding the issue. The third time the topic arises, I will ask the student to explain the scientific topic back to me to get an accurate sense of what they actually understand. Then, I will challenge their understanding and fill in gaps as needed. In the context of a voice lesson, additional use of voice science most frequently comes up to reinforce the student's body awareness or observed experience, to validate why something is challenging, or to challenge habits and misperceptions. For example, if a student reflects on singing a high passage by saying their tone felt and sounded "stuck", I may take a few moments to talk about how tension in the back of the tongue impacts the function of the larynx.

Gillyanne Kayes

I almost always use voice science to help students, although the ways I explain it vary depending on their interest, or their ability to grasp concepts. I use applications, models, drawings, hand modelling, and elastic bands. I have a working model of a paper larynx that shows the cricoid, thyroid, and arytenoid cartilages, together with the epiglottis. We created the template for our voice education company (Vocal Process[4]) and it is used all over the world. Applications that I use are Essential Anatomy and Vocal Folds ID. I also have videos of the larynx that we have created for our training company. Out of these, I mostly use videos that show: the difference between modal and falsetto vibrations in male and female voice; the constriction and release of the false vocal folds; and a two-octave glide in male voice showing how the vocal folds elongate and thin for the higher pitches

Matthew Edwards

Voice science informs everything I do. I believe students sing best when they understand how their instrument works, so therefore I begin by introducing them to the basics of anatomy. I have several videos and animations that I use so that students understand the moving parts and how they affect vocal production. This also allows me to establish a common language from which we can build.

I am always thinking about vocal function while I teach and listen for faults in the system that may be preventing the student from achieving the result they desire. Every article I read makes me question what I know and what I do. When students ask questions, I give them a fact-based answer. However, once they get the sound they are looking for, we identify a term that means something to them. If the student uses a placement term to describe their experience, that is what we use from then on. If they think technically like I do, great. As my colleague David Meyer says, "Science has helped today's high school athletes break records

---

4   More information may be found at vocalprocess.co.uk/gillyanne-kayes-jeremy-fisher/.

set by the first Olympians". I think by using science to inform our work with singers, we can get better results in a shorter amount of time.

Robert Edwin

Since my pedagogy is fact-based, my students learn the basic anatomy, physiology, acoustics, and function of their singing systems. Pre-science voice pedagogy that is not fact-based has no place in my studio. Diaphragms do not sing; we do not have voices in our chest or in our head; phonation is produced by the vocal folds in the larynx in the throat; we do not fill our stomachs with air; and sound comes out of the mouth and nose, not the top of the head. In my studio, the use of imagery is usually restricted to emotional contexts and character development.

Wendy DeLeo LeBorgne

I do not think I can separate my voice science brain from my voice teaching brain. In my studio, I use laryngeal models and a diaphragm model of how respiration works. I try to use functional anatomy and physiology, and voice science, in each and every lesson that I teach. I try to help students to understand the laws of tubes in order to understand acoustics better. We can explore this by singing into different sized straws or blowing into a duck call. I try to use tangible items to teach voice science within the singing studio. If they really want to know more about anatomy and physiology, I am happy to delve into it with them.

I teach a lot of imagery, but the imagery is based in my scientific knowledge of why things work. For example, if a student is singing in chest voice, and I ask them to describe how it feels to them, they may say to me "That is my dark-red voice" (because they decide to use color terminology to best describe their own voice). If I want them to lighten the sound up a little bit, I might say to them "Can you sing in a slightly lighter shade of red here, maybe verging towards pink?". To the student, it means singing lighter. To me, it means using less thyro-arytenoid engagement. If that doesn't work, we start to have a different conversation that may involve more anatomy and physiology, but I try to meet the students where they are and build our conversation and knowledge together. As another example, if a student feels like the breath is constricted, I will ask what that feels like. If they may say "It feels like I'm singing through a coffee-stirrer" I will suggest trying to imagine singing through a smoothie-straw. For me, this means they are opening up their pharynx. To them, they are using the imagery of the bigger law of tubes. However, I do not necessarily have to go into the acoustics of tubes to explain what is happening.

Irene Bartlett

I most definitely use voice science to help students. The knowledge I have gained through the study of voice science is key to my teaching model. To minimize the possibility of confusion caused by the inference that surrounds imagery (my concept or interpretation of an image might be different to yours), I train my students to work with the factual language of anatomy and physiology. I have found that this approach assists students to be independent learners as they practice building an efficient, reliable, technique on their own, outside of studio lesson times. I believe that it is important to be ever mindful of the singer's particular learning mode (aural, visual, kinesthetic), as the effectiveness of any teaching is impacted by the student's ability to conceptualize knowledge rather than just respond on rote. Once the student is trained in the basics of voice anatomy and physiology, fact-based body mapping, imagery, and sound-making can be employed independently or in combination to assist the student to produce healthy but style-appropriate sounds. I draw pictures and diagrams and use models, videos, and spectrographic software, to encourage each student to develop a factual body map. These are particularly powerful pedagogical tools when the student is a visual learner. I also use hand gesture, primal (emotion based) sounds, and, when called for, imagery to engage and hold the singer's attention throughout a lesson.

Kimberly Steinhauer

The Estill Voice Model™ and Estill Voice Training® are founded in scientific principles that I use daily with students. High expectation leads to high performance. Students of all ages embrace the scientific terms and principles as they explore their artistic goals.

Marcelle G. Gauvin

I use voice science in my teaching. To explain it to students, I use lectures, handouts, Powerpoint®, videos, photos, and casual conversation, over coffee when possible.

Tracy Marie Bourne

I use voice science to help students. I have found it really useful in my own understanding of vocal function. I will go through some basic vocal physiology with adult students, especially when we are working on the tongue, soft palate, and mouth shapes. I don't talk much science with my very young singers, but it underlies all of the work I do with them.

Elisabeth Howard

To help students understand voice science, I use a model replica of the larynx that you can look at from all directions and down into the vocal folds. I explain basic principles of how the cricoid and arytenoid cartilage work the vocal folds. I explain how the intercostal and subcostal muscles work for breathing and support. More information than that is too much and not necessary for most students. I recommend my own book *SING!*[5] and a few other good books if they really want to know more about the scientific aspects of singing.

Kevin Wilson

My students clearly understand anatomy and basic physiology. We use anatomical diagrams, videos, charts, and physical/palpation exercises to aid in vocal discovery. Additionally, I have a breathing bootcamp sequence, which is about 30 minutes of getting into your physical body and finding muscles, that all of my students are taught.

Trineice Robinson-Martin

Yes. Anatomical Awareness is a major part of my teaching philosophy. Students need to identify aspects of the sound-making process aurally, visually, and kinesthetically. This is important because CCM singers are not always in environments that allow them to hear themselves, so they have to use kinesthetic awareness to help monitor vocal effort. When teaching I use diagrams and videos on anatomy to help singers understand how the various components of the voice function. I then have students look in the mirror, while physically touching their

---

5   Elisabeth Howard, *Sing! The Vocal Power Method* (New York: Alfred Music, 2006).

bodies and doing exercises that help them become more acquainted and aware of how the voice works, and how they perceive the voice working in their body.

Edrie Means Weekly

I use voice science in the studio to help students. I discuss with each student the anatomy and physiology of voice production. To explain this to students, I use the SpectrumView[6] application, Human Anatomy Atlas application, videos, illustrations, and hands-on models to help explain voice science. I always try to explain at a level they can understand and ask them to repeat/ explain it back to me. I will also use examples aurally, kinesthetically, or visually, depending on their learning style. Many of my clientele have downloaded the above-mentioned apps and have found them useful. With SpectrumView, one can visualize a real time spectrogram and spectrum analyzer. Although the app can be used for all sorts of acoustic analysis, some of my singers find it interesting and useful for a visual feedback on a much more basic level. The Human Anatomy Atlas is the anatomy reference in 3-D and has interactive animations of muscles.

Jeff Ramsey

I show students a diagram of the basic anatomy of the larynx and the vocal folds. However, the best way I have found that works is giving my students a rubber band to explain the mass or thickness of the folds, versus the thinning and stretching of the folds. It seems to be the best way to give them a visual and kinesthetic feel for what is going on when they sing.

Jan Shapiro

I use some vocal science terms but not TOO much! I do show a diagram of our breathing anatomy.

Mary Saunders Barton

I am committed to communicating technical information to students as factually and accurately as I can. The exciting new partnership between voice scientists and artist-teachers has fundamentally changed the way we think and speak about the singing voice. This new knowledge has enhanced my teaching in countless ways, although I am careful to keep my focus on the developing artist.

Kim Chandler

A passion for, and understanding of, voice science from a pedagogical angle underpins my whole approach to vocal coaching. How much detail I go into with a client is entirely dependent on their needs, learning style, and interest level.

Cate Frazier-Neely

Most students are interested in anatomy. Many teenagers and adults love to know more about the science of their singing, but I keep it short and relevant to what they are learning. I recommend articles, applications, videos, and other resources for their own further exploration, but rarely take lesson time to actually look at these things unless they have a question. Professional CCM singers usually just want to get on with practical application,

---

6   More information may be found at http://www.oxfordwaveresearch.com/products/spectrumviewapp/.

and if you spend too long on technique only, you will lose them, unless they need medically recommended rehabilitation or have come from a culture of technical training. Voice teachers or educators in both CCM and classical who work with me do want voice science, and enjoy correlating what we are doing with the information that is available.

Mark Baxter

Absolutely, I use voice science to help students, but I buffer any technical discussions with the fact that humans sang long before the word "science" was uttered. I find the physical sciences such as physiology and acoustics to be informative for teachers but not instructive for singers. So, I will explain what is occurring inside the body if someone is curious, but in my experience, it is redundant to instruct the body as to how to behave naturally. Example: a genuine toothy grin versus the awkward outcome after a friend yells "Smile!" but fails to immediately take the shot. Instructing the face to smile does not create a natural result. A trust of one's reflexes combined with a focus on the sentiment to be conveyed is how actors ply their craft. The same approach is what connects popular singers to their audience. Therefore, I find that the observations of social sciences, such as psychology and musicology, provide students with the important understanding that the invisible forces at play when singing are cultural and emotional. If anything, cognitive neuroscience is the branch of science that best connects the physical and social aspects of singing. So, I reference the mind/body connection often in lessons.

Lisa Popeil

Unfortunately, most of my students get fairly glassy-eyed if I get too "*sciency*" so I keep it simple and occasionally show photos and videos of vocal folds. Some students actually get squeamish and I have to remember who is interested and who is not when looking inside the body. Anything I can teach by touching makes the process more palatable and interesting, so I like to have them feel my larynx move and also demonstrate various vocal mechanisms with a mirror and a small flashlight. Most people love comparing their mouth to mine!

Jeannette LoVetri

Occasionally, I use science to explain something but only after I get the student to understand the basics. Science is very important, and we need it to prevent us from making up ridiculous ideas about where the sound goes or how it is being produced, but understanding it is the booby prize. It doesn't help you sing.

Dane Chalfin

If you cannot make it meaningful and applicable, #whocares? I say this a lot when I speak. I am criticized by my colleagues, sometimes for providing "science for dummies", but I will fly that flag with a lot of pride. This is my entire modus operandi: no methods, no brands, no bullshit. I am not here to look clever, I am here to help you do your job more easily and in a way that makes sense. Whatever language people want to use is fine by me. I have to find a way in that is fun, easy, and playful. A science lesson only makes sense when people ask for it. Knowing that the back third of the vocal fold is only cartilage and mucosa does not actually matter. No one cares. They are interested in "How do I hit that note the way I want more easily, every show?

How do I communicate that better? How do I look after my instrument in a party environment? What can I get away with, and what can't I get away with?". I only introduce anatomical and physiological terminology if students ask for it. You get geeky students sometimes and I love them, but you have to keep them focused on what is practically applicable.

My clientele comes in two packages, either high level professionals who are having a problem or have a checklist to fix a few things, or rehab clients who came through the voice clinic or one of the medical charities that help performers. Mostly I am working with disordered voices, either organic or functionally disordered. They often need more explanation because they do not know how they became disordered in the first place. They do not know how any of it works. They do not know what is doing what. This process is slower, and it includes a lot more explanation. It really depends on the person. If they want the science, I will absolutely give it to them. I often ask if a student wants to know how something is happening, and if they say "No, not really" then I just move on.

Cathrine Sadolin

I use the knowledge from voice science, but I do not always talk about the science as such, depending on the occasion. Usually, singers need help with a specific issue and it is our job as teachers to explain the techniques in a simple and concrete way. For this I have developed an extensive number of charts which explain all the issues in an easy understandable manner.

Sometimes I work with high level professional singers who develop some kind of trouble while on tour or recording in the studio. These are typically one-time only gigs with time pressure. I work on releasing the uncontrolled constriction that has formed around the vocal cords. I can usually find a way to release this tension in about an hour. I do not work with anatomy and physiological terms because we only have an hour. For these lessons, I translate my terms into the singer's own language or preferred terminology.

For those who want to become an authorized Complete Vocal Technique (CVT) teacher, then of course, they have to have a solid background in voice science. They also have to be able to perform all styles themselves. For instance, it is not a good idea to teach a classical sound to a rock singer, unless the rock singer specifically wants this. Often singers understand sound before they understand terminology. For this reason, it is very important for teachers to be able to demonstrate the sounds. No matter what your specialization, you must learn how to make every sound in order to teach every sound. So, the "classical" authorized CVT teacher also has to learn to scream and distort. The "rock" authorized CVT teacher must also learn Baroque trills and to make classical sounds in order to teach it.

Marci Rosenberg

I do think it is very important for students to know what is involved in singing and have a strong kinesthetic reference for where these parts are and what they "feel like". I will often show an anatomical picture or an animation of various structures to help close the loop on establishing an internal reference after the students have attempted to do some sort of experiential mapping on their own. However, I do not use this kind of language while working technically. I never say things like "lift your palate" or "use your diaphragm" because I find these types of cues to be fairly meaningless for actually integrating movement patterns. I believe it is much more useful to simply provide an exercise that allows the student to find the target production experientially, without excessive and redundant verbal input from me, because focusing extensively on internal structures when singing tends to be counterproductive and can lead to "over analysis paralysis". Simple is best and working slowly gets you there faster.

Seth Riggs and Margareta Svensson Riggs

For half a century while "vocal establishments" looked down on and disregarded "pop-vocal technique", Seth Riggs successfully taught the vast majority of stars in the commercial fields. Therefore, looking to the fairly new voice science to help someone learn how to sing is not what we tend to do. In recent history, many teachers have fallen victim to what has been termed "voice science". It seems any time you associate something with the word "science" it automatically assumes an aura of truth. That is very attractive to both teachers and students, who are anxious to grab onto anything that seems to offer them hope of understanding what has unfortunately become a very confusing subject.

Of course your voice works, as does everything else, according to scientific principles. But those principles can be abused by those who mostly observe, and who are not able to apply them. Prominent vocal "scientists" have attempted now for years to translate scientific findings into usable vocal technique. Some of those methods have had in common the manipulation of the muscles in and around the larynx, and even the larynx itself. Not only does that prevent the larynx from resting in a speech-level condition, allowing balancing of the bridges (*passaggi*), but it is also damaging to the vocal cords.

To its merit, "voice science" has contributed to some remarkable observations as to what happens to voices during the process of singing. But that is all they are - observations. Science however is not only knowledge derived from observation, but the skill resulting from that knowledge. In singing, that skill can only be developed through singing, (not discussion or reading) but singing special exercises that balance your vocal co-ordination so that speech-level tone production is possible. This is dependent on your larynx resting in the general area where you speak, proper breathing and support, narrowing the vowels in the bridges and – not to forget – by marrying vocal skill with artistic expression through music, which seems to be more or less forgotten in voice science.

References and recommended reading

Behrman, Allison. *Speech and Voice Science*. 2nd ed. San Diego: Plural Publishing, 2013.

Bozeman, Kenneth. "A case for voice science in the voice studio." *Journal of Singing* 63, no. 3 (January/February 2007): 265–270.

Bozeman, Kenneth W. *Kinesthetic Voice Pedagogy: Motivating Acoustic Efficiency*. Gahannah, OH: Inside View Press, 2017.

Bozeman, Kenneth W. *Practical Vocal Acoustics: Pedagogic Applications for Singers and Teachers*. Hillsdale, NY: Pendragon Press, 2014.

Callaghan, Jean. *Singing and Science: Body, Brain, and Voice*, 2nd ed. Oxford: Compton Publishing, 2014.

Collyer, Sally. "Singing teaching and science: An ancient symbiosis." In *Perspectives on Teaching Singing: Australian Vocal Pedagogues Sing their Stories*, edited by Scott D. Harrison, 83-100. Bowen Hills, Qld.: Australian Academic Press, 2010.

Gill, Brian P. and Christian T. Herbst. "Voice pedagogy—what do we need?" *Logopedics, Phoniatrics, Vocology* 41, no. 4 (2016): 168–173. www.doi.org/10.3109/14015439.2015.1079234.

Harris, Tom and David Howard, eds. *The Voice Clinic Handbook*, 2nd ed. Oxford: Compton Publishing, 2018.

Helding, Lynn. "Voice science and vocal art, part one: In search of common ground." *Journal of Singing* 64, no. 2 (November/December 2007): 141–150.

Helding, Lynn. "Voice science and vocal art, part two: Motor learning theory." *Journal of Singing* 64, no. 4 (March/April 2008): 417–428.

Howard, David M and Damian Murphy. *Voice Science, Acoustics and Recording.* San Diego, CA: Plural Publishing, 2008.

Howard, Elisabeth. *Sing! The Vocal Power Method.* New York: Alfred Music, 2006.

Ihasz, Daniel and Dillon R. Parmer. "Practical pedagogy and voice spectrography: A proposal for using technology in pursuit of artistic excellence." *Journal of Singing* 63, no. 1 (September/October 2006): 65–70.

LeBorgne, Wendy D. and Marci Rosenberg. *The Vocal Athlete.* San Diego: Plural Publishing, 2014.

McCoy, Scott. "Pedagadgets." *Journal of Singing* 74, no. 5 (May/June 2018): 533–536.

McCoy, Scott. *Your Voice: An Inside View.* 2nd ed. Delaware, OH: Inside View Press, 2012.

McCoy, Scott. "Singing pedagogy in the twenty-first century: A look toward the future." In *Teaching Singing in the 21st Century,* edited by Scott D. Harrison and Jessica O'Bryan, 13–20. Dordrecht: Springer, 2014.

Michael, Deirdre. "Dispelling Vocal Myths. Part I: 'Sing from your diaphragm!'" *Journal of Singing* 66, no. 5 (May/June 2010): 547–551.

Michael, Deirdre. "Dispelling Vocal Myths: Part II 'Sing it *off* the chords!'" *Journal of Singing* 67, no. 4 (March/April 2011): 417–421.

Michael, Deirdre and George S. Goding. "Dispelling Vocal Myths. Part 3: 'Sing OVER your cold!'" *Journal of Singing* 68, no. 4 (March/April 2012): 419–425.

Michael, Deirdre. "Dispelling Vocal Myths: Part IV 'Talk higher!'" *Journal of Singing* 69, no. 2 (November/December 2012): 167–172.

Michael, Deirdre. "Dispelling Vocal Myths: Part V 'Sniff to raise the palate!'" *Journal of Singing* 71, no. 3 (January/February 2015): 319–324.

Murry, Thomas, Danielle M. McRoy, and Nooshin Parhizkar. "Common medications and their effects on the voice." *Journal of Singing* 63, no. 3 (January/February 2007): 293–297.

Nix, John. "Mission possible: Starting a voice lab at your music school." *Journal of Singing* 65, no. 2 (November/December 2008): 187–193.

Roth, Douglas F. and Katherine Verdolini Abbott. "Vocal health and singing pedagogy: Considerations from biology and motor learning." In *Teaching Singing in the 21st Century,* edited by Scott D. Harrison and Jessica O'Bryan, 68-89. Dordrecht: Springer, 2014.

Sataloff, Robert Thayer. *Voice Science.* 2nd ed. San Diego, CA: Plural Publishing, 2017.

Sataloff, Robert T. *Vocal Health and Pedagogy: Science, Assessment, and Treatment.* 3rd ed. San Diego, CA: Plural Publishing, 2017.

Seikel, J. Anthony, David G. Drumright, and Douglas W. King. *Anatomy & Physiology for Speech, Language, and Hearing.* 5th ed. Clifton Park, NJ: Cengage Learning, 2015.

Sundberg, Johan. *The Science of the Singing Voice.* Dekalb, IL: Northern Illinois University Press, 1987.

Titze, Ingo R. "An appeal for patience and long-suffering by singing teachers in their assessment of the value of voice science." *Journal of Singing* 64, no. 5 (May/June 2008): 593–594.

Titze, Ingo R. *Fascinations with the Human Voice.* Salt Lake City, UT: The National Center for Voice and Speech, 2010.

Titze, Ingo R. *Principles of Voice Production.* Iowa City, IA: The National Center for Voice and Speech, 2000.

Titze, Ingo R. "Voice science and voice pedagogy vocabularies: Can they merge?" *Journal of Singing* 73, no. 3 (January/February 2017): 291–292.

Titze, Ingo and Katherine Verdolini Abbot. *Vocology: The science and practice of voice habilitation.* Salt Lake City, UT: The National Center for Voice and Speech, 2012.

Ware, Rachel. "The use of science and imagery in the voice studio: A survey of voice teachers in the United States and Canada." *Journal of Singing* 69, no. 4 (March/April 2013): 413–417.

Welch, Graham F., David M. Howard, Evangelos Himonides, and Jude Brereton. "Real-time feedback in the singing studio: An innovatory action-research project using new voice technology." *Music Education Research* 7, no. 2 (July 2005): 225–249. doi.org/10.1080/14613800500169779.

Wilson, Pat. "Sinful modern music: Science and the contemporary commercial singer." *Australian Voice* 9 (2003): 12–16.

Winnie, Brian J. "Service the students: developing a *Mise en Place.*" In *The Voice Teacher's Cookbook: Creative Recipes for Teachers of Singing* edited by Brian J. Winnie, 130–132. Delray Beach, FL: Meredith Music, 2018.

Zemlin, Willard R. *Speech and Hearing Science: Anatomy and Physiology.* 4th ed. Boston, MA: Allyn and Bacon, 1998.

19

Teaching young singers

Demand for teaching voice lessons to minors has increased in the past few decades. Anecdotally, many independent studios have a large client base of minors, and vocal study may begin at almost any age. College audition preparation is big business, with specialist college audition coaches making thousands of dollars to help high school students get into the competitive musical theatre school of their choice. One can find children starring in musical theatre productions from the community theatre to the Broadway theatre, in everything from *Oliver* to *Fun Home*. In a classical paradigm, it is logical that vocal study would begin at the age of maturity in order to avoid a Charlotte Church or Jackie Evancho situation. Any time children are stuck on imitating adult sounds there is cause for pedagogical concern. However, these CCM pedagogues encourage natural and age-appropriate sounds based in functional training. Most of the pedagogues (88%) teach singers under the age of 18, either regularly (50%) or occasionally (38%). They are careful to select age-appropriate repertoire. They also point out that once the lyrics have been determined to be age-appropriate, pop/rock music may be sung in any key and often uses a small range, making it ideal material for the changing voice.

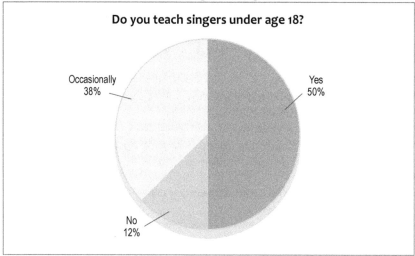

Of those pedagogues who teach singers under the age of 18 (*n* = 18), 61% say that they modify their approach with younger students. This majority is reflective of the trend toward flexibility and customizing pedagogical approaches for each individual student. Fewer (39%) say that they do not change their pedagogical approach, with the exception of selecting age-appropriate repertoire. There are valid reasons on both sides and it is possible that divergent pedagogical choices may produce equally effective results. Many highlight the benefits and rewards of working with a student at the beginning of their vocal development.

Those who do not teach singers under the age of 18 are the minority (12%), but there are strong reasons behind that choice. Some do not see satisfying results with this age group due to students being over-scheduled, lack of student effort, and the climate of modern parenting. Others harshly criticize the performing industry for putting children to work in spite of child-labor laws against such practices. Other concerns surrounding teaching minors include increased liability for the teacher, requiring a chaperone to facilitate "hands-on" pedagogies, and managing parental expectations.

This chapter includes responses to the prompt "Do you teach singers under age 18? If so, what is unique or different about teaching these singers?". The responses are presented in order from those who do teach students under age 18 and also modify their approach, followed by those who teach them but do not modify their approach, and ends with those who do not teach singers under age 18.

Robert Edwin

Half of my students are under the age of 18. My DVD, *The Kid & The Singing Teacher*,[1] was one of the first to pioneer and address child voice pedagogy in all styles of singing, and I have covered the topic extensively in my writings.[2] What is unique and challenging about teaching children is scaling down pedagogic language and concepts to fit their learning abilities without giving up fact-based explanations. The other challenge is to have child voice expectations and not impose adult vocal standards on the kids. Their voices are not fragile, but they are ever-changing, especially during puberty, so we have to be sensitive to the growth of their bodies which, of course, includes the singing system. As teachers, we need to tap into their play mode by using creative and engaging exercises to develop a solid technical base. Since I do that with my adult students as well, it's not a big shift for me. Age-appropriate technique and repertoire are at the core of my child voice pedagogy. Common sense says children should not copy adult voices and should not be singing about the broken love affairs they have never had. They need to find their own voices and tell stories in rep that relate to their experiences and their understanding of the world.

Mary Saunders Barton

I occasionally work with talented teenagers these days, and earlier in my teaching career I taught children as young as 5 and 6 and loved every minute of it.

With teenagers who have career aspirations, I want to introduce them to a lifelong respect for the care of their instrument. In developing voices, I will always look for weaknesses and begin to fill in any "holes". There are times when teachers have to steer young people away from unhealthy vocal behaviors in their day to day lives that they might not be aware of. It is important to choose repertoire that is developmentally appropriate, that they are inspired to sing. Knowing just how much to push a shy 15- year-old, or to restrain an over-enthusiastic one, takes a delicate approach.

---

1   Robert Edwin and Barbara Arboleda, *The Kid & The Singing Teacher*. DVD. Voicewize, 2008. http://www. voiceinsideview.com/kid_sing.html.

2   Robert Edwin, from "The care and feeding of young voices," *The Journal of Singing/The NATS Journal* 43, no. 4 (March/April 1987), 44, to "Vocal parenting revisited," *Journal of Singing* 70, no. 3 (January/February 2014), 341–344.

Teaching little kids is just plain fun if they love to sing. The technique part of things is blended into the process, like medicine in apple sauce. Occasionally, we encounter a wildly gifted 10-year-old. Then it is our job to let them sing, sing, sing and "do no harm".

Tracy Marie Bourne

Yes, I teach a number of young singers under age 18. I do technical work with all of them, but I keep it to one concept at a time. Some younger singers have trouble with pitch accuracy and I have found that consistent attention to this with simple songs and exercises resolves the issue over time. We also work on alignment and singing with ease. I take young singers through the whole of their range at every lesson. My experience is that if I keep it simple, and work through a few key concepts, young singers tend to improve in a natural way. Young singers often have great instincts and fewer tension issues than adults. There are fewer bad habits to deal with and children can be really fast learners!

Marcelle G. Gauvin

Yes, I teach singers under the age of 18. If they are boys, the abrupt voice change can be challenging. I deal with parents who might have unrealistic expectations. Airiness can occur due to the vocal fold "chink" in many young teen females. Finding age-appropriate material is challenging.

Matthew Edwards

I work with singers around the age of 15 and up. I think you can safely teach students younger than 15, it is just not where I excel as a teacher. With younger students, I am very cautious about allowing them to sing near extremes (range, volume, etc.). If the student is overly ambitious, which many are, they will take everything you show them and practice 100%+ at home. If they just learned to belt a C5, they will go home and try to sing "Defying Gravity" for several hours a day. That can quickly get them injured. Therefore, I always tell them slow and steady wins the race, voice training is a marathon not a sprint. I also think it is critical to develop the head voice in this age group. I never use foreign language repertoire unless the student is drawn to it. Instead, we use vocal exercises and simple word phrases to explore the upper part of the voice. If the student is a musical theatre performer, we sing a lot of Golden Age ballads alongside their contemporary rep.

Lisa Popeil

I teach singers as young as 6-years-old. My attitude is that as long as a child is interested in singing, and is singing around the house or perhaps on stage, they should learn to sing properly. As for repertoire, I normally begin with classic Disney™ songs and kid-friendly musicals they might be performing at school. In addition, I like to show them the basics of the piano, such as the names of the notes, and if they're a bit older and bright, I will introduce them to reading music. Since I had such an interest in languages, if I notice that same ability in young people, I will pull out songs in French, German or Italian and observe if they enjoy learning to sing in a foreign language. On occasion, I will introduce classical singing to a young person, since normally they are not being exposed to it elsewhere. I feel responsible for at least providing an introduction to this type of singing. For very young students, I try to stay away from pop music that they are already hearing, though by the time a singer is 11 or 12, they will often have a great interest in singing pop/R&B, and we'll work together using karaoke while I coach them during the recording process (headphones, mic, professional recording program, and mixing on large speakers), which is very exciting to them.

Edrie Means Weekly

I teach professionals, amateurs, and beginners under the age of 18. I teach the individual and adapt to how they learn, whether they are young or old. Each singer is unique with different needs. There is no cookie cutter recipe for all singers. The young pre-pubescent voice and body will be going through many changes in the next several years, and has to be guided gently and worked with differently. Both pre-pubescent female and male voices go through changes. I maintain working on healthy vocal function, evenness of register balance, and flexibility, as I do with all clients/students. I strongly believe they need to understand why we are doing certain vocalizes or body stretches, and how it affects the voice. I adjust to their learning style – aural/visual/kinesthetic. I try to explain things in a simplistic way. The amateur and younger singers require more practice in strengthening and co-ordination due to weaker intrinsic muscles.

As with all of my clients/students, I am working with singers who have a uniqueness and style. Together we are working towards producing better co-ordination and control of a certain style or sound they want to make.

I am also careful about the repertoire I pick for them, as well as advising them on the potential problems with repertoire they bring in. For example, if the song is too high and loud for too long.

Mark Baxter

I work with singers as young as 7 if they are in performing situations and exhibiting signs of vocal fatigue. I adjust my approach to the individual needs and capabilities of each singer I work with. The mind and physiology of a child are always taken into account. The major difference in working with children is managing the expectations of parents. Unfortunately, non-singing adults glean their knowledge of the music business via TV competitions and overnight success fables. Being a parent, I understand the filter they view their children through, and their desire for success without sacrifice. I spend a great deal of time educating parents on the reality of the life of a performing artist. I usually end my discussions with "If you really want your children to find the grit and passion necessary to become a professional singer – just call them delusional and forbid them from throwing their lives away. It worked like a charm on me!".

Kathryn Paradise

I occasionally teach singers under the age of 18. The main difference in my mind is the intensity and pace of the training. Frequently, these lessons take on a more general and exploratory nature unless we are working towards a specific audition or performance. If students are serious about pursuing music, I often incorporate basic music theory and piano skills into the lesson. Technically, I use more metaphor and take less time directly covering the science of singing, but I still address basic vocal health. The main challenge with these young singers is helping them find repertoire that they are both interested in and are technically capable of mastering. Frequently, we adjust keys and discuss how comparing oneself to an edited studio recording is unrealistic. We focus on building foundational vocal technique and basic musicianship.

Marci Rosenberg

I do work with younger singers (not younger than 12) if they are higher level singers on a pre-professional trajectory. For a typical adolescent, the main focus should be balance and flexibility, and developing strength in the breathing musculature. If the student is quite young, then a slower approach may be necessary. If these students come in having only done hefty belting, then I will work in the opposite direction to make sure they are balanced. I think younger girls are much better off focusing on head voice and gentle chest register strengthening but avoiding loud, high belting until they are teenagers. The belt quality will sometimes emerge on its own in a younger instrument that has been trained in a balanced manner. These singers will often have a much stronger mix and a lot more vocal options as they mature. It is often difficult to manage over-zealous parents who want their child to be singing material that is too difficult for them. These singers often pay a price when they are older.

Jan Shapiro

Yes, I teach singers under age 18, but I only teach some grade school ages within specific circumstances. Generally, I encourage children to sing naturally and freely, and to study an instrument first.

Trineice Robinson-Martin

I try to play off their natural creativity, more so than with adults. Adults tend to have more mental blocks when learning to improvise, and often are afraid to sound "bad" or "do it wrong". In terms of voice training, I still teach them voice science and make them aware of how their body works when singing. I limit repertoire based on story rather than technicality. In other words, is the singer old enough or mature enough to tell this story? The repertoire and stylistic choices correlate to their vocal development (Note: this is not exclusive to under 18).

Seth Riggs and Margareta Svensson Riggs

Yes, absolutely, and the process is the same as for grown-ups. The vocal cords of a child are shorter than those of grown-ups, but the bridging (*passaggio*) process is the same. They just happen in a higher register.

Technically, including for the male voice that is transitioning from boy soprano to the beginning of adult male voice, it is always about monitoring and ensuring as balanced a voice co-ordination as possible. Again, connecting the chest with the head, keeping the larynx down, proper breath support, and narrowing the vowels to keep the good line.

We tailor the training for each student so that they can succeed.

Kevin Wilson

I rarely teach singers under the age of 18. When I do, however, I try and stay true to my teaching process of slow and steady progress technically, and assign age- and technique-appropriate repertoire.

Wendy DeLeo LeBorgne

The singers in my studio who are under 18 are either professional artists, or pre-professional artists, so they are generally not beginners. They are either on track to audition for college or are currently performing professionally, so they generally have fairly well-developed instruments by the time I see them. I do not train these singers any differently than my adult artists. We train like vocal athletes and I work to choose repertoire that is age-, emotionally-, and vocally-appropriate for a given artist. We want them to grow, so we provide them with a bit of a challenge, but we do not want to over-train and create injury.

Kimberly Steinhauer

Yes, I teach singers under age 18. Singers of all ages learn the Estill Voice Training® Figures[3] and apply them to age-appropriate repertoire. Since vocal health is paramount, not much changes when teaching young singers.

Dane Chalfin

I only take clients under 18 who are already working professionally, and they must bring a parent or guardian to the lesson because I teach occasionally with "hands-on". I need to be able to do that to teach effectively. I do not really change my approach with these students. I worked with one of the Young Michaels from *Motown* and I did not feel that I was the right match to teach him. I know others who are really good at that, so I pass them on. A young professional performer will get the same training from me that an adult would. However, I always tailor to every individual that is in front of me. Performers need to know what kind of industry they are going into. I spend a lot of time reminding them not to buy into the media and press, stop chasing the Instagram photo, stop sucking in your stomach on stage because you cannot breathe. I think body-positivity is a bigger issue with the under-18 group, particularly the girls. In my studio, they have to make a choice to trust me and let go of the things that do not help them get better at singing, like that constant tummy-holding.

Elisabeth Howard

I have taught hundreds of students under the age of 18. In fact, I had 10 winners on Ed McMahon's Star Search back in the 80s. I had seven 1st place winners in the prestigious classical high school competition, the Los Angeles Music Center Spotlight Awards.

The fun and advantage of teaching students this age is that you get them before they have developed bad habits. I was able to give solid foundations to hundreds of singers who are now out in the professional world singing in opera houses all over the world, and recording artists who are well known in pop to jazz.

Jeff Ramsey

I have not had much experience with younger singers under 18 but the couple I have taught were old enough to understand certain principles. I try to teach them about breath and healthy singing.

---

3   An EVT Figure is a vocal exercise that establishes control over one structure within the vocal mechanism by isolating and moving the structure through different conditions. There are 13 figures in the EVT model. More information may be found in Kimberly Steinhauer, Mary McDonald Klimek, and Jo Estill, *The Estill Voice Model: Theory and Translation* (Pittsburgh: Estill Voice International, 2018).

Gillyanne Kayes

I teach singers under the age of 18 very occasionally and only if they are exceptional. The difference is knowing that during adolescence, voices are subject to change. I have taken two young men through voice change recently and it can be a challenging time for them.

Kim Chandler

Generally, I do not teach singers under age 18, only in exceptional cases.

Irene Bartlett

I do not currently teach students under age 18. However, I did for around 20 years and "The Ever-Changing Voice - From Infant to Adult" is a study area within the master's degree in Voice Pedagogy that I lead at the Queensland Conservatorium, Griffith University.

All care should be taken to protect and strengthen the developing voice. I believe strongly that children should be encouraged to sing in all styles, but with their own voice rather than *mirror-image* vocal copies of their adult idols. I do this by asking them to sing a wide range of repertoire from all genres. In my experience, a teacher has the power to open young students' minds to a world of music. In this way, they can be eased away from a fixation on a particular "star" performer. I start by finding similar repertoire in terms of style and rhythm and, as in CCM we are not required to sing in any set key, I can offer repertoire from singers of the opposite gender

When working with children and adolescents, teachers must be aware that young voices are anatomically and physiologically immature. Voice science informs us that growth changes in the body (including the respiratory system and the laryngeal cartilages and muscles) are constant from birth, with major changes occurring through puberty when the rate of development becomes both unique to the individual and influenced by gender.

I believe that best practice teaching of young singers demands a knowledge of the physiological stages of voice development, as each stage affects the singer's potential vocal strength, endurance, range, and tessitura. We know that the most dramatic voice change occurs at puberty especially for boys, but awareness of mutational change is equally important when teaching girls.

Cate Frazier-Neely

Half of my private studio used to be for ages 13-18. I developed and taught junior high voice classes for years, which I really enjoyed.

You cannot treat a child, tween, or teen as a small adult. The teacher must either intuit or understand basic child psychology, and their stages of physical and mental development. Many people who teach this age group are wonderful classical singers, but they are trying to apply what they learned in their classical adult pedagogy or performance classes. They attend workshops hoping for "tips" because working with younger singers makes up part of their livelihood, but they do not seem to understand that younger singers require a different set of teaching skills than what they have acquired. This age group has become a "cash cow", with unsuspecting parents paying thousands of dollars for anyone or any program that claims expertise or has impressive credentials.

When our second child was in her last years of high school, I decided I could not work with this age group because of the physical and psychic strength needed to parent in the U.S., which is not very family-friendly. I now have a few students of this age, but they are highly vetted to make sure their parents will support our work together. Even then, the regularity needed for true growth over the years does not happen due to schedules, peer group pressures, and the attitude that just by taking lessons someone becomes a good singer. I often end up teaching solely to the next audition or performance. This is not a way to build a voice or even lay the groundwork for music education that will last a lifetime.

Cathrine Sadolin

No, I do not teach singers under age 18. We are a professional institute (CVT), and in my personal political view, no children under 18 should be involved in the professional music industry. I know that it happens, but I think that it is abuse. Child labor has been outlawed all over the world, except in the professional music industry. Why is it illegal everywhere else, but not in music? I think working as a child is not in the best interest of the children. I believe that this is wrong, and we do not want to help a young person get into trouble by teaching them how to get into the industry before the age of 18. I do not want to participate in that because I do not think it is right.

References and recommended reading

American Academy of Teachers of Singing. "Keeping music in the schools: Advocating for the arts as core curriculum." *Journal of Singing* 69, no. 2 (November/December 2012): 129–135.

Barlow, Christopher and Jeannette LoVetri. "Closed quotient and spectral measures of female adolescent singers in different singing styles." *Journal of Voice* 24, no. 3 (May 2010): 314–318. doi.org/10.1016/j.jvoice.2008.10.003.

Barlow, Christopher and David M. Howard. "Voice source changes of child and adolescent subjects undergoing singing training: A preliminary study." *Logopedics, Phoniatrics, Vocology* 27, no. 2 (2002): 66–73. www.doi.org/10.1080/140154302760409284.

Barlow, Christopher and David M. Howard. "Electrolaryngographically derived voice source changes of child and adolescent singers." *Logopedics Phoniatrics Vocology* 30, no. 3-4 (2005): 147–157. doi.org/10.1080/14015430500294031.

Benack Spadaro, Esther, Kimberly McInnis, Kimberly Steinhauer, and Mary McDonald Klimek. *The Estill Adventure: Figures for Beginners.* Estill Voice Training Systems International, in press.

Burdick, Barbara. "Vocal techniques for music theater: The high school and undergraduate singer." *Journal of Singing* 61, no. 3 (January/February 2005): 261–268.

Brunssen, Karen. *The Evolving Singing Voice: Changes Across the Lifespan.* San Diego: Plural Publishing, 2018.

Cooksey, John M. *Working with Adolescent Voices*, rev. St. Louis, MO: Concordia Publishing House, 2005.

Edwin, Robert. "Repertoire for child singers." *Journal of Singing* 68, no. 4 (March/April 2012): 443–444.

Edwin, Robert. "The care and feeding of young voices," *The Journal of Singing/The NATS Journal* 43, no. 4 (March/April 1987): 44.

Edwin, Robert. "Vocal parenting revisited." *Journal of Singing* 70, no. 3 (January/February 2014): 341–344.

Edwin, Robert and Barbara Wilson Arboleda. *The Kid & The Singing Teacher.* DVD. Dedham, MA: Voicewize, 2008. http://www.voiceinsideview.com/kid_sing.html.

Freer, Patrick K. "The changing boy's voice: From rocky road to sublime smoothie." In *The Voice Teacher's Cookbook: Creative Recipes for Teachers of Singing* edited by Brian J. Winnie, 44–45. Delray Beach, FL: Meredith Music, 2018.

Greene, Novie. "Developing healthy children's voices in a noisy world." *Journal of Singing* 70, no. 5 (May/June 2014): 591–595.

LeBorgne, Wendy D. and Marci Rosenberg. *The Vocal Athlete.* San Diego: Plural Publishing, 2014.

McAllister, Anita, Elisabeth Sederholm, Johan Sundberg, and Patricia Gramming. "Perceptual and acoustic analysis of vocal registers in 10-year-old children." *Logopedics Phoniatrics Vocology* 25, no. 2 (2000): 63–71. doi.org/10.1016/S0892-1997(05)80294-2.

Mecke, Ann-Christine, Johan Sundberg, Svante Granqvist, and Matthias Echternach. "Comparing closed quotient in children singers' voices as measured by high-speed-imaging, electroglottography, and inverse filtering." *Journal of the Acoustical Society of America* 131, no. 1 (January 2012): 435–441. www.doi.org/10.1121/1.3662061.

Mondelli, Peter. "From the Bel Canto stage to reality TV: A musicological view of opera's child prodigy problem." *Journal of Singing* 75, no. 1 (September/October 2018): 7–15.

Pomfret, Bonnie. "How young is too young? Teaching the unchanged voice." *Journal of Singing* 68, no. 4 (March/April 2012): 445–449.

Sanderson, Ana and Gillyanne Kayes. *Singing Express: Discovering the Singer in Every Child.* London: A & C Black, 2009.

Schneider, Berit, Michaela Zumtobel, Walter Prettenhofer, Birgitta Aichstill, and Werner Jocher. "Normative voice range profiles in vocally trained and untrained children aged between 7 and 10 years." *Journal of Voice* 24, no. 2 (March 2010): 153–160. doi.org/10.1016/j.jvoice.2008.07.007.

Skelton, Kevin D. "The child's voice: A closer look at pedagogy and science." *Journal of Singing* 63, no. 5 (May/June 2007): 537–544.

Stathopoulos, Elaine T., Jessica E. Huber, Joan E. Sussman, and Robert Schlauch. "Changes in acoustic characteristics of the voice across the life span: Measures from individuals 4-93 years of age." *Journal of Speech, Language, and Hearing Research* 54, no. 4 (August 2011): 1011–1021. www.doi.org/10.1044/1092-4388(2010/10-0036).

Trollinger, Valerie. "Pediatric vocal development and voice science: Implications for teaching singing." *General Music Today* 20, no. 3 (Spring 2007): 19–25.

Warwick, Jacqueline and Allison Adrian, eds. *Voicing Girlhood in Popular Music: Performance, Authority, Authenticity.* New York: Routledge, 2016.

Williams, Jenevora. *Singing and Teaching Singing to Children and Young Adults*, 2nd ed. Oxford: Compton Publishing, 2018.

Williams, Jenevora. *Teaching Singing to Children and Young Adults. Disc. 1. Vocal technique for young singers -- Disc. 2. Adolescent male voice change.* DVDs. Oxford: Compton Publishing, 2013.

Willis, Elizabeth. "Registration in young voices: A balancing act." In *Perspectives on Teaching Singing: Australian Vocal Pedagogues Sing their Stories*, edited by Scott D. Harrison, 141–154. Bowen Hills, Qld.: Australian Academic Press, 2010.

Wilson Arboleda, Barbara. "Strength training and rock singing for the young." *Journal of Singing* 69, no. 4 (March/April 2013): 463–465.

SECTION IV:
Aesthetic Context

20

Singers to admire

This chapter presents personalized playlists from pedagogues who have spent their lives listening to voices. What a gift! A study published in the *New York Times* showed that the majority of us develop our musical tastes for life by age 16, and as adults, we listen most frequently to the music that captivated us during our adolescent years.[1] However, data indicate that the great CCM pedagogues have never stopped listening to new music. They listen to the classics *and* the newest artists, and appreciate them both with equal reverence. Great voices transcend musical genre. In fact, most of the pedagogues produced a stylistically varied list, spanning Luciano Pavarotti to Stevie Wonder, or Barbra Streisand to Lady Gaga. Many identify the most essential traits of a truly admirable singer as a unique sound and an emotionally compelling performance. The two most commonly named singers had these traits in spades: Aretha Franklin and Ella Fitzgerald.

One of the easiest ways to explore new music is by turning on your FM radio. It's free and is available in your car or on your smartphone. Another good option is Sirius XM radio, a subscription service that has more than 150 genre-specific channels. A terrible injustice within the music industry is the fact that commercial artists are not paid fairly for their recorded music. Companies like Pandora, Spotify, and YouTube are the worst offenders. The best way to support musicians is to purchase live concert tickets, purchase merchandise at those concerts, and promote favorite musicians on social media. Another good tactic is to purchase CDs and MP3 file downloads, and to encourage students to do the same. In spite of unfair compensation to creative artists, Spotify, Pandora, and YouTube provide undeniably convenient ways to explore new music before purchasing concert tickets. There are free and paid subscription versions, and all three services allow you to listen to an endless variety of music. Pandora is especially helpful because you can enter the name of someone like "Taylor Swift" and Pandora takes you on a virtual music tour of similar artists. Pandora plays "Teardrops on my guitar", one of Swift's early singles from 2007, then "Hello" by Adele, then "Blown Away" by Carrie Underwood, then "Closer" by The Chainsmokers, and so on. Follow the example of these great CCM pedagogues, and never stop exploring.

To explore the latest developments in musical theatre, seeing a high-production-value musical is ideal. However, if you cannot fly to New York City to see a Broadway show in person, BroadwayHD.com[2] offers a streaming subscription to top level archived productions, concerts, cabarets and more, for less than the cost of a movie ticket. PBS curates a large archive of "Great

---

1   Seth Stephens-Davidowitz, "The Songs That Bind," *The New York Times*, February 10, 2018, accessed August 1, 2018, www.nytimes.com/2018/02/10/opinion/sunday/favorite-songs.html?rref=collection%2Fbyline %2Fseth-stephens-davidowitz&action=click&contentCollection=undefined&region=stream&module=stream_ unit&version=latest&contentPlacement=1&pgtype=collection.

2   More information may be found at www.broadwayhd.com/index.php.

Performances" from theatre, musical theatre, opera, concerts, and popular music, which may be streamed through a subscription service.[3]

A special plea for those who may not have embraced rap and hip hop in the singing voice studio: note that several pedagogues below report *enjoying* listening to rap and hip hop artists. In 2017, rap/hip hop music song consumption was the highest of all genres, accounting for 20.9% of all song consumption in the United States.[4] If you have even one student who loves Lin-Manuel Miranda's *Hamilton: An American Musical* (for which Miranda received a MacArthur Genius Grant and a Pulitzer Prize), rap has already crossed your studio threshold. It is time to explore this complex and multi-faceted genre. An excellent starting place, especially for the well-trained musician, is Martin E. Connor's *The Musical Artistry of Rap*.[5] Another powerful step can be to ask your students which artists they enjoy listening to and let them guide your listening journey. There are some broad stereotypes which generalize all rap and hip hop as violent, profane, and misogynistic, but in reality, the genres are significantly more multi-facetted.[6] No singer should miss out on the elements which *accurately* define the genre: sophisticated prosody and sublime rhythmic virtuosity.

This chapter includes responses to the prompt "Whose singing do you admire?". The responses are presented in random order.

Edrie Means Weekly

That's a tough question. There are so many singers that I admire! Judy Garland (young Judy and MGM years, not 1960s) is one of my top. I have several for each style.

- Broadway: Julie Andrews, Ron Raines, Robert Goulet, Norbert Leo Butz, Gavin Creel, Stephanie J. Block, Kristin Chenoweth, George Hearn, Bernadette Peters, Norm Lewis, Patti LuPone, Marin Mazzie, and Audra MacDonald.
- Jazz/swing: Louis Armstrong, Ella Fitzgerald, Ann Hampton Callaway, Dianne Reeves, Diana Krall, Frank Sinatra, and Sarah Vaughan.
- Contemporary Christian/gospel: The Gaither Brothers, Sandy Patti, Steven Curtis Chapman, Point of Grace, Larnelle Harris, and Michael W. Smith.
- Country: Trace Adkins, Johnny Cash, Patsy Cline, Loretta Lynn, Carrie Underwood, and so many others in different genres of country.
- Pop/R&B: Barbra Streisand, Barry Manilow, Bette Midler, Michael Jackson, Aretha Franklin Whitney Houston, Ray Charles, Celine Dion, Christina Aguilera, and Stevie Wonder.
- Rock: Heart, Pat Benatar, Lady Gaga, Justin Timberlake, Ricky Martin, and Sting.

Matthew Edwards

Luciano Pavarotti, Thomas Quasthoff, Thomas Hampson, Samuel Ramey, Lisette Oropesa, Giorgio Tozzi, Laura Osnes, Jeremy Jordan, Ben Platt, Sutton Foster, Jessie Mueller, Neil Diamond, Bob Dylan, Nina Simone, Adam Lambert, Freddie Mercury, Michael Jackson, Ed Sheeran, Mariah Carey, Stevie Wonder, and Ariana Grande. I know I am forgetting many others.

---

3 More information may be found at www.pbs.org/show/great-performances/.

4 Statista, "Share of music song consumption in the United States in 2017, by genre," accessed on August 27, 2018, www.statista.com/statistics/694862/music-song-consumption-genre/.

5 Martin E. Connor, *The Musical Artistry of Rap*, (Jefferson, NC: McFarland, 2018).

6 Sherri Williams, "Cardi B: Love & Hip Hop's unlikely feminist hero," *Feminist Media Studies* 17, no. 6 (December 2017), 1114-1117, http://www.doi.org/10.1080/14680777.2017.1380431.

Kim Chandler

Stevie Wonder, Donny Hathaway, Layla Hathaway, Karen Carpenter, Melonie Daniels, Beady Belle, Matt Corby...

Mary Saunders Barton

I admire many, many singers from many different eras and genres. Among my favorites are: Maria Callas, James Taylor, Cynthia Erivo, Barbra Streisand, Alix Korey, Eva Cassidy, Luciano Pavarotti, Kelli O'Hara, Audra McDonald, Jussi Björling, Nancy LaMott, Sutton Foster, Leontyne Price, Carolee Carmello, Lea Salonga, Judy Kuhn, Judy Collins, Harry Chapin, Bruno Mars, Bobby McFerrin, Betty Buckley, Beverly Sills, Billy Joel, Linda Ronstadt, to name a few, and many of the simply extraordinary singers I had the privilege of working with at Penn State.

Mark Baxter

I admire anyone who is courageous enough to reveal an honest aspect of his or herself in a song.

Robert Edwin

I listen to everything, so the list would be extensive. I have my favorite rappers (Eminem and Chance the Rapper) right through to my favorite opera singers (I grew up listening to old 78 rpm records featuring artists such as Enrico Caruso, Antonio Scotti, Rosa Ponselle, and Eva Gauthier). My parents started this whole "Bach to rock" thing with me when I was a child. They taught me to listen for a story within the style and to try to understand what the artist was trying to say. I pass that advice on to everyone, especially my students who have trouble embracing a variety of musical aesthetics.

Cathrine Sadolin

I admire everyone that is doing something which is "out there" or "touches" people. When we talk about what I personally like, it is in the niche area. This doesn't mean that I think some singers are better than others, they are just sounds that I happen to like. I favor heavy metal singers, I love the way they sing. The late-singer Ronnie James Dio of Black Sabbath was fantastic and inspiring to me personally. I studied his voice a lot to learn his technique. Of course, I love the traditional singers like Aretha Franklin and James Brown. I also love Bob Dylan. I know a lot of people say he cannot sing, and I think they are absolutely wrong. He is one of the most amazing singers and I love his sound. I love his treatment of rhythm, and how he plays guitar at the same time, also in interesting rhythmic patterns. Of course, his lyrics are brilliant. I also like a singer named Dick Gaughan, a Scottish singer. He has a fantastic approach to small ornamentation and very interesting rhythmic styles when singing on consonants.

I can mention brilliant singers in every style. I especially like ethnic styles, and I even like those singers who sing completely out of tune. I can enjoy that a lot, even though I am a singing teacher. Singing out of tune can have a lot of heart and meaning. I like when the pitch is used for expression. Once there is expression, I do not care about the voice, I just want the expression.

Gillyanne Kayes

This is an enormously difficult question to answer. I enjoy the *song* itself, and not just the voice, so I tend to admire a particular song or performance. Examples that spring to mind are: Lady

Gaga "I'm on the Edge"; Christina Aguilera's opening number in *Burlesque*; the young Aretha Franklin singing "Say a little prayer"; and John Owen Jones singing "Rise Like a Phoenix". Some voices that I admire are Ramin Karimloo, Donny Hathaway, Alison Krauss, and Jessie J. I think that JJ, Sia, Jason Mraz, and Ed Sheeran are all interesting songwriters.

Kevin Wilson

Dmitri Hvorostovksy, Bryn Terfel, Maria Callas, Beverly Sills, Kelly O'Hara, Stephen Pasquale, Cynthia Erivo, Jessie Meuller, and Audra McDonald.

Elisabeth Howard

First of all, I admire my student, Paige O'Hara, voice of Belle in the film, *Beauty and the Beast*.
- Jazz Women: Eva Cassidy, Ella Fitzgerald, Billy Holiday, Cleo Laine, and Diana Krall.
- Jazz Men: Bobby McFerrin, Al Jarreau, Kurt Elling, George Benson, Michael Bublé,
- Michael Feinstein, and Tony Bennett.
- Pop Women: Barbra Streisand, Celine Dion, Whitney Houston, Anita Baker, Aretha Franklin, Patty Labelle, Gladys Knight, Adele, Cristina Aguilera, Bonnie Raitt, Alicia Keys, Sara Bareilles, Ricky Lee Jones, Laura Nyro, Lady Gaga, Amy Winehouse, Katy Perry, Kelly Clarkson, Mariah Carey, Beyoncé, Shakira, Pat Benatar, Karen Carpenter, Natalie Cole, Dionne Warwick, Diann Summer, Eydie Gorme, Judy Garland, Liza Minnelli, Melba Moore, Tina Turner, Roberta Flack, and Donna Summer.
- Pop Men: Billy Joel, Elton John, Sam Smith, Ed Sheeran, Tony Bennett Lionel Richie, Nat King Cole, Elvis Presley, Bing Crosby, Johnny Mathis, Sammy Davis Jr., Bruno Mars, Justin Timberlake, and John Legend.
- Rock Women: Janis Joplin, Stevie Nicks, Tina Turner, Sheryl Crow, Pat Benatar, Melissa Etheridge, Kelly Clarkson, Heart, Amy Winehouse, and Alanis Morissette.
- Rock Men: Rolling Stones, Aerosmith, Sting, The Who, Motley Crue, Mick Jagger, Jeff Buckley, Axl Rose, Jon Bon Jovi, Bono, Chris Cornell, the Eagles, Jim Morrison, John Bon Jovi, and Led Zeppelin.
- Country Women: Alison Krauss, Anne Murray, Dolly Parton, Emmy Lou Harris, Faith Hill, Linda Ronstadt, Carrie Underwood, Lee Ann Rimes, Reba McEntire, Shania Twain, and Trisha Yearwood.
- Country Men: Alan Jackson, Clint Black, Dwight Yoakam, Garth Brooks, Kenny Chesney, Randy Travis, Tim McGraw, Trace Adkins, Travis Tritt, Vince Gill, Charlie Daniels Band, George Jones, George Strait, Chris Kristofferson, Larry Gatlin, Glen Campbell, Merle Haggard, and Willie Nelson.

Jan Shapiro

I admire any singer who uses his or her voice well – freely and naturally. So that could be Billie Holiday, Ella Fitzgerald, Barbra Streisand, Michael Jackson, or Bruno Mars.

Tracy Marie Bourne

Australian Singers: Anthony Warlow, Amanda Harrison, Rachel Beck, Silvie Paladino, Matt Hetherington, Marcia Hines, John Farnham, Simon Gleeson, and Queenie van der Zandt.

Audra McDonald, Linda Eder, Barbara Cook, Kristen Chenoweth, Brian Stokes Mitchell, Sutton Foster, and Theresa McCarthy.

Trineice Robinson-Martin

Nancy Wilson, Darryl Coley, Gregory Porter, CeCe Winans, Kim Burrell, and Rachelle Farrell.

Wendy DeLeo LeBorgne

There are so many singers I admire. I like Betsy Wolfe, Audra McDonald, Sutton Foster, Patti LuPone, and the list could go on and on. I personally am influenced by, and enjoy, old jazz artists like Sarah Vaughan and Rosemary Clooney. These are just my personal preferences. I love to listen to unique voices, and whether it is commercial or classical, I love to listen to singers who are interesting. I like to listen to Adele, Ariana Grande, Christina Aguilera, Katy Perry, to name a few. I do not think that any of those voices I just mentioned are what I would consider "totally normal" voices. For example, people love the voice of Grace VanderWaal, who won America's Got Talent last year. I would not say that I necessarily like her voice, but I can say that it is very likely a pathologic voice, and she won a million dollars singing that way. How long it will last is another question. It creates a generation of young singers who want to sound like her, but if a young singer has normal vocal cords, there is likely no way they can sound like VanderWaal. This is a bit of a disconnect. However, I like listening to those artists every now and again. I think a lot of our commercial artists probably are not totally "healthy", but they are so interesting and unique and that is what makes them awesome.

In music theatre, I like the voices of Mandy Patinkin, Stephen Pasquale, and Brian Stokes Mitchell. I also like commercial artists like Adam Levine.

Dane Chalfin

The top 5: Whitney Houston, Freddy Mercury, Shirley Bassey, Luciano Pavarotti, and George Michael. I admire each singer for different reasons, but they all share a relentless commitment to emotional communication.

Irene Bartlett

Regardless of style, any singer who engages me emotionally, or is singing in their chosen style on a healthy sustainable vocal production. Many of my early influences are listed in the chapter on training, but I should add that I love to listen to some the amazing singers of today, such as Beyoncé, Jennifer Hudson, Alicia Keys, P!nk, and Sarah Bareilles; Steve Balsamo, Michael Bublé, Jamie Cullum, and Keith Urban, amongst many others.

Kathryn Paradise

Aretha Franklin, Kurt Elling, Sarah Bareilles, Ella Fitzgerald, Joni Mitchell, Stevie Wonder, Frank Sinatra, Nat King Cole, Annie Lennox, Joe Williams, Steve Perry, Dolly Parton, Tom Waits, Björk, Lauren Hill, Celine Dion, Carol King, Whitney Houston, Adele, Billie Holiday, Marvin Gaye, Amy Winehouse, Donny Hathaway, Lady Gaga, Justin Timberlake, Bill Kenny, Sarah Vaughan, Michael Jackson, Sting, Linda Ronstadt, Barbra Streisand, Bonnie Raitt, Esperanza Spaulding, Merle Haggard, Blossom Dearie, James Taylor, Annie Ross, Rufus Wainwright, Brittany Howard, Jeff Buckley, Louis Armstrong, and Ray Charles.

Jeff Ramsey

There are many singers I admire, but some of the ones who stand out for me come mostly from R&B and gospel music; singers such as Aretha Franklin, Donny Hathaway, Luther Vandross, Gladys Knight, Vanessa Bell Armstrong, Daryl Coley, Lalah Hathaway, Ledisi, and Rachelle Ferrell are just a few of the singers I have admired over the years.

Cate Frazier-Neely

Ella Fitzgerald, Cleo Lane, Sarah Vaughan, Mel Torme, Nina Simone, Betty Carter, Lisa Fisher, Tarriona Ball of Tank and the Bangas, Roger Daltry, Brian Wilson, Ann Wilson, Annie Lennox, Vern Gosdin, Vince Gill, Randy Travis, Patsy Cline, Shania Twain, Alison Krauss, CeCe and Whitney Houston, Bonnie Raitt, Donna Summer, Linda Eder, Barbara Cook, Alanis Morissette, Freddy Mercury, Pete Seeger, Odetta, Julie Andrews, Elis Regina, and Celia Cruz.

Lisa Popeil

There are so many singers I admire, but mostly I admire classic pop singers, those who make the difficult look easy. Some of my favorites include Barbra Streisand, Fergie (a great rock singer), Edye Gorme, Judy Garland, Kelly Clarkson, Mariah Carey, Christina Aguilera (though sometimes I wish she would riff less and sing the melody more), and towards the top of the list, Tom Jones. He had it all; the whole package.

Seth Riggs and Margareta Svensson Riggs

There are many singers we admire, but two that come to mind immediately are Jussi Björling and Barbra Streisand.

Jeannette LoVetri

I like so many different people. I loved Luciano Pavarotti, Joan Sutherland, Marilyn Horne, and many other classical singers. I love Ella Fitzgerald, Mel Tormé, Tony Bennett, Sarah Vaughan in jazz, and Kelli O'Hara, Audra McDonald, Marin Mazzie, Brian Stokes Mitchell on Broadway. I like Reba McEntire, Dolly Parton, and many other country artists, and I am unashamedly a fan of many of my own students including Meredith Monk, Theo Bleckmann, Kate McGarry, Luciana Souza, Rondi Charleston, Scott Hamilton, Trineice Robinson-Martin, Val Mindel, and quite a few others. It would be impossible for me to choose just one or two.

Marcelle G. Gauvin

Yolanda Adams, Linda Eder, Stevie Wonder, Michael Jackson, Luther Vandross, Audra McDonald, Ella Fitzgerald, Sarah Vaughan, Kurt Elling, Dianne Reeves, Steve Perry, Aretha Franklin, Bobby McFerrin, Al Jarreau, Joni Mitchell, James Taylor, Cynthia Erivo, Barbara Hannigan, Heather Hadley, Beyoncé, Lady Gaga, Bruno Mars, Ed Sheeran, Amy Lee, Freddie Mercury, Whitney Houston, and Luciano Pavarotti.

Marci Rosenberg

I admire any singer who is true to their style and gives a moving performance. There are many singers I enjoy listening to. Currently in the pop world I like Sara Bareilles and Ed Sheeran. I love the clear brilliant soprano vocal quality of both Beverly Hoch and Youngok Shin. I do tend to prefer clear and brighter qualities in classical sopranos. Billy Gillman from The Voice has a nice effortless country/pop belt style. Adam Lambert is a phenomenal pop/rock belter. Celine Dion is another great belter who has a very specific vocal quality that is unique to her. Of course, we cannot forget about Luciano Pavarotti who was one of the greatest belters of them all.

Kimberly Steinhauer

I admire any singer who is offering her or his vocally athletic talents by performing live on stage. I sing in a variety of styles and my "favorites" rotate. Currently, I love to listen to Cecile McLorin Salvant for jazz, Eliane Coelho for opera, and Smokie Norful for everything.

References and recommended reading

Bennett, Andy and Ian Rogers. "Popular music and materiality: Memorabilia and memory traces." *Popular Music & Society* 39, no. 1 (February 2016): 28–42. www.doi.org/10.1080/03007766.2015.1061339.

Bicknell, Jeanette. "Just a Song? Exploring the Aesthetics of Popular Song Performance." *The Journal of Aesthetics and Art Criticism* 63, no. 3 (2005): 261–70. www.doi.org/10.1111/j.0021-8529.2005.00206.x.

Connor, Martin E. *The Musical Artistry of Rap.* Jefferson, NC: McFarland, 2018.

Gomes, Ricardo Milani. "Audio quality X accessibility: How digital technology changed the way we listen and consume popular music." *Revista Vortex* 4, no. 2 (December 2016): 1–14.

Gracyk, Theodore. *Listening to Popular Music: Or, How I Learned to Stop Worrying and Love Led Zeppelin.* Ann Arbor: University of Michigan Press, 2007.

Gracyk, Theodore. "The Aesthetics of Popular Music." *Internet Encyclopedia of Philosophy.* Accessed on August 12, 2018. www.iep.utm.edu/music-po/#H3.

Kayes, Gillyanne and Graham F. Welch. "Can genre be 'heard' in scale as well as song tasks? An exploratory study of female singing in Western Lyric and Musical Theater Styles." *Journal of Voice* 31, no. 3 (May 2017): 388.e1-388.e12. doi.org/10.1016/j.jvoice.2016.09.015.

Mitchell, Helen F. "Perception, evaluation and communication of singing voices." In *Teaching Singing in the 21st Century,* edited by Scott D. Harrison and Jessica O'Bryan, 187–200. Dordrecht: Springer, 2014.

Nowak, Raphaël. *Consuming Music in the Digital Age: Technologies, Roles and Everyday Life.* Basingstoke: Palgrave Macmillan, 2016.

Pontara, Tobias and Ulrik Volgsten. "Domestic space, music technology and the emergence of solitary listening: Tracing the roots of solipsistic sound culture in the digital age." *Swedish Journal of Music Research* 99 (2017): 105–123.

Ratliff, Ben. "Seeking genuine discovery on music streaming services." *New York Times,* June 29, 2015. LexisNexis Academic.

Rogers, Jim. *The Death and Life of the Music Industry in the Digital Age.* New York: Bloomsbury Publishing, 2013.

Rhys, Dan and Gail Mitchell. "Music's judgement day: Spotify's new rules governing the conduct of artists and creators are lauded by some, but many fear fair enforcement is impossible, while innocent acts face losing their livelihoods." *Billboard* May 19, 2018. LexisNexis Academic.

Sisario, Ben. "Spotify's licensing deals are putting labels on edge." *New York Times,* September 6, 2018. LexisNexis Academic.

Statista. "Share of music song consumption in the United States in 2017, by genre." Accessed on August 27, 2018. www.statista.com/statistics/694862/music-song-consumption-genre/.

Stephens-Davidowitz, Seth. "The Songs That Bind." *New York Times,* February 10, 2018. Accessed August 1, 2018. LexisNexis Academic.

Tobias, Evan S. "From musical detectives to DJs: Expanding aural skills and analysis through engaging popular music and culture." *General Music Today* 28, no. 3 (April 2015): 23–27. www.doi.org/10.1177/1048371314558293

Weisbard, Eric, ed. *Listen Again: A Momentary History of Pop Music.* Durham and London: Duke University Press, 2007.

Williams, Sherri. "Cardi B: Love & Hip Hop's unlikely feminist hero." *Feminist Media Studies* 17, no. 6 (December 2017): 1114–1117. http://www.doi.org/10.1080/14680777.2017.1380431.

Williamson, John and Martin Cloonan. "Rethinking the music industry." *Popular Music* 26, no. 2 (May 2007): 305–322. www.doi.org/10.1017/S0261143007001262.

21

Success

In an Australian survey of "successful contemporary musicians", musicians reported that the most significant aspect of their music education was an inspiring teacher.[1] The job of the pedagogue is clear for most of us: serve the students and help them exceed their goals. However, it is less clear what a student should do in order to become "successful".

According to the pedagogues, the most common "it" factor which contributes to a student's success is excellent vocal talent and skill (48%). Versatility and technical mastery were often listed as the first and most necessary element for success. After these foundational elements, the pedagogues point to tenacity, determination, drive, and stamina (36%).

Twenty-eight percent of the pedagogues indicate the importance of the following: dance ability/excellent physical fitness, media savvy, and a distinctive/unique vocal sound. The physical rigors of musical theatre and concert performance schedules have been previously discussed in this text. In chapter 17, Beyond the Voice Studio, media savvy was not identified as a critical topic of study beyond the voice studio: only 8% indicated that they recommended knowledge of marketing to their students. However, here, media savvy is identified by 28% as a necessary skill for *success*, and one that is expected by the industry. Uniqueness, or a distinctive sound, may be both a blessing and a curse. To work in musical theatre as an emerging artist often means ensemble work as a swing or understudy. This work requires a vocal sound that "blends", or is even capable of many different sounds. Having a "unique" or "distinctive" sound is often what makes someone successful as a pop star or musical theatre star, but this does not work as a member of the ensemble or as a backup singer. It is nevertheless a critical component of success, and one of those ineffable "it" factors.

To achieve success, a high work ethic and authenticity in performing were also commonly listed (24%), as well as the ability to "play well with others", and to care for and maintain contact with fans (20%). The most commonly listed elements that contribute to success are summarized in the chart below.

---

1   Richard Letts, "Survey of successful contemporary musicians," *Music in Australia Knowledge Base*, May 2013, accessed August 8, 2018, http://musicinaustralia.org.au/index.php/Survey_of_Successful_Contemporary_ Musicians.

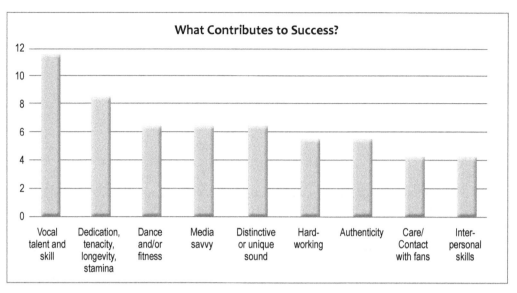

Several pedagogues have significant concerns about what determines "success" within the commercial singing industry and these are summarized in the chart below. While attractiveness can be a helpful quality for success, it can also become the focus of a marketing strategy, and there is a long history of objectifying CCM singers in order to sell more products. When sexiness becomes sexual objectification, it undermines the potency of the talent, which is especially concerning among female performers. In a post-#MeToo world, perhaps more women may be able to dictate how they are marketed. Unfortunately, sexual objectification has a long history of successfully boosting sales.

Other concerns include the fact that fame and "success" correlate in many ways, and fame may be influenced or determined by the public. The sale of merchandise and the gathering of social media followers are now marketing elements that performers are expected to provide. They are also expected to maintain a lot of contact with and care for their fans, in order to maintain and enhance the number of social media followers. Due to the connective power of the internet, the public plays a significant role in the continued success of a CCM singer.

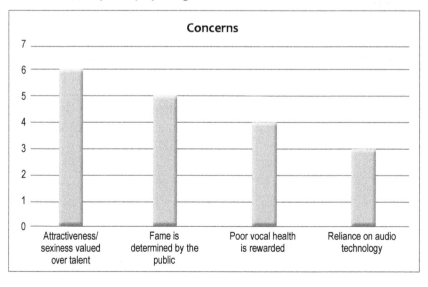

Pedagogues point out that the public often confuses pathologic voices with authentic voices because they sound emotional. A dangerous vocal habit may be the very sound that makes a voice distinctive. Such a voice can walk a very fine line between being an asset (which Dane Chalfin calls a "sustainable flaw") or a recipe for a very short career (vocal abuse/injury). Because pirating music has sadly become commonplace and it is almost impossible to make any money from records, the best way for a performer to earn is through touring. Longer and more intense tours can push performers beyond the limits of safety. Grueling touring schedules and the pressure of not cancelling concerts due to illness or fatigue can also lead to vocal injury.[2] Some very famous artists have recently come forward to publicly disclose vocal injuries after cancelling tours, including Adele (2017), Sam Smith (2015), and Meghan Trainor (2015).[3] They have been very candid about the conditions of touring, leading to exhaustion, lack of sleep, illness, and pressure to perform no matter what.[4] Admittedly, these established artists were already famous enough that they could afford to take time off for treatment and recovery. Lesser known artists may not have the same luxury. Disclosure of vocal injury in the musical theatre industry is less common,[5] even though the performance schedules are no less grueling.

The final concern most commonly expressed in the responses below is the trend toward the over-use of auto-tune and audio engineering tricks to "correct" poor technique, poor musicianship, and to obfuscate the natural sound of the voice. Pedagogues prefer the unobstructed sound of the human voice. This preference is perfectly understandable, as they have devoted their life's work to cultivating such a sound. However, "success" in CCM singing is largely determined by the general public, not by voice specialists, and the average lay listener may not even perceive that the natural voice has been disguised.

This chapter includes responses to the prompt "What is your perception of successful commercial singers today?". In some cases, the prompt was clarified to "What does it take to succeed?", or "What do singers need to have in order to succeed?". The responses are presented in a loose order according to shared values or concerns.

Marci Rosenberg

Well, one could define "successful" as "commercially successful" or "vocally successful", and the two often do not go hand in hand. In fact, in the pop/rock genre, there seems to be an inverse relationship between them in many cases. My perception of commercial success is the more successful the singer is the higher the stakes are. Touring schedule, press obligations, and performance demands frequently increase exponentially, often with very little consideration for the artist's health and well-being, and vocal health very often takes a big hit. We see this happen repeatedly. Unfortunately, young budding artists who win nationally televised talent competitions are thrust into the same kinds of schedules and demands. They have no-one

---

2   Deirdre D. Michael and George S. Goding, "Dispelling vocal myths. Part 3: 'Sing OVER your cold!'" *Journal of Singing* 68, no. 4 (March/April 2012), 419-425.

3   Bernhard Warner, "Why do stars like Adele keep losing their voice?" *The Guardian*, August 10, 2017, accessed on August 1, 2018, www.theguardian.com/news/2017/aug/10/adele-vocal-cord-surgery-why-stars-keep-losing-their-voices.

4   Nicole Sands, "Meghan Trainor: Needing vocal cord surgery 'was a big slap in the face,'" *People* October 15, 2017, accessed on August 1, 2018, people.com/celebrity/meghan-trainor-on-vocal-surgery/.

5   Natalie Bradshaw and Amy L. Cooper, "Medical privacy and the professional singer: Injury stigma, disclosure, and professional ramifications on Broadway," *Journal of Singing* 74, no. 5 (May/June 2018), 513-520.

guiding them and protecting their vocal health and long-term interests. It is an unfortunate situation of "not knowing what you don't know", and the children pay a price.

Several pop/rock artists have come out publicly in recent years about their vocal difficulties and struggles with vocal health. This does a great service to singers in general because it highlights that it is a very real problem, and illustrates the point that these artists are vocal athletes and are at very high risk for injury. It is disappointing when such artists are criticized by other singers or voice teachers, who blame their musical style or faulty technique. Often, it is simply the very unrealistic performance schedules these singers are required to keep. The classical world is not quite so forthcoming around issues of vocal health, but they are also at high risk and not at all immune to vocal injury. Perhaps famous and successful commercial artists will set a standard of greater transparency and the other genres will follow suit.

Gillyanne Kayes

The key word here is *commercial*. Some singers are aggressively marketed beyond their ability to sing night after night on a grueling tour schedule, plus interviews during the day. Not all of them are sufficiently well prepared for these rigors.

Seth Riggs and Margareta Svensson Riggs

There are some very good singers today, though mediocrity has invaded a lot of the entertainment world over the last 15-20 years, not just in music. Therefore, a successful singer is not necessarily a good singer.

At the same time there seems to be a growing craving for authenticity again, where each singer's unique sound, style, and quality is recognizable, with songs about real life and emotions, with singable melodies, solid chord progressions, and at times, quite bare productions. Hopefully those singers, some with better technique than others, after having suffered vocal problems and the agony of cancelling concerts, will come around and get the vocal technique they need to support their artistry, so that they can go on for as long as they want.

Matthew Edwards

Unique is what sells. The commercial music industry does not seem to care whether or not singers will last more than a few years on the road. In fact, the industry often rewards risky vocal production and pathologic voices. That is unfortunate, and it makes it difficult to convince students to think about their long-term vocal health. However, that is the reality we live in right now because many audience members connect to the perceived emotional connection of voices that are right on the edge of damaging behavior. Singers can be trained to make aggressive sounds without causing damage, but convincing them that is the case can be very difficult.

Musical theatre is slightly better, but profits still drive decision-making so artists must advocate for themselves. There are certain roles, such as Elphaba in *Wicked*, that are extremely difficult to perform eight times a week. Some performers can pull it off, but others struggle. Young singers need to realize that just because they can sing a song once through does not mean that they are ready to tackle the role eight times a week. Part of our job is to teach students their limits and convince them to wait until they are ready to take on roles that are just barely within their reach.

While type used to be a driving factor, there seems to be a move towards individualism and diversity in casting. Diversity in this context includes ethnicity, body type, and gender identity. What is most important is that the students show their authentic selves in the audition room. The students need to know who they are and choose audition songs that are similar in character. The one consistent factor I notice is hard work. If a performer consistently shows up prepared, is technically capable of performing the part, and is easy to work with, he/she will book work. It does not mean they will be a Broadway star, but they will find places that will pay them to perform.

Trineice Robinson-Martin

A successful commercial singer is measured by audience appeal, often depicted by the number and consistency of people following shows and buying merchandise.

Tracy Marie Bourne

I think music theatre singing is a different form than pop singing. Professional music theatre singers are expected to be at a very high level of skill (as actors and dancers too); they tend to be well prepared for auditions and performances, and are aware of the risks of fatigue and vocal abuse. At the same time, I have seen some casting choices that were based on the fame and popularity of the actor rather than on whether they were the best actor for the role, and these performances can be disappointing.

Edrie Means Weekly

Successful commercial singers are not always the most talented vocally. Success is industry-driven, and the public pretty much dictates it. Successful singers must be hard working, have the market covered, have a great network, and have established themselves through many venues. I believe there are some very talented commercial singers. However, a lot seems to be put into sexualizing popular musicians and this tends to lead to too much emphasis being put on their image and not enough on their ability.

Good stage presence, audience connection, dancing, captivating and charismatic performers stand out from others. Catchy tunes or lyrics with a good melody and a good hook (chorus) that get stuck in your head are often successful. A performer who communicates real emotion that audiences want to relate to will have a strong fan connection. Performers should have a strong image and know what they stand for.

Mark Baxter

I define a successful singer as anyone who is able to reproduce the sounds he or she hears in their imagination. When voice and vision are one, the singer has succeeded. I do not appreciate the terms "commercial singer" or "commercial music" when referring to modern music styles because it implies money and/or fame is the driving intention. I use the terms popular or contemporary as all-inclusive labels, and individual sub-genres such as rock, pop, R&B, jazz, etc., to be more specific. *All* aspiring singers wish to connect with as large an audience as possible, regardless of genre or style. Yet, regardless of genre or style, most singers will not achieve the ability to sustain themselves financially in the art form they desire. However, those that pursue a popular form of singing are thought of as commercially driven, while those that pursue a classical form are artistically pure. This feels like Bel Canto snobbery to me!

My experience working with financially successful singers for the last 35 years is that they are extremely dedicated to their craft. The days of drunken debauchery have long past for those at the upper echelon. Artists constantly train and seek ways to improve their conditioning because their performances are incredibly demanding. A typical headlining show is 90 to 120 minutes of non-stop pressure on the vocal folds. Audiences have nanosecond attention-spans, so performers stay in constant motion, either with elaborate dance choreography or by exaggerated physical antics. It is common for performers to drop a few pounds during a show. Also, the itineraries of popular singers are the most daunting in the performing arts due to the constant travel and endless promotional duties.

My experience working with financially unsuccessful singers is exactly the same, minus the travel and fans. They are dedicated to their craft and passionate about improving their skills. Most are as vocally capable as their successful counterparts. The difference is in their promotional skills. Creating and maintaining public awareness is the second full-time job of every professional performer. Any singer who does not have a passion for self-promotion will eventually learn: the music business is mislabeled, it really should be called the promotion business.

Jeff Ramsey

I see success being less about the actual vocal ability of the artists, and more than ever about the allure of an artist. This has always been true, but it seems to be more important than the vocal chops. That seemed to go out the door after singers such as Whitney Houston, Mariah Carey, and Celine Dion. Beyoncé, Jessie J., and a few others are the exception, and not the rule among today's pop stars.

Lisa Popeil

Unfortunately, I am quite cynical about the true talent in many of today's young singers. Talent often is overshadowed by sex appeal and how one looks in a scanty outfit. I have nothing against looking sexy, I just think that musical innovation and artistic vision can easily be squashed by the pressures of having a hit. Also, I will always value musicianship in addition to singing excellence, and many singers seem to have such limited musical backgrounds and are really the pawns of producers. I am aware that there are thousands of talented singers out there, with little opportunity to make a living, so I do not begrudge singers doing what they feel they need to do to be heard and make an opportunity happen.

Marcelle G. Gauvin

To be successful, commercial singers must be physically fit to endure rigorous touring schedules or show runs, be generally charismatic or physically attractive, have a large social media fan base, generally possess a highly developed chest register and a strong mixing ability, and have a unique sound and performance style. Many are also songwriters.

Kimberly Steinhauer

Successful commercial singers today inspire with a unique creative sound that complements their marketable, unique physical traits.

Jan Shapiro

In my perception, there are some very good singers, some bad singers, and those that use auto-tune and effects to hide the lack of vocal control.

Elisabeth Howard

At this moment in time, I do not believe that there are new and innovative directions in commercial contemporary vocal music. The legends, the household names, go on tour and are still very popular. The trend towards rap has its place but is more philosophic in nature. The record industry is not what it used to be in the 70s and 80s. Singers and songwriters are pretty much left on their own, to record themselves in home studios with independent producers, and market themselves on social media such as Facebook, Instagram, iTunes, YouTube, etc. The future is anyone's guess.

Jeannette LoVetri

There are a few people who have strong voices and whose singing I like, such as Christina Aguilera, Beyoncé, Adam Lambert, Michael Feinstein, and others. What I don't like is the heavy emphasis on electronic technology on the production side. I think the robotic repetition of patterns, the distortion of the sound for the sake of effect, and the multiple layers of adjustment on the live voice, make it really hard to hear a human being expressing honest communication. This is a terrible loss, particularly when the person singing has a phenomenal voice and ends up sounding like everyone else.

Kim Chandler

There are some truly great artists out there who are amazing live performers, such as Ed Sheeran, Bruno Mars, Lady Gaga, and Beyoncé, but there is an over-reliance currently on overtly tuned vocals in recorded music in the charts. Personally, I hope there is a trend away from this fake, manufactured sound soon, as it tends to strip the humanity and individuality out of a voice. Young singers are being brought up on the auto-tuned vocal sound not necessarily aware that real human voices do not sound like that naturally; it's a studio construct (somewhat the audio equivalent of Photoshop). The evidence of this is the recent phenomenon of "sideways yodeling" where a singer is able to replicate the (overt) effects of Auto-tune with their acoustic voice.

Cathrine Sadolin

I hear all kinds of styles of singing which are successful. I cannot say that I personally like everything, but I can say that I often understand why they are famous or successful. Usually, this is because the choices they make define them as an artist. Their choices are related to expression. If they want to sing a very soft song and then scream in the middle of the song, this is usually validated by the expression or emotion of the song. I do not think it is valid to say that everyone who sings high notes or ornaments a lot will be successful. These choices only make sense if they support the expression of the song. High notes or ornaments for the sake of showing off can be quite tiring. Everything has to fit the expression. If it fits, a singer could whisper or scream an entire song, and I do not mind. What makes people successful is when their expression is backed up by good choices in their singing sounds.

Kathryn Paradise

Modern day commercial singers are asked to be vocal athletes, entrepreneurs, songwriters, musicians, spokespeople, and creative innovators. In order to be successful, they have to have a clear artistic point of view and a uniquely identifiable vocal sound while maintaining a rigorous performance and travel schedule required of few other professions. Those who succeed are under constant scrutiny and risk becoming obsolete overnight. I am personally in awe of those who choose to devote their lives to the craft of commercial singing despite these challenges, and believe the profession of voice teaching should uplift and encourage these individuals in every way possible.

Mary Saunders Barton

Because my orientation is theatrical, I can only speak about what applies to successful musical theatre performers. Actors want to be hired again. Talent and skill are essential, but a reputation for professional ethics, artistic discipline, generosity, and kindness will always win the day.

Cate Frazier-Neely

"Successful" is certainly a moving target. For me, successful CCM singers are those who have managed to cultivate that sweet spot between technical facility and stamina, their uniqueness through heart-felt motivations, and the ability to "play well" with other musicians and audio technicians. They have managed to cultivate healthy personal boundaries and an inner locus of control to navigate the music industry in ways that allow them to be themselves. These are pretty much the same criteria for successful classical singers.

Dane Chalfin

Successful commercial singers have longevity and personal fulfilment, which I believe are tied together. I have seen a lot of artists come and go. The ones who stick around tend to have some key characteristics in common. They tend to be really in love with other people and other people's needs. They tend to really care about audiences, and that people get it and feel it, and are getting their money's worth. They work hard. They are warm to everybody. I have never met anyone ridiculously ego-driven that stuck around for very long. I know they are out there, but luckily, I haven't worked with many.

The hallmark of success and sustainability is somebody who is warm and considerate and a decent human being, who really cares about everyone around them. Everyone has up and down moments in their career. You have to get used to that up/down cycle. Great singers stay focused on being a great human being.

Kevin Wilson

I think of commercial music as pop, but for musical theatre and pop success is all the same thing: technique, physical awareness, stamina, healthy lifestyle, and balance. To be an employable musical theatre singer you must be very genre-flexible and know how to use your voice appropriately in each style.

Irene Bartlett

Successful commercial singers have to be very hard-working, multi-skilled (singing, dancing, acting), and multi-media and business savvy.

Wendy DeLeo LeBorgne

If you enjoy making a living doing what you do and staying vocally, mentally, and physically healthy, you are successful.

Robert Edwin

Elite artists tend to rise to the top in every field. In general, they tend to be highly talented, very motivated, disciplined, opportunistic, well-managed, and a little bit lucky.

With the advent of the internet, so many more performers than before are getting their voices out to the public. The quantity and quality of music are staggering to me. It's hard to sort through it all, but I continue to try to stay on top of who is the best of the best in all singing genres and styles.

References and recommended reading

Bartlett, Irene. "More than just style: A profile of professional contemporary gig singers." In *Teaching Singing in the 21st Century*, edited by Scott D. Harrison and Jessica O'Bryan, 367-382. Dordrecht: Springer, 2014.

Baym, Nancy K. "Fans or friends? Seeing social media audiences as musicians do." *Participations: Journal of Audience & Reception Studies* 9, no. 2 (November 2012): 286-316. http://www.participations.org/Volume%209/Issue%202/17%20 Baym.pdf.

Bennett, Lucy. "Patterns of listening through social media: Online fan engagement with the live music experience." *Social Semiotics* 22, no. 5 (November 2012): 545-557. www.doi.org/10.1080/10350330.2012.731897.

Bicknell, Jeanette. "Just a Song? Exploring the Aesthetics of Popular Song Performance." *The Journal of Aesthetics and Art Criticism* 63, no. 3 (2005): 261-70. www.doi.org/10.1111/j.0021-8529.2005.00206.x.

Bradshaw, Natalie and Amy L. Cooper. "Medical privacy and the professional singer: Injury stigma, disclosure, and professional ramifications on Broadway." *Journal of Singing* 74, no. 5 (May/June 2018): 513-520.

Chalfin, Dane. "From 'me' to 'we': Audience-focused practical tools for interpretation and performance." In *The Singer-Songwriter Handbook*, edited by Justin A. Williams and Katherine Williams. New York: Bloomsbury Academic, 2017.

Cazden, Joanna. "Dionysus, Demi Moore, and the cult of the distressed voice." *Voice and Speech Review* 3, no. 1 (2003): 243-246. doi.org/10.1080/23268263.2003.10739409.

Frisby, Cynthia M. and Jennifer Stevens Aubrey. "Race and genre in the use of sexual objectification in female artists' music videos." *Howard Journal of Communications* 23, no. 1 (January/March 2012): 66-87. www.doi.org/10.1080/10646 175.2012.641880.

Gilman, Marina, Albert L. Merati, Adam M. Klein, Edie R. Hapner, and Michael M. Johns. "Performer's attitudes toward seeking health care for voice issues: Understanding the barriers." *Journal of Voice* 23, no. 2 (March 2009): 225-228. doi. org/10.1016/j.jvoice.2007.08.003.

Hughes, Diane, Sarah Keith, Guy Morrow, Mark Evans, and Denis Crowdy. "What constitutes artist success in the Australian music industries?" *International Journal of Music Business Research* 2, no. 2 (October 2013): 61-80.

LeBorgne, Wendy D. and Marci Rosenberg. *The Vocal Athlete*. San Diego: Plural Publishing, 2014.

Letts, Richard. "Survey of successful contemporary musicians." *Music in Australia Knowledge Base*. May 2013. Accessed August 8, 2018. http://musicinaustralia.org.au/index.php/Survey_of_Successful_Contemporary_Musicians.

Lingel, Jessa and Mor Naaman. "You should have been there, man: Live music, DIY content and online communities." *New Media & Society* 14, no. 2 (March 2012): 332-349. www.doi.org/10.1177/1461444811417284.

McLean, Rachel, Paul G. Oliver, and David W. Wainwright. "The myths of empowerment through information communication technologies: An exploration of the music industries and fan bases." *Management Decision* 48, no. 9 (2010): 1365-1377. doi.org/10.1108/00251741011082116.

Michael, Deirdre D. and George S. Goding. "Dispelling vocal myths. Part 3: 'Sing OVER your cold!'" *Journal of Singing* 68, no. 4 (March/April 2012): 419-425.

Moody, Nekesa Mumbi. "Plain Janes need not apply: For today's female singers, sex appeal is a must." *The Associated Press*, May 17, 2007. LexisNexis Academic.

Phyland, Debra J., Julie F. Pallant, Michael S. Benninger, Susan L. Thibeault, Ken M. Greenwood, Julian A. Smith, and Neil Vallance. "Development and preliminary validation of the EASE: A tool to measure perceived singing voice function." *Journal of Voice* 27, no. 4 (July 2013): 454-462. doi.org/10.1016/j.jvoice.2013.01.019.

Phyland, Debra J., Julie Pallant, Susan L. Thibeault, Michael S. Benninger, Neil Vallance, and Julian A. Smith. "Measuring vocal function in professional music theater singers: Construct validation of the evaluation of the ability to sing easily (EASE)." *Folia Phoniatrica et Logopaedica* 66, no. 3 (March 2015): 100-108. www.doi. org/10.1159/000366202.

Phyland, Debra J., Susan L. Thibeault, Michael S. Benninger, Neil Vallance, Kenneth M. Greenwood, and Julian A. Smith. "Perspectives on the impact on vocal function of heavy vocal load among working professional music theater performers." *Journal of Voice* 27, no. 3 (May 2013): 390.e31-390.e39. doi.org/10.1016/j.jvoice.2012.12.003.

Rogers, Jim. *The Death and Life of the Music Industry in the Digital Age.* New York: Bloomsbury Publishing, 2013.

Sands, Nicole. "Meghan Trainor: Needing vocal cord surgery 'was a big slap in the face.'" *People* October 15, 2017. Accessed on August 1, 2018. people.com/celebrity/meghan-trainor-on-vocal-surgery/.

Sataloff, Robert T. *Vocal Health and Pedagogy: Science, Assessment, and Treatment.* 3rd ed. San Diego, CA: Plural Publishing, 2017.

Sataloff, Robert T., Mary J. Hawkshaw, Jaime Eaglin Moore, and Amy L. Rutt. *50 Ways to Abuse Your Voice: A Singer's Guide to a Short Career.* Oxford: Compton Publishing, 2014.

Spivey, Norman and Mary Saunders Barton. *Cross-Training in the Voice Studio: A Balancing Act.* San Diego, CA: Plural Publishing, 2018.

Soukup, Charles. "Hitching a ride on a star: Celebrity, fandom, and identification on the world wide web." *Southern Communication Journal* 71, no. 4 (December 2006): 319-337. www.doi.org/10.1080/10417940601000410.

Smith, Gareth Dylan. "Seeking 'success' in popular music." In *Music Education: Navigating the Future*, edited by Clint Randles, 183-200. New York: Routledge, 2015.

Spencer, Jennifer. "Performing arts training in the age of #MeToo." *Voice and Speech Review*, in press, 2018. doi.org/10.1 080/23268263.2018.1488461.

Vellar, Agnese. "The recording industry and grassroots marketing: From street teams to flash mobs." *Participations* 9, no. 1 (May 2012): 95-118.

Warner, Bernhard. "Why do stars like Adele keep losing their voice?" *The Guardian*, August 10, 2017. Accessed on August 1, 2018. www.theguardian.com/news/2017/aug/10/adele-vocal-cord-surgery-why-stars-keep-losing-their-voices.

Williamson, John and Martin Cloonan. "Rethinking the music industry." *Popular Music* 26, no. 2 (May 2007): 305-322. www.doi.org/10.1017/S0261143007001262.

22

Excellence

The definition of "excellence" is highly subjective. This inquiry is meant to remove the commercially-driven concept of "success" and reveal the unfettered ideals of excellent CCM singing and performing. These two concepts do not always correlate. The public can reward an artist with success even if they are not excellent. Likewise, excellent singing may be achieved without "success". I hoped to reach answers to the question of "what is the *special something* about the voice that makes a truly excellent singer"?

A significant majority of the pedagogues (75%) placed advanced, optimal, efficient, and easy vocal technique at the top of the "excellence" list. This was followed by stamina/longevity (58%) and genuine expression/storytelling (54%), which were ranked at nearly equal importance. Fifty percent of pedagogues listed an exciting stage persona which connects to the audience, which has more to do with "entertainment" than with artistry, but the pedagogues report that it is of significant value. Under excellence, a unique or distinctive sound was identified as important by 42% of the pedagogues. In the previous chapter, under *success*, a unique or distinctive sound was identified as important by only 28% of the pedagogues. This discrepancy may be due to the fact that "success" requires a certain income, and a unique sound may impede entry level work, such as back-up singing or music theatre ensemble work. Conversely, someone with no distinctive individual sound would not be excellent as a CCM soloist or music theatre star. In pursuit of *excellence*, a distinctive sound is more valuable to the pedagogues.

Several pedagogues pointed out that excellent qualities would vary depending on the job at hand. A high level of musicianship (29%) and versatility/flexibility (29%) are valued more in music theatre performing and session singing in the CCM industry. Consistency (25%) was most often listed in relation to consistent vocal technique, and the ability to consistently deliver excellent performances over the long-term duration of a career. The most valued trademarks of excellence appear in the chart below.

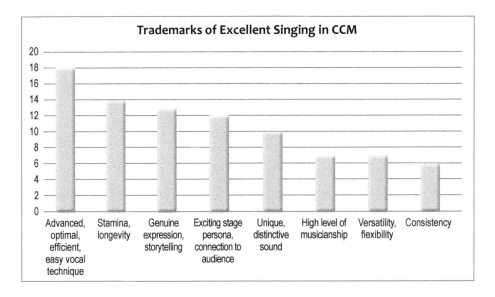

Some pedagogues expressed that the elements of "excellence" were challenging to list, perhaps due to the trend toward separating personal preferences from pedagogical offerings. Especially in the extraordinarily broad umbrella term "CCM", teachers are bound to have personal preferences for certain styles. However, the majority of these pedagogues see themselves as "in service" to the student and therefore, their personal tastes do not play a role in their pedagogical approach. Some core values will be universal, like "good technique", but the teacher's aesthetic point of view does not determine what is "good". The pedagogues define "good technique" as consistently healthy and easy singing, *and* the ability to make all the sounds required to serve the desired style of music. For some genres, this might mean helping the student learn to scream sustainably and easily. Not only is this possible, but exemplary pedagogues are prepared to offer strategies to achieve this goal, regardless of personal tastes.

This chapter includes responses to the prompt "What are the trademarks of excellent singing in commercial music?". The responses are presented in an order loosely grouped according to the qualities or concerns highlighted.

Gillyanne Kayes

This is an extremely difficult question to answer. I feel more equipped to talk about musical theatre here than CCM generally, as this is my area of specialism. For musical theatre I would say excellence is the ability to act through the song and commit to the material, and to have a sufficiently strong technique to be able to sing for eight shows a week for a year-long contract. For CCM I would say excellence is commitment to the song material, and a passion for singing the song that is shared with the audience first and foremost. I would like to add here that one thing I regard as a hallmark of excellence is the ability to deliver a good cover of someone else's song. There is a wonderful recording of Sara Bareilles singing Elton John's "Yellow Brick Road". It is a re-working of a classic CCM rock ballad and she absolutely nails it while making it her own. Similarly, if you listen to Jessie J. singing "Killing me Softly" in the version she delivered for the competition in China, it is a unique performance, yet truthful to the original concept with her own interpretation. So different from how she normally sings. For me, this is about artistry. Isn't that what we are looking for? Not just a voice, not even just a great song, but a vocalist with imagination and creativity.

Wendy DeLeo LeBorgne

From an excellence standpoint, the commercial genre covers so much. Excellence in jazz is different from excellence in music theatre, which is different from excellence in country. If you can meet market demand, and have some longevity in your career, this constitutes excellence. People would say that Willie Nelson has had excellence in his career as a country artist. Do I think he has an excellent voice? Maybe not, but I think he is an excellent country music artist. This definition of excellence goes way beyond vocal quality. It has to do with writing, connection to the audience, and so much more than just the voice.

Jeff Ramsey

It is pretty subjective to define what is excellent as it means many different things for the lay person as well as for my fellow colleagues. I believe it is a personal preference. I think, for me, it is a sound that is fairly easy to produce and does not sound strained. I know that is a pretty generic answer, but I believe that it should not matter what style of music you sing: you should be able to get the sound you want, with minimum resistance from muscles that negatively affect the desired sound the singer is working to make.

Kim Chandler

Excellence depends on whether it is an artist or a more generic "jobbing" singer that is being discussed, as the parameters are different for these roles. Both benefit from having a reliable vocal technique, high-level musicality, and engaging performance abilities. However, an artist needs to have a distinctive "signature sound", while a professional singer does not and generally benefits from being stylistically generic but versatile in order to optimize employability.

Kathryn Paradise

Successful commercial vocalists are frequently *either* unique or versatile, so I find myself most impressed with those who are capable of being both unique *and* versatile. Additional markers of excellent singing in commercial music include longevity, consistency, strong musicianship, and a genuine understanding of music rooted in the African-American musical tradition. Commercial music is largely performer-, rather than composer-centered, so a great commercial vocalist typically needs to read as "authentic" and must have something to say.

Cathrine Sadolin

I am just one out of millions. I do not know if my ideas are any more important or interesting than anyone else's. I would say that if you have something to express, that is what I really go for. The singing does not matter as much, I want expression. This is what I look for and really enjoy. Again, I am only one out of millions.

Marci Rosenberg

To me this is a very straightforward question to answer. The successful CCM singer must be able to produce the vocal sounds consistent with the aesthetic of the style they are singing, in the most efficient way possible, and they must be able to duplicate it consistently without significant strain or effort. How this is achieved will likely vary depending on the style and on the singer.

Kimberly Steinhauer

Trademarks of excellent singing in commercial music are creativity, commitment, and longevity.

Tracy Marie Bourne

Singers use their sound to tell a story and to express the thoughts and feelings of a character. Excellent singers are able to consistently produce an appropriate and attractive sound in a broad range of vocal styles. They can maintain a healthy voice throughout a long performance season. It is essential that they are exciting and committed performers on-stage.

Lisa Popeil

Trademarks of excellent singing are being able to sing live in tune, having vocal ease throughout the range, thrilling high notes, consistency in quality and skill, the ability to manage the vocal challenges of touring and performing multiple sets nightly, or singing eight shows a week without vocal damage. This is a challenging list of goals, to be sure!

Irene Bartlett

Trademarks of excellent singing are a unique and *free* vocal sound that supports optimal voice production with genuine emotional story-telling and expression, the appropriate voice production for the individual singer's need (their specific style choice, personality, and level of expertise), performance stamina and longevity, and a great stage persona that excites and connects them with their audience.

Elisabeth Howard

I look for expressivity and honoring the lyric and music. Vocal technique should be solid enough to ensure the longevity of the singer. What the classical world might consider ugly, in terms of vocal tone quality, might in fact be appropriate for the genre of music that is being expressed in CCM.

Marcelle G. Gauvin

The trademarks of excellence in CCM singing are a conversational manner of communicating the lyric, a voice that is unique with interesting vocal color, control over chest, mix, head and belt used in a stylistically appropriate way, a great grasp of dynamics and the ability to build an emotional arc during a song, the ability to maintain a signature sound throughout one's career, yet display flexibility within that sound to surprise and interest your audience, a great rhythmic feel in phrasing, great interpretation of the lyric enhanced by phrasing development, ornamentation, or riffing, and the ability to convey a song both in the studio and in live performance.

Edrie Means Weekly

Excellent singers are healthy singers. They are vocally talented, with a sense of style and a unique instrument. They must have a good vocal range. They should have brilliant technique and consistency throughout the range. They should sound great in live performance and be able to sustain a career over a long period of time.

Trineice Robinson-Martin

Excellent commercial singers are not limited in their ability to produce a multitude of sounds and colors. Excellent commercial singers are skilled in their ability to use various aspects of musicality to tell a story.

Seth Riggs and Margareta Svensson Riggs

In purely technical terms it is pitch, duration, and quality. Singers who have a sincere and secure knowledge of bridge (*passaggio*) balance, from low to high, are free to explore the untrammeled ease of the extra notes with which to build style. Proper breathing and support give duration, and vibrato gives quality. Do not be fooled; analyze the most successful, great singers of today and you will find those elements.

Kevin Wilson

For successful commercial singers like P!nk, Beyoncé, and Adele, to Audra McDonald or Jessie Mueller, the trademarks of excellent singing are endurance and flexibility. For musical theatre singers it is the move from standards to contemporary belt without applying the same aesthetic principles, yet still staying true to their sound.

Robert Edwin

I go back to the days when singers had little or no technology to help their singing. Bad singers were easily exposed. It is rare now to hear a natural, acoustic, self-amplified vocalist outside of opera houses and concert halls. Today's commercial music is very heavily processed, so with software such as Pro Tools, which can alter pitch, tonal quality, and phrasing, it is hard to tell if the singers are naturally good or if they are bad singers with a very good recording engineer and producer. That said, the trademarks of all good singers, not just CCM singers, is the ability to tell a story in song with accurate pitch, stylistically-appropriate phrasing and tonal quality, and emotion that captures our hearts.

Matthew Edwards

For musical theatre, excellence is a voice that is guided by the actor. I want to see a committed performance with a technique that leaves no doubt the performer will make it through not only the show, but the entire run.

For commercial singers, excellence is consistency. I want to see performers who can deliver no matter what the situation, whether it be in a studio, live on TV, in a small club, or an outdoor festival. I also think "excellent" singers avoid auto-tune and other forms of manipulation as much as possible, except for artistic purposes.

Jan Shapiro

Excellent singing in any style has good intonation and sustains notes appropriate to a specific style.

Dane Chalfin

Trademarks of excellence in commercial singing are believability and sustainable flaws. A perfect voice is a boring voice. You have to have something different. There is a danger with being too technically proficient. You cannot take away what makes a student unique. When a label sends a singer to me, they say "Singer losing his voice, do not change the sound". Sometimes you have to leave the sustainable flaws in place.

The litmus test for me is "Do I believe you?". Someone made a meme of a quote of mine which says "Singing made simple: Stand up. Take a breath. Tell the truth". That is it for me. If I believe it and I feel it, I am in. But you need a very flexible, well-honed technique to make this possible.

Mark Baxter

The trademark of excellent singing in 1601 was the ability to fill a hall with the sound of your voice. The trademark of excellent singing in 2018 is the ability to fill a hall with people. Identity is the hallmark of popular singers. The connection between contemporary artists and listeners is more about personality than proficiency. This is not to suggest vocal skills are not a factor. They are for some listeners, just not for all.

The only common denominator connecting all successful contemporary singers is their courage to highlight a unique aspect of their sound. No matter if it is discovered by accident or default, their style must be cultivated via skill to become a signature sound. There is no blueprint to follow for popular singers. Voice classifications and the *Fach* system do not apply well to contemporary music due to the extremely wide spectrum of accepted vocal timbres.

Since popular and classical audiences are so different, a more fitting comparison for a contemporary singer pursuing excellence would be as a contemporary writer. Aspiring popular singers face the same challenges as aspiring authors. The trademark of excellent writing is that the author establishes a unique "voice". He or she will spend years cultivating this voice without any indication that acceptance awaits. These days, digital word programs manage the standard mechanics of writing, such as correct spelling and proper grammar, just like digital recording programs manage a singer's pitch and pacing. The criteria for deeming one an excellent singer is left to the public, based on style choices that may or may not connect with a wide audience. Just as an author must produce a book before knowing if he or she will be accepted as a worthy writer, singers of popular music must establish a signature sound and then present it to the public. Often, it is simply a lack of public awareness that sidelines many admirable voices. Fame is not a filter for excellence – it is merely the fuel that drives a career in the promotion business.

Mary Saunders Barton

Successful Broadway singing requires stamina, flexibility, range, a powerful need to communicate, and a certain "*je ne sais quoi*" that separates a voice from all the others. That special sound can certainly be encouraged, but not taught.

Jeannette LoVetri

I want to hear the voice and the person. I want to be captured by the quirkiness of being human and not lulled into a stupor by repetitive robotic sound. I want to hear the voice such that I can recognize who is singing five seconds after I hear the song's beginning. That is a rare occurrence now.

References and recommended reading

Adessa, Michelle, Tara Stadelman-Cohen, Lauryn Zipse, A.J. Guarino, and James T. Heaton. "Factors affecting voice therapy completion in singers." *Journal of Voice* 32, no. 5 (September 2018): 564–571. doi.org/10.1016/j. jvoice.2017.06.021.

Borch, Daniel Zanger. *Ultimate vocal voyage: The definitive method for unleashing the rock, pop or soul singer within you.* Milwaukee: Hal Leonard, 2008.

Borch, Daniel Zanger, Johan Sundberg, P.-A. Lindestad, and M. Thalen. "Vocal fold vibration and voice source aperiodicity in 'dist' tones: Study of a timbral ornament in rock singing. *Logopedics, Phoniatrics, Vocology* 29, no. 4 (2005): 147–53. doi.org/10.1080/14015430410016073.

Chalfin, Dane. "From 'me' to 'we': Audience-focused practical tools for interpretation and performance." In *The Singer-Songwriter Handbook*, edited by Justin A. Williams and Katherine Williams. New York: Bloomsbury Academic, 2017.

Cross, Melissa and D. Korycki. *The Zen of Screaming: Vocal Instruction for a New Breed.* DVD and CD. New York: Loudmouth, Inc, February 21, 2006. Alfred Music, February 1, 2007.

Cross, Melissa. *The Zen of Screaming 2: Vocal Instruction for a New Breed.* DVD. New York: Alfred Music, June 1, 2007.

Edgerton, Michael Edward. "Finding the ingredients towards yummy, unusual tastes: Extra-normal voice." In *The Voice Teacher's Cookbook: Creative Recipes for Teachers of Singing* edited by Brian J. Winnie, 36–38. Delray Beach, FL: Meredith Music, 2018.

Edgerton, Michael Edward. "The Extra-Normal Voice: EVT in Singing." In *Teaching Singing in the 21st Century*. Edited by Scott D. Harrison and Jessica O'Bryan, 109–132. Dordrecht: Springer, 2014.

Edwards, Matthew. "Icing the song: Onsets and releases in rock singing." In *The Voice Teacher's Cookbook: Creative Recipes for Teachers of Singing* edited by Brian J. Winnie, 39–41. Delray Beach, FL: Meredith Music, 2018.

Gaunt, Helena. "Understanding the one-to-one relationship in instrumental/vocal tuition in higher education: Comparing student and teacher perceptions." *British Journal of Music Education* 28, no. 2 (July 2011): 159–179. doi.org/10.1017/S0265051711000052.

Gilman, Marina, Albert L. Merati, Adam M. Klein, Edie R. Hapner, and Michael M. Johns. "Performer's attitudes toward seeking health care for voice issues: Understanding the barriers." *Journal of Voice* 23, no. 2 (March 2009): 225–228. doi.org/10.1016/j.jvoice.2007.08.003.

Green, Lucy. *How Popular Musicians Learn: A Way Ahead for Music Education.* Abingdon-on-Thames: Routledge, 2017.

Hughes, Diane. "'Art' to artistry: A contemporary approach to vocal pedagogy." In *The Routledge Research Companion to Popular Music Education*. Edited by Gareth Dylan Smith, Zack Moir, Matt Brennan, Shara Rambarran, and Phil Kirkman. Abingdon-on-Thames: Routledge, 2017.

Hughes, Diane. "Contemporary vocal artistry in popular culture musics: Perceptions, observations, and lived experiences." In *Teaching Singing in the 21st Century*. Edited by Scott D. Harrison and Jessica O'Bryan, 287–301. Dordrecht: Springer, 2014.

Katz, Bruce. "A measure of musical preference." *Journal of Consciousness Studies* 11, no. 3–4 (2004): 28–57.

Morton, Jennie. *The Authentic Performer: Wearing a Mask and the Effect on Health.* Oxford: Compton Publishing, 2015.

Paradise, Kate. "Swinging lasagna." In *The Voice Teacher's Cookbook: Creative Recipes for Teachers of Singing* edited by Brian J. Winnie, 88–89. Delray Beach, FL: Meredith Music, 2018.

Phyland, Debra Jean, Jennifer Oates, and Kenneth Mark Greenwood. "Self-reported voice problems among three groups of professional singers." *Journal of Voice* 13, no. 4 (December 1999): 602–611. doi.org/10.1016/S0892-1997(99)80014-9.

Robinson-Martin, Trineice. "Soul Ingredients™: Onsets in African American folk-based music." In *The Voice Teacher's Cookbook: Creative Recipes for Teachers of Singing* edited by Brian J. Winnie, 99–101. Delray Beach, FL: Meredith Music, 2018.

Reinhert, Kat. "Singers in the academy: Training the popular music vocalist." In *The Bloomsbury Handbook of Popular Music Education*. Edited by Zack Moir and Bryan Powell. Bloomsbury Academic, 2019.

Sataloff, Robert T., Mary J. Hawkshaw, Jaime Eaglin Moore, and Amy L. Rutt. *50 Ways to Abuse Your Voice: A Singer's Guide to a Short Career.* Oxford: Compton Publishing, 2014.

SECTION V:
Conclusion

23

CCM voice pedagogy: diversity, unity, and core values

Throughout this text, diverse approaches have been celebrated and championed. With 26 contributing authors from all over the world, representing (approximate) ages of between 40 and 75 years, and from stylistic backgrounds of every possible CCM specialization, a surprising number of common trends emerge from the data. Across all four sections of the text (approaches, elements of training, special demands from the industry, and aesthetic context) elements of majority consensus emerged. These are summarized in the tables below.

Approaches	
Have classical training	84%
Entry into the field of CCM voice pedagogy facilitated by a significant mentor	60%
Choose to teach and pursue performing at the same time	50%
Choose to teach and not pursue performing at the same time	50%
Participate in formal voice research and scholarship	48%

Special Demands from the Industry	
Recommend that singers also train in acting	50%
Recommend that singers also train in dance	54%
Teach improvisation	76%
Use audio equipment in their voice studios	63%
Use voice science regularly in their teaching	60%
Use voice science either occasionally or regularly in their teaching	96%
Teach singers under the age of 18 regularly	50%
Teach singers under the age of 18 either occasionally or regularly	88%

Aesthetic Context	
Value an exciting stage persona that connects to the audience in the pursuit of excellence	50%
Value storytelling/expression in the pursuit of excellence	54%
Value longevity/stamina in the pursuit of excellence	58%
Value optimal, efficient and easy vocal technique in the pursuit of excellence	75%

In approaches, the data show that a majority of the pedagogues share elements of training and mentoring, and value both the practice of research and the choice to perform or not. In special demands from the industry, pedagogues share values in auxiliary training in dance and acting. The majority of pedagogues teach improvisation and use both audio technology and voice science in their teaching. The majority of pedagogues also teach students under the age of 18, which could be viewed as a significant philosophical difference between classical and CCM voice pedagogy. In aesthetic context, the pedagogues share the values of engaging stage personae, career longevity, stamina, storytelling, expression, and optimal vocal technique in the pursuit of excellent singing.

Elements of training	
Posture/alignment: Avoid prescribing a fixed position for optimal alignment	52%
Posture/alignment: Agree that optimal alignment seeks to minimize tension	68%
Breath: Believe that "breathing" includes both inhalation and exhalation	65%
Support: Favor a flexible or efficient model of support, which can work in any physical situation and can be manipulated for expressive purposes	52%
Support: Agree that during supported exhalation/phonation the abdominals contract and ribcage remains expanded	65%
Tension: State that tension can be good or bad	52%
Registers: Frame the voice in terms of registration/source activity (as opposed to voice quality/filter activity)	64%
Registers: Use the terms "head" and "chest" to refer to M1 and M2	73%
(In)Consistency: State that a smooth transition between M1 and M2 is not always desirable in CCM singing and they train both consistency and inconsistency	52%
(In)Consistency: Say that "mix" is the predominant sound that we hear most of the time in female singing and may be used to describe any coordinated sound engaging both TA and CT muscles	71%
Belt: Use the term "belt"	88%
Belt: Believe that "belting" is more than one sound, aka a "multiplicity"[1] of sounds	94%
Belt: Believe that belting is always loud	64%
Belt: Believe that "belt" is not interchangeable with "mix" (the term "mix" is not the same as "chest-dominant mix")	79%
Belt: Believe that belting is a registrational event (as opposed to voice quality/vocal tract shaping)	53%
To train belt: Work to strengthen head voice/M2 singing	50%
To train belt: Work to strengthen chest voice/M1 singing	67%
To train belt: Work to strengthen some type of "mix"	67%
To train belt: Work on "twang"[2]	58%
Expression: Use techniques to evoke an emotional response to the material	67%

Within the broad topics covered in elements of training, there were many different priorities and tactics, but also much in common. In posture and alignment, the majority seek an optimal posture which attenuates tension. To prevent the development of additional unnecessary tension, they

---

1   Lisa Popeil, "The Multiplicity of Belting," *Journal of Singing* 64, no. 1 (September/October 2007), 77–80.

2   In this instance, "twang" refers to aryepiglottic (or epilarynx) narrowing, which often results in a strengthened singer's formant. More information on "twang" may be found in Johan Sundberg and Margareta Thalén, "What is twang?" *Journal of Voice* 24, no. 6 (November 2010), 654–660, doi.org/10.1016/j.jvoice.2009.03.003, Ingo R. Titze, Christine C. Bergan, Eric Hunter, and Brad Story, "Source and filter adjustments affecting the perception of the vocal qualities twang and yawn," *Logopedics Phoniatrics Vocology* 28, no. 4 (December 2003), 147–155, and Eiji Yanagisawa, Jo Estill, Steven T. Kmucha, and Steven B. Leder, "The contribution of aryepiglottic constriction to 'ringing' voice quality: A videolaryngoscopic study with acoustic analysis," *Journal of Voice* 3, no. 4 (December 1989), 342–350, doi.org/10.1016/S0892-1997(89)80057-8.

avoid prescribing any fixed postural or alignment position. In breath and support, the majority interpret "breath" to include both inhalation and exhalation, and "support" to result from the abdominal muscles contracting while the ribs remain expanded during exhalation/phonation. The majority also favor a flexible model of support, which can function efficiently in any physical position and may be purposely manipulated for expressive purposes. Under tension, the majority underline that some tension is required for energetic singing. However, too much tension may undermine singing efforts, and should be carefully monitored. Under registration and (in)consistency, the majority frame vocal development in terms of registration, and use the terms "head" and "chest" to refer to mechanism 1/TA-dominant registration and mechanism 2/CT-dominant registration. Pedagogues point out that a smooth and seamless transition between M1 and M2 may not always be desired in CCM styles. The majority define "mix" as the predominant sound that we hear most of the time in female singing, and use the term to describe any co-ordinated sound engaging both TA and CT muscles. The majority define belting as a loud, registrational event (source-level activity), and believe that it is more than one sound and not interchangeable with mix. To train belt, the majority of pedagogues build strength in the M1/chest register and M2/head register, and then work to strengthen "mix" and evoke "twang." Expression is viewed as an indispensable aspect of technical training, and the majority of pedagogues use tactics to evoke an emotional connection to repertoire within voice lessons.

These data illustrate the preferred approaches of a majority of exemplary pedagogues. They do not present consensus, by any means, and contrasting approaches are presented with equal enthusiasm in this text. Diverse perspectives should always be welcome in any creative field. The key to exemplary CCM pedagogy is to remain flexible and to customize approaches for every student's individual needs. This text presents diverse approaches so that teachers may have a multitude of tried and tested tools available to them.

Topics with Highest Consensus (more than 75%)	
Have classical training	84%
Believe that belting is more than one sound, or that it is a multiplicity of sounds	94%
Believe that belting is not interchangeable with "mix"	79%
Teach improvisation	76%
Teach CCM students under the age of 18, occasionally or regularly	88%
Use voice science in their teaching, occasionally or regularly	96%
Value optimal, efficient, and easy vocal technique in pursuit of excellent singing	75%

Topics which have been at the center of much heated debate, such as teaching children CCM styles, belting, and the utility of voice science in the voice studio, have a surprisingly high rate of agreement. Shared elements of training and aesthetic values also enjoy a strong consensus. The prevalence of training in improvisation would suggest that teachers who are currently not offering training in improvisation might consider finding a colleague with these strengths for referral or endeavor to add this skill to their offerings.

The number of common trends is not as surprising when one considers how often the pedagogues refer to one another. Many have studied several of the pioneering methodologies, or taken lessons from each other, or collaborated on research and scholarship with one another. The data show that the community of CCM voice pedagogues is bound together by several common interests, goals, and values.

From the data collected, it is possible to distill the following core values in the CCM voice pedagogy community.

Core Values
A commitment to life-long learning
A commitment to a constantly evolving, flexible, student-centered pedagogy
A commitment to separating personal taste from student-selected repertoire
A commitment to maintain one's own technique for demonstration but enjoying the choice to maintain an active performing career or not
A commitment to participate in mentoring and training

A commitment to life-long learning has been emphasized many times throughout this text. The pedagogues expressed an insatiable curiosity, which often catalyzed their exploration of CCM voice pedagogy and has sustained long and rewarding careers. The pedagogues continue to explore all that is new in voice science, research, technology, and pedagogical approaches. They attend conferences and workshops, generously sharing their own expertise and learning from their colleagues. Between conferences, they are active on social media, in email discussions, in blog-writing, and in traditional publishing. They perform research and enthusiastically share findings with the community. They are driven by a never-ending mission to improve their understanding of the human voice. They are the living examples of NATS Past President Norman Spivey's advice to be "generous enough to learn from your colleagues, bold enough to share what you know with others, and humble enough to acknowledge what someone else does well".[3] This requires raw honesty and nerves of steel, which these pedagogues have in droves.

A commitment to a continually evolving, flexible, student-centered pedagogy was revealed as a consistent trend in CCM voice pedagogy. The pedagogues expressed the need to customize their approach for the specific situation at hand. Students have different needs and goals, and the job of the teacher is to meet their needs and to lead them to achieve their goals. Several referred to a "rolodex"[4] or "toolbox" of skills, gathered from training in several methodologies, reading science, their own vocal study, and trial and error in the voice studio. There is a reverence for the pioneering methodologies, and a desire to evolve the field by drawing stronger and deeper connections between voice pedagogy and voice science. The commitment to life-long learning fuels the acquisition of skills and knowledge. Drawing from this extensive collection, practical solutions to any challenge may be found quickly. Many pedagogues expressed a willingness to use any vocabulary or pedagogical syntax that makes sense to the student, in pursuit of the most effective solution to the challenges in front of them. This reflects a pedagogical style that is solution-focused, rather than process-focused. Several also practice the act of referral. If a student needs expertise that the primary teacher cannot provide, they will not hesitate to refer that student to another practitioner, be it a speech-language pathologist, bodywork expert, improvisation coach, or style specialist. There is not the same sense of exclusivity in CCM voice study as in the classical mentor-apprentice model. Students come and go, and CCM teachers believe that students should have access to the best experts to meet their needs.

---

3   Norman Spivey, "Building bridges: Paths to a multifaceted career," *Journal of Singing* 72, no. 1 (September/ October 2015), 5.

4   Marci Rosenberg, Chapter 3: Philosophy.

The pedagogues are committed to separating personal taste from student-selected repertoire. They never stop exploring what is new in musical tastes and trends, regardless of genre. They meet their students where the student's interest lies and learn alongside them. In a recent interview, Neil deGrasse Tyson (prompted by criticism of his interviewing Katy Perry on his radio show) encouraged academics to abandon "high-falutin standards". He explained, "if I can have a conversation with [Perry] about how science has touched her craft, then that brings science to her following", which includes more than 100 million Twitter followers. If academics continue to reside in ivory towers, they will miss critical opportunities to "add value" to their fields.[5] Among these exemplary CCM pedagogues, no genre is "lesser" or "unworthy" of serious exploration.

CCM pedagogues are open to the integration of audio technology in the voice studio. Many pedagogues use a sound system in training singers, or they refer students to colleagues who specialize in this area. Universities can provide supplementary coursework for students in audio technology. Some voice teachers train students on microphone technique, as well as audio software, especially if their genre calls for this type of expertise. This is another manifestation of putting personal tastes aside in favor of what is best for students. While a teacher might prefer to teach in an all-acoustic (unamplified) studio, they do not ignore the necessity of audio training for their students.

Many pedagogues underline a commitment to maintain one's own technique in order to demonstrate. It is not acceptable to demonstrate only classical sounds, and then try to teach CCM sounds through theoretical descriptions alone. The pedagogues maintain that one should first be familiar with all of the required sounds of a given genre, and then one should be able to demonstrate the sounds required in *every genre* in which one is offering training. For heavy metal and punk rock, this would include extreme vocal techniques, such as scream and growl.[6] Some pedagogues suggest that savvy students should request to hear a teacher perform as a measure of pedagogical ability. For perhaps the first time in the culture of higher education, university voice teachers have a *choice* in whether to maintain an active performing career or to pursue other "creative scholarship" alongside a teaching career. Continuing to perform is still a highly-valued option, but universities have become more informed about the multi-faceted career contributions of an artist-teacher.[7] Pedagogues who can devote themselves exclusively to pedagogy may develop into master teachers at a faster rate than those who attempt to maintain both a teaching and a performing career. For example, in the NATS Intern program, Matthew Edwards moved from intern to master teacher in just nine years (2009-2018). Less time spent performing also means more time to contribute to the field through research, conferences, teaching, and mentoring, which has long-term benefits for the field as a whole.

A commitment to mentoring and training the next generations of pedagogues is the central mission of the pioneering methodologies. Their systems were organized and codified first for their own understanding, but then to help others attain more in-depth knowledge and facility in their own pedagogy. In addition to this type of formal training in specific methodologies,

---

5   Neil deGrasse Tyson, quoted in Vimal Patel, "What Neil deGrasse Tyson thinks higher ed gets wrong," *The Chronicle of Higher Education*, September 16, 2018, accessed on September 21, 2018, www.chronicle.com/article/What-Neil-deGrasse-Tyson/244522.

6   A recommended reading list may be found at the end of chapter 1.

7   American Academy of Teachers of Singing, "Research and creative accomplishment in promotion and tenure: A realistic look at expectations for teachers of singing in academia," *Journal of Singing* 71, no. 2 (November/December 2014), 141–143.

there are now some summer training programs with no central methodology. Instead, they have a CCM specialization within voice pedagogy (Shenandoah and Boston Conservatory at Berklee). The pedagogues in this text are committed to strengthening and developing university CCM pedagogy programs, such as those at Shenandoah (Edwards, Means Weekly) and Penn State (founded by Mary Saunders Barton). There are also countless champions for the cause of CCM singing who are implementing and strengthening CCM components into pre-existing classical pedagogy programs in order to prepare teachers to meet the needs of the real world. A growing number of formal and informal mentoring programs, through the National Association of Teachers of Singing and other professional organizations, help build up new pedagogues and strengthen the network within which we all may learn from each other. These mentoring networks demonstrate the presence of collegiality and a sincere wish to see each other succeed and help each other along the way.

There are many valid ways to approach a pedagogical challenge. Some are more common than others. Nevertheless, this text demonstrates that a wide variety of approaches may yield equally successful results. Surely, with so many shared values, we can abandon the desire to label any single approach as better than the next. Every methodology, method, system, or approach is flexible, malleable, and capable of responding to both the needs of a given student and the development of science. The *art* of teaching is a constant evolution. The field of CCM voice pedagogy celebrates its shared practices, values, and goals, and at the same time, respects and applauds the many different roads traveled in the pursuit of excellent singing.

References and recommended reading

American Academy of Teachers of Singing. "In support of contemporary commercial (nonclassical) voice pedagogy." *Journal of Singing* 65, no. 1 (September/October 2008): 7–10.

American Academy of Teachers of Singing. "In support of fact-based voice pedagogy and terminology." *Journal of Singing* 71, no. 1 (September/October 2014): 9–14.

American Academy of Teachers of Singing. "Research and creative accomplishment in promotion and tenure: A realistic look at expectations for teachers of singing in academia." *Journal of Singing* 71, no. 2 (November/December 2014): 141–143.

Austin, Howard and Elisabeth Howard. *Born to sing: The Vocal Power Method (the next generation) – A fully integrated, cross-referenced multimedia program.* United States: Music World, Vocal Power School, 2007.

Bartlett, Irene. "Reflections on contemporary commercial singing: An insider's perspective." *Voice and Speech Review*, 8, no. 1 (2014): 27–35. www.doi.org/10.1080/23268263.2013.829711.

Bartlett, Irene. "Unique problems and challenges of contemporary voice: What do teachers think?" *Australian Voice* 5 (1999): 45–49.

Bartlett, Irene. "One size doesn't fit all: Tailored training for Contemporary Commercial Singers." In *Perspectives on Teaching Singing: Australian Vocal Pedagogues Sing their Stories*, edited by Scott D. Harrison, 227–243. Bowen Hills, Qld.: Australian Academic Press, 2010.

Bartlett, Irene. "More than just a style: A profile of professional contemporary gig singers. In *Teaching Singing in the 21st Century*. Edited by Scott D. Harrison and Jessica O'Bryan. Dordrecht: Springer, 2014.

Baxter, Mark. *The Rock-And-Roll Singer's Survival Manual.* Milwaukee: Hal Leonard, 1990.

Benson, Elizabeth Ann. "Modern voice pedagogy: Functional training for all styles." *American Music Teacher* 67, no. 6 (June 2018): 10–17.

Borch, Daniel Zanger. *Ultimate vocal voyage: The definitive method for unleashing the rock, pop or soul singer within you.* Milwaukee: Hal Leonard, 2008.

Bos, Nancy. "Where we were then and where we are now: A singing teacher's perspective." *Journal of Singing* 71, no. 3 (January/February 2015): 347–348.

Chalfin, Dane. "From 'me' to 'we': Audience-focused practical tools for interpretation and performance." In *The Singer-Songwriter Handbook*, edited by Justin A. Williams and Katherine Williams. New York: Bloomsbury Academic, 2017.

Chandler, Kim. "Teaching popular music styles." In *Teaching Singing in the 21st Century* edited by Scott D. Harrison and Jessica O'Bryan, 35–51. Dordrecht: Springer, 2014.

Delp, Roy. "Now that the belt voice has become legitimate…." *Journal of Singing* 57, no. 5 (May/June 2001): 1–2.

Edwards, Matthew. *So You Want to Sing Rock 'N' Roll: A Guide for Performers*. Lanham, MD: Rowman & Littlefield, 2014.

Edwin, Robert. "Are we the National Association of Teachers of Classical Singing? (Revisiting 1985)." *Journal of Singing* 67, no. 5 (May/June 2011): 589–590.

Edwin, Robert. "Personal and pedagogic aesthetics." *Journal of Singing* 66, no. 5 (May/June 2010): 575–577.

Fantini, March, Franco Fussi, Erika Crosetti, and Giovanni Succo. "Estill Voice Training and voice quality control in contemporary commercial singing: An exploratory study." *Logopedics Phoniatrics Vocology* 42, no. 4 (2017): 146–152. http://www.doi.org/10.1080/14015439.2016.1237543.

Freeman, Robert. *The Crisis of Classical Music in America: Lessons from a Life in the Education of Musicians*. Lanham, MD: Rowman & Littlefield, 2014.

Friedlander, Claudia. *Complete Vocal Fitness: A Singer's Guide to Physical Training, Anatomy, and Biomechanics*. Lanham, MD: Rowman and Littlefield, 2018.

Garner, Kelly K. *So You Want to Sing Country: A Guide for Performers*. Lanham, MD: Rowman & Littlefield, 2016.

Gerbi, Elizabeth. "The music theater specialist: Jack (or Jill) of all trades and master of all?" *Journal of Singing* 72, no. 5 (May/June 2016): 605–608.

Green, Lucy. *How Popular Musicians Learn: A Way Ahead for Music Education*. Abingdon-on-Thames: Routledge, 2017.

Hall, Karen. *So You Want to Sing Music Theatre: A Guide for Professionals*. Lanham, MD: Rowman & Littlefield, 2014.

Harrison, Scott D. ed. *Perspectives on Teaching Singing: Australian Vocal Pedagogues Sing their Stories*. Bowen Hills, Qld.: Australian Academic Press, 2010.

Harrison, Scott D. and Jessica O'Bryan, eds. *Teaching Singing in the 21st Century*. Dordrecht: Springer, 2014.

Harrison, Scott D. and Jessica O'Bryan. "Postlude: The future of singing pedagogy." In *Teaching Singing in the 21st Century*, edited by Scott D. Harrison and Jessica O'Bryan, 411–413. Dordrecht: Springer, 2014.

Howard, David M. and Damian T. Murphy. *Voice Science, Acoustics and Recording*. San Diego, CA: Plural Publishing, 2008.

Howard, Elisabeth. *Sing! The Vocal Power Method*. New York: Alfred Music, 2006.

Hughes, Diane and Jean Callaghan. "Advocating for change: Interdisciplinary voice studies in Australian school education." In *Perspectives on Teaching Singing: Australian Vocal Pedagogues Sing their Stories*, edited by Scott D. Harrison, 306–316. Bowen Hills, Qld.: Australian Academic Press, 2010.

Kayes, Gillyanne. *Singing and the Actor*. New York: Routledge, 2004.

Latimerlo, Gina and Lisa Popeil. *Sing Anything: Mastering Vocal Styles*. G. Latimerlo and L. Popeil, 2012.

LeBorgne, Wendy D. and Marci Rosenberg. *The Vocal Athlete*. San Diego: Plural, 2014.

LoVetri, Jeannette. "Editorial: Contemporary Commercial Music." *Journal of Voice* 22, no. 3 (May 2008): 260–262. doi. org/10.1016/j.jvoice.2006.11.002.

LoVetri, Jeannette. "The necessity of using functional training in the independent studio." *Journal of Singing* 70, no. 1 (September/October 2013): 79–86.

LoVetri, Jeannette. "Contemporary commercial music: More than one way to use the vocal tract." *Journal of Singing* 58, no. 3 (2002): 249–252.

LoVetri, Jeannette, Mary Saunders Barton, and Edrie Means Weekly. "A brief overview of approaches to teaching the music theatre song." In *Teaching Singing in the 21st Century*. Edited by Scott D. Harrison and Jessica O'Bryan, 53-66. Dordrecht: Springer, 2014.

McPherson, Gary and Graham Welch, eds. *The Oxford Handbook of Music Education*. New York: Oxford University Press, 2012.

Meyer, David and Matthew Edwards. "The future of collegiate voice pedagogy: SWOT analysis of current practice and implications for the next generation." *Journal of Singing* 70, no. 4 (March/April 2014): 437–444.

Miller, Richard. "Pop Music, Non-Western European and Efficient Vocal Function." *The Journal of Singing/The NATS Journal* 51, no. 4 (March/April 1995): 37–38.

Mindel, Valerie. *So You Want to Sing Folk Music: A Guide for Performers*. Lanham, MD: Rowman & Littlefield, 2017.

Patel, Vimal. "What Neil deGrasse Tyson thinks higher ed gets wrong." *The Chronicle of Higher Education*. September 16, 2018. Accessed on September 21, 2018. www.chronicle.com/article/What-Neil-deGrasse-Tyson/244522.

Popeil, Lisa. "The Multiplicity of Belting." *Journal of Singing* 64, no. 1 (September/October 2007): 77–80.

Popeil, Lisa. *The Total Singer*. DVD and CD.

Riggs, Seth and John Dominick Carratello. *Singing for the Stars: A Complete Program for Training Your Voice*. Van Nuys, CA: Alfred, 1998.

Riggs, Seth. *Singer's Advantage: Female*. DVD. In Tune Product, 2007.

Robinson-Martin, Trineice. *So You Want to Sing Gospel: A Guide for Performers*. Lanham, MD: Rowman & Littlefield, 2017.

Robinson-Martin, Trineice. "Take my hand: Teaching the gospel singer in the applied voice studio." In *Teaching Singing in the 21st Century*, edited by Scott D. Harrison and Jessica O'Bryan, 335–350. Dordrecht: Springer, 2014.

Rosenberg, Marci and Wendy D. LeBorgne. *The Vocal Athlete: Application and Technique for the Hybrid Singer*. San Diego: Plural Publishing, 2014.

Sabey, Paul. "Developing a tertiary course in music theatre." In *Teaching Singing in the 21st Century*, edited by Scott D. Harrison and Jessica O'Bryan, 383-387. Dordrecht: Springer, 2014.

Sadolin, Cathrine. *Complete Vocal Technique*. Copenhagen: CVI Publications, 2012.

Sadolin, Cathrine. *Complete Vocal Technique Application*: completevocal.institute/app/.

Saunders Barton, Mary. *Bel Canto, Can Belto*. DVD. University Park, PA: Penn State Media Sales, 2007.

Saunders Barton, Mary. *What About the Boys?* DVD. State College, PA: Mary Saunders Barton, 2014.

Shapiro, Jan, *So You Want to Sing Jazz: A Guide for Professionals*. Lanham, MD: Rowman & Littlefield, 2016.

Sieck, Stephen. "Inclusive pedagogy: Cooking in a way that feeds all singers." In *The Voice Teacher's Cookbook: Creative Recipes for Teachers of Singing* edited by Brian J. Winnie, 109–110. Delray Beach, FL: Meredith Music, 2018.

Spivey, Norman. "Building bridges: Paths to a multifaceted career." *Journal of Singing* 72, no. 1 (September/October 2015): 1–5.

Spivey, Norman and Mary Saunders Barton. *Cross-Training in the Voice Studio: A Balancing Act*. San Diego: Plural Publishing, 2018.

Steinhauer, Kimberly, Mary McDonald Klimek, and Jo Estill, *The Estill Voice Model: Theory and Translation*. Pittsburgh: Estill Voice International, 2018.

Sundberg, Johan and Margareta Thalén. "What is twang?" *Journal of Voice* 24, no. 6 (November 2010): 654–660. doi.org/10.1016/j.jvoice.2009.03.003.

Titze, Ingo R. *Principles of Voice Production*. Iowa City, IA: The National Center for Voice and Speech, 2000.

Titze, Ingo R. "Some reflections on speech-like singing and related contemporary approaches." *Journal of Singing* 70, no. 1 (September/October 2013): 57–58.

Titze, Ingo R., Christine C. Bergan, Eric Hunter, and Brad Story. "Source and filter adjustments affecting the perception of the vocal qualities twang and yawn." *Logopedics Phoniatrics Vocology* 28, no. 4 (December 2003):147–155.

Tracy, Neal. "Music theater rocks! Organic Rock singing 101 and beyond." *Journal of Singing* 70, no. 2 (November/December 2013): 209–213.

Wigginton, James R. "When 'proper' is dead wrong: How traditional methods fail aspiring artists." *Journal of Singing* 66, no. 4 (March/April 2010): 447–449.

Wilson, Pat H. "Sinful modern music: Science and the contemporary commercial singer." *Australian Voice* 9 (January 2003): 12–16.

Winnie, Brian J., ed. *The Voice Teacher's Cookbook: Creative Recipes for Teachers of Singing*. Delray Beach, FL: Meredith Music, 2018.

Yamin, Eli. *So You Want to Sing the Blues: A Guide for Performers*. Lanham, MD: Rowman & Littlefield, 2018.

Yanagisawa, Eiji, Jo Estill, Steven T. Kmucha, and Steven B. Leder. "The contribution of aryepiglottic constriction to 'ringing' voice quality: A videolaryngoscopic study with acoustic analysis." *Journal of Voice* 3, no. 4 (December 1989): 342–350. doi.org/10.1016/S0892-1997(89)80057-8.

Zangger Borch, D. and Johan Sundberg. "Some phonatory and resonatory characteristics of the rock, pop, soul, and Swedish dance band styles of singing." *Journal of Voice* 25, no. 5 (September 2011): 532–537. doi.org/10.1016/j.jvoice.2010.07.014.

Glossary

A

Accent Method: A holistic therapy regime designed to co-ordinate respiration, phonation, articulation, and resonance to produce clear and well-modulated speech. It originated with Danish Phonetician, Svend Smith, and is widely used in Scandinavia and Europe. (The British Voice Association). It has been adapted for classical singers by Ron Morris and Linda Hutchison[1] and is widely used by CCM pedagogues in the U.K. and Australia.

Acoustic singing: Singing without amplification or the use of audio processing technology.

Ad-libbing: (1) Improvisation. (2) In musical theatre, "ad-lib" can refer to a free tempo with *rubato*, or a section of music which is paced as the singer chooses.

Alexander Technique: A bodywork modality created by Frederick Mathias Alexander; founded on the principles of reeducating the body and discovering new balance by releasing unnecessary tension.

Amplified singing: Singing with the use of a sound system. CCM genres are performed or recorded with amplification and some degree of sound processing. However, some CCM training and auditions may still be conducted in unamplified settings.

Amplitude (dB): An objective measure of the size of a sound wave vibration, and perceived as the "volume" of a sound.

Anchoring: A term used in Estill Voice Training® to refer to muscle engagement which stabilizes the head, neck, and torso.

Appoggio: The Italian term meaning "to lean on", used in singing to refer to expanding the ribcage upon inhalation and then keeping the ribs expanded during phonation. A type of support.

Articulators: The anatomical structures of the mouth and throat which interact to create phonemes, including lips, tongue, teeth, soft palate, hard palate, uvula, jaw, alveolar ridge, glottis, and pharyngeal wall.

Aryepiglottic folds (also called "epilarynx"): The sides of the epiglottic funnel found at the top of the larynx. Shaping this area impacts twang or ring in the sound. In the Estill Voice Model™, the aryepiglottic folds comprise part of the aryepiglottic "sphincter" (AES), which may be narrowed to increase the sound energy between 2-4 kHz.

Aspirate onset: An onset which begins with airflow through abducted vocal folds. The vocal folds are then adducted into the airflow, resulting in a breathy onset of phonation. In CCM singing, it is often used as a vocal stylism for expressive purposes.

Authenticity: A performance which is not copied or fake, but represents the genuine nature of the individual performer. It is an essential ingredient in expression, success, and excellence in CCM singing.

Auto-tune: A vocal processing effect used to correct pitch errors both recorded and live sound processing. It may be used to varying degrees, and for both corrective and artistic purposes.

---

1   Ron Morris and Linda Hutchison, *If in Doubt, Breathe out! Breathing and Support for Singing Based on the Accent Method*, (Oxford: Compton Publishing, 2016).

B

Back beat (or backbeat): In common time, an emphasis on the 2 and the 4 (as opposed to the 1 and the 3). The presence of a back beat is a defining characteristic of most CCM genres.

Back phrasing: A variation of phrase synchronization wherein the singer pushes their own tempo forward or drags it backward, while the backing band or piano maintains a steady beat. This effect is common in jazz, and to varying degrees in some CCM genres and musical theatre.

Bel Canto/Can Belto: An organized pedagogical point of view developed by Mary Saunders Barton, Professor Emeritus of Penn State University and Independent Voice Teacher in New York City. The approach focuses on musical theatre vocal technique and may be explored through workshops and DVDs.

Belt: A loud and intense sound used for expressive purposes in CCM singing. It is frequently described as a registrational state (TA-dominant) with a distinctive ring or vocal color. In Complete Vocal Technique, this sound is called Edge Mode.

Belter: A singer who has a particularly remarkable belt sound, or who specializes in making belt sounds efficiently and expressively.

Belting: The act of singing a belt sound.

Belt-mix: (1) The highest part of the belted-range above approximately C5 for female voice and F4 for male voice. (2) Another term for chest-dominant mix in any part of the range. However, the definition may vary. This hybrid term can be confusing because "belt" (chest-dominant) may also be contrasted with "mix" (head-dominant). See "belt" and "mix".

Belt quality: One of the six voice qualities in the Estill Voice Model™, heard in the American musical theatre, ethnic music, pop music, and in children's voices on the playground. (The Estill Voice Model: Theory & Translation)

Bend or bending the note: A vocal stylism or effect used for expressive purposes wherein a note is sustained with a slight movement under or over the center of the pitch, followed by a return to the center of the pitch. In country music, this is also known as a "dip".

Body map: One's self-representation within the brain.

Body mapping: The conscious correcting and refining of one's body map to produce efficient, coordinated, effective movement. Developed by William Conable and carried on by Barabara Conable through the Andover Educators® group.

Bodywork: A therapeutic modality which involves the human body. Some modalities commonly used by singers include Alexander Technique, Body Mapping, and Feldenkrais®.

Bridge: The term for *passaggio* used in Speech Level Singing™.

C

Call-and-response: A performance structure wherein one musician executes a short phrase (the call), and another musician repeats the phrase (the response). This structure continues within a constant rhythmic pulse of the music, while the musical material varies. The pattern is used for training vocal improvisation, and in the improvisational performance practices of blues, gospel, and jazz music.

CCM: Abbreviation for Cincinnati Conservatory of Music.

CCM: Abbreviation for Contemporary Christian Music.

CCM: Abbreviation for Contemporary Commercial Music.

Chest-dominant mix (also called "chest-mix" or "belt-mix"): Vocal production of mixed registration wherein the thyroarytenoid muscles are dominant but the cricothyroid muscles are also active to a lesser extent.

Chest-mix: See "chest-dominant mix".

Chest register (also called "mechanism 1", "modal voice", or "TA-dominant register"): The lower part of the singing range for both men and women. Phonation in chest register has a higher closed quotient than phonation in head register.

Circle singing: A term used to describe an improvised process of community-singing. One common structure is when singers form a circle around one person who leads the group by introducing different motives to create a multi-part harmonic groove and then improvises a solo or invites others to improvise a solo over the groove. The individual motives of the harmonic groove may evolve through group improvisation. The phrase is said to have been coined by improvisational singer Bobby McFerrin.

Closed-quotient: The percentage of time the glottis is closed during each vibratory cycle of phonation. Phonation in chest register has a higher closed quotient than phonation in head register.

"Comping" a vocal: Compiling the best vocal performance from multiple takes, a common editing task for digital audio workstation (DAW) users.

Complete Vocal Technique (CVT): The singing methodology founded and developed by Danish pedagogue Cathrine Sadolin. Training in the methodology is offered at the Complete Vocal Institute (CVI) in Copenhagen. The method is called "complete" because it covers all the sounds the human voice can produce in any style of singing. The method aims to explain the voice simply and understandably and to ensure that the desired sounds are produced in a healthy way.

Compression: A vocal processing effect that regulates the amplitude or volume of the signal.

Condenser microphone: A type of highly sensitive microphone used in recording studios and in live musical theatre performance.

Constriction: In singing, this often refers to excessive squeezing/tightening within the vocal tract. The extrinsic muscles of the larynx may also be involved in some types of constriction.

Constrictors: Muscles that tighten the throat and are used in swallowing.

Contemporary Commercial Music (CCM): A term coined by Jeannette LoVetri to replace the previously used term, "nonclassical". CCM includes genres such as pop, gospel, jazz, R&B, soul, folk, blues, country, hip hop, rap, metal, and rock. LoVetri originally conceived of "musical theatre" as part of CCM (it is "nonclassical"), but there is now some debate about its emergence as a distinctive umbrella term, neither classical nor CCM.

Creak (also called "vocal fry" or "mechanism 0 (M0)"): (1) The lowest vocal register which is produced by aperiodic vibrations of the vocal folds with a loose glottal closure. (2) A stylism used in CCM singing in onsets and offsets, as a vocal distortion, or as an expressive tool.

Cricothyroid (CT) muscles: A pair of laryngeal muscles which connect the cricoid cartilage to the thyroid cartilage, and contract to lengthen the vocal folds. They are the principle muscles used in head register or M2.

Cricothyroid-dominant (also called "CT-dominant", "head-dominant", or "mechanism 2"): Refers to a registration configuration in which the cricothyroid muscles are dominant (as opposed to the thyroarytenoid muscles). In CT-dominant mix (head-mix), the thyroarytenoid muscles are also involved, but to a lesser extent than the dominant cricothyroid muscles.

Cross-training: (1) training to perform both classical and CCM styles. (2) Conditioning the voice using contrasting elements such as both low and high range components, or both legit and belting registration configurations.

Cry: A vocal stylism or effect which sounds similar to crying.

CT-dominant: Abbreviation for cricothyroid-dominant.

Curbing mode: One of the four vocal modes used in Complete Vocal Technique. Curbing is the half-metallic mode and the mildest of the metallic modes. The sound is often slightly plaintive and restrained. (CVT Application Glossary).

CVT: Abbreviation for Complete Vocal Technique.

D

Damping: The term for phonation used in Speech Level Singing™.

DAW: Abbreviation for Digital Audio Workstation.

Decibel (dB): A unit of measurement for the volume or amplitude of a sound.

Digital Audio Workstation (DAW): A device or software used for recording, editing, and processing audio recordings.

Distortion: (1) An effect which may be added to a vocal sound for expressive purposes, often using "noise" created by the false vocal folds or other supraglottic structures. (2) An effect which may be added to a signal chain by an audio engineer or sound designer.

Dynamic microphone: A robust workhorse microphone which is less sensitive than a condenser microphone. The handheld Shure SM-58 is the most commonly used dynamic microphone in live performance venues.

E

Edge mode: One of the four vocal modes used in Complete Vocal Technique. It is a full-metallic mode. The character of Edge is lighter and sharper than Overdrive. Edge has a non-breathy character. (CVT Application Glossary).

Effect: A term used in Complete Vocal Technique to refer to sounds that underline the singer's expression or style, such as distortion, creak, rattle, growl, grunt, scream, intentional vocal break, air added to the voice, vibrato, or ornamentation. (CVT Application Glossary). These elements are also known as "vocal stylisms."

Efficient singing: Using the least amount of effort required to achieve the desired sound. Efficient singing is also used to refer to singing which is sustainable over a long-term and intensive performance schedules, such as a lengthy tour or 8-show week.

EGG: Abbreviation for Electroglottograph.

Electroglottograph (EGG): A non-invasive instrument that measures vocal fold contact patterns (open and closed quotients) during phonation using an electric current passed between two electrodes placed on the neck.

Embellish: To modify a melodic line for expressive purposes by adding vocal stylisms or riffs.

EQ: Abbreviation for equalization.

Equalization: A vocal processing effect which adjusts frequency volumes within a sound spectrum, or boosts/attenuates targeted harmonics for aesthetic purposes.

Estill Voice Model™ (EVM): A detailed physiological model of voice production, developed by Jo Estill (1921-2010) "over a lifetime of singing, teaching, and researching". (The Estill Voice Model: Theory and Translation).

Estill Voice Training® (EVT): A methodological training program founded by Jo Estill (1921-2010), focused on the craft of singing. The method identifies and isolates the structures responsible for vocal sound within the larynx and vocal tract, and develops conscious control of the voice through targeted exercises, called Figures for Voice™. Estill Voice International, LLC offers three levels of EVT certification through training, exams, and membership.

EVM: Abbreviation for Estill Voice Model™.

EVT: Abbreviation for Estill Voice Training®.

Extended vocal technique: The use of vocal stylisms or effects which produce extremes of vocal expression, such as rattle, growl, grunt, scream, or squall.

F

Fall-off: A vocal stylism or effect often used at the ends of phrases, in which the pitch sounds and then quickly descends (in pitch), while attenuating the volume to an almost inaudible level and stops.

Fall-up: A vocal stylism or effect often used at the ends of phrases, in which the pitch sounds and then quickly ascends (in pitch), while attenuating the volume to an almost inaudible level and stops.

False vocal folds: A pair of structures in the larynx located directly above the true vocal folds (vocal folds). They are not involved in typical phonation, but they may play a role in vocal distortions or extended vocal effects such as rattle, growl, grunt, scream, or squall.

Falsetto: A term for CT-dominant register, head register, loft, or mechanism 2. In CCM singing, falsetto is used in reference to both male and female voices.

Falsetto quality: One of the six voice qualities in the Estill Voice Model™, a breathy voice heard in the voices of children, boy choirs and certain early music classical singers. (The Estill Voice Model: Theory & Translation).

Feedback: A high whining sound produced when a microphone faces a speaker or monitor and captures its own sound over and over.

Feldenkrais Method®: A bodywork methodology founded by Moshé Feldenkrais, often used by singers to increase self-awareness, facilitate ease, and reduce limitations in movement while performing.

Figure (also called "compulsory figure"): In Estill Voice Training®, a vocal exercise that establishes control over one structure within the vocal mechanism by isolating and moving the structure through different conditions.

Filter: In the source-filter model of voice acoustics, the vocal tract is the filter of the sound. This tube runs from the glottis to the lips/nostrils and may be shaped to attenuate or boost harmonics provided by the sound source (vocal folds).

Fitzmaurice Voicework®: A bodywork modality which "combines adaptations of classical voice training techniques with modifications of yoga, shiatsu, bioenergetics, energy work, and many other disciplines" in order to "support people in finding and using their unique voices". (www.fitzmauriceinstitute.org/fitzmaurice-voicework).

Frequency (Hz): An objective measure of vibrations per second. Frequency is also perceived, less precisely, as pitch.

Fry: See "vocal fry".

Fry-glide onset: See "gravel onset".

Functional training: (1) Training the voice using the scientific principles of anatomy and physiology within the vocal mechanism. (2) A tenant of Somatic Voicework, the LoVetri Method™. Exercises are crafted to elicit functions of the voice based on anatomy and physiology to strengthen the vocal mechanism, producing the freest and healthiest sound.

G

Glottal onset: An onset which begins by adducting the vocal folds and building subglottal air pressure. The release of this pressure initiates an abrupt phonatory onset with an articulated edge in the sound. In CCM singing, it is often used as a vocal stylism for expressive purposes.

Gravel sounds: Rough or aggressive vocal textures used for expressive purposes at an emotional climax. The four basic types in gospel singing are squalls, whoops, growls, and midvoice.

Gravel onset (also called "fry-glide onset"): An onset used as a vocal stylism or effect for expressive purposes, wherein the tone starts as vocal fry (M0) and then slides up into a pitched tone, usually in M1, but it is also possible in M2.

Groove: A repeated rhythmic pattern.

Growl: (1) A type of vocal stylism, effect, or distortion with a rough vocal quality. It is most often used in heavy metal, death metal, screamo, and occasionally in other genres as a type of onset. (2) One of the gravel sounds used for expressive purposes in gospel singing. It is a vocal stylism or effect which sounds like a rough vocal quality at the start of a word but is immediately followed by a clearer sound.

Grunt: A vocal stylism, effect, or distortion with a rough vocal quality.

H

Head-dominant mix (also called "head-mix"): Vocal production of mixed registration wherein the cricothyroid muscles are dominant, but the thyroarytenoid muscles are also active to a lesser extent.

Head-mix: See "head-dominant mix".

Head register (also called "CT-dominant register", "loft", "falsetto", or "mechanism 2"): The higher part of the singing range for both men and women. Phonation in head-register has a higher open quotient than phonation in chest-register.

Hook: The catchy melodic or rhythmic part of a popular song, consisting of a short section or phrase. The hook is often found in the chorus, but not always.

I

iReal Pro™: An application for phone, tablet, and Mac, which creates a real-sounding band to accompany a singer during practice and collects chord charts.

K

Kinesensic: A descriptor used in Lessac Kinesensic Training. It comes from a combination of the words: "Kine + Essence + Sense + Sic", meaning "movement + marrow + feeling + original", and is defined as "learning to sense/feel innate movement/motion of the body, and then gathering the information from that feeling process and using it for optimal body function". (lessacinstitute.org/about-us/kinesensic-training/).

L

Laryngeal lean: A term coined by Lisa Popeil and used in the Voiceworks® Method to refer to a specific laryngeal posture used in belting wherein the thyroid cartilage is perceived to lean forward (but not tilt downward) as the anterior space between the thyroid and cricoid cartilages widens. In the Estill Voice Model™, this is referred to as the cricoid cartilage tilt.

Legit: The style of singing used commonly in the Golden Age of musical theatre, circa 1925-1965. This style uses traditionally lyric singing, similar to classical style singing, with pervasive vibrato and frequent use of legato. However, the vowels are modified to a lesser extent than in classical singing and more closely resemble American speech vowels.

Lessac Training (Lessac Kinesensic Training): A system of voice and body training described as "a comprehensive and creative approach to developing the voice and body in a holistic way, resulting in greater flexibility and power and improved expressiveness and communication". (lessacinstitute. org/about-us/kinesensic-training/).

Lick: A melodic embellishment which may be improvised, or used as a stock pattern or phrase within a song.

Linklater (Kristin Linklater Voice): A system of speaking voice work, defined as "a series of step-by-step practical exercises that include relaxation, awareness of breathing, the experience of voice vibrating in the body, how to open the throat, the development of resonance and range, and the articulating activity of lips and tongue". (www.linklatervoice.com/linklater-voice/about-linklater-voice).

Lisa Popeil's Voiceworks®: See "Voiceworks®".

Loft: A term for CT-dominant register, head register, falsetto, or mechanism 2, often used in contrast with "modal".

M

Mechanism: A term which may be used interchangeably with "register", but only when register refers exclusively to source-level (glottal) activity and does not also include vocal tract shaping or timbral qualities. Also called "laryngeal vibratory mechanism", it is discussed by Roubeau et al.[2] in a study focusing on laryngeal source activity measured by electroglottograph (EGG) and acoustic spectrographic analyses. Mechanism 0 (M0) corresponds to vocal fry/creak; mechanism 1 (M1) corresponds to chest/modal; mechanism 2 (M2) corresponds to head/falsetto/loft; and mechanism 3 (M3) corresponds to whistle/flageolet/flute.

Microphone technique: The art of using a microphone to enhance a vocal sound with the goals of minimizing vocal load and maximizing expression. This may involve choosing the right microphone, holding the microphone, regulating the distance between the microphone and the mouth, adjusting diction, and adjusting the singer's spectrum of volume, among other techniques. In CCM singing, the microphone is considered an extension of the vocal mechanism.

Midvoice: One of the gravel sounds used for expressive purposes in gospel singing. It is an effect or vocal stylism that sounds like a sustained gravel sound through several sung phrases.

Mix: (1) The word used to describe the registrational state for any combination of TA- or CT-dominant singing. In the female voice, "mix" is the registrational state used most of the time in songs. Mix may be further divided into chest-mix, and head-mix, referring to the register of dominance within the mix. (2) Within the musical theatre industry in the U.S., "mix" refers to CT-dominant

---

2   Roubeau, Bernard, Nathalie Henrich, and Michele Castellengo. "Laryngeal vibratory mechanisms: The notion of register revisited". *Journal of Voice* 23, no. 4 (July 2009): 425–438, doi.org/10.1016/j.jvoice.2007.10.014.

registration and is often used to describe the opposite of "belt" (meaning TA-dominant singing). The word "mix" may be used differently in other countries.

Modal: A term for TA-dominant register, chest register, or mechanism 1, often used in contrast with "loft".

Mode: (1) The ancient melodic modes: Ionian, Dorian, Phrygian, Lydian, Mixolydian, Aeolian, and Locrian. (2) Abbreviation for "vocal mode", as used in Complete Vocal Technique. See "vocal mode".

Monitor: A speaker which faces the performer and enables self-regulation of sound production. In-ear monitors are commonly used in CCM and professional musical theatre because they allow a performer to move around the stage and still hear themselves consistently.

N

Nasal: (1) Term used to describe singing with the velopharyngeal port partially closed or closed. (2) A term used to describe character voices in musical theatre.

Necessary twang: Twang is created by narrowing the aryepiglottic funnel. See "twang". Complete Vocal Technique maintains that "necessary twang" is always required to a certain degree, in order to have correct technique and achieve easy and unhindered use of the voice, regardless of the vocal mode, sound color, and effect used. (CVT Application Glossary)

Neutral mode: One of the four vocal modes used in Complete Vocal Technique. It is the only non-metallic mode. It is very extensive and contains many different sounds and sound colors. The sounds are softer and milder than the other modes. (CVT Application Glossary)

O

Offset (also called "release"): The ending of a vocal sound, or the exact moment when phonation ceases. Offset may be used as a vocal stylism or effect for expressive purposes. In the Estill Voice Model™, there are four different types of offset, including glottal, aspirate abrupt, aspirate gradual, and smooth. Other types of offset include inhalation, yodel, hitch, flip, and fall-off.

Onset (also called "attack"): The beginning of a vocal sound, or the exact moment when phonation begins. Onset may be used as a vocal stylism or effect for expressive purposes. The most common types of onsets are glottal, coordinated/smooth, and aspirate. However, these exist on a spectrum. Other types of onset can include gravel, fry-glide, or growl, among others.

Open quotient: The percentage of time the glottis is open during each vibratory cycle of phonation.

Opera quality: One of the six voice qualities in the Estill Voice Model™, heard in the stage speech of Shakespearean actors or in the "ringing" quality of singers on the operatic stage. (The Estill Voice Model: Theory & Translation).

Overdrive mode: One of the four vocal modes used in Complete Vocal Technique. It is a full-metallic mode. Its character is often direct, loud, and shouted, like when someone calls "hey" in the street. (CVT Application Glossary).

P

Palette: A spectrum of expressive sounds, akin to a painter's palette of colors.

PA System: Abbreviation for public address system.

Passaggio: The Italian term for the point of transition from one register to another.

Pentatonic scales: A scale with five notes per octave. In CCM singing, the major and minor pentatonic scales are commonly used in riffs and in improvisation. The major pentatonic scale is built on scale degrees 1-2-3-5-6. The minor pentatonic scale is built on scale degrees 1-♭ 3-4-5-♭ 7.

Primal Voice: An approach to CCM sounds developed by Dane Chalfin, adapted from primal voice theory as taught by Janice Chapman[3]. The four gestures (qualities) in primal voice are sigh, whimper, whinge, and yell.

Public address system (also called "PA system"): A simple sound system comprised of a microphone and speakers, at a minimum. It may also include an amplifier, mixer, or other components.

R

Rattle: In Complete Vocal Technique, an effect that occurs from vibrations of the arytenoid cartilages or by vibrations in the back of the tongue or soft palate, or by making the mucosa over the arytenoid cartilages vibrate, used in Complete Vocal Technique. (CVT Application Glossary).

Register: A group of sounds made the same way. In current CCM pedagogy, register usually describes the activity of the thyroarytenoid and cricothyroid muscles and does not include shaping of the vocal tract or timbral qualities. Functionally, there are two main registers in singing: chest (modal/TA/mechanism 1) and head (falsetto/loft/CT/mechanism 2).

Release: See "offset".

Resonance: As the sound moves from the source (vocal fold vibrations) through the filter (vocal tract), harmonics are attenuated or amplified by bone structure, size and conditions of the structures within the vocal tract, muscular tone, and craft. These components are unique to each singer; therefore, the resulting sound is distinctive. While resonance is a considerable component of classical vocal training to maximize volume and formant configurations in order to sing unamplified over an orchestra, no such need exists in CCM singing. Instead, CCM pedagogues train resonance (vocal tract shaping) to maximize the expressive palette. Some do not use the term at all due to its affiliation with a classical signature sound.

Riff: Several notes sung quickly to embellish an otherwise simple melody for expressive purposes.

Rock: (1) An umbrella term to refer to all popular music since circa 1950, in general. (2) A genre of music characterized by the use of electric guitar, blues-influenced structures, and the artistic application of audio technology.

Run: Five or more notes sung quickly, and often used for expressive purposes to embellish an otherwise simple melodic phrase. Interchangeable with "riff".

S

Scoop: A vocal stylism or effect used for expressive purposes wherein the singer slides up to the intended pitch.

Scream: (1) A vocal effect or stylism used in heavy metal and screamo genres, among others. (2) In Complete Vocal Technique, scream refers to a sudden, often ferocious, loud, and high-pitched note. (CVT Application Glossary).

Screlting: (1) High-pitched belting with excessive constriction or tension. (2) An unsuccessful attempt at belting which sounds so unpleasant that it may as well be screaming.

---

3 Janice L. Chapman, *Singing and Teaching Singing: A Holistic Approach to Classical Voice*, 3rd ed. (San Diego: Plural Publishing, 2016).

Semi-occluded vocal tract (SOVT) exercise: Any vocal exercise where the vocal tract width is narrowed (occluded). Examples include humming, straw phonation, lip buzz, among others. SOVT exercises may be used for both vocal habilitation and rehabilitation.

Session singer: A singer hired by the session to make recordings, usually someone of impeccable technical control with strong sight-singing abilities.

Sigh: One of the four gestures (qualities) in the Primal Voice Model. It is breathy phonation which uses registration in either mechanism 1 or mechanism 2, and is modeled after the sound of a sigh.

Slide: A vocal stylism or effect in which the singer slides from one pitch to the next, also known as a glissando.

SLS: Abbreviation for Speech Level Singing™.

Sob quality: One of the six voice qualities in the Estill Voice Model™, heard in the speech of those who mourn or in the classical singing of art songs or lullabies. (The Estill Voice Model: Theory & Translation).

Somatic Voicework™ The LoVetri Method: The singing methodology created by Jeannette LoVetri. It is a body-based method of functional vocal training which draws from many disciplines, including voice science, medicine, traditional classical vocal training, complementary modalities, and bodywork approaches.

Soul Ingredients®: An organized pedagogical approach to soul singing developed by Trineice Robinson-Martin which shows students how to take their musical influences and models and execute the different components in a manner that is personalized and expressive.

Soul singing: Term used to describe singing in historically African-American folk-based music genres including gospel, jazz, blues, and R&B, in which the expression and communication of emotion supersede the lyrics and melody.

Sound color (also called "vocal color" or "timbre"): Sound color is created by shaping the vocal tract. In Complete Vocal Technique, sound color is one of the three main descriptors of voice production (along with vocal mode and effect) and is described using terms such as "light" and "dark". In Elisabeth Howard's Vocal Power Method, the four main vocal colors used are chest, mouth, nasal, and head.

Sound designer: In musical theatre, this is the person in charge of the overall sound aesthetic, but also works in close collaboration with the director, producer, technical director, and music director to determine how the music will be sonically presented.

Sound engineer (also called "audio engineer"): A trained professional who helps to produce a recording or live performance. This person specializes in the technical elements of the sound and music such as placing speakers and microphones, setting levels, and mixing.

Source: In the source-filter model of voice acoustics, the vocal folds are the source (sound source).

SOVT: Abbreviation for semi-occluded vocal tract.

Speech Level Singing™(SLS): A trademarked singing methodology created by Seth Riggs and continued by Seth Riggs and Margareta Svensson Riggs, with a foundational principle that allows the larynx to rest in a speech level condition. Due to the common usage of the term "speech level singing", the trademarked methodology of the same name is in development, please see http://www.theriggsvocalstudio.com for the most up to date information.

Speech quality: One of the six voice qualities in the Estill Voice Model™, heard in the everyday speech of most newscasters and in popular and folksongs. (The Estill Voice Model: Theory & Translation).

Split-Second Singing: Moniker for a pedagogical perspective developed by Mark Baxter, which focuses on functions of the autonomic nervous system.

Squall: One of the gravel sounds used for expressive purposes in gospel singing. It is a vocal effect or stylism that sounds like a short yell with a rough vocal quality.

Structure: In the Estill Voice Model™ there are 13 anatomic structures within the vocal mechanism which move through various conditions to produce changes in the vocal sound.

Stylism: See "vocal stylism".

Support: The muscles and actions which control the outflow of air during phonation.

SVW: Unofficial abbreviation for Somatic Voicework™, The LoVetri Method. This abbreviation is used by members of the Somatic Voicework™ community but is not an official abbreviation.

Syncopation: Rhythms that accent the weak beats or upbeats of a given meter.

T

Tail: No more than 4 notes added to the very end of a phrase, either descending or ascending in stepwise motion. Used for expressive purposes to embellish an otherwise simple melody.

TA-dominant: Abbreviation for thyroarytenoid-dominant.

Temporomandibular joint disease disorder (TMJ): An unconscious and habitual clenching of the jaw muscles, which can interfere with free and efficient singing.

Thyroarytenoid (TA) muscles: A pair of intrinsic laryngeal muscles which connect the thyroid cartilage to the arytenoid cartilages, form the body of the vocal folds, and contract to shorten the length of the vocal folds. They are the principle muscles used in chest register or M1.

Thyroarytenoid-dominant (also called "TA-dominant", "chest-dominant", or "mechanism 1"): Refers to a registration configuration in which the thyroarytenoid muscles are dominant (as opposed to the cricothyroid muscles). In TA-dominant mix (chest-mix), the crycothyroid muscles are also involved, but to a lesser extent than the dominant thyroarytenoid muscles.

Timbre: A term used to describe vocal color, usually created by shaping the vocal tract but also may involve registration and bone structure.

TMJ: Abbreviation for temporomandibular joint disease disorder.

True vocal folds (also called "vocal folds", but called "true vocal folds" in the Estill Voice Model™): Folds of tissue in the larynx which vibrate against each other to produce speech or singing sounds.

Turn: Short riff in which first and last pitches are the same, used for expressive purposes to embellish an otherwise simple melody.

Twang: A distinctive vocal color (vocal tract configuration) used in country and bluegrass styles of singing and used to train belting in CCM singing. Sundberg and Thálen describe it as a resonatory effect which raises F1 and F2 and lowers F3 and F5 in the sound spectrum.[4] Both The Estill Voice Model™ and Complete Vocal Technique identify twang as a bright and piercing quality which is produced by narrowing the aryepiglottic sphincter (epilarynx) within the vocal tract. Twang is not interchangeable with nasality, which is a result of singing with a partially closed or closed velopharyngeal port.

---

4   Sundberg, Johan and Margareta Thálen. "What is twang?" *Journal of Voice* 24, no. 6 (November 2010): 654–660. doi.org/10.1016/j.jvoice.2009.03.003.

Twang quality: One of the six voice qualities in the Estill Voice Model™, heard in the speech of many cultures, modern musical theatre, bluegrass, and some country music. (The Estill Voice Model: Theory & Translation).

V

Vibrato: Regular fluctuations in pitch during sustained singing. In CCM styles, vibrato is often reserved for use as an expressive tool, controlled by regulating its presence, speed, and width.

Vocal agility: The ability to change vocal register and vocal color at will, while moving through pitches rapidly, accurately, and clearly. This skill is often showcased in "riffs".

Vocal distortion: Intentionally distorted sounds used for expressive purposes.

Vocal folds: Folds of tissue in the larynx which vibrate against each other to produce sound (phonation). In the source-filter model of voice acoustics, the vocal folds are the source. They are constructed of muscle (thyroarytenoids), three layers of lamina propria (gel), and stratified squamous epithelium. Their primary function is to protect the airway from choking. They also regulate the flow of air in and out of the lungs and vibrate to produce speech and singing sounds.

Vocal function: How the sound is made, or the anatomy and physiology within the vocal mechanism.

Vocal fry (also called "creak" or "mechanism 0"): (1) The lowest vocal register which is produced by aperiodic vibrations of the vocal folds with a loose glottal closure. (2) A stylism used in CCM singing in onsets and offsets, as a vocal distortion, or as an expressive tool.

Vocal mechanism: (1) A generic term referring to the anatomical and physiological components of the body which are responsible for creating sound, including the lungs, larynx, and vocal tract. (2) Used in reference to registration. Also called "laryngeal vibratory mechanism", see "mechanism".

Vocal mode: In Complete Vocal Technique, these are four primary singing sounds categorized based on volume, pitch, and sound color. These are labeled Neutral, Curbing, Overdrive, and Edge.

Vocal Power Method: The singing methodology created and developed by Elisabeth Howard with the motto "Let it shine". The Vocal Power Method specializes in pop, rock, musical theatre, jazz, and country music genres and has foundational principles in vocal technique, vocal style, and the communication of feelings through music.

Vocal Process: A company providing teacher training by multidisciplinary, multimedia voice educators Gillyanne Kayes and Jeremy Fisher.

Vocal stylism: Term coined by Edrie Means Weekly for extra nuances or effects added to a song for expressive purposes. These are not written in the music but are critical for stylistic authenticity. Common vocal stylisms include cry, fall-off, fall-ups, fry, bending the note, pop-appoggiatura, shadow vowels, licks, riffs, runs, waves, vibrato, dips, hitch, flip, growl, squall, whoop, midvoice, uvula trill, among others.

Vocal tract: The cavity of the throat from the glottis to the lips/nostrils. In the source-filter model, the vocal tract is the filter, and may be shaped to attenuate or boost harmonics provided by the sound source (vocal folds).

Vocology: Voice science, or the science and practice of voice habilitation. It encompasses speech and language pathology, laryngology, speech therapy, voice therapy, voice training, singing voice pedagogy, and voice and speech training for professional voice users.

Voice quality: (1) A generic term used to describe timbre or color, usually having to do with the shape of the vocal tract (filter), but sometimes also impacted by the activity of the vocal folds (source). (2) Used in the Estill Voice Model™, each voice quality results from a combination of structures in particular conditions (figure combinations), with a unique "recipe" for each voice quality. The six voice qualities in EVM™ are Speech, Sob, Twang, Opera, Falsetto, and Belt. (The Estill Voice Model: Theory and Translation).

Voiceworks® (also called "Lisa Popeil's Voiceworks®"): The singing methodology created and developed by Lisa Popeil. The Voiceworks® Method takes the mystery out of singing and shows singers exactly "what to do" to sing their best in any style.

Vowel distortion: Purposely changing the vowel to the point that it is unrecognizable. Sometimes used for expressive purposes in certain CCM genres.

Vowel modification: A modification of the shape of the vocal tract and/or actions of the articulators, often performed in order to facilitate ease of production and consistency of ring in the sound.

W

Whimper: One of the four gestures (qualities) in the Primal Voice Model. It is produced using mechanism 2 throughout the range, and is modeled after the sound of a whimper.

Whinge: One of the four gestures (qualities) in the Primal Voice Model. It is produced using mechanism 1 throughout the range, and is modeled after the sound of crying out.

Whoop: One of the gravel sounds used for expressive purposes in gospel singing. It is a vocal stylism or effect which sounds like an elongated squall (short yell with a rough vocal quality) sustained on one or more pitches.

Y

Yell: One of the four gestures (qualities) in the Primal Voice Model. It is produced using mechanism 1 throughout the range with a narrowed vocal tract, and is modeled after the sound of a yell.

Yodel: A vocal stylism or effect used for expressive purposes which is produced by a rapid and audible leap or alternation between registers (M1 and M2), with a contrast in dynamic level. In country music, the ascending version is also called a "vocal flip", and the descending version is also called a "hitch".

Index of Responses by Name

Index of Responses by Name

Shapiro, Jan: Audio Technology. Belt. Breath. Beyond the Voice Studio. Excellence. Expression. Improvisation. (In)consistency. Methods. Performing. Philosophy. Posture/Alignment. Registration. Singers to Admire. Success. Support. Teaching Younger Singers. Tension. Training. Voice Science. Vowels.

Steinhauer, Kimberly: Audio Technology. Belt. Breath. Beyond the Voice Studio. Excellence. Expression. Improvisation. (In)consistency. Methods. Performing. Philosophy. Posture/Alignment. Registration. Singers to Admire. Success. Support. Teaching Younger Singers. Tension. Training. Voice Science. Vowels.

Wilson, Kevin: Audio Technology. Belt. Breath. Beyond the Voice Studio. Excellence. Expression. Improvisation. (In)consistency. Methods. Performing. Philosophy. Posture/Alignment. Registration. Singers to Admire. Success. Support. Teaching Younger Singers. Tension. Training. Voice Science. Vowels.

Index of Terms

About the Author

Praised for her 'delightful' (*The Boston Globe*) and 'delicately compassionate' (*Times Herald Record*) singing, Elizabeth Ann Benson is recognized as a dynamic and versatile performer. In her Carnegie Hall début, she created the title role of *Lucy* by Tom Cipullo, and her performance was acclaimed as 'excellent' (*The Big City*). She specializes in performing and teaching crossover vocal styles, spanning from opera to musical theatre to rock. She is trained in Somatic Voicework™, the LoVetri Method, Lisa Popeil's Voiceworks® method, and Estill Voice Training™. She is a 2016 graduate of the Intern Program of the National Association of Teachers of Singing (NATS) and a 2012 recipient of the NATS Emerging Leader Award. She has published research on contemporary voice pedagogy in *American Music Teacher* and has presented at national conferences for The Voice Foundation, the National Association of Teachers of Singing, the Association for Popular Music Education, and the College Music Society. She is a graduate of Occidental College (BA), New England Conservatory (MM), and The City University of New York Graduate Center (DMA). At Auburn University, she is Assistant Professor of Music Theatre and serves as the music theatre singing specialist for the Department of Theatre. www.elizabethannbenson.com

Lightning Source UK Ltd.
Milton Keynes UK
UKHW030028080922
408487UK00004B/16